PROGRESS, POVERTY AND EXCLUSION

AN ECONOMIC HISTORY OF LATIN AMERICA IN THE 20TH CENTURY

Rosemary Thorp

DISTRIBUTED BY THE JOHNS HOPKINS UNIVERSITY PRESS
FOR THE INTER-AMERICAN DEVELOPMENT BANK
AND THE EUROPEAN UNION

© 1998 Inter-American Development Bank
1300 New York Avenue, N.W.
Washington, D.C. 20577

Produced by the IDB Publications Section
Distributed by The Johns Hopkins University Press
2715 North Charles Street
Baltimore, Maryland 21218-4319

Cover photo: © Peter Menzel/Stock Boston/PNI.
Photos for Chapters One through Six are reproduced with permission of the Columbus
Memorial Library of the Organization of American States. All other photos are from the
Photo Library of the Inter-American Development Bank.

Graphic design: Dolores Subiza

Cataloging-in-Publication data provided by the
Inter-American Development Bank
Felipe Herrera Library

Thorp, Rosemary.
    Progress, poverty and exclusion: an economic history of Latin America in the 20th
century / Rosemary Thorp.
    p. cm.
    Includes bibliographical references.
    ISBN: 1886938350

    1.Latin America—Economic conditions—20th century. 2.Economic history—20th cen-
tury. 3.Economic development—20th century. 4.Poverty—Latin America—20th century.
I.Inter-American Development Bank.
330.09 T57—dc21   98-73731

For Carlos Díaz-Alejandro

PREFACE

THE PRESIDENT OF THE INTER-AMERICAN DEVELOPMENT BANK, Enrique V. Iglesias, decided in 1995 that to mark the end of the century the Bank should sponsor a history of the Latin American economies over the past 100 years. The president's personal inspiration was that development could be illuminated by a historical account tracing the interplay between policymaking and economic, social and political structures and institutions. The book would not be about theoretical approaches, but rather seek to place in proper historical context the development efforts, strategies, choices, successes and failures of the different Latin American countries. At a time when the role of the state was being radically rethought, the idea was that a balanced historical account could contribute to current debate by examining the evolving state role and different approaches to policymaking.

The issue of procedure then became very important. President Iglesias wanted the book to reflect the very best of Latin American scholarship, yet a sympathetic outsider had a certain comparative advantage in coordinating and synthesizing experience across the continent. We agreed on a procedure using workshops and consultancies, with an Advisory Committee bringing together outstanding scholars from Latin America, the United States and Europe. But at the end of the day—literally, a year—I would write the book. President Iglesias then set me free to pursue the project entirely as I wished—a remarkable act of confidence.

Two workshops were established to cover what were felt to be the major gaps in the comparative literature. Each produced academic volumes being published in parallel with this book under the editorship of Enrique Cárdenas, José Antonio Ocampo and myself. This has been in itself a happy and fruitful collaboration. The parallel volumes are frequently referred to in the text as "companion volumes," and contain much of the detailed documentation and references that could not be as-similated within the covers of the present text. I also requested consultancies that produced additional papers and assistance. Those who participated are listed in the Appendix, along with the titles of the companion volumes and the contributors. I was also able to draw on earlier collaborative work, in particular that which gave rise to the second companion volume, on the impact of the 1929 Depression. These companion volumes provide part of the solution to one of the greatest challenges posed by President Iglesias, which was to make this book accessible to economists and noneconomists alike.

The approach of this book is to attempt to capture in depth the comparative reality within Latin America, rather than to explain why Latin America is not East Asia or indeed any other part of the world. The emphasis is on a combination of quantitative data with what is known as "political economy." This term is short-hand for the interface between political forces, institutional inheritance and eco-nomic outcomes. The book thus draws on and owes a huge debt to the substantial Latin American school of economic historians and political economists. This rich foundation begins with Raúl Prebisch himself.[1] Outside Latin America, particular mention must be made of Albert Hirschman, who from an early date contributed unique inspiration to the mixing of economics and politics in a historical perspective. The dedication of the book to Carlos Díaz-Alejandro, the spontaneous choice of both President Iglesias and myself, is testimony to the special role he played in Latin American economic history and in bringing together scholars from inside and outside Latin America.

Even with such a solid base in collaboration, the book was clearly extraordi-narily difficult to write, particularly in terms of doing justice to individual country experiences, while maintaining an overall vision. The challenge was particularly difficult in regard to the English-speaking Caribbean. President Iglesias was deter-mined that the Caribbean have its proper place, but its complexity and distinct tra-jectory—along with my own limited background in Caribbean affairs—made the task all the more daunting. Though I have included as many insights from Caribbean

---

[1] Among the early notable books (listed in alphabetical order) are those by Cardoso and Faletto, 1971; Cariola and Sunkel, 1982; Cortés Conde and Hunt (and their contributors), 1985; Díaz-Alejandro, 1970; ECLA, 1951; Ferrer, 1963; Furtado, 1970; Pinto, 1964; Solis, 1963; Sunkel and Paz, 1970; and Urquidi, 1964.

experience as possible, and learned much in the process, I would suggest to the IDB that there should be in due course a companion volume on the Caribbean economies.

Given the collaborative procedures that underpin this book, the acknowledgments take on special importance. Indeed, I would have preferred some kind of corporate authorship, but it would have been impracticable, particularly given the IDB's time frame. In the end, I had to take responsibility, but there are many debts.

My first and greatest is clearly to President Iglesias himself. He gave me the invitation, the resources and the confidence to accept. At the IDB, Nohra Rey de Marulanda managed the project with her usual effectiveness and flexibility, while keeping me encouraged, and Peter Kalil worked tirelessly to make the whole project happen. Many Bank staff members helped patiently with my search for materials and documents.

I also owe a debt of gratitude to the European Union, whose additional finance made the project possible.

The Advisory Committee set up by the IDB (and listed in the Appendix) was very much engaged with the project. After the committee held a two-day meeting in Washington to review the manuscript, I received 62 pages of written comments. These were supportive, tough and searching, and precipitated some energetic rewriting on my part. One member, José Antonio Ocampo, had difficulty participating owing to the singularly good excuse that he was made Colombia's Minister of Finance shortly after the project began. I owe him a special debt of gratitude for reading my draft immediately after leaving office and making extensive and exceptionally useful comments. Special thanks go as well to Alan Knight, who in addition to making extensive comments on substance also drove me relentlessly to rewrite the text in clear and nontechnical English, and to Osvaldo Sunkel and Albert Fishlow, who read and commented on the entire manuscript a second time.

In Oxford, Pablo Astorga worked with me throughout the year as research fellow, and has contributed significantly to the book. He and Valpy Fitzgerald were responsible for much of the quantitative work, which as revealed in the Statistical Appendix was a tour de force that we hope may result in a separate publication. Leila Jazayery worked tirelessly as a research assistant. Karen Kemmis Betty, Renato Colistete, María Cristina Dorado, Monika Lutke-Entrup, Truman Packard, Ben Driggs, Caterina Ruggeri Laderchi and Catalina Sanint all contributed to the project at different times. My colleagues, both in the Latin American Centre and in Queen

Elizabeth House, took over all my usual jobs with exceptional good grace, and Alan Knight, Alan Angell, Malcolm Deas and Valpy Fitzgerald struggled with my first draft and improved it enormously. Laurence Whitehead also provided insights, material and commentary. St. Antony's College provided financial management.

My thanks also go to the consultants, who were all extraordinarily generous with their ideas and insights. People told me to "take their text and use it as I wished." I have tried to signal clearly in the text where I have done this, but there was no way to footnote adequately the intellectual origin of such a vast range of insights.

I keep the really special thanks to the last. I could not possibly have managed without the unreserved commitment of the Latin American Centre's office in Oxford. Margaret Hancox is an outstanding administrator, and a continual source of moral support. Thanks go as well to Elvira Ryan, Ruth Hodges and Laura Salinas. And, of course, I could not have managed without Tim, my husband, who kept me calm, offered encouragement, tolerated my obsession and sorted my computer problems.

Rosemary Thorp

TABLE OF CONTENTS

OREWORD

THIS COMPREHENSIVE ECONOMIC HISTORY examines the political, institutional and social forces that have shaped the complex and often paradoxical development process of Latin America and the Caribbean over the 20th century.

For the world, it was a century that perhaps saw as much change and tumult as any in the history of mankind. Rosemary Thorp writes of Latin America's century, but notes in her introduction of how difficult it is to capture a period whose hue is shaded by so many "lights and shadows." And the sands of history shift as our perceptions and analyses change. Today's conventional wisdom for Latin America heralds export-led economies fueled by technical innovation, but in 1900, the same idea was in vogue. The social cost of excluding poor and marginalized people is singled out as a crucial issue today, while only two generations ago exclusion was so thoroughly woven into the fabric of Latin America that it was simply accepted. The focus now is on the shortcomings of import substitution industrialization, in the process seemingly wanting to forget it was once reasonably considered to be the pillar of progress upon which a modern Latin America would be built.

The author relentlessly poses the question: What did the Latin American economies achieve in the course of a hundred years? The closest we can come to answers is that per capita income increased fivefold, yet today it is lower in proportion to the industrial countries than it was a century ago; modern infrastructure was built and industry grew to 25 percent of GDP, but the region's share of world trade was halved; social indicators such as life expectancy and literacy improved dramatically, but inequity and poverty worsened.

This analysis of the experience of the 20th century can be immensely instructive for those building for the future. For this reason, the Inter-American Development Bank and the European Union—both devoted to economic and social development—commissioned this examination of the Latin American century.

The Bank was created in 1959 in response to a longstanding desire on the part of the Latin American nations for a development institution that would focus on the pressing problems of the region. Today it is the world's largest regional development bank and the leading source of multilateral credit for Latin America and the Caribbean. The Bank finances projects that address practically every social and economic issue discussed in this book.

The European Union and Latin America have longstanding historical and cultural ties, and since the 1970s have steadily improved their political relations. A formal regional and subregional political dialogue was established through such efforts as the Groups of Rio and San José, and there have been numerous interparliamentary meetings and extensive cooperation agreements. The European Union is also Latin America's largest source of public development aid, and since 1993 its support has been complemented by lending to the region by the European Investment Bank.

Only history can provide the perspective that shapes vision—in the Latin American case, clearly a vision that can reconcile growth with equity along the twin paths of increased productivity and participation. The gains and setbacks of the century are guideposts to help shape that vision, and for determining the best path for the development of Latin America and the Caribbean in the years ahead.

ENRIQUE V. IGLESIAS
President
Inter-American Development Bank

MANUEL MARIN GONZALEZ
Vice President
European Commission

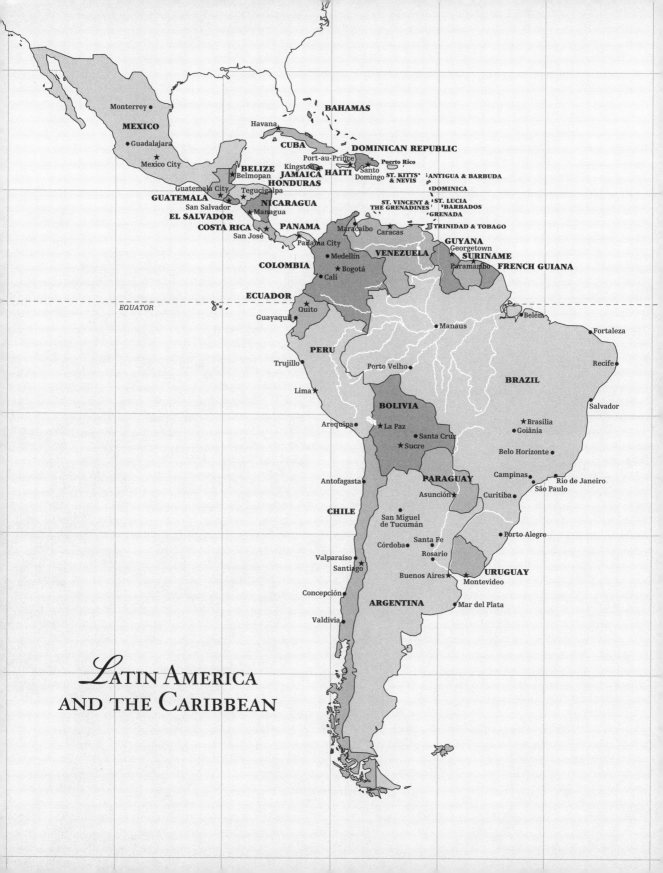

Monterrey ●

MEXICO

● Guadalajara

Havana ●

Mexico City ●

BAHAMAS

CUBA

Port-au-Prince ● **DOMINICAN REPUBLIC**

Kingston ● Santo **Puerto Rico**

★ Belmopan **JAMAICA HAITI** Domingo ● ANTIGUA & BARBUDA

BELIZE **ST. KITTS'**
& NEVIS

Guatemala City ● **HONDURAS** **DOMINICA**

GUATEMALA ★ Tegucigalpa ★

San Salvador ● **NICARAGUA** ST. VINCENT & **ST. LUCIA**
THE GRENADINES ★ **BARBADOS**

EL SALVADOR ★ Managua **GRENADA**

COSTA RICA Maracaibo ● **TRINIDAD & TOBAGO**

★ San José **PANAMA** Caracas ●

Panama City ● **VENEZUELA** **GUYANA**
Georgetown ★

Medellín ● **SURINAME**

COLOMBIA ★ Bogotá Paramaribo ★ **FRENCH GUIANA**

● Cali

EQUATOR **ECUADOR**

Quito ★

Guayaquil ● Belém ●

Manaus ● Fortaleza ●

PERU

Trujillo ● Porto Velho ● Recife ●

Lima ★ **BRAZIL**

BOLIVIA Salvador ●

Arequipa ● ★ La Paz

● Santa Cruz Brasília ★

★ Sucre Goiânia ●

Belo Horizonte ●

Antofagasta ● **PARAGUAY** Campinas ● Rio de Janeiro ●

Asunción ★ Curitiba ● São Paulo ●

CHILE San Miguel
de Tucumán ●

Santa Fe ● Porto Alegre ●

Córdoba ● Rosario ●

Valparaíso ● **URUGUAY**

Santiago ★ Buenos Aires ★ ★ Montevideo

Concepción ● Mar del Plata ●

Valdivia ● **ARGENTINA**

ℒatin America
and the Caribbean

CHAPTER 1

INTRODUCTION

THE YEAR 2000 INVITES A RETROSPECTIVE analysis of the century. The challenge of this book is to capture that century, with its lights and shadows—the positive and the negative. It asks the basic question: What did the Latin American economies achieve in the course of a hundred years, and how did those achievements come about? For the continent certainly changed. In 1900, there were some 70 million Latin Americans; by the year 2000, there will be 500 million. Three-quarters of the population lived in the countryside when the century began; today, two in three live in cities. In 1900, three-quarters were illiterate; at the century's end, seven of eight adults can read and write. Life changed dramatically for ordinary people in four generations.

The economy also grew. In the year 2000, the continental per capita income will be five times higher than in 1900 (Figure 1.1). Yet, while Latin America progressed economically, it failed to gain ground on the developed world. Average per capita income of the larger Latin American economies was 14 percent that of the United States in 1900 and 13 percent in the 1990s. Income relative to Northern Europe rose by mid-century, only to decline again.[1] Industry grew from

---

[1] Using data from Maddison (1983), Latin American GDP was around 16 percent of that of the average of France, Germany and Britain at the turn of the century, and rose to 23 percent by mid-century. Latin America's GDP was about 30 percent of that of Spain and Italy in 1900, reaching 40 percent by 1950. Positions were reversed in the second half of the century.

Photo: Sugar harvest in Cuba, circa 1900.

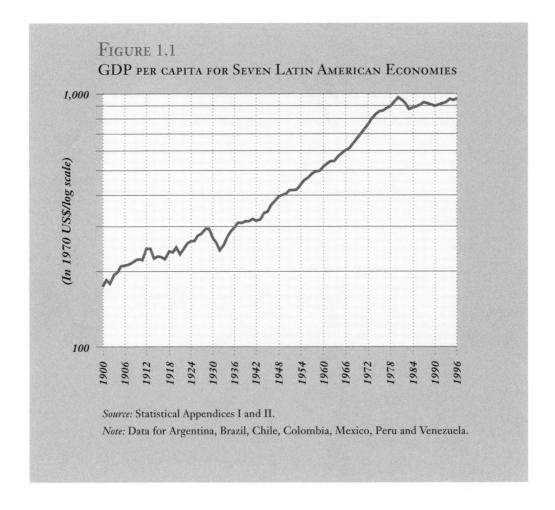

FIGURE 1.1
GDP PER CAPITA FOR SEVEN LATIN AMERICAN ECONOMIES

Source: Statistical Appendices I and II.
Note: Data for Argentina, Brazil, Chile, Colombia, Mexico, Peru and Venezuela.

some 5 to 25 percent of GDP, but the continent's share of world trade fell from 7 to 3 percent, and at the end of the century over half of exports were still primary products such as coffee, oil, sugar, iron ore and copper. Financial dependence grew as foreign debt increased and Latin America remained vulnerable to external shocks.

Life expectancy increased from 40 to 70 years, and literacy rates rose from 30 to 85 percent of adults. However, income distribution almost certainly worsened: it was probably the worst in the world by the 1960s, and deteriorated even further as the continent struggled to adjust in the 1980s. Today, two in every five Latin American families rank as poor.

Behind the aggregate growth performance lay a transformation of the basic economic structures of the Latin American countries. Not even the smallest country in 1900 could have been considered an integrated nation. In every country, remote regional economies and societies had little interaction with the rest of the economy, and links, if there were any, might well have run outward. In Mexico, the Yucatán peninsula had no rail connection with the rest of the country and traded principally with the United States. When a thirsty customer ordered a "foreign" beer in Mérida he was sold a glass of Dos Equis—from Orizaba.[2] So-called "internal" trade was conducted by strange routes: Peruvian timber destined for Lima arrived by way of the Amazon and a long sea journey around Cape Horn. Southern Brazil exported hides, skins and jerked beef but sold almost none to the rest of the country. Sugar and cotton economies in the Brazilian Northeast and the rubber economy in the Amazon formed similar islands.[3]

With this went a lack of national monetary integration. Bolivian currency circulated in the south of Peru and Guatemalan pesos in the south of Mexico. In some villages, trade was still based on barter: maize, beans, dried chili and tortillas were common means of exchange in parts of rural Mexico.[4] Pure subsistence economies were rare, since small-scale local commerce existed everywhere and used money, but a recognizably "modern" economy absorbed only a small part of the population. At the turn of the century, Haber reckons, some two-thirds of the Mexican population remained outside the consumer economy.[5] As late as the 1930s, more than half of the Venezuelan economy was still described as precapitalist.[6] International trade involved only primary commodities, with little processing. In-

---

[2] See Knight in Companion Volume 1. He vividly describes the lack of regional integration during the period.

[3] See Abreu in Companion Volume 1.

[4] Tannenbaum, cited by Knight in Companion Volume 1.

[5] Haber, 1989: 27. Estimating the amount of production that was subsistence is virtually impossible, since estimates of production were made from the area planted or sown, thus automatically incorporating, at least in principle, subsistence farming.

[6] Córdova, in Silva Michelena and Córdova, 1967.

dustry existed, and, indeed, had a significant tradition behind it in Brazil, Argentina and Mexico. Factory production had begun in Chile and Peru in the 1870s. But nowhere did the share of manufacturing in GDP exceed 10 percent, and industry produced only for the national market.

By mid-century, a revolution in infrastructure and national integration had occurred. Transport costs fell nationally and internationally between 1880 and 1920 and the change was only beginning. By the end of the century, a further revolution had occurred, with air travel and transport, telex, fax and the internet further easing communication and movement.

Implicit in the economic history of this century is a story of institutional transformation. By institutions we mean both the usual organizations, such as the judiciary, central banks, planning ministries and firms, as well as the rules of the game such as property rights, and even social customs, all of which are an important part of the fabric that conditions behavior and response of economic agents. The 1920s were a decade of substantial institutional innovation, with central banks becoming almost universal for the first time, and customs and tax collection agencies taking new shape. From the 1940s to the 1960s, the principal institutional growth was in public enterprises, development banks, industrial development institutions, and agricultural development agencies promoting technology and credit. With the shift in the development model in the 1970s and 1980s away from state intervention and towards free markets, Latin America entered a phase during which many organizations were abolished, downgraded or privatized. Establishing or strengthening other types of institutions, such as stable rules of the game and regulatory bodies, assumed pivotal importance.

Within this process of overall growth, the continent experienced a clear pattern of waves of expansion that responded to the growth phases of the world economy. The first phase of expansion was already well under way at the start of the century, its starting date anywhere after 1850 depending on the country in question. In a few cases, internal disorder was such that the expansion only really began with the new century. The second phase began with the renewed expansion of the world economy after the disruptions of the two World Wars and the Great Depression. While world expansion was important to this wave of growth, the principal focus in Latin America was inward looking. In many countries, expansion was for the first time faster than the growth of the purchasing power of exports (Figure 1.2). Each phase

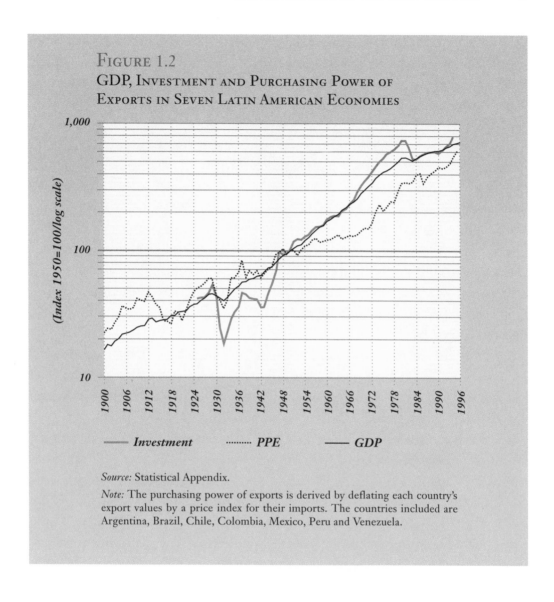

FIGURE 1.2
GDP, INVESTMENT AND PURCHASING POWER OF
EXPORTS IN SEVEN LATIN AMERICAN ECONOMIES

Source: Statistical Appendix.

Note: The purchasing power of exports is derived by deflating each country's export values by a price index for their imports. The countries included are Argentina, Brazil, Chile, Colombia, Mexico, Peru and Venezuela.

ended with a decade when growth was still strong but sustained by forces which, with hindsight, can be seen to have spelled danger: while expansion of exports continued for some countries in both the 1920s and the 1970s, growth was prolonged throughout the region by a flood of foreign loans. When external conditions abruptly became less favorable, problems of debt were added to continuing problems of dependence on foreign markets. Each phase gave way to a period first of recession, then transition. Following the first expansion, these phases lasted, for some countries, from 1929 to the 1950s. The second recession began with the debt crisis of 1982, and the ensuing transition is still in process as the century ends. These phases can be traced out in the pattern of exports, GDP, per capita GDP and investment shown in Figures 1.1 and 1.2.

The first wave of expansion was essentially a period of primary export-led growth. But labor was scarce, a problem only partially remedied by immigration. This scarcity led perversely not to a good income distribution with high returns to labor, but rather to institutions that repressed and controlled labor and created a labor supply by dispossessing peasants. Indian communities in particular were often dispossessed and evicted, while various forms of forced labor helped to secure a cheap supply of workers. These developments simply extended the colonial inheritance of land concentration and the subjugation of Indian peoples. Inequality was thus knit deeply into the fabric of the model and was part of its effectiveness in generating growth.

Each national story of export expansion had different consequences for vested interests, for policymaking, and for the links between the two. The result was that the ability of policymakers to manage change varied, but, as we shall see, was always embedded in unequal structures.

When expansion ended with the Great Depression of 1929, the fact that the motor of growth was damaged did nothing to change social and political structures. As the transition period melded slowly into the new pattern of expansion, significant institutional change occurred, but not in patterns of ownership. There was growth of a middle class and even of indigenous social movements, but the traditional elite groups remained extremely powerful. The institutional change involved expansion and redirection of the role of the state in promoting growth. But governments and private sectors were in large measure responding to the existing socioeconomic structure, so the significant gains in building institutions did little to ameliorate the inequality embedded in the status quo. In the previous expansion phase, export-led growth had actually shaped and cemented the structure of income distribution and the institutions delivering it. Inequality was functional to the efficiency of the growth path. In this second phase, the distribution of resources was a given from the start and not radically modified. Major institutional development occurred, but was directed principally at enlarging and focusing the role of the state. In most countries, this expansion was funded by indirect taxation, exchange rate manipulation, profits of state enterprises, and borrowing, and did not involve any direct confrontation with traditional power groups (such as increasing direct taxes). Thus the deep entrenchment of sociopolitical structures in an unequal system persisted through the first shift in the development model. In fact, the new patterns actually reinforced the existing distribution of income, since the expanding economic activities were capital-intensive, employment creation was slower than the growth of demand for jobs, and the structure of production catered to existing demand, producing consumer durables for upper- and middle-class urban residents.

Income concentration was not optimal for the dynamics of the new industrialization model, since it would have been desirable to have a wider national market, more broadly-based domestic savings, more flexible policymaking, and more investment in human resources. However, the existing power structure, vested interests, and the short-term economic costs of change all militated against a decisive policy of redistribution. Efforts tended to fall short for both political and economic reasons, as with land reform, which was at once technically difficult and opposed by vested interests. Technical failures further strengthened support for the status quo.

The period of transition of Latin America's next expansionary phase is still in progress as the end of the century approaches. Once again, crisis has brought a new policy approach, a change more abrupt and ideological than in the first transition. Once again, the new approach is embedded in the existing structure, exacerbating inequality by worsening income distribution, a clear empirical finding for the 1980s. However, in the 1990s, policy is perceptibly shifting, becoming more pragmatic and diverse. Social issues appear to be moving up the agenda in a number of countries. These developments frame the questions and challenges at the end of the century. Are any of the disadvantages that lack of equity brought to the postwar model still relevant today? How far is inequality in fact functional to the new approach? Can growth-friendly policies be made compatible with social equity?

STRUCTURE OF THE BOOK

This book considers the dramatic transformation in output and in institutions over the century, and the equally dramatic record of inequity and poverty. The analytical approach we use combines quantitative data with what is known as "political economy," a shorthand for the interface between political forces, institutional inheritance and economic outcomes. Political economy studies how economic policies and their results emerge from a particular balance of political forces, are executed with varying degrees of efficiency in the interests of a distinct group or several groups, and are refined by mechanisms of consultation or accountability. For a "political" economist, it is significant that outcomes vary greatly in both growth and equity terms depending on political and institutional factors.

Chronological analysis of the century begins in Chapters Three and Four with the period from 1900 to 1945. This is preceded by a preliminary scene-setting in Chapter Two, which tries to quantify progress and poverty for the century. It also begins to elucidate exclusion by exploring important interactions between such factors as gender, literacy, poverty and the environment.

Chapters Three and Four overlap chronologically; the first explores the nature of export-led growth across the continent up to 1930. By comparing experiences in different countries, the chapter seeks an explanation for the very different experiences of growth, institution building, development of policymaking capacity, concentration of income and wealth, and environmental damage. Explanations are found in a wide range of factors, but they point in particular to the nature of the export commodity, relations with international capital and markets, and preexisting conditions. For example, it made a difference for equity whether or not there was an indigenous population that had to be displaced or dispossessed for export expansion to occur. Chapter Four examines the impact of external shocks between 1914 and 1945–wars and depression–and seeks patterns in the responses of countries to the threats and opportunities represented by such shocks.

The next period, 1945 to 1973, is considered in Chapters Five and Six. This period saw significant growth of the role and functions of the state and an associated development of institutions. The larger countries industrialized significantly, the smaller countries less so, aided in some cases by economic integration. Agriculture and primary exports were widely neglected and income distribution generally worsened, though standards of living improved, in contrast with the later period. Inflation became a widespread problem among the larger economies. Again, national capacities for managing the process and adjusting are examined, as the pitfalls of excess protection of industry and discrimination against exports and agriculture became more visible.

The final period begins with the quadrupling of the price of oil in 1973. The analysis traces the impact of a sudden increase in external funds and of no less sudden a withdrawal after 1982. We follow the evolution through years of mismanaged adjustment to the shock of the debt crisis, and then to the major shift in model in the 1980s, which it is to be hoped will slowly evolve into a new period of growth—and possibly even greater concerns with equity—by the end of the century.

The final chapter reflects on what the analysis of the century teaches us and attempts to draw it together, even though the story itself suggests the impossibility of writing a book about "Latin America" per se. We are dealing with countries radically different in size, both of territory and population, ranging from Brazil, today with 150 million people, to the smallest states of the Caribbean. The ethnic composition of the countries varies as well: compare Mexico, Peru, Ecuador, Bolivia and Guatemala, with their large indigenous populations, to Argentina, 30 percent of whose population was foreign in 1914, largely European in origin.[7] The commodity lottery, to use Carlos Díaz-Alejandro's striking phrase, accounts for further differences in both wealth and fortune, with the important outcomes that are the story of Chapter Three. Even *within* countries, the differences are so great, and the lack of integration at least for the first 40 years so marked, that some writers speak of national economies as archipelagos of distinct regions and localities.

There remains an irresistible temptation to draw out common threads and seek systematic explanations of different outcomes. But the objective here is to include as much comparative analysis among countries and as much micro detail as the text can bear—perhaps *more* than it can bear, but that seemed the better direction in which to fall off the tightrope. The "Companion Volumes" described in the preface are a second part of the strategy and, to continue the metaphor, provide an important safety net.

---

[7] Sánchez-Albornoz, 1986: 137.

THE ACTORS

From an economist's perspective, the driving forces of growth are the accumulation of capital and the technical change embodied in it. Behind this process lie three principal classes of economic actors, each with its distinct way of working. First are the small or medium-sized local enterprises, known as SMEs, typically family-owned. These entrepreneurs often have an ambiguous attitude toward growth, since a larger firm brings the threat of loss of family control. Second are public sector enterprises, their distinctive characteristics being a lack of budget constraints, and vulnerability to pressures to view providing employment as a goal in itself. Third are the large, profit-oriented firms, ranging from multinationals based in developed countries, and their Latin American versions (all referred to here as transnationals, or TNCs), to domestic groups that shade down to the SME end of the scale. At the start of the century, the SMEs dominated. Public enterprises were almost nonexistent and TNCs few in number, though they often accounted for much if not all export production.

Since political economy is the analytical tool being used to examine the century's economic development, the range of actors must be extended to include business groups, civil society organizations such as unions, popular groupings such as women's organizations and peasant associations, political parties, nongovernmental organizations (NGOs), and the state itself, which comprises the civil service bureaucracy, the government in power at the time, and public enterprises. Government itself is never a single actor, but comprises the central executive, the ministries, and local governments, in addition to public enterprises, each with its own agenda and varying levels of competence.

The military has also been an important actor. In the 1930s and 1940s, its influence was seen both within government and without, building up industry and influencing its structure (see Chapter Five). In the 1950s and more so in the 1960s, the military often attempted to impose economic as well as political order. By the 1980s, they had returned to barracks.

Finally, there are external actors: foreign governments, international financial institutions (increasingly after the 1940s), and an important homegrown international organization in the shape of the Economic Commission for Latin America and the Caribbean.

The nonspecialist reader may reasonably ask where ordinary people might appear in such a list. They are indeed the heart of the story, but it is impossible to tell this kind of history through individual cases. A few brief histories have been included in order to give a sense of what lies behind the statistical categories with which we have to work.

CHAPTER 2

GROWTH AND THE QUALITY OF LIFE OVER THE CENTURY

THAT THERE WAS ECONOMIC GROWTH in Latin America over the course of a century is a given, but what was the *quality* of that growth? The most obvious impact of growth on the quality of life concerns the distribution of the benefits of that growth. But other aspects also affect quality, such as the security and sustainability of the growth process, particularly in terms of the stability of income and prices. Both can affect the gains from growth and its viability. Instability can be linked to vulnerability to external shocks emanating from an unstable world economy: we need to explore the ways in which growth might have become more or less resilient to such shocks. Lastly, environmental costs (and benefits, perhaps) affect the quality of growth, though there are few data to explore how far such costs have in fact undermined the viability of the growth path.

This chapter first documents growth itself in terms of output, productivity and infrastructure. It then examines the four elements that help determine the quality of growth: stability of growth, stability of prices, economic dimensions of external dependence, and environmental costs. We then attempt to explore social welfare, first via poverty and income distribution, which requires analysis of demographic

Photo: Tin miners in Bolivia, 1940.

trends. Finally, the chapter examines literacy and life expectancy, concluding with an attempt to build a Historical Living Standards Index for the century. Most of the data has been consigned to the Statistical Appendix, in the interest of readability.[1]

ECONOMIC GROWTH AND INFRASTRUCTURE

Aggregate economic growth for Latin America over the century was over 4 percent a year.[2] The century can be broken down into phases of faster and slower growth, which shape the structure of the following chapters. The initial rapid growth of the early century, based on primary exports and capital inflow, gave way to somewhat slower growth starting with the First World War, followed by the fastest period of growth between 1945 and 1973, then by a decline (Table 2.1). Most countries for which we have data experienced their most rapid growth in the post-WWII period, except for Argentina, Chile, Cuba and, probably, Uruguay, all of which had faster growth in their initial export economy phase.[3] Thus a major change in ranking occurred: the leaders of the early period were overtaken by Brazil and Mexico in the second half of the century.

Exports fueled growth in the early period, with one remarkable exception: from 1900-29, Brazil grew faster than her export sector (Appendix Table VI.2). Chapter Four explores how all but the smallest countries were forced into a change of direction by the shocks of the first half of the century. After 1945, the rate of

---

[1] The data collection comes primarily from original work for this project by Pablo Astorga and Valpy Fitzgerald (economic growth, productivity and vulnerability), Andre Hofman (GDP and investment), Oscar Altimir (income distribution) and Shane and Barbara Hunt (life expectancy and literacy).

[2] The estimate is based on data for eight countries for the whole century, reported in Appendix Tables II.2 and II.3, weighted by income size. Comparison between the period from 1920-92, for which we have 13 countries, and 1945-96, for which we have data for 19, suggests that the eight are a reasonable proxy for total GDP growth, with the per capita figure being slightly exaggerated, as the new entrants tend to have higher population growth rates.

[3] There are no early GDP figures for Uruguay. Cuba becomes difficult to incorporate in the comparative analysis after 1959. With the revolution, the country adopted the Communist system of material balances for its accounting of growth, which excludes all services and commerce. The Caribbean cannot be incorporated in any full way in the early part of the century, for lack of data.

TABLE 2.1
GDP RATE OF GROWTH BY PERIOD
(In percent)

	1900-29	1900-13	1913-29	1929-45	1945-72	1972-81	1981-96	1900-80	1900-96
Argentina	3.8	6.3	4.1	3.4	3.8	2.5	1.9	3.5	3.3
Brazil	4.2	4.1	5.1	4.4	6.9	6.6	2.4	5.5	5.5
Chile	2.9	3.6	3.7	3.0	4.1	3.6	5.4	3.2	3.3
Colombia	4.5	4.4	4.9	3.8	5.1	5.0	4.0	4.7	4.7
Ecuador		5.0	4.1	3.3	5.3	7.0	2.6	4.8	4.8
Mexico	3.4	3.4	1.4[a]	4.2	6.5	5.5	1.5	5.2	5.0
Peru	4.5	4.5	5.3	2.8	5.3	3.4	0.4	4.2	3.9
Venezuela	5.0	2.3	9.2	4.2	5.7	4.7	2.2	6.5	5.9
LA-8	3.6	4.3	3.3	3.8	5.6	5.2	2.3	4.3	4.3
Central America		3.8[b]	2.9	5.4	3.8	2.7	4.2[b]	4.0[b]
Latin America				5.3	3.7	2.2		

Note: LA-8 is comprised of the countries listed above. Central America includes Costa Rica, Guatemala, Honduras, El Salvador and Nicaragua.
[a] Figures for Mexico during this period exclude the years of the revolution (1911-1920).
[b] Data begin in 1920.
Source: Statistical Appendix II.

growth of the aggregate economy for most countries generally exceeded growth of exports. What lay behind this fact is explored in Chapter Five.

The same sense of cyclical growth and similar timing is seen in the "productivity" per capita of the economically active population.[4] Data for the larger economies, given in Statistical Appendix IV, show initial rapid and fluctuating growth in output per person, both sectorally and in aggregate. This was followed typically by a period of more unstable and rather slow growth, then a change of trend, particularly in industrial productivity, sometime in the 1940s or 1950s. Sustained increases in productivity then continued in a rather stable way until the 1970s. These periods are summa-

---

[4] This is value added per worker recorded for census purposes as belonging to the sector, whether employed or not. So it is hardly productivity in the usual sense (see Statistical Appendix). These data are presented and analyzed much more fully in a forthcoming paper by those responsible for building the series for this book, Pablo Astorga and Valpy Fitzgerald.

TABLE 2.2
PHASES OF PRODUCTIVITY GROWTH, 1900-90

	Argentina	Brazil	Chile	Mexico	Venezuela
Early high growth, unstable	1900-13	1900-20	No data	1900-10	No data
Period of relatively slow growth, high instability	1914-50s	1921-47	1908-38	1910-40	1926-50
Accelerating stable high growth	1950s-74	1947-80	1938-72	1940-81	1950-77
Deceleration with increased instability	1975-90	1986-90	1972-90	1982-90	1977-90

Source: Statistical Appendix IV.

rized in Table 2.2, which indicates when the change in trend occurred, based on the three indicators: industrial, agricultural and total output per economically active person.[5]

Another way to approach the claim to substantial progress over the century is to explore the growth of infrastructure. The end of the 19th century and the early part of the 20th century saw a wave of investment in railways (Table 2.3). This surge was based on substantial external financing. At the same time, there was expansion of ports and development of financial infrastructure in the form of private banks. In the early period, three countries led the process—Argentina, Uruguay and Cuba—with Chile and Mexico close behind. Brazil's indicators were of course affected by the enormous extension of the country: its relatively low ranking underestimates the level of development of certain regions in Brazil. In terms of social infrastructure in the form of social welfare networks, the five pioneers in the 1920s and 1930s were Argentina, Uruguay, Cuba, Chile and Brazil, with social security programs including pensions and sickness benefits.[6]

---

[5] The Statistical Appendix gives the data on which this is based, and also the standard deviations of the growth rates, as an indicator of the degree of stability.

[6] The term pioneer is Mesa-Lago's. For example, 11 countries had industrial accident insurance by the 1920s. Mesa-Lago, 1994: 15.

TABLE 2.3
GROWTH OF INFRASTRUCTURE IN LATIN AMERICA
(Compound annual growth rates in percent)

	Length of railways	Electric energy	Telephones in use	Motor vehicles[a]
1880-1900	7.9	...	...	...
1900-13	4.3	...	...	...
1913-30	1.1	...	7.8	...
1930-50	0.4	9.1	5.3	3.5
1950-70	-0.3	9.5	6.6	8.7
1970-95	-0.3	6.9[b]	8.2[c]	6.9[c]

Note: Measurements are based on kilometers for length of railway track, kilowatts per hour for output of electric energy, and number in use for telephones and motor vehicles.
[a] Roads have not been included, as the sources available could not be reconciled. Motor vehicles are given as a poor proxy for roads, which no doubt failed to expand proportionately.
[b] Data end in 1994.
[c] Data end in 1990.
Source: Statistical Appendix X.

The post-World War II period saw strong growth of infrastructure decade by decade. Brazil and Venezuela moved up the ranking, and generally the gap between countries closed somewhat.[7]

QUALITY OF GROWTH

Instability, Vulnerability and the Environment

By its very nature, growth may be more or less unstable. The recent consensus, although there is debate over this, is that greater instability in Latin America has adversely affected investor confidence and thus investment.[8] The Statistical Appendix tests for the variability of the growth rate and finds that the instability of growth was reduced from 1930 onwards, but that instability increased again after

---

[7] See Appendix X to appraise levels of infrastructure by country.
[8] Inter-American Development Bank, 1996.

1973 (Appendix Table II.4). This is an important finding for the analysis of the later period.

A further aspect of instability is more obvious: prices. Inflation can slow growth by aggravating uncertainty and reducing savings (unless indexation is more or less complete, as in Brazil from the 1960s to the 1980s). The account in Chapter Five of the Argentine immigrant entrepreneur, Samuel, demonstrates how credit systems and small businesses can be undermined (Box 5.2). Inflation can prompt repeated efforts at stabilization, which in the 1950s and 1960s damaged growth and often failed to cure inflation. Price rises may also hit the poor more than the rich, since the poor have fewer ways of defending themselves. The record on inflation (Appendix Table V.1) shows that in the first half of the century it was moderate, with a few exceptions: Colombia had hyperinflation during the Thousand Days War at the start of the century, Chile had rates consistently above the average over decades, and Mexico suffered inflation in the first years of the revolution. The problem became severe for many of the larger countries towards the end of the 1960s, but improved somewhat in the 1990s—an important part of the story of Chapter Eight. By the mid-1990s, even Brazil's high rate had come down.

External shocks can also cause economic instability, and exposure to such shocks may increase or decrease with time. If an economy grows but in so doing increases, say, its dependence on imported foodstuffs, its export concentration on a few products and markets, and its level of debt, it seems important at least to note these facts. We have constructed a data set to look at these aspects of external dependence over the long run. The preliminary results, summarized in Appendix VII, suggest that over the century the major countries did reduce their degree of exposure in a number of areas. In particular, commodity concentration of exports became far less pronounced by the 1980s and 1990s, geographical concentration of exports and imports was reduced, and the dependence of fiscal revenue on the level of trade fell noticeably from mid-century. Dependence on oil imports varied greatly. Between countries, it was a function of local production possibilities, and for any given country, it was also a result of the instability of the price of oil. Dependence on food imports fell somewhat, though some highly dependent countries remained so.

Financial exposure increased in the 1970s and 1980s, with increased debt, greater vulnerability to interest rate changes and a higher propensity to move capital internationally (see Chapter Six). And the increased diversity of trade, while on the whole positive, in part represented a new dependence on fragile intraregional trade, which tended to transmit the effects of recession between neighbors.

What happened in the smaller countries, however, was a more unhappy tale. The Caribbean forms the extreme case. Here, trade measures of openness remained extraordinarily high. For example, in 19 of the 26 states (on the widest definition of the Caribbean), the ratio of exports and imports of goods and services to GDP in the 1990s was over 100 percent, and often far over. The larger countries—the Dominican Republic, Haiti and Trinidad and Tobago—still had ratios of around 50 to 70 percent.[9] Exports remained concentrated in a very small number of primary products: 78 percent of exports for Jamaica, and 76 percent for Trinidad and Tobago.[10] In addition, new forms of financial exposure were simply added to old forms of vulnerability, including geopolitical vulnerability and the ecological vulnerability of small island economies in a region prone to hurricanes and volcanic eruptions.

These three aspects of the quality of growth—instability of growth itself and of prices, and external vulnerability—can interact in any number of ways to make the development path less secure. We shall try to tease out the interrelations and the consequences as we narrate our story period by period.

The fourth and final qualification to the gains from growth occurs when they are associated with environmental destruction, to the point of endangering long-run growth. Obviously, resource consumption is a necessary part of progress. Defining what is "too much" involves weighing both present competing interests and the interests of future generations. Measuring the latter is often complicated, since it implies quantifying imponderables such as which resources will be most in demand in the future.

Just as for other parts of the world, lack of concern historically means that there is little information from which to calculate the environmental costs of growth for Latin America. Contemporary data suggest the cost has clearly been high, but there is no way to determine exactly when and where those costs were incurred, nor to match one country or one product against another. Sensitivity to these

---

[9] Girvan, 1997, Table A2.

[10] Harker, El Hadj and Vinhas de Souza, 1996.

issues is extremely important for the future, however, so it is important to review what little historical background is available. Latin America in the 19th century was marked by incipient environmental interest, mostly that of "amateur enthusiasts in natural sciences," while by the 1920s and 1930s some enhanced perception of new environmental problems worked toward the adoption of legislation and the creation of forest agencies, notably in Mexico and Brazil.[11] But in the postwar period, economic growth took over as the overwhelming goal. Only by the 1980s was there a hesitant acceptance of environmental concerns. Still, in comparative terms, there is no reason to think that the environmental cost of Latin America's growth has been any higher than anywhere else—possibly the cost has been lower, since the continent has been relatively well endowed with natural resources and has had lower population density than, say, Asia. Subsequent chapters try to introduce the more qualitative evidence where it exists; here we would make six points in summary of the continent's historical experience.

First, the rapid expansion of most crops in Latin America was associated with some degree of resource abuse, leading to deforestation, erosion, and, where irrigation was practiced, salinity. In Mexico, 79 percent of arable land is eroded, 28 percent severely so, and 16 percent denuded. In the Andes, erosion affects 30 to 80 percent of arable land, depending on the region.[12] Any crop requiring irrigation is open to mismanagement and thus salinity: it is estimated that today 8 percent of Latin America's agricultural land is thus affected.[13]

Second, large estates and export crops together often led to monoculture, which was usually damaging to soil quality and prone to disease. An example was banana expansion in Central America, which illustrates the two severe problems of monoculture: disease and pollution, the former caused by repeated use of land for one crop, the latter often resulting from the methods used to treat disease and falling soil fertility.

Third, the deficiencies or absence of institutions constrained implementation of progressive policies. For example, a code to induce replanting of trees was introduced surprisingly early in Brazil, but was ignored. The first reforestation program

---

[11] Dean, 1995.

[12] Altieri and Masera, 1993: 100.

[13] Sunkel, 1980: 36.

was developed in 1862, but was ineffective and few trees were planted. In 1933-34, the Vargas government set up a forest code, denying absolute rights of property, prohibiting the cutting of trees along water courses or those harboring rare species or protecting watersheds, and forbidding owners to cut more than three-quarters of the trees on their property. The code was unsuccessful both because it was not enforced and because of the many problems in the way it was designed. There were easy ways to evade the law. Implementation required that each county set up a forest delegation for enforcement, but few were established.[14]

Fourth, mining has often had knock-on effects on agriculture. The problems have typically been those of contamination, such as arsenic in the water supplies of the area surrounding Southern Peru Copper Corporation in Ilo in the 1960s, or contamination of land by smelter fumes around Cerro de Pasco in Central Peru in the 1920s and 1930s. For the sheer quantity of pollutants released into the air and water, the mining sector has been the most important source of industrial pollution.[15]

Fifth, urban industrial problems, present throughout the century, emerged as the chief environmental cost of growth as the century closed, reflecting the extraordinary levels of urbanization and industrial concentration that had developed by the 1960s.[16] Since the developed world began to show concern for pollution only in the 1970s,[17] it was hardly to be expected that Latin American governments should do so earlier. From the end of the 1950s, industrial production followed the developed country trend toward capital-intensity and energy (oil) intensity, while the mechanization of agriculture took agribusiness in the same direction. The most dynamic industries were characterized by high degrees of toxicity, releasing mercury, lead, manganese, chromium, cadmium and even radioactive materials, all elements which directly destroy the organic compounds of the environment.[18]

Sixth, these technological trends have reinforced the traditional geographical concentration of industrial production in Latin America. In consequence, pollution problems have been severe for those living in large cities. By the end of the 1970s,

---

[14] This paragraph is based on Dean, 1995: 225, 262.

[15] Meller, Ryan and Solimano, 1996: 265.

[16] Tolba, 1980; Sunkel, 1980; Tomassini, 1980.

[17] With a few exceptions, such as London's smog and clean air legislation in the 1950s.

[18] Sunkel, 1980: 32. This kind of pollution is more expensive to treat than organic pollution.

seven states or provinces in three countries (Buenos Aires, Santa Fé, Guanabara, Rio de Janeiro, São Paulo, Mexico City and Monterrey) accounted for 75 percent of the industrial product in Latin America.[19] By the 1990s, 80 million people were living in cities with permanent air pollution problems; several cities (Mexico City, Rio de Janeiro, São Paulo, Santiago) exhibited some of the worst urban pollution problems in the world.[20]

Demography, Distribution and Poverty

The starting point for a discussion of distribution and poverty has to be population growth, if only in a purely accounting sense, since the expansion of population reduces high output growth rates to the distinctly more modest rates of per capita income growth reported earlier in Figure 1.1.

Population growth rates are given in Table 2.4. Where immigration occurred, population growth in fact helped economic growth in the early years, since immigration to certain countries brought the labor supply needed for the export boom. The fall in the birth rate began as early as the 1920s in Argentina, Uruguay and Cuba,[21] but in general the population growth rate was still rising strongly as mortality rates fell.

From 1930, with those exceptions, Latin America became a region of extremely high population growth—the highest in the world by mid-century. Immigration now played only a small role. Governments began to invest heavily in public health. The Rockefeller Foundation played an increasing role from the 1920s, partly responding to foreign investors' concern about health risks.[22] The Foundation started Schools of Public Hygiene and ran vaccination campaigns in such countries as Mexico, Costa Rica, Chile and Colombia. As countries benefited from such public health interventions, death rates began to fall more significantly after the Second World War. Declines in deaths from infectious diseases accounted for 21 percent

---

[19] Sunkel, 1990: 32-33. São Paulo, for example, has 56 percent of Brazil's chemical industry, 80 percent of transport equipment, 90 percent of the rubber industry, and 66 percent of the paper industry.

[20] Altieri and Masera, 1993: 100.

[21] Sánchez-Albornoz, 1986; Merrick, 1994.

[22] Abel, 1996: 20.

TABLE 2.4
COMPOUND RATE OF POPULATION GROWTH
(In percent)

	1900-30	1930-50	1950-70	1970-95
Argentina	3.1	1.8	1.7	1.5
Bolivia	1.0	1.1	2.2	2.3
Brazil	2.1	2.4	3.0	2.1
Chile	1.3	1.7	2.3	1.6
Colombia	2.2	2.0	3.1	2.5
Costa Rica	1.6	2.4	3.9	2.8
Cuba	2.8	2.1	2.2	1.0
Dominican Republic	2.6	2.6	3.2	2.7
Ecuador	2.5	2.5	2.9	2.6
El Salvador	2.0	1.3	3.1	2.1
Guatemala	2.3	2.4	3.2	2.8
Haiti	2.2	1.2	1.6	2.1
Honduras	2.8	2.1	3.1	3.1
Mexico	0.8	2.4	3.1	2.4
Nicaragua	1.6	2.2	2.8	3.3
Panama	1.9	2.8	2.9	2.5
Paraguay	0.9	2.5	2.4	3.2
Peru	1.0	1.6	2.5	2.6
Uruguay	2.2	1.2	1.0	0.7
Venezuela	0.9	2.2	3.8	2.9
Latin America	1.8	2.1	2.7	2.2

Source: Statistical Appendix I.

of the decline in mortality between 1950 and 1973. Birth rates continued to rise after the Second World War, except in Argentina, Uruguay, Cuba, Chile and southern Brazil. It was only in the 1960s or even the 1970s that the fertility decline spread to most other countries, though not even then to the Caribbean and much of Central America.[23]

   Population growth reduced high growth rates to more modest levels in terms of growth of per capita income. Interestingly, the expected further effect—that popu-

---

[23] Merrick, 1994.

176643

lation growth would weaken the rate of growth of income itself—failed to occur. Growth weakened or disappeared in response to external shocks in mid-century, but reasserted itself in the 1950s and 1960s, and difficulties since 1980 have had other origins. It was in fact a Latin American country, Mexico, that played a key role in the evolving analysis of the population issue. A study done in 1956, around the peak time for rapid population growth, noted that in Mexico, despite rising incomes and urbanization, birth rates were not declining as they had done in Western Europe.[24] The study predicted that the resulting high ratio of dependents in the population would drag down the growth of income. Coale, one of the authors, revisited Mexico 20 years later and found that while his population predictions had been correct, his income growth predictions had not: Mexico had grown contrary to his prediction.[25] The reason for the earlier error, however, was that Coale had assumed that with a rising proportion of dependents in the population, governments would actually divert expenditure to cover increased social needs, thus taking resources from directly productive investment. This typically did not happen.

This analysis gives an important insight into the significance of a high and increasing rate of population growth: it may not affect GDP growth, but it may worsen income distribution in two principal ways. First, it fails to lower the growth rate only because resources are not allocated to social spending, which can for the most part only help growth and income distribution in the medium term, whereas children need care immediately. Secondly, birth rates tend to be higher among poorer families with less access to education. It is always difficult to assign causal relations in explaining fertility decline, since education, social class and urbanization overlap, but a consensus is emerging that if there is a single most important factor, it is women's education. This is one among many reasons why the analysis of literacy below pays close attention to this topic.[26]

Population growth may or may not have worsened income distribution, but there was already an extreme degree of inequality throughout Latin America by the beginning of the 20th century. The social and economic processes of export-led

---

[24] Coale and Hoover, 1956.

[25] Coale, 1978.

[26] Birth control has now been put into context: it is important that the means to regulate fertility are available but it could never be the single most important factor, as the 1960s neo-Malthusian literature tended to suggest.

growth, building on the land grants and monopolies of the colonial period, had cemented inequality. The Spanish and Portuguese crowns had made generous land grants to colonists as a way of colonizing without using resources and as a form of royal patronage. The monopolies and privileges of the colonial system were also highly exclusive, subjugating Indian populations. The colonial period had seen establishment of a complex, ethnically segmented society. From the later 19th century on, export economy expansion increased land concentration and reinforced social and political inequalities. Here it is illuminating to consider alternative paths as they occurred elsewhere.[27] In the United States, for instance, the Civil War may not have destroyed the southern cotton and sugar plantations, but it did confirm the predominance of Northern industrial and farming interests in the country's political economy. In Australia, the colonial regime itself fostered smallholding and promoted industry.[28] In Latin America, however, there was no such offsetting force to the power of landed elites, who were able to prevent the imposition of taxation. This perpetuated inequality by assuring an inadequately funded state. Governments' failure to spend on education and health was as important as their failure to tax the better off. The landed elites were also able to secure systems to obtain cheap labor supplies. These methods varied with the circumstances. The "empty" countries towards the South relied on immigration, with systems to control access to land ownership (notably in Brazil). In countries where substantial Indian populations remained, the answer often took the form of forced labor, with many variations. In the sugar plantation economies, variations on the theme of slavery and indenture were used.

Some insight into the resulting structures can be gained by looking at returns to land and labor. By 1913 in Argentina (admittedly an extreme case), the ratio of wages to the value of land had fallen to one-fifth of its mid-1880s level.[29] Chapter Three will document in qualitative terms the various processes that led to increasing concentration of land and other natural resources in national and foreign hands, and thereby increased rents as expansion occurred. The process of concentration became a part of the growth model itself and was gradually embedded in mecha-

---

[27] This draws on a consultancy document for this book by Alan Knight.
[28] Dyster, 1979.
[29] Williamson, 1996: 13. The value of land is used as a proxy for rental income.

nisms of social control and attitudes.[30] The process was halted by the 1929 Depression; the 1930s may have seen some improvement in income distribution, though not in poverty (we have no data). But monopoly structures and methods of social control were typically not modified.

This account is based on an understanding of the historical process as it is discussed in a wide literature: quantification is impossible. It is, however, suggestive that a recent study finds that on a worldwide basis, concentration of land and distribution of educational opportunities are the most important explanations of inequality.[31] The study is based on observations from 108 countries, the earliest dating from the 1960s. The difficulties of such research, involving as it does comparison of measures of inequality between countries and indeed continents, make us hesitate to place too much weight on the results. But the consistency is worth noting.

The partial exceptions to this picture were the countries where there was earlier progress in education, where immigration affected social structure, and where Indian populations were smaller or died out early on. Policymakers in Uruguay and Costa Rica pursued policies that built on these early differences, as described in Chapters Three and Five. Both countries—along with Argentina, which had high income and rural productivity—still showed concentration of incomes, but by 1970 were at least less overwhelmingly unequal than other countries for which we have data.[32]

Degrees of inequality can begin to be documented by mid-century, with the earliest estimates putting Latin America high up the world scale. By the time when figures are available for a wide range of countries, around 1970, the income share of the top 20 percent as a multiple of the bottom 20 percent was 21 in Brazil, 24 in Venezuela, and 17 in Colombia—while for developed countries the average was 5.5.[33] Estimates by the World Bank for 1960 suggested an income

---

[30] In the previous chapter we used the phrase "effective" for growth. It would be pushing counterfactual history too far to claim that the inequality was necessary, and indeed it is not clear that it was, but it certainly functioned in growth terms, while building exclusion deep into the economy and society in institutional terms.

[31] The database and its analysis is found in Deininger and Squire, 1996. An interesting analysis is that of Birdsall and Londoño, 1997.

[32] As mentioned in the text, the experts who work most closely with these data warn us severely against putting much weight on cross-country comparisons. See Altimir, 1997a.

[33] Quoted from Kakwani by Cardoso and Helwege, 1992.

share for the poorest 20 percent in Latin America that was lower than for any other region of the world.[34]

While researchers agree on the extreme inequality of income for the 1950-70 period, defining trends is another matter. Even the most painstaking and detailed single country studies over time have produced only very qualified conclusions: there are so many variations in the definition of data and the form of each survey that comparison is hazardous. There tend to be two principal sources of underestimation: among the poor, nonmonetary income is difficult to estimate, and often omitted, while among the rich, the failure to include in household surveys income other than that from employment leads to a grave underestimation. Some studies attempt to correct for one or other of these biases; most do not.

Bearing in mind all the difficulties, a conclusion reached by a number of careful studies is that some countries probably experienced continued worsening of income distribution through the 1960s and 1970s, while for one or two others there is reasonable evidence of incipient improvement.[35] [36] Colombia, Mexico and Argentina have the most extended data set, summarized in Table 2.5. In Colombia, it seems that inequality worsened between roughly 1938 and 1970, as migration to cities helped tighten rural labor markets but worsened urban income distribution, exacerbated by the pattern of industrialization, as Chapter Six will explore. A turning point occurred around 1970 as continued modernization of agriculture closed the rural/urban gap and urban wage earners improved their position. As a result, poverty lessened, from its previous high levels.[37] Somewhat similar processes were at work in Mexico, where worsening inequality arrived at a turning point, probably a little earlier than for Colombia.[38] A third path is that of Argentina, which had

---

[34] World Bank, 1980: 461. The data difficulties were so great that this set of estimates was discontinued.

[35] See Berry, 1997, for a survey; also Altimir, 1997. See Londoño and Székely, 1997, for a massive review of country data and an extrapolation to the Latin American level.

[36] This paragraph is based on Altimir, 1997a, a consultancy paper prepared for this book. In various works by Altimir cited in the bibliography, he stresses the tremendous problems of comparability, since in addition to the underestimation mentioned in the text, surveys at particular points in time are heavily affected by short-run effects of the economic cycle, and so can only with much care be used for an analysis of results over time. The results reported here have been derived from Altimir's best effort at scrutinizing the data. For the details and references to the original work behind the analysis, the reader is referred to his original text.

[37] Urrutia, 1976; Londoño, 1995.

[38] Navarrete, 1960; Székely, 1996; Altimir, 1997a, consultancy document for this book.

TABLE 2.5

DISTRIBUTION OF INCOME BY INCOME GROUPS: ARGENTINA, COLOMBIA AND MEXICO
(In percent)

Argentina	Poorest 40% of households	Top 10% of households
Nationwide		
1953	18.1	37.1
1961	18.0	39.0
Urban only		
1953	19.9	35.2
1961	18.1	38.4
1970	17.5	27.6
1980	14.8	30.5
1994	13.7	32.4

Colombia	Poorest 50% of individuals	Top 10% of individuals
Nationwide		
1938	19.9	34.9
1951	16.7	43.5
1964	14.9	45.5
1971	16.1	42.2
1978	18.7	37.6
1988	18.9	37.1
1993	18.7	35.7

Mexico	Poorest 40% of households	Top 10% of households
Nationwide		
1950	12.6	44.7
1963	10.2	42.2
1967	10.4	42.2
1977	11.5	36.3
1984	14.3	32.8
1989	12.9	37.9
1992	12.7	38.2

Sources: Argentina: Altimir, 1997a; Colombia: Altimir, using Londoño, 1995, because of its long time period; Londoño builds on Urrutia, 1985; and the basic material is Dane, several years. Mexico: Altimir, using Navarrete, 1960; Altimir, 1982; Lustig, 1992.

higher per capita income, higher rural productivity, better income distribution and, by mid-century, a very small percentage of the population below the poverty line. Here, policy produced many fluctuations in relative incomes but no long-run trend towards greater inequality by the postwar period.

Other cases suggest a pattern of continued worsening, but the data are too weak for a clear conclusion. In the case of Brazil, data only begin in 1960, but they suggest a worsening, the explanation of which has been the focus of much controversy.[39] Peru and Chile also appear to have suffered increasing inequality.[40]

What is far more clear is that all countries—and the trend was very general—suffered a major economic reversal with the debt crisis, and any trends toward improvement stopped, with the single and notable exception of Uruguay (see Chapter Seven).[41] The worsening was centered in the deterioration in the labor market, which saw declining employment and wages and a sharp attack on unions in the name of "labor market flexibility."[42] Very limited data suggest that in countries such as Brazil and Peru, the turning point noted for Colombia and Mexico had not happened prior to the debt crisis: rather there was a persistent and gradual worsening of distribution.

Even more than with distribution, the degree of poverty was highly variable. The first estimate on a comparable basis across a range of countries was done by Altimir for 1970. He found a variation from 5 percent of urban households in absolute poverty in Argentina, to 35 percent for Brazil and 38 percent for Colombia. Rural poverty shares ranged from 19 percent in Argentina to 73 percent for Brazil, closely followed by Peru and Panama at 68 percent.[43] Altimir's estimates over time indicate fairly general improvement through the 1960s and 1970s, ceasing in the

---

[39] Cardoso and Helwege, 1992: 28. For a careful review and an agnostic conclusion, see Pfefferman and Webb, 1982.

[40] For Peru, Webb (1977: 39) shows worsening income distribution for 1950-66.

[41] Colombia and Costa Rica showed no worsening, although whether there was in fact continued improvement is still controversial. In Colombia, urban income distribution worsened in the 1990s.

[42] See Meller, O'Ryan and Solimano, 1996, for the Chilean case.

[43] See Statistical Appendix, Section VII. Absolute poverty is defined in Altimir's study with reference to a basic food basket. A person is poor if his or her income is no more than 1.75 times the money value of that minimum basket, in a rural area, and twice its value in an urban area. ("Absolute" poverty is distinguished in the literature from "relative" poverty, which looks at an individual's or family's resources relative to the rest of the society in which they live.)

1980s and often reversed. Even Argentina began in the 1980s to register significant poverty—12 percent of urban households were poor by 1994.[44]

How Poverty and Inequality Were Reinforced by the Context

The degree of poverty and inequality was determined over time by a complex interaction between income growth itself and a wide-ranging set of factors. These included political, social and economic structures and the institutions resulting from those structures. The institutions took on a life of their own, becoming causal factors in their own right. Thus, for example, racial prejudice, or attitudes towards education, were generated by a particular set of social and economic structures, but tended to become part of the way society operated (though if they started to conflict with economic or political interests they might gradually erode). Further, people's capacities crucially influenced their access to income opportunities; these capacities in turn were influenced by racial, class and gender attitudes, by the availability of resources, and by the resulting access to health and education. Finally, poverty and the use and abuse of resources interacted, as the poor had to survive in the short term. The abuse of the environment under economic pressure might then set up feedbacks affecting health, for example, and therefore productivity and income.

These complex interactions are perhaps easiest to see in real life examples. Box 2.1 tells a story of poverty spanning three generations and almost the entire century. The subject of the interview, María, was living in 1976 in Cajamarca in the highlands of Peru. What the interview reveals is how poverty persisted despite María's extraordinary industry and initiative. Much of the reason has to do with the deficiencies of the social and institutional fabric. The key in María's case was perhaps the legal struggle that wasted 15 crucial years. A judicial system that takes that long to produce an answer, and then only with the intervention of the local grandee, is almost worse than useless, as it ties up energies and hopes. This crucially affected what emerges as a key livelihood issue: access to land. Health and education are crucial, too: María's grandmother could be cruelly taken advantage of because she was illiterate. María cared about education, but it was an effort to achieve two years of schooling for her daugh-

---

[44] ECLAC, 1997, Table 16.

ters, and there is little indication that this was enough to change their prospects. Her sons' deaths, we now know, could easily have been prevented, and possibly her own incapacity from injury could have been cured.

Obviously, much of this tragedy is the result of gender. Starting with her grandmother's loss of land, María's story is an example of how women lacked the protection of education or legal recourse when abandoned. Economic development further marginalizes women in this story: when the road arrives in the 1940s, the men have better access to wage-earning employment on the coast, the women lose their key source of monetary income and independence, small-scale commerce, and with that the outlet for their handicrafts.

The example of María leads us to the issue of labor market segmentation, which played an important part in the interactions between institutions and income distribution. Such segmentation often applied, as in this instance, to both gender and ethnic aspects. The inheritance of an ethnically segmented society from colonial times, with the Indian in a clearly inferior position, evolved during the export economy period into a range of exploitative methods, from informal coercion to horrendous violence in remote areas such as the rubber territory of the Putumayo. As labor shortages eased, the need for such systems was reduced, but a residue of prejudice remained as a basis for more informal discrimination. The extent of that prejudice in contemporary labor market segmentation is difficult to evaluate for lack of data.

As regards gender, there are more data. Over time in Latin America, we see a huge increase in female participation in the urban labor market, the positive side of which is increased (independent) income opportunities. But the negative side is that labor market segmentation has continued. "Segmentation" in gender terms refers to the stereotyping of jobs as suitable or not for women. A World Bank study of 15 Latin American countries found that only 20 percent of the difference in earnings between men and women could be explained by differences in their human capital. Allowing 20 percent for women's own choice, this left 60 percent attributable to "cultural aspects which segregate the labor market and establish a limited number of jobs considered suitable for women."[45] Data for 13 urban areas for the 1990s show that the average income of women was 44 to 77 percent that of men. New

---

[45] Psacharopoulos and Tzannatos, 1992.

Box 2.1

María

María was born in 1912 in Pariamarca, in the Cajamarca highlands of Peru. Interviewed in 1976, she told how she was brought up by her grandmother, Celestina, who provided all the income for the family by trading and weaving. She often traveled for days at a time, leaving the children behind. María as a very small child collected wood for boiling up the dyes—it took her and her sister three to four days of collecting to get enough to dye 30 pounds of wool. They also helped spin the wool and cared for the sheep. At 12 she went for a year to school; after that the money ran out. Celestina needed a man for the agricultural work so she married again. She managed all the cash and they eventually saved enough to buy a hectare of land. But Celestina's husband took advantage of her illiteracy, and put the land in his name. Shortly after, he ran off with Celestina's sister-in-law and then claimed the land, which he later sold. Celestina had no recourse.

When María was 15, her grandmother died. She inherited 0.4 of a hectare and tried to stay in the area, living with each of her aunts in turn. But none of the arrangements worked out. So she sold her sheep, put her land to sharecropping and went to Cajamarca as a servant. Her first job gave her 2.50 soles per month, the second double that—enough to buy material for a blouse and save a little. In three years she had saved enough to leave and start up as a trader, buying in Pariamarca and selling in Cajamarca. Soon she was traveling the valley with her donkey. This became her way of life for the next 15 years. She had married for the first time at 19, a common law marriage. Her husband went to the coast after two years and never came back—her in-laws had needed cash and persuaded him to accept an advance from the labor contractor for the coastal sugar plantation, Casa Grande. María was convinced her bitterness towards him was transmitted with her milk and killed her child. She went back to the tiny house left to her and her sister by their grandmother. Now for the first time, she said, she understood the value of property: "I had somewhere to hole up when my man threw me over."

In 1933, María married Manuel Aguilar. His mother died shortly after their marriage, with no will. She left 4.5 hectares. Aguilar's four brothers had all moved away and left him to work the land, but now they came to grab the best bits. The legal fight was to take 15 years. Meanwhile all they had between them was María's 0.4 hectares. She continued her commercial activities, taking with her whichever child she was breastfeeding. (She had a child every two years. Four girls survived, and three boys died at two to three years old of diarrhea). Trade was reasonable in the 1930s—there was little competition then. Manuel tried working on the coast but didn't like it. María arranged sharecropping for them because Manuel was too proud to approach people. He did the agricultural work, but the girls also worked from the age of six or seven. It was important to her that her eldest had one year in school, the others two.

Then their house burned down. The relative of her previous husband living in Celestina's house refused to let her have it back. It took five years to save enough to build another house.

At last, in 1949 a legal judgment gave Manuel one hectare (and this only with the intervention of the local *hacendado*). This enabled María to slow down on her trading activities—a relief, because by this date they were being undercut with the coming of the road to the coast. With her two donkeys she could not compete with trucks.

The interview says little on the 1950s and 1960s. María's daughters eventually left, and she took in a granddaughter. Then came tragedy: in 1974, Manuel left her. She was 72, she couldn't walk because of a fall, and he had another woman. Her girls did what they could. At the time of the interview, María was living with her daughter Simona in a very small adobe house with a straw roof. She was very bitter—she should have had boys, she said, who would have been earning and could have supported her. The girls provided food but there was nothing for clothes or medicine.

Source: Rewritten from Deere, 1992. Carmen Diana Deere interviewed María extensively over a 12-month period.

technology is repeating the pattern of segmentation.[46] With the crisis of the 1980s, as we shall see in Chapter Seven, the increased role of the informal sector led to a disproportionate number of women finding low-paid, unskilled and precarious work. The welfare side has a further dimension: as women participated more in the labor market, they typically retained the burden of the household and the family, especially if they were poor.[47]

Finally, we consider poverty and the environment. Here again, the relationships are often complex, frequently involving health, and sometimes education. A central role has usually been played by institutions, and the political and social structures behind them. For example, in urban areas, the better off typically would take control of the good residential housing land and force up the price of housing. The poor then would have to settle on marginal land vulnerable to flooding and landslides. Lack of services would lead to silting up of what drainage there might be. A scarcity of services, especially clean water, and worsening pollution would make for health problems, reducing productivity and income in a familiar vicious circle. The burning of firewood with no ventilation would produce further pollution and health problems.

In rural areas the problems were in part similar, though vulnerability to nature was often greater. Industrial contamination could still be a problem in mining regions. Drought and poor harvests could lead to destructive farming practices, out of necessity.

Inadequate institutions and a lack of concern for laws were often part of the problem. The failure to protect indigenous land rights had serious consequences. For instance, indigenous peoples lost the motivation to improve land as squatters or migrants would claim it. In the early 20th century, squatting and claim jumping were standard procedures for acquiring land for subsequent sale, and the land companies assisted by creating a market.[48] Courts bestowed titles on land that had been acquired by claim jumping, which therefore became an accepted method of procuring property.[49] The marginalization of indigenous peoples and failure to protect their land

---

[46] See Rangel de Paiva Abreu, 1993, on the microelectronics sector.

[47] Beneria, 1992.

[48] See Dean, 1995, on the exploits of the Northern Paraná Land Company, formed in London in 1925. It bought 13,600 km^2 from the state and private owners.

[49] Fearnside, 1990; Pearce and Brown, 1994.

rights had many knock-on effects. In order to survive, some indigenous people, for example, took to poaching rare plants and trees to sell to collectors.

HUMAN DEVELOPMENT: LITERACY AND LIFE EXPECTANCY

Pioneering work by Shane and Barbara Hunt for this book has made it possible to construct a Historical Living Standards Index for the whole of the century. We first present their detailed work on literacy and life expectancy, then the summary measure of relative performance.

Literacy

Educational attainment is an important aspect of developing people's capabilities, the heart of human development. Adult literacy, as self-assessed for census records, is an imperfect proxy for only the most basic goal of formal education. Its inadequacies are such that it has been replaced where possible by more precise concepts such as functional literacy, as well as by measures of higher levels of attainment, such as primary and secondary school completion. Nevertheless, self-assessed adult literacy measures have the great virtue of being included in nearly all Latin American censuses of the late 19th and early 20th centuries. Thus literacy is the only measure of educational achievement allowing us to view the century as a whole.

Progress over the century in Latin America is remarkable: the illiteracy rate declined from 71 percent in 1900 to 47 percent in 1950, and to 10 percent in 1995.[50] This substantial decline in illiteracy rates nearly closed the gap in literacy between Latin America and the developed countries. Taking the United States as a representative developed country and using the median values of the 20 republics, this gap stood at 60 percentage points in 1900 and had been narrowed to 10 points by

---

[50] These figures apply to adults ages 15 and over. The regional total is the median of the figures for individual countries, preferred to the simple average because in recent years, as many countries have achieved very low illiteracy rates, the average is greatly influenced by a few outliers such as Guatemala and Haiti. An average weighted by population gives very similar results: 68.2 percent in 1900, 42.1 percent in 1950, 13.5 percent in 1995.

TABLE 2.6

ILLITERACY RATES IN LATIN AMERICA VERSUS THE UNITED STATES
(In percent)

	Latin America	United States[1]	Gap
1900	70.9	11.2	59.7
1910	67.6	8.2	59.4
1920	63.0	6.5	56.5
1930	61.0	4.8	56.2
1940	55.0	4.2	50.8
1950	46.5	2.6	43.9
1960	35.0	2.1	32.9
1970	26.9	1.0	25.9
1980	17.8	0.5	17.3
1990	12.1	0.5	11.6
1995	10.2	0.5	9.7

[1] The most recent figure available for the United States, 0.5, is for 1979. It is used as the estimate for 1980, 1990 and 1995.
Source: Hunt, 1997.

1995. Nearly all this narrowing has been accomplished since 1930. Table 2.6 shows the decade-by-decade progress in this comparison.

The other way to view these figures, however, is that despite a century-long effort to expand literacy, by the early 1990s Latin America had still only reached a level achieved by the United States in 1900. In fact, since the weighted-average illiteracy figure for 1995 is 13.5 percent, it can be said that, in the expansion of basic literacy to the adult population, Latin America is lagging behind the United States by almost a hundred years.[51] This is a far longer lag than that observed in measures of public health, such as life expectancy.

Within the overall improvement, the differences in timing are striking. Data by decade show that countries generally experienced a period of rapid decline in adult illiteracy, lasting 30 to 50 years, reflecting a substantial effort at primary education beginning some 10 to 15 years earlier. At the end of the period of rapid

---

[51] From this 1995 figure, a reasonable forecast for adult literacy in the year 2000 would be 11.5 percent, i.e., two percentage points less.

TABLE 2.7
TIMING OF LITERACY IMPROVEMENT, 1870-1995

Period	Countries achieving their significant improvement in this period[1]	Ranking according to literacy in 1995
18??-1908	Uruguay[2]	1
1870-1920	Argentina	3
1890-1930	Chile	4
	Cuba[3]	2
1900-1940	Costa Rica	5
1930-1980	Mexico	11
	El Salvador	16
	Panama	9
1940-1980	Paraguay	6
	Peru	12
	Dominican Republic	15
	Venezuela	8
1950-1980/1990	Brazil	13
	Colombia	7
	Ecuador	10
	Bolivia	14
1960-	Honduras	18
	Guatemala	19
	Nicaragua	17
1970-	Haiti	20

[1] The definition of "significant" is a change of more than seven points.
[2] First data are for 1908, showing that the improvement has already occurred.
[3] Data from 1900.

decline, illiteracy would still be 25 to 30 percent, and would then decline more slowly, principally as the less-educated cohorts reached the end of their lives. Table 2.7 lists countries according to the timing of that period of educational breakthrough. It will be seen that the group divides sharply into two. First came the countries where large numbers of relatively educated European immigrants arrived in the 19th and early 20th century.[52] Here the data show the effects of ef-

---

[52] Argentina, Cuba, Chile, Uruguay (in part indirectly through Argentina) and Costa Rica. Brazil received many immigrants, but with lower educational levels in general, who replaced slave labor in coffee.

forts at primary education beginning in the 19th century, responding to demands like that of Samuel's family, described in Box 5.2 in Chapter Five.[53] Immigrants also supplied teachers, especially in Argentina and Uruguay.[54] Then came a pause: apart from the effect of immigration, export-led growth did not induce educational efforts. Notably, *no* country began its spurt in the two decades from 1910 to 1930, which suggests that education was not a priority in the first years of the century. In the 1920s and 1930s, presumably reflecting urbanization and social awareness, primary education made progress, and this is reflected in a wave of results. At least 10 countries significantly reduced illiteracy in the period from 1930 to 1960. After 1960, only Haiti and much of Central America had failed to begin their serious attack on illiteracy. The more patchy data on enrollment confirm this story.[55]

Within this overall picture, how did women fare? The question is of particular importance, given the solid finding of much recent research that education of women brings population growth rates down, which in its turn is one of the most effective means of eventually improving income distribution through increasing scarcity of labor.[56] Once it becomes sufficiently extensive, education will also contribute by increasing equality of access to the labor market.

Again, the results are striking in terms of the country variations they reveal. Defining the gender gap as the absolute difference between the illiteracy rates of adult males and females, a pattern of early widening can be seen, as education efforts initially reached principally boys. The gap then narrowed, as Table 2.8 shows, at varying speeds for different groups of countries.

The first group, represented in the table by Brazil, consists of those countries where the gender gap has been declining steadily to very low levels in recent decades. Other countries with a similar pattern are Costa Rica, Panama, El Salvador, Ecuador and Paraguay.

The second group, represented by Cuba, resembles the first, except that at some point the gender gap was closed and the female illiteracy rate actually became lower than that of the male. This is also true of Uruguay and Jamaica. The third

---

[53] We do not have the data to confirm this, but our hypothesis is that immigrants provided a demand for education, rather than significantly affecting the data simply by their presence.

[54] Newland, 1991. In Uruguay in 1876, 54 percent of school teachers were foreign; in Argentina, 41 percent.

[55] These data are discussed in Hunt, 1997.

[56] Some studies find that primary education is enough, others find that secondary education has a further effect.

TABLE 2.8
PATTERNS OF GENDER GAPS IN ILLITERACY RATES
(Absolute difference in percentages)

	Brazil	Cuba	Argentina	Peru	Guatemala	Mexico
1869			9.2			
1895			10.7			
1900		3.0	10.1	15.9		8.3
1910		3.3	9.0	18.0		8.1
1920	15.7	1.6	7.6	20.1	2.3	6.3
1930	14.2	-3.1[a]	5.8	22.2	5.0	9.7
1940	12.7	-2.3	4.1	24.3	7.7	7.9
1950	10.6	-3.5	2.7	25.2	10.4	7.0
1960	7.9	-2.7	2.2	26.0	11.8	9.5
1970	6.3	-0.6		22.3	14.2	7.8
1980	3.5	-0.5	0.7	16.8	15.4	6.3
1990	0.7		0.3	12.5	18.3	5.4

[a] A negative number indicates that the male illiteracy rate is higher than the female rate.
Source: Hunt, 1997.

group, represented by Argentina, has data going far enough back that we can trace the initial widening of the gap, making it possible to estimate when the gender gap reached its maximum. In the case of Argentina, this appears to have occurred close to the turn of the century. Other countries whose data also show the gender gap peak are Chile, Colombia, Venezuela, Honduras and the Dominican Republic.

The fourth and fifth groups are remarkable for the size of the gender gap. Peru and Bolivia show gender gaps in excess of 20 percentage points. Guatemala's gap is still rising, as is that of Haiti. The final group consists only of Mexico. There the gender gap remained essentially unchanged for several decades, although some decline did occur after 1970.

The data suggest, then, that, within the range of experience presented by Latin America, while some poor Caribbean countries have tended to have rather small gender gaps in illiteracy (e.g., Jamaica and the Dominican Republic), countries with significant indigenous populations have had rather large gaps. The cases of Bolivia, Peru and Guatemala are particularly striking in this regard.

However, the gender gap overlaps with a second gap, that between urban and rural illiteracy, since countries with large indigenous populations tend also to be those with large rural sectors. Data distinguishing urban and rural literacy rates started only in 1950. They reveal that at mid-century, the majority of Latin American countries had gaps of 40 percentage points or more between urban and rural populations.

Summing up on literacy, then, it is the country variation as much as the extent of overall progress that is striking. The breakthrough to widespread literacy occurred at widely different dates. Countries with large European immigrant populations made the breakthrough at the beginning of the century, while the poorest Central American countries and the non-English-speaking Caribbean have yet to make it. The gender variation also is huge, with a general narrowing occurring, but with large Indian populations showing a large gender gap even at the end of the century.

Life Expectancy

Life expectancy serves as a proxy for the quality of life, because various studies show that people who live longer are healthier.[57] In particular, their incidence of chronic illness is lower.[58] It also seems reasonable to suppose that a longer life is good in itself. This can be understood in the following illustration taken from Peru in the early 1990s: a community was reflecting on the death of one of its older members, and the comment was made, with some envy, that the man had died "at the end of his life." When else can one die, one might ask? But in Peru, indeed, at a time of acute violence, repression and economic recession, many were not dying "at the end of their lives," but very near their beginning, with infant mortality at 64 per 1,000 live births.[59]

---

[57] Life expectancy directly measures the length of life. It summarizes the mortality experience of a population for a given year by stating what the average age at death would be for a cohort born in that year, providing that the cohort sustained mortality rates at different ages in life that were identical to the mortality rates of the different cohorts making up the population in the given year. The average expectation of life for those born in the given year would actually be greater than this figure, because we generally expect health conditions to be improving in the future.

[58] Fogel, 1991 (studies of Norwegian males and U.S. Civil War soldiers).

[59] This reflection was made in a lecture by Gustavo Gutiérrez at Oxford University in 1993. The infant mortality figure is from UNDP, 1996: 148.

Life expectancy has increased dramatically in Latin America during the 20th century. According to available estimates, average life expectancy was 29 years in 1900, 47 in 1950, and 68 in 1990. Over 90 years, the average length of life has more than doubled. This accomplishment was made possible by having started from such a low level of life expectancy, not uncommon in the world of 1900 but, except for a few unfortunate countries devastated by war, unknown in the world today.[60]

In terms of life expectancy, Latin America in 1990 was 40 years behind the United States: a life expectancy level of 68 years had been reached by the United States in 1950. This is a long lag, but not nearly so long as the 100-year lag found for literacy. This reflects the fast progress which could be made once there was a wide diffusion of medical and public health interventions such as drainage, running water and vaccinations. During the first three decades of the century, the gap in life expectancy between the United States and Latin America actually widened. The detailed country figures in the Statistical Appendix show a pattern of accelerated improvement in life expectancy over a period of some 35 to 40 years, which raises life expectancy from around 45 years to nearly 70, at which point the improvement tails off. This same process took 60 years in the United States. The wholesale application of public health measures has compressed the process in recent years, irrespective of the level of economic development. Again we can distinguish groups of countries, as in Table 2.9. A first group began their improvement before World War II—as early as the 1910s for Argentina, Uruguay and Cuba (that is, later than the literacy drive). This group includes most of the countries that made an earlier attack on literacy (with the exception of Chile) and also includes the two principal British colonies in the Caribbean. A second group began to accelerate its improvement in the 1950s, sometimes reaching a leveling-off point by the 1990s, sometimes not. A third began very late and still shows relatively low levels of life expectancy: Bolivia, Haiti and three of the Central American republics.

In summary, life expectancy increased more rapidly than literacy and was less closely correlated with income levels, reflecting the impact of generalized public health improvements. Nevertheless, in both cases a strong pattern remains of inter-country variation, with the leading and lagging countries substantially overlapping.

---

[60] The lowest life expectancy listed in a recent issue of the *World Development Report* is that of Guinea-Bissau, at 38 years. World Bank, 1997: 214.

TABLE 2.9
PERIOD OF SUBSTANTIAL IMPROVEMENT IN LIFE EXPECTANCY

Group 1: Begins before WWII, levels off by 1970-75

	Ranking by life expectancy in 1990
Costa Rica	1
Cuba	2
Trinidad and Tobago	4
Jamaica	5
Uruguay	6
Argentina	8

Group 2: Begins in the 1950s, some already leveled off, others not

Leveled off	Rank	Not yet leveled off	Rank
Chile	3	Paraguay	13
Panama	7	Ecuador	14
Venezuela	9	Brazil	16
Mexico	10	El Salvador	17
Colombia	11	Peru	17
Dominican Republic	12		

Group 3: Begins in the 1960s or later

	Rank
Honduras	15
Nicaragua	19
Guatemala	20
Bolivia	21
Haiti	22

Source: Statistical Appendix IX.

Historical Living Standard Index

One way of summarizing the results in Latin America regarding literacy and life expectancy, though without entering into questions of distribution, is to calculate an index, which we are calling a Historical Living Standards Index. It is similar to the UNDP's summary measure, the HDI, but the latter is strictly only a ranking

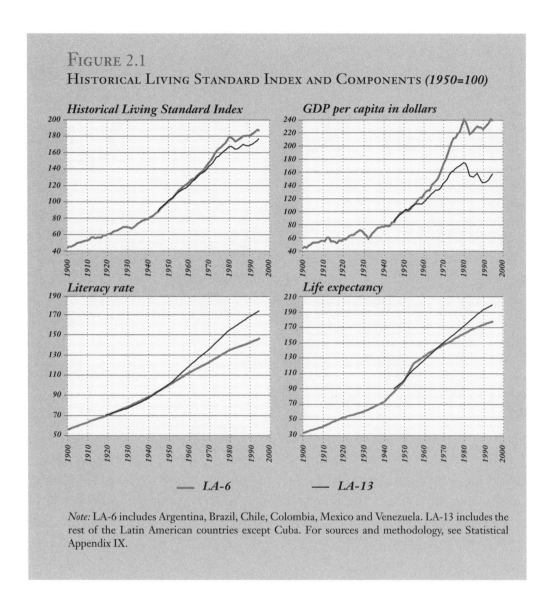

FIGURE 2.1
HISTORICAL LIVING STANDARD INDEX AND COMPONENTS *(1950=100)*

Note: LA-6 includes Argentina, Brazil, Chile, Colombia, Mexico and Venezuela. LA-13 includes the rest of the Latin American countries except Cuba. For sources and methodology, see Statistical Appendix IX.

within a given year. We have used the three indicators the UNDP originally worked with—literacy, life expectancy and GDP per capita—and combined them in an index with arbitrary equal weights. The results are given in Figure 2.1. Table 2.10 shows the movement relative to the United States.

There are many difficulties with such an index, whether it is used to rank countries within a given year or to track change over time. The first and most obvi-

TABLE 2.10

RATIOS OF SELECTED WELFARE INDICATORS TO U.S. LEVELS IN THE SAME YEAR
(In percent)

	LA-6					Latin America		
	1900	1930	1950	1970	1995	1950	1970	1995
GDP per capita	35	36	35	37	36	37	37	35
Life expectancy	61	62	70	86	91	69	86	91
Literacy	38	50	62	75	88	60	73	87
Relative Living Standard Index	45	49	156	66	72	55	65	71

Note: GDP per capita figures correspond to scaled values. LA-6 includes Argentina, Brazil, Chile, Colombia, Mexico and Venezuela. For sources and method, see Statistical Appendix IX. The scaling, explained in the Statistical Appendix, accounts for this figure being higher than that cited in Chapter One.

ous is the arbitrariness of trying to capture "welfare" with only three indicators, and giving the three equal weight, for want of any better decision-taking principle. A further problem is that over time both literacy and life expectancy approach a maximum value as development occurs. Thus some part of the catching up to the United States in literacy and life expectancy is nothing more than a reflection of the fact that the variables had by the end of the century come close to their maximum in many countries as well as the United States. A more accurate plotting of relative performance should draw on more variables. While this is possible for the later years it cannot be done for the whole period. The data should therefore be taken with considerable caution.

Subject to all these qualifications, the index serves to bring out some interesting points. The most notable is the lack of correlation between progress in health and education and short-term fluctuations in the GDP per capita indicator—a fact that has been particularly analyzed in relation to the crisis of the 1980s. A second is that while the region catches up to the United States in literacy and life expectancy, it manifestly does not do so in per capita income.

Conclusion

Substantial progress indeed occurred in Latin America over the course of the century in terms of modernization, improvement in real income, health and literacy. The gains were concentrated in the period from the Second World War to the 1970s, and by that stage were widespread across the continent. Behind this also lay a substantial development of organizations and institutions—from central banks and social security systems to vaccination programs—as well as more intangible gains such as changes in behavior, for example the desire to give one's daughters an education. There were also major improvements in physical infrastructure, such as transport systems and power supplies.

But at the same time, there was continued exclusion based principally on the form of economic expansion, its displacement of traditional activities, limited employment possibilities, various institutional arrangements, and attitudes embodying discrimination. Considerable fragility remained: if exposure to the international market declined in some respects, it rose in others, and ecological problems almost certainly increased as soil erosion and urban pollution worsened.

CHAPTER 3

THE EARLY 20TH CENTURY: CAPITAL, EXPORTS AND INSTITUTIONS

THE BEGINNING OF THE 20TH CENTURY found Latin America in the middle of an expansionary phase responding to growth of the world economy. Only a few countries had failed to take substantial advantage of the new growth surge, usually for reasons of internal disorder, previous bankruptcy or poor resource endowment. Demand for primary products and the capital inflow this attracted were powerful catalysts for change, interacting with varying local conditions. In some cases, relatively empty lands required an accompanying inflow of immigrants; in others, land and labor had to be exacted, often forcibly, from the substantial Indian population. In several countries, foreign-financed building of infrastructure had been under way for 30 or more years. In others it had barely started. A relatively consolidated state already existed in some countries and could attempt negotiations with foreign investors and governments. Other states, including much of the Caribbean, were still colonies. Panama was still part of Colombia. Puerto

---

Photo: The Panama Canal, 1913.

Rico and Cuba each had its own peculiar status of dependence on the United States.

The twin phenomena of export demand and capital inflow had a profound impact on the diverse economic, social and political structures that characterized Latin America and the Caribbean during this period. The "commodity lottery"[1] was profoundly influential, but so too was size, meaning a country's effective economic size—a function of population, income and territorial extension. "Size" can therefore vary considerably over time. Also important were geography, prior political relationships, and underlying political and social characteristics.

The next section outlines the external forces at work between 1870 and 1930, then reviews the different country experiences, laying the groundwork for understanding response capacity when the model had to change because of growing instability of the world economy and its collapse in 1929.

Development of an International Economy

Rapid expansion of world trade was one of the outstanding features of accelerating economic growth of the industrial "center" in the 19th century.[2] This process continued in the early 20th century, but decelerated sharply in 1914 with the outbreak of the First World War. At 1990 prices, world exports increased from $7.3 billion in 1820 to $56.2 billion in 1913 and $334.4 billion in 1929.[3] Up to 1913, trade expanded at a faster rate than GDP in the industrial center and its offshoots in North America and Oceania; the subsequent slowdown was sharper for trade. The high share of raw materials was a distinguishing feature of world trade throughout the period. The dominance of Western Europe, particularly Great Britain, was also a major characteristic up to the First World War, but the balance gradually shifted towards the United States.[4]

---

[1] What nature has blessed or cursed you with, plus what nature permitted man to introduce: coffee, cattle and grain were all deliberately introduced.

[2] The term "center" was much used in the writing of Raúl Prebisch and means the developed world. The rest is described by him as the "periphery."

[3] Maddison, 1995, Table 1.4.

[4] Maddison, 1995; Ashworth, 1987.

Behind this lay a revolution in technology and transport, supported by major institutional developments. The breakthroughs in technology that were the heart of the first Industrial Revolution[5] in Britain—particularly the use of steam—had already happened by 1850. But it took the confluence of institutional change and technological development to generate the growth in production and trade that would have a strong impact on Latin America as well as on almost every area of the world.

Technological breakthroughs included commercial use of the Bessemer process and the Siemens open-hearth process to produce steel more cheaply. Another landmark was the discovery in 1878 of how to adapt either process to make steel from phosphoric ore. The institutional structures that allowed this potential productivity to multiply included the organization of firms and credit and capital markets. Joint stock companies, stock exchanges and banks, as well as accompanying regulatory legislation, spread throughout much of Europe and eventually the United States. Landmarks such as the U.K. Bank Charter Act of 1844 and the invention of the Registrar General of Companies were the unglamorous but necessary background to rising prosperity. The less obvious landmarks lay in civil service and judicial reforms that had a radical impact on corruption and efficiency.

The consequences for Latin America followed with the application of steam and iron to transport. Railways and steamships revolutionized what and who could move efficiently. Technological development led to an extraordinary need for minerals, the demand for which grew faster than industrial output between 1880 and 1920.[6] Increasing division of labor and rising incomes meant more demand for food, initially met by mechanization of agriculture in the developed countries but increasingly motivating the settlement of new temperate lands. Latin America played a role in responding to demand for both temperate and tropical products, and capital and labor moved to make this possible. Between 1820 and 1930 (primarily 1860-1914), 62 million people emigrated to the Americas from Europe and Asia. Of those, 61 percent went to the United States and 12 percent to Canada, but Argentina and Brazil came next with 10 percent and 7 percent, respectively. Uruguay, and to a

---

[5] Landes, 1969, identifies two Industrial Revolutions: first, steam, railways and textiles, and second, the impact of cheap steel, machine tools and electricity in the late 19th and early 20th century.

[6] Ashworth, 1987: 225.

lesser extent Chile, received immigrants both directly and indirectly via Argentina and Brazil. Tropical and subtropical agriculture needed labor, too, but acquired it through systems ranging from thoroughly coercive (slavery), semi-coercive (indentured workers and debt peonage), to free wage labor. These various systems allowed plantation-style agriculture to expand throughout the Caribbean, the Caribbean coasts of South America, and Peru and Ecuador. In Cuba, elements of slave, indentured and free labor systems coexisted and progressively displaced each other with the passage of time.

Capital also moved, principally from Britain, Germany and France and into the financing of railways and, to a lesser degree, other public utilities and mines. By 1913, 20 percent of U.K. capital overseas was in Latin America, and half of that in Argentina. Increasingly, capital moving into Latin America was not necessarily connected to prospective export expansion. Lending as opposed to direct investment, for example, was often unrelated to export prospects. Its availability generally responded to developments in the center countries. This was to become one of the most threatening aspects of the new international order.

Trade and factor movements also needed institutional support. In the early 19th century, trade still ran predominantly in bilateral channels. But stimulated by increasing specialization and new needs and resources, trade became increasingly multilateral, supported by the availability of sterling as a reserve currency and by the stability of the international system. Contrary to perceptions at the time, recent research has shown that the gold standard was the product of that stability rather than its cause; the equilibrium in flows and the resulting stability were extraordinarily important in allowing the development of international financial instruments and channels. Political stability helped, too, given the relative absence between 1870 and 1914 of wars and disturbances sufficient to disrupt the emerging international economy. Hence, Ashworth characterizes this expansion as "both unique and mortal."[7]

In light of recent debates, it is important to note that only in Britain was this expansion supported by enthusiasm for free trade. In the rest of Europe, and especially in the United States, policies were protectionist. With or without protection, however, both the U.K. and U.S. governments tended to support their private sectors' economic expansion. For Latin America, on rare occasions this might involve

---

[7] Ibid.

outright military intervention, undertaken for reasons both economic and geopolitical; usually, however, it involved the deployment of economic power within unequal relationships (such as that between the United States and Cuba).

The economic transformation of this period was profound, but it varied in its impact. Geography and natural resource endowment greatly affected how the transformation impinged on national realities. The experience of Argentina was profoundly different from, say, Ecuador or Haiti.

NATIONAL EXPERIENCES

The fastest growing countries during this period were nearly all among the largest countries in terms of population: Argentina, Mexico up to the Revolution of 1910, and Chile. (The dollar growth rates of exports are given in Table 3.1, together with GDP growth rates for those countries for which we have data. Quantum series for exports appear in the Statistical Appendix.) Colombia's 19th century political instability may account for its late start, though rapid growth ensued.[8] Brazil was a complex partial exception that we shall discuss in detail.

Of the small countries, the exceptions to the pattern of relatively slower growth were Uruguay, which benefited from foreign investment along with Argentina, though not to the same extent, and the countries ripe for an inflow of U.S. direct foreign investment into sugar: Cuba, Puerto Rico and the Dominican Republic. Thus, size alone did not determine foreign investors' interest, as Table 3.2 shows. Geography, political relationships and political stability also mattered: countries just emerging from 19th century turbulence formed the bottom of the list.

To elaborate what lies behind this diverse picture, this section considers individual country experiences. Size is the main organizing principle, but, particularly within each of the subgroups, the order follows theme rather than size where similarity of product allows the more coherent development of an argument. The principal export products are indicated in Table 3.3. The first section discusses four of the largest economies, taking Brazil and Colombia first, followed by Argentina and

---

[8] But see Deas, 1982, for two-way causation between instability and economic conditions.

TABLE 3.1

EXPORTS AND GDP RATE OF GROWTH, 1900-29

(Annual compound rates, in percent)

	Exports	GDP
Argentina	6.4	3.8
Brazil	3.2	4.2
Chile	0.9	2.9
Colombia	9.6	4.5
Cuba[1]	7.3	4.1
Mexico[2]	6.6	3.4
Peru	8.2	4.5
Venezuela	7.2	5.0

Note: Export figures are in current US$ millions. GDP figures are in constant US$ millions at 1970 prices (PPP-adjusted). The estimation of export trends is subject to large error terms, owing to the large instability. See Statistical Appendix for the degree of error.
[1] GDP figures correspond to national income estimates beginning in 1903. Brundenius, 1984.
[2] The years 1913-19 are not included, as no data exist for the years following the revolution.
Source: Statistical Appendix.

TABLE 3.2

FOREIGN INVESTMENT AND SIZE, CIRCA 1914

(Ordered by ranking of DFI to population)

	Population[1]	Area[2]	DFI[3]	Railways[4]	DFI/pop[5]	Rail/km[6]
Argentina	7,885	2,777	3,217	31,859	408	11
Uruguay	1,262	187	355	2,576	281	14
Cuba	2,539	115	386	3,752	152	33
Chile	3,537	757	494	8,069	140	11
Costa Rica	386	51	44	878	114	17
Guatemala	1,166	109	92	987	79	9
Panama	374	76	23	479	62	6
Venezuela	2,899	912	145	1,020	50	1
Brazil	24,152	8,512	1,196	24,737	49	3
Peru	4,162	1,285	180	2,970	43	2
Paraguay	652	407	23	410	35	1
Honduras	620	112	16	241	26	2
El Salvador	1,059	21	15	320	14	15
Dominican Rep.	802	49	11	644	13	13
Nicaragua	582	130	6	322	10	2
Colombia	5,330	1,139	54	1,061	10	1
Haiti	1,862	28	10	180	5	6

[1]Population in 1914 in thousands of inhabitants. [2]Territory, 1971, in thousands of km[2].
[3]Direct foreign investment circa 1914 in millions of US$. [4]Length of railways in km circa 1913.
[5]Dollars of direct foreign investment per person. [6]Meters of railway per km[2] of territory.
Sources: Bulmer-Thomas, 1994, Tables 4.3 and 4.4. For territory and population, see the Statistical Appendix.

TABLE 3.3
EXPORT COMMODITY CONCENTRATION RATIOS, CIRCA 1913

Country	First product	Percentage	Second product	Percentage	Total
Argentina	Maize	22.5	Wheat	20.7	43.2
Bolivia	Tin	72.3	Silver	4.3	76.6
Brazil	Coffee	62.3	Rubber	15.9	78.2
Chile	Nitrates	71.3	Copper	7.0	78.3
Colombia	Coffee	37.2	Gold	20.4	57.6
Costa Rica	Bananas	50.9	Coffee	35.2	86.1
Cuba	Sugar	72.0	Tobacco	19.5	91.5
Dominican Rep.	Cacao	39.2	Sugar	34.8	74.0
Ecuador	Cacao	64.1	Coffee	5.4	69.5
El Salvador	Coffee	79.6	Precious metals	15.9	95.5
Guatemala	Coffee	84.8	Bananas	5.7	90.5
Haiti	Coffee	64.0	Cacao	6.8	70.8
Honduras	Bananas	50.1	Precious metals	25.9	76.0
Mexico	Silver	30.3	Copper	10.3	40.6
Nicaragua	Coffee	64.9	Precious metals	13.8	78.7
Panama	Bananas	65.0	Coconuts	7.0	72.0
Paraguay	Yerba mate	32.1	Tobacco	15.8	47.9
Peru	Copper	22.0	Sugar	15.4	37.4
Puerto Rico	Sugar	47.0	Coffee	19.0	66.0
Uruguay	Wool	42.0	Meat	24.0	66.0
Venezuela	Coffee	52.0	Cacao	21.4	73.4

Source: Bulmer-Thomas, 1994: 59.

Mexico. This ordering enables us to compare across two large coffee economies,[9] and allows Mexico to form a link in terms of commodity to the next group, comprised of medium-sized countries which were all principally mineral-based economies: Chile, Bolivia, Venezuela and Peru. The other sizable economy, Cuba, introduces a theme that has entered only marginally up to this point: the interplay between U.S. economic and political interests and export-led growth. This in

---

[9] Colombia at the turn of the century was large in population and territory but not in terms of national income. But by the 1920s, Colombian GDP was larger than that of Chile.

turn leads to the rest of the Caribbean, where the theme dominated. Finally, we turn to the remaining small economies of South and Central America.

Brazil: Strong Elites and the Expanding Role of the State

The most complex story is that of the largest country, which covers half the continental land mass. Brazil's expansion in terms of GDP was substantial but not exceptional in this period: faster than the rate of growth of exports, but below the average for the eight countries for which we have data for the first decades of the century (Appendix Table II.1). Coffee took off in the early 19th century, and such was Brazil's size and potential that by the 1830s it was already supplying nearly 30 percent of world exports. Brazil's coffee exports by volume rose to 5.5 percent between 1880 and 1900, and the country produced over 60 percent of world coffee in every year from 1896 to 1942. The expansion was supported by the political consolidation which took place with the transition to a Republican regime in 1889, building on prior strength helped by the peaceful transition to independence. The coup of 1889 resulted from an alliance between the military and the Paulista coffee growers.[10] The political influence of the Paulistas consolidated powerful policies of support to the coffee sector, promoting and subsidizing immigration once the use of slaves was no longer possible, and regulating tenure so that immigrants might not become independent farmers. This guaranteed a supply of labor to the plantations in varying sharecropping arrangements. Coffee elites and government together promoted the building of infrastructure by and with foreign capital. One notable producer managed to get six kilometers of a publicly-funded railroad line built on his own estate.[11] Railways were typically state-owned and leased to foreign companies. Both government and business groups had enough coherence to negotiate with foreign capital from a position of some strength.[12]

Economic expansion was helped by geography and the land tenure inherited from the colony: coffee in Brazil can grow on the relatively open flatlands of Paraiba and the Paulista plateau, and estates are large. Big farms had 82 percent of

---

[10] Abreu and Bevilaqua in Companion Volume 1.
[11] Topik, 1996.
[12] Ibid.

coffee trees by 1927, and the average farm had a production level six times that of the average Colombian holding.

Thus, although in the last decade of the 19th century in Brazil rubber contributed 14 percent of exports, sugar 6 percent and cotton 3 percent, it was coffee that provided the dynamism and the formative element for growth. Brazil's market dominance enabled the government to pioneer the creation of price maintenance schemes, though these ultimately would hurt the country. Abreu and Bevilaqua show that the long-run effect of devaluation in Brazil was to raise the world price of coffee in foreign currency, since the increase in domestic costs resulting from devaluation was passed on to the foreign consumer. And in parallel, market power meant that when Brazil imposed tariffs on her imports, this also resulted in increases in cost for domestic producers, which were ultimately passed on to the coffee consumer abroad.[13]

These policies were, of course, not developed without difficulty. Size again enters the analysis, since coffee was produced across three large states, which required that the different elements of the elite negotiate with each other and with Brazil's relatively developed political institutions. Transactions within the coffee elite lent a certain sophistication to the political process.[14]

The economy, however, was based on much more than coffee, and other exports did not fare so well. Sugar in the Northeast was affected throughout the 19th century not only by competition in the sugar market but also by the consequences of coffee exports on the exchange rate. Indeed, it is argued that the Northeast would have gained by being a separate nation, and it is not surprising that there were separatist moves. Rubber boomed with international demand, but collapsed after 1910 as Asian production undermined Brazil's market share. It is a salutary counterweight to the rather strong image of Brazil exemplified by São Paulo and the coffee expansion to consider the fragility and instability of the rubber sector: local business groups in Pará could not muster the capital and state support necessary to develop the plantation crop developed by Europe's Asian colonies, which had abruptly undermined the Amazonian product.[15]

[13] All this is given econometric substantiation in Abreu and Bevilaqua in Companion Volume 1.
[14] See Bates, 1997, for a fascinating account of this period of Brazilian coffee policy.
[15] Weinstein, 1983.

GDP figures for Brazil before 1912 are unreliable, but it is argued by Leff (1997) that for the end of the 19th century the figures would show growth as less than export growth, since there was a large rural sector not integrated into any commodity boom, producing beans, maize and manioc for its own needs and for local trade. This sector was still largely outside the national economy, with huge transport barriers that only began to be reduced by the end of the 19th century. Per capita GDP can reasonably be assumed to have grown very little.

Coffee, however, was already stimulating diversification. The noncoffee economy was concentrated in industry and associated services and experienced its first solid boom in the 1890s.[16]

The role of coffee merchants and planters in this period has been extensively documented, initially by Dean. By 1901, about 45 percent of industrial workers in São Paulo were employed in firms controlled by coffee interests.[17] Coffee production did not need sizable reinvestment of surplus, as the technology was simple and unchanging. This explains the tendency of coffee economies to diversify, size permitting, since surplus funds sought profitable use outside the sector. But Brazil had a further advantage: since the effect of tariffs on costs could be passed on to the consumer, the powerful coffee elites felt no pressure to lobby against protection, which further cemented their alliance with industrial groups. This is surely an important explanation for the relatively high tariffs in Brazil from an early date, in contrast to Argentina, but paralleling Colombia.

The result was a combination of high protection and strong industrial growth, which meant that industrial output increased almost fivefold between 1900 and 1930, while total output increased only 3.5 times.[18] By 1919, the share of imports in the total supply of industrial production was reduced to only 25 percent.[19]

By the early 20th century, coffee expansion, diversification and infrastructure growth was driving Brazilian GDP to grow faster than export, the only instance in Latin America along with Chile where this was true, as far as our data allow us to judge. (In Chile, this was the result of the collapse of nitrate exports in the 1920s.)

---

[16] Fishlow, 1964; Dean, 1969.

[17] Dean, 1969: 37-38.

[18] Haddad, 1978.

[19] Abreu and Bevilaqua in Companion Volume 3.

The proportion of exports in GDP fell from around 30 percent at the turn of the century to some 18 percent by 1913, and 14 percent by the late 1920s.[20]

The negative side of this story was the resource cost and the social characteristics of growth. The Atlantic rain forest was virtually destroyed as coffee expanded, and the quality of the soil much damaged by farming methods. The initial burning of the forest produced high fertility, which then declined rapidly; monoculture produced problems of disease, while planting even on relatively gentle slopes led to erosion. A combination of such causes could lead to trees failing after 20 years. What followed, however, was even worse: the trees were uprooted and burned and the land used as pasture for cattle, preventing the regrowth of secondary forest.[21] The grass that invaded was typically the inedible Imperata grass, and pasture yields deteriorated rapidly because of depletion of the soil nutrients, compacting of the soil, and invasion.[22] These effects were elsewhere reduced by shade and intercropping of foodstuffs. In Brazil, the use of shade was largely abandoned, since the trees used for shade were considered to compete with coffee for limited moisture. With the move to gang labor on large estates, the intercropping of food products also disappeared.

The social consequences of expansion were determined by the nature of share-cropping and by the way the structure of power was used to consolidate the supply of cheap labor to the coffee sector. Sharecroppers used unpaid family labor and received no cash for their output; conditions were tolerable only because they could at least produce their own food. However, when coffee prices rose, planters would forbid intercropping of food and coffee, and gave wage increases that rarely made up for lost self-provisioning, particularly as food prices rose.[23]

These negative aspects of course did not affect the functioning of the macroeconomy: indeed they made it possible, through policies that cheapened labor and through high soil fertility in the short term. In macroeconomic terms, the model functioned more successfully as characteristics of coffee and the consequences

---

[20] Calculated in current prices in local currency and using the GDP calculations of Haddad, 1978. The figures quoted are three-year averages.

[21] For problems caused by cattle, see Fearnside, 1990; Hecht, 1990.

[22] Dean, 1995.

[23] Stolcke, 1988, Chapter 2.

of size came together. Thus, coffee provided expansion but did not need surplus reinvested in it: intersectoral links were already developing, leading to rather successful diversification, helped by a political economy that gained from political consolidation and from size. These factors together led to considerable political trading between the elites of the major states (São Paulo, Rio de Janeiro and Minas Gerais), with positive effects on the development of policymaking machinery. And market power was enough to allow the impact of tariffs on producer cost to be passed on.

Colombia: Small Producers and Institution Building

Colombia was also to be a coffee success story, though it came late to the table. Establishing conditions for economic growth in the 19th century proved extraordinarily difficult, though some growth occurred thanks to gold mining in Antioquia, tobacco exports via the Magdalena River in the mid-century, and three bursts of coffee expansion from the 1860s on. Gold mining in particular promoted institutional development through establishment of a mining code, banks, technical education and roads, led by the state government of Antioquia. There also was a strong culture of trust, indispensable for market exchange when formal institutions are weak. In Antioquia, particularly, "my word is my bond" meant a great deal, as illustrated in Box 3.1, which draws on the remarkably frank autobiography of Marco Restrepo, a local entrepreneur in the making.[24] A resolute individualist, Restrepo exemplifies anything but a culture of trust, but knows he can rely on it in others.

However, many steps backward were taken with the War of a Thousand Days (1899-1902). The turn of the century found Colombia's coffee industry in a deep crisis due to the fall in international prices, high inflation and devastation, the latter two resulting from the war. A degree of political consolidation was subsequently reached and rapid growth soon followed, based on coffee and to a lesser extent on the two foreign-owned enclaves, bananas from the first decade and oil from the 1920s.[25]

The earlier expansion of coffee had been in Cundinamarca, characterized by large *haciendas*. The new expansion in the hills of the Central Cordillera in the west

---

[24] See Brew, 1977, on the entrepreneurial culture of Antioquia.

[25] This summarizes Ocampo and Botero in Companion Volume 1.

was in the hands of new settlers, who had begun with slash and burn cultivation only after resolving battles over adjudication of *tierras baldías*—literally "empty lands" unclaimed and in the public domain. A mixed agriculture then developed involving coffee, using shade and interplanting, as well as livestock.[26]

Colombia's exports grew 7 percent a year on average in real terms between 1905-09 and 1925-29; coffee led with 7.3 percent. Transport was one key to achieving growth. At the turn of the century, Colombia was almost without railways; the main transport artery from the coffee area to the coast was the Magdalena River, and this was seasonally so low in water as to make it impassable to boats. Foreign investors were not keen, and Colombia had lacked access to international capital markets for over 100 years, having failed to settle the debt from the War of Independence. The expanding coffee and commerce sectors together had to pressure the government for action. So began a public/private partnership that was to have important consequences.

But there was a further "institutional" need: the exceptionally high quality coffee was produced by many small producers. Both aspects differentiated Colombia from Brazil, where coffee quality was good, but not as good, and there were more large estates. The Colombian situation presented a special institutional challenge, since high-quality coffee had to be particularly well treated, processed and warehoused, and marketed with quality guarantees, if it was to be profitable. But small producers were not likely to collaborate spontaneously to achieve these ends. This challenge led to the formation at an early date (1927) of the *Federación Nacional de Cafeteros*, endowed from its inception with quasi-state capacities, in particular the right to collect taxes, despite its private sector nature. This very special institution was to grow significantly in the next two decades. Always run by financiers and merchants, it made the most of another characteristic of coffee—that it required little surplus to reinvest. Thus, these merchant financiers mediated the transfer of surplus and developed a web of intersectoral interests, at the heart of which lay the Coffee Fund, created in 1940. This institutionality had a dimension of social

---

[26] Le Grand, 1986. She claims that few small settlers obtained titles, despite a land policy intended to give them rights. Even if, as others claim, some settlers did in fact obtain titles, her material makes clear the complexity of institutional development. The law took no account of the many hidden costs, such as surveyor's fees, travel, postage, etc.

Box 3.1

"El Rey de la Leña"
Autobiography of a Self-made Man: Marco Restrepo

Marco Restrepo was born in 1889 of a landowning Antioqueñan family whose origins he traces back to immigration from Spain in the 16th and 17th centuries. The family properties and enterprises were dislocated by the wars and disturbances of the 19th century, and Restrepo had to go into hiding to avoid being conscripted for the War of a Thousand Days (he claimed they were conscripting 10-year-olds). He began his entrepreneurial life in farming, then joined his father in commerce. His father, however, prone to excessive and imprudent purchases, was a thorn in the side of his business-minded 20-year-old son. One disastrous day Restrepo bought beans in the market, only to find that his father had also bought huge amounts of the same product. Restrepo rescued the family from bankruptcy by taking advantage of the strength of the local institution of trust: "my word is my bond." The most important businessmen in the local town were three brothers. Restrepo waited until lunch-time, then quickly located one brother in his house, the second in the street and the third minding the shop, and persuaded each separately to buy beans, knowing that they would not go back on their word. By these and similar strategies he disposed of all the beans before the price collapsed.

At the age of 26, Restrepo was in jail, accused of killing one of his workers. He escaped and fled the country, intending to go to Argentina; but, having stopped in Ecuador for a time, he stayed on and made his fortune there. His first strategy was to find the names of the local rich and see how they made their money. This led him nowhere so he started to seek out Antioqueños living in the area. He soon decided none of them were trustworthy, so he opted to follow his own way. He spotted an opportunity: lack of shipping meant that Australian coal was no longer available for the Ecuadorian railways (it was the time of World War I). He started to buy up properties for their wood, and rapidly made money supplying firewood and later railway sleepers. His enterprises were based on tough labor relations and homemade discipline. His initiation of new workers took place "with money in his hand and a revolver in the belt." He is explicit that he himself dealt with wrongdoing. While he denied charges of murder and arms-dealing, his application of "order" is presented as what any sensible man would do. He continued to buy and sell, anything from mules to banknotes. His entire life appears from his own account to have been lived without collaboration, and with unashamed forcefulness and self-reliance. But for persecution by José María Velasco, Sr. (who held office three times during Restrepo's career), he would have been, he claims, "one of the big ranchers of the Andes."

control, as the federation built up paternalistic relations with small coffee producers, who in turn both cooperated and depended on the federation and local government.

This unusual and highly Colombian-specific institutional development occurred alongside a significant diversification, fed by the intersectoral character of the institutions described here, but also benefiting from coffee itself and from geography. Geographical fragmentation had been a negative factor throughout the 19th century; once growth began, however, it became a positive factor, for the incipient capital goods industry developing around coffee processing had natural protection. More important was policy; the protectionist trend already in evidence in the 19th century, notably that of Rafael Núñez in the 1880s, was consolidated by the major tariff reforms of 1905 and 1913, supported by government purchasing policies.[27]

The complementarity of coffee and industry was not principally that coffee provided a direct market for industry. It did so, to an extent, but incomes were low and there was little consumption of factory goods by small farmers. What coffee provided at the macro level was the impetus to infrastructure, general growth in incomes, urban development, surplus for reinvestment, and a political economy where those controlling surplus were *interested* in a more diversified economy. There was also much rural poverty and increasing rural violence, but these aspects did not impede the efficient growth process; in fact, low incomes were part of the mechanism leading to the accumulation of surplus at the intermediate stage.

In summary, Colombia as an export-led model had a number of resilient characteristics:

• Political economy, that is, the particularly constructive relationship between the public and private sectors, which complemented Colombia's political system and facilitated communication between the elites of coffee commerce and government.

• Complementarity between coffee and food, an unusual characteristic of an export economy and important for sustainability and for reducing the vulnerability of the poor.

• Agricultural practices and different organizational characteristics, which led to somewhat healthier environmental effects than in Brazil.

• Interest of the coffee elite in diversification and in an active role of the state.

---

[27] Ocampo and Botero in Companion Volume 1.

Argentina: Success or Failure?

Viewed from the traditional "staple theory" perspective of export economies,[28] Argentina is the closest to the textbook case in Latin America. Carlos Díaz-Alejandro eloquently describes how growth was closely related to successive booms in the export of land-intensive commodities, with land having very low opportunity cost. "Pre-1930 growth can be said to have been 'export-led' not because exports and their associated capital inflows provided growing aggregate demand (in a Keynesian fashion) but because, more fundamentally, exports and capital inflows led to an allocation of resources far more efficient than the one which would have resulted from autarkic policies. In particular, the domestic cost of capital goods, which would have been astronomical under autarky, say in 1880, was reduced to a low level by exports of commodities produced by the generous use of an input—land—whose economic value under autarky would have been quite small."[29]

Capital certainly poured in: by 1914 there was $3.2 billion of direct foreign investment and the public external debt was another $784 million. Investment went principally into railways and public utilities. Labor poured in, too: of the 3.25 percent annual population increase between 1880 and 1930, 44 percent—i.e., 1.4 percent per annum—was immigration, chiefly from Europe, and in particular Italy. (Brazilian immigration over the same period accounted for only 15 percent of population growth.)[30] This eased the labor constraint, though some immigrants in fact stayed in the cities or made their way there as fast as possible.[31] It should be noted that those going into the rural sector did not encounter "free" land, as happened in the American Midwest. Land was already in the hands of large landowners, dating both from colonial grants and later land policies. The newcomers entered into tenancy arrangements, often poorly regulated: this phenomenon was to have repercussions with time as the percentage of tenancy grew.

---

[28] Where foreign factors of production arrive to give value to a previously unused or underused natural resource.

[29] Díaz-Alejandro, 1970: 11.

[30] Sánchez-Albornoz, 1986.

[31] This seems to have been particularly true of Central Europeans brought to Argentina under charitable schemes to give Jews a fresh start in land settlement schemes. Many city dwellers of Central Europe typically lost little time in moving out of agriculture into trade and thence to Buenos Aires, though there were colonies, such as Colonia Baron Hirsch, where it was the second generation who sought the city lights. Gerchunoff, 1936.

In fact, the pure "staple" vision omits important factors. First, technical advance played a large role in the increase in production, and second, there were impending problems in the model, which would only appear with time. The first important technical advance was the arrival of wire fencing in the 1870s. Fencing radically reduced the need for labor in ranching. But while in neighboring Uruguay the decline in labor demand was producing a large, unstable surplus rural population, in Argentina the rich land of the Pampa allowed labor absorption through the alternation of wheat and alfalfa so that wheat and meat could prosper together. As the limit of the land frontier was reached in the 1910s, technical improvements in cattle raising allowed increased productivity of existing land, sustaining the model. Already at that point the model had led to substantial diversification: industry was 17 percent of GDP in 1913, led by the food sector based on meatpacking and grain products. Tariffs were quite low and the buoyant exchange rate did not encourage industry, but linkages from exports were rather strong.[32]

Second, this apparently ideal staple story had serious elements of fragility even while it yielded exceptionally rapid growth. These elements concerned financial exposure, the institutions and practices in agriculture and their consequences for sustainability, and the general shaping of the economy and infrastructure under the staple model.

On financial exposure, the inflow of capital had a high component of loans. This produced a degree of vulnerability shown at its most extreme with the Baring Crisis in 1890[33] and again with the Balkan Crisis in 1912, when funds were withdrawn both by investors seeking liquidity and governments needing to supplement their war chests.[34]

On institutions and practices in agriculture, the growing numbers of tenants were farming with inadequate tenure arrangements, and the soil of the Pampas was being badly abused, a clear case of "mining agriculture." By the 1930s this would lead to seriously declining yields.

On the general shaping of the economy, the expansion of infrastructure—principally railways, banks, commercial houses and ports—were all geared to the

---

[32] Cortés Conde in Companion Volume 1 provides more detail and documentation for this paragraph.

[33] See Ferns, 1992.

[34] Ibid.

extraction of export commodities for external markets. The most graphic representation of the way in which the shaping was not necessarily optimal for the longer run is given by the railway map of Argentina, a visual demonstration of how all links ran outwards. The railway system facilitated growth within this period but eventually would limit the integration of the national market.

Another influence of export-led growth was the close and initially beneficial relationship with a single trading partner, the United Kingdom. This would prove an irresistible force against change even once the writing was on the wall and the relationship was no longer so rewarding.[35]

The final aspect of the influence of the export model concerns political economy. While expansion was strong, growth was nonconflictual, since all could gain. But once crisis came—as with World War One, aggravated by vulnerability to drought and capital movements—then the government, faced with a severe recession, confronted labor resistance on the one hand and, on the other, demands from exporters for state support. Yet there were no state institutions that might help navigate such stormy seas. A wide franchise had been granted in 1912, but a population with a strong immigrant element was disinclined to become politically involved. On the other side, the elite groups who had led the export expansion enjoyed a dominant position, centered geographically in the Province of Buenos Aires and buoyed by support even from nonagrarian interests. Though controversy over the nature and role of these interests is intense in the literature, the recent work of Sabato shows their intersectoral links and their internal strength.[36] The author argues that this confluence of agrarian and nonagrarian interests supported the export-led phase and allowed industry to expand alongside agriculture, helped by the importance of the meat-packing industry, which provided a strong linkage effect. However, the relative self-sufficiency of these groups and the resulting lack of need to build relations with other groups in society limited the capacity of the country in due course to deal with change, since consensus-building networks that would be needed later were never developed.

---

[35] See Abreu in Companion Volume 2.

[36] Hora, 1997. The central references are Donghi, 1995; Sabato, 1988; Schvartzer, 1996; Sabato, 1987 and 1989; and Pucciarelli, 1986.

This interpretation coincides with the recent emphasis of another large literature: that comparing Argentina with Australia.[37] This argues that in Australia the powerful merchant groups had a strong interest in the internal market developed by colonial spending on wages and salaries, which in turn produced a demand for the goods they imported.[38] This resulted in a "model" in which relatively high rural wages and land prices favored commercial interests. The literature emphasizes not only the economic consequences of this, but also both the political and institutional results. Politically, land-based elites were forced to compromise and build alliances with urban commercial groups; and institutionally, Anglo-Australian banks and financial regulatory mechanisms developed with strong Australian participation. This contrasts with the dominance of Argentinean rural elites and the integration of early large-scale industry into the agro-exporting model, with meat-packing playing a central role. It is significant that the leading manufacturing firms of the period, such as Bunge and Born, were exporting both goods and capital in the 1920s.[39] The absence of challenge to this elite was quite different from what happened in Brazil and Colombia, where challenges arose from the regionally diffuse elite structure.

All these points of weakness were to act as counterweights to the major strengths represented by the extensive and intensive growth provided by the export economy, and its significant stimulus to industrialization.

Mexico: Revolution and the Export Economy

Mexico also came late to the table, especially considering its size and geographical proximity to the United States. The stormy nature of the struggle for independence and the ensuing political instability deterred foreign investment and growth, with stagnation aggravating instability in a vicious circle.[40] The result was a lack of progress in infrastructure. Mexico lagged behind Brazil, Argentina and Cuba. However, the

[37] See Dyster, 1984, for a stimulating discussion.

[38] It is argued that convicts and ex-convicts were incorporated economically, if not politically.

[39] See Katz and Kosacoff in Companion Volume 3.

[40] The following paragraphs are based on Knight in Companion Volume 1. Knight gives extensive documentation as well as a much more nuanced discussion than space allows here.

last quarter of the 19th century, under the regime of Porfirio Díaz (1876-1911), brought political stability, authoritarianism and a rapid catch-up in economic terms. The export boom was led by both mining and agriculture. Nonprecious metals—copper, lead and zinc—gained relative to the precious metals, and coffee, henequen, rubber and cotton all contributed to the 6 percent per annum growth of exports. The export boom was accompanied by industrial growth, helped not only by tariffs but by the depreciation of the silver currency, a story that will reappear in Peru.

The liberal elite in power understood well a lesson that would have to be learned again a century later: that where institutions were weak, the state had to create the appropriate conditions for market-led growth. "In pursuit of a distant economic liberalism"[41] and in a reciprocal relationship with export growth, substantial interventions produced new mining and commercial codes, a banking system, tariffs, and subsidies to the railway system. The government modernized ports, promoted communications, legislated to facilitate colonization, impeded labor organization and repressed social protest. Yet the state's capacities and possibilities were far less than in Brazil, given the need to battle constantly against internal and external threats.[42]

The missing element, compared to Brazil and Argentina, was immigration. A substantial indigenous population and the relative lack of need for labor in mining account for this. The consequences of the nature of the labor force were major, particularly in the southern regions of the country, where there was labor coercion and exploitation and the cementing of authoritarianism. This combined with recession and falling real wages in the early 1900s to produce the largely independent, vigorous political opposition to the Díaz dictatorship. Thus ensued the Revolution of 1910. As Knight argues, there was an intimate association with the export-led model:

"Most of the socioeconomic ingredients were to be found elsewhere in Latin America: an authoritarian, racist and positivistic regime, bent on export-led development; a dynamic commercial agriculture, linked to peasant dispossession and a degree of labor coercion; a growing manufacturing sector (especially in textiles), catering to a shallow domestic market; and a falling death rate, hence a growing

---

[41] Knight in Companion Volume 1.
[42] Topik, 1996: 140.

population, which, coupled with urban and rural proletarianization, eased the labor market, to the advantage of employers who usually had the ear of the state. Mexico differed only in degree: its growth came late and was unusually rapid, spurred by the close U.S. connection; aggressive state-building, coupled with a 'successful' project of *desarrollo hacia afuera*, benefited a minority but increasingly offended the majority; and this majority—mostly peasants—possessed valuable collective resources which, for example, Brazil's peasants, subject to the 'paternalist' control of the *coronel*, often lacked: village solidarity, a degree of local autonomy, a historical consciousness of previous popular struggles. Meanwhile, the growing middle class, like their counterparts in the Southern Cone, sought responsible, constitutional rule (not, of course, social revolution); the peasantry, threatened by the loss of land and political autonomy, looked to arrest Porfirian state-building in the name of a nostalgic popular liberalism. Díaz's failing powers and faulty judgment encouraged an anomalous alliance between these disaffected groups."[43]

The immediate economic consequences of the revolution were savage inflation, considerable hardship, and default on debt, but the oil industry boom in the years after 1910, followed by the revival of mining in the 1920s, led to surprising continuity in the export economy pattern: exports and GDP grew from 1910 to 1930.[44] How far the revolution was anti-foreign is a matter of controversy: U.S. investment certainly flowed into the export sectors and to industry in the 1920s.[45] Ford, Dupont and Colgate-Palmolive were to be found among the new arrivals.

The more powerful consequences, as Knight points out, were internal, significantly modifying Mexican capacity to react to the coming external shocks. By an extremely indirect and violent route, the Mexican version of the export economy model produced not only growth but remarkable institutional development, as both the state and civil society were fundamentally changed, allowing the late starter to catch up.

---

[43] Knight in Companion Volume 1.

[44] Reynolds, 1970, initially demonstrated this.

[45] Earnest efforts were made to negotiate on debt: twice in the 1920s agreements were reached with foreign bankers and bondholders, but economic downturns prevented resumption of debt payments.

The Classic Mineral Exporting Stories: Chile, Bolivia, Peru and Venezuela

Mining economies have well-known and clear-cut negative characteristics: not only are they particularly subject to "boom and bust" cycles, but their modus operandi also deters diversification and thus the long-run sustainability of growth. Sustainability is also constrained by contamination problems, with their knock-on effects on agriculture. Historically, returned value[46] tends to be low because of the interrelated characteristics of capital-intensive technology and foreign ownership, so profits are exported and equipment bought from abroad. Thus linkage through demand effects is low. Direct linkage effects through infrastructure are good, but limited by geography—that is, the usefulness of the resulting infrastructure depends on where the deposits are located.[47] Direct linkage effects through the purchase of inputs are also limited, though at the beginning of the 20th century in Latin America such purchases stimulated numerous small foundries and repair shops—an incipient capital goods industry. This promising start was eroded over the next two decades, however, through the combined effects of falling international transport costs, technical advances in metal-working and smelting technology, and transnationals' purchasing practices. The shift from nitrates to copper in the case of Chile further weakened such effects, as the requirements of the copper sector were more complex. So the wider effect of mining typically became heavily dependent on the indirect linkage through the government's taxing and spending.

The stories are different in the various instances of economies heavily dependent on mining.[48] In *Chile*, strong path dependence[49] effects worked in a favorable direction. Development in the early 19th century of a strong state and military

---

[46] Returned value is that part of export revenues that stays in the host economy, such as wages, local purchases, construction expenditure and other investment, and taxes.

[47] Chile's nitrate deposits were actually quite helpful in that regard since they extended over a huge distance. By contrast, "mining" the guano on offshore islands of Peru provided little spillover.

[48] Although mineral products were its principal export, Mexico is not included here as a mineral economy because the country's most important events were not strongly related to mining. It did not help Mexico's early development that mineral exports were important. Despite its unusually diverse export mix, Mexico suffered some of the same problems as the mining economies.

[49] A term introduced by Douglass North as a shorthand for the cumulative effects of history, through inherited resources, institutions, and social forces and culture molded by a particular historical path.

capacity, and the determination to keep national unity in the face of an unusual geography, resulted in relative stability and early institution building—the exact opposite of the Mexican story. Economic crisis in the 1870s was overcome by Chile's initiation of the War of the Pacific and the consequent acquisition of nitrate deposits (the British interest in the sector being unaffected by the transition). This unusual supply-side discontinuity was accomplished at the perfect moment, for Chile gained a world monopoly just as demand increased for nitrates both from the explosives industry and from European agriculture. The ensuing boom would normally be expected to have had severe supply-side consequences, by causing revaluation of the currency and erosion of protection (public revenues from taxing the booming export usually leading by default to the erosion of other sources of revenue). In fact, helped by the relatively favorable linkages from nitrates to domestic demand, the domestic economy prospered, aided by policy. An organization of industrialists, the *Sociedad de Fomento Fabril* (SOFOFA), had already come into existence in 1883, and large landowners, having faced the decline of export demand for wheat and other agricultural exports, were already interested in industry as well as the protection of agricultural products. In 1883, SOFOFA and the *Sociedad Nacional de Agricultura* (SNA) proposed tariff increases, and in 1897 they formed the *Centro Industrial y Agrícola*. In the same period, numerous industrial training schools were opened, at SOFOFA's initiative, and in the early 1900s a special office was opened to promote and subsidize the immigration of foreign technicians.[50]

Consonant with this private sector interest and activity, tariffs were increased on numerous occasions, rather than eroded, and the exchange rate kept pace despite substantial domestic inflation. The gold standard was abandoned. In addition, government expenditure rose and contained an unusually high "development" component. Following the War of the Pacific, Balmaceda's government created the Ministry of Public Works and Industry and endowed it with a rapidly expanding budget. Education was also expanded: there were 79,000 primary and secondary pupils in the country at the start of the Balmaceda government in 1886, and double that number by its end. This reflected a clear perception that the deposits were exhaustible and that the revenue from them had to be invested.[51]

---

[50] See Muñoz, 1968; Palma, 1979; and Kirsch, 1977, on the early history of Chilean industry.

[51] Blakemore, 1974.

All of this represented a coherent response to the threat of overvaluation—a coherence rarely seen in other countries a hundred years later. The result was continued industrial expansion. Applying a Chenery-style[52] calculation to data for 1914-16, Muñoz finds that Chile's level of industrialization was 1.7 times the level predicted from population and per capita income.[53]

Copper gradually emerged as nitrates collapsed because of failure to meet the productivity challenge from synthetic nitrates, and then from the replacement of nitrate in final use. The modus operandi of the export economy remained similar, however, with the sector in foreign hands, excluding locals, and with limited direct linkages. But a relatively strong and development-minded state and an unusually coherent private sector with a multisectoral base were already taking shape, able to withstand continued exclusion from copper, the principal source of wealth. Institutional development was pushed on the economic and social side, with Chile leading the way with Uruguay in social security reforms in the 1920s.[54] What suffered throughout, however, was agriculture for the domestic market. Food imports were 7 percent of total imports in 1912 and twice that by 1928.

Chile shows how, given appropriate preconditions, prior institutions and government-business collaboration, foreign-owned and capital-intensive mining can facilitate considerable development. In turn, *Bolivia* shows that substantial domestic ownership is not of itself sufficient to generate development on the basis of mining. Bolivian tin had the distinction of producing the earliest and most substantial instance of a Latin American international capitalist—Simón Patiño. In 1928, 41 percent of the Bolivian tin industry, by then 70 percent of exports, was nationally owned.[55]

At the turn of the century, tin was not Bolivia's principal export—silver and rubber were both higher proportions of the total. But both were soon to collapse for reasons of the international market, while tin was set fair for a strong demand expansion, linked to the development of the canning industry in the United States and Argentina. In 1900, Bolivia was producing 11 percent of world production, and

---

[52] Chenery's 1960 cross-section analysis, based on some 40 countries, provides a basis for predicting what a country's level of industrialization will be if it follows usual patterns.

[53] Muñoz, 1968: 32.

[54] Mesa-Lago, 1994.

[55] This section draws on Contreras in Companion Volume 1.

by 1910, 20 percent. Tin gave Bolivia rapid growth through the three decades up to the Great Depression.

However, wider effects of the tin boom were limited. The central problem was the poverty and isolation of Bolivia, where the 19th century had been characterized by political instability and economic stagnation. Despite a population only slightly more than half that of Chile in 1900, Bolivia was far poorer. Its geographic problems worsened when Bolivia lost its only access to the sea with the War of the Pacific.

The tin industry was primitive in its early days, financed in limited fashion by trading houses.[56] When Patiño was setting up in business in the first five years of the century, local purchases were an impossibility. He brought mules from Argentina, flour and fodder from Chile, and jute sacks from Europe, and had forms printed in Antofagasta. By 1905, he was bringing in a $1 million plant for metals smelting. A Chilean firm imported it from Europe for him and sent German engineers to assist with its installation.[57] Patiño began to accumulate a surplus with extraordinary speed, and claimed in an interview in 1911 that he wanted to invest in Bolivia: "Using my judgement as a Bolivian and an industrialist I have come to the conclusion that, instead of piling up in Europe what is left over from my mining and banking profits, it would be more advantageous to leave them in my country, benefiting it and me."[58] He did create a bank in 1912—the Banco Mercantil—with $5 million of his own money, but many of his other plans were frustrated. He laid plans for colonization of the east of the country to develop supplies of food and wood for the mines, with a railway to bring the goods, but Congress refused the concession. So he tried to invest in cement, but a price could not be agreed upon with the Foundation Company, the parent company of his designated target. Meanwhile, every step involved him in legal battles, settled with difficulty and expense. The fragile fabric of institutions provided neither the basis for trust nor the instruments to settle disputes, and his investments never happened.

Given the ineffectiveness of direct linkages and the limits on the reinvestment of private surplus, what of the route through taxation and government spend-

---

[56] Patiño started in this way, with credit from his former employers, Fricke and Co.
[57] Geddes, 1972.
[58] Ibid.: 155.

ing? By the 1920s, the government was succeeding in taxing the tin sector—at the cost of considerable friction and transaction costs. But its use of the money, and of that borrowed from abroad, in prestige projects and corruption, became notorious.[59] The miners opposed both taxation and the external borrowing that led to higher taxes.

However, even with such a classic story of limited spread effects, there were gains. Railways were built in the first 20 years of the century, principally making connections to the sea but subsequently linking the main cities.[60] The liberal governments of Montes (1904-09 and 1913-17), in particular, expanded education, including technical education.[61]

Growth also encouraged inequality, and the Indian population was, as elsewhere, the loser, though with a mining economy the pressures for land were less extreme than in a mixed economy like Mexico. But the issue of supplying the mines with food and with coca—an important part of wages—was central throughout the export economy period. Patiño may have imported flour, but mining generally needed to rely on local supplies. The result of such dependence was that even where the export commodity was not directly land-using, pressures were placed on Indian lands by expansion of *haciendas*. How far this was successfully resisted in some regions is a matter of controversy in the literature.[62] Overall, within a general pattern of dispossession of communal land, there was a pattern of varied Indian response. The net result was increased parcelization and harm to those peasants already on the margins of the structures of property and power.

Peru, like Mexico, is labeled a mining economy only by abusing the truth. But it does usefully illustrate the possible costs of foreign control, as well as the negative side of export diversity. Peru has the lowest indicator of commodity concentration in Table 3.3, yet its diversity, while only marginally greater than Mexico's, was even more regionally specialized. Each export product had its distinct regional base with its own regional dynamism, labor and land market characteristics, yet at the same time the elite's economic interests were rarely exclusively regional. This may be a

---

[59] McQueen, 1926.
[60] Contreras, 1990a.
[61] Ibid.
[62] Dunkerley, 1997. The key references are Grieshaber, 1980; Klein, 1993; Langer, 1987; Rivera, 1984.

particularly unrewarding set of circumstances for successful development. And running through each regional dynamic in some form is the need for labor and land to be exacted from a preexisting indigenous population.

Wool was produced in southern Peru, with foreign merchant houses providing the marketing and powerful landlords encroaching on Indian lands. Population pressure and social differentiation undermined community bonds, increasing vulnerability and causing eventual crisis with the collapse of wool markets in the 1920s. The resulting peasant rebellion was forcibly and successfully crushed, but wool never recovered its external market. The coast, suitable for sugar and cotton, faced labor shortages following the abolition of slavery. Once the Chinese indentured labor supply ceased in the 1870s, the system of *enganche* slowly developed, whereby contractors in the Sierra would offer loans to induce people to work on the coast in a form of tied labor. Indians coming to work in cotton came under sharecropping arrangements. Mining was concentrated in the Central Sierra, with foreign capital entering Cerro de Pasco in the early 1900s and coexisting with local mines, which supplied copper. Environmental damage was localized but extreme, via the contamination of agricultural land by fumes. Under pressure, foreign firms would then buy the contaminated land and subsequently develop livestock activity in addition to mining. Labor contractors used methods similar to the *enganche* system, but with modernization in the 1920s a more stable workforce was needed. Oil formed an enclave along the northern coast after 1910, while during the same period the Amazon saw its rubber boom dying out, as was happening elsewhere.

At the start of the century, Peru's development potential looked promising. In the 1890s, the collapse of silver brought the same relative price stimulus that it did to Mexico, while the prior effect of the guano boom had been to eliminate many sources of revenue. This meant that there was a strong incentive to raise tariffs for revenue purposes, given a combination of weak government and strong export elites resisting taxation. This led to impressive industrial growth in the 1890s, accompanied by the development of banking and infrastructure.[63] However, the industrial base was easily eroded, as sugar, copper and eventually oil generated the classic overvaluation effects

---

[63] Thorp and Bertram, 1978.

on the exchange rate, and the sectorally-fluid elite moved their interests into export sectors and abandoned industry. In addition, the incipient capital goods industry, stimulated initially by local purchasing by copper and sugar sectors, suffered the same fate as in Chile.[64] This was one effect, in part, of a foreign presence: the deeper consequence was that the development needs of the different export sectors were satisfied by foreign firms that built infrastructure and supplied technology and marketing contacts and expertise. The elite groups had ample opportunity in various export sectors and did not need government, either to protect new risky ventures or to market or develop other services around their export interests.

Unlike Chile, the foreign presence, while it brought technology and increased the rate of growth, had an intangible negative effect in Peru: the disincentive to local groups to support a new role for government or to sustain industrial and other initiatives of the 1890s.[65] The various competing interests implied by export diversity did not help, since this discouraged Chilean-style early development of large producer associations.

The need for labor, land and water and the specific characteristics of each regional experience tended to perpetuate and deepen inequalities. Exploitation produced social and ethnic tensions, but these were generally concentrated in a particular locality, making protest movements vulnerable to repression, as with the peasant rebellions of the south. Thus, unlike in Mexico, economic growth in Peru affected neither state formation nor class or race relations. The most serious threat was the worker-based movement emerging out of the sugar economy of the northern coast, which gave rise in due course to the Aprista Party.

The last example of the medium-sized, mineral-based economies suggests quite different lessons. *Venezuela* became a mineral economy only in the course of this period, beginning as an agrarian, coffee and cacao-based economy. But once oil appeared, Venezuela became Latin America's closest example to a "pure" rentier export economy within this early period, and so is helpful in defining the conditions and tendencies that allow such a model to emerge.

---

[64] A further negative aspect was the practice of large plantations and mining firms to maintain company stores supplied largely with imports, or at least goods from outside the region.

[65] For example, the training and technological development efforts of the *Cuerpo de Ingenieros de Minas y Aguas*.

The country had a violent and disturbed political history into the 20th century, characterized by military governments and dictators, and leading to a culture that tended to see government as war booty and to confuse the political and the personal.[66] A military dictator would be surrounded by a group of collaborators and friends, military and nonmilitary, looking to benefit from their access to sources of patronage.

Nevertheless, Venezuela was a coffee economy of some importance in the late 19th century. It was the second largest coffee producer in the world after 1881. However, the weakening of coffee prices and internal political instability meant negative growth in the 1890s and into the first decade of the 20th century. Thereafter, some growth occurred, but there were problems of limited land and labor supply.[67] Slow growth and lack of stability meant that the surplus did not lead to diversification, as in Colombia; it accumulated in the hands of merchants and facilitated imports. The tendency to fluctuations in export revenue further inhibited any ability to accumulate the resources that might have established an economic or political elite capable of transformation. There was relatively little artisan industry of the type to be found virtually everywhere in Latin America by the turn of the century.

It was with the entry into power of Juan Vicente Gómez in 1908, who ruled until his death in 1935, that enough political stability was created to encourage foreign investors to come exploring Venezuela's oil. In 1912, the oil companies invested $44 million (Venezuela's total exports in that year were only $25 million). The first field came into production in 1917. Oil rose from 2 percent of exports in 1920 to 47 percent by 1925 and 85 percent by 1930. Three companies—Standard Oil, Shell and Gulf—controlled 99 percent of output. Venezuelans sold their concessions to the foreign companies, but whereas in Peru there were options for surplus, in Venezuela there was too small a domestic base for the proceeds to be used for anything but consumption and construction.[68] By the 1930s, both coffee and cacao declined even in absolute terms, as was to be expected. The government circulated oil revenue by three means: revaluation of the currency, which cheapened

---

[66] Moncada, 1995.

[67] Rangel, 1969.

[68] Vandellos, 1938, cited by Kornblith, 1984.

imports, reduction or elimination of other taxes, and public spending. The latter was used to build the central state and implement effective control for the first time, but always with two characteristics. First, the continued blurring of private and public, which made President Gómez the richest man in the country. At his death his personal fortune was estimated to be larger than the national budget.[69] Second, the "development" component characteristically took the form of subsidies. For example, in 1928 the Agricultural and Livestock Bank and the Worker Bank were created, the former for cheap credit and the latter for cheap housing.

In summary, the essence of this particularly extreme version of a rentier economy includes the following characteristics:

- Income is channeled through government.
- The entrepreneurial role is carried out exclusively by foreign companies.
- Oil income *is* the country's income—other sources are relatively small or quickly eliminated.
- The prior culture confuses the political and the personal and sees control of government in terms of access to sources of patronage.
- The previous level of development is low.

Caribbean Sugar

The final medium-sized economy, *Cuba*, takes us to the sugar economies of the Caribbean, which included a number of the area's fastest growing economies during this period. At the start of the century, most of the English, French and Dutch-speaking Caribbean states were still colonies, with the exception of Haiti, which was occupied by the United States in 1915.[70]

Cuba is not only the largest island in the Caribbean, but is also endowed with superb sugar land. Its history exhibits with painful clarity, however, the characteristics common to many Caribbean nations. Two aspects intertwine: the nature of the commodity and the consequences of geography for political as much as economic dependence—more specifically, proximity to the United States. Three other aspects

---

[69] Sullivan, 1976.

[70] Of the 26 Caribbean states, nine today remain dependent territories of European powers or the United States. Fourteen more have only become independent since 1960.

in turn result from commodity and geography: diverse interests within the export sector, institutions formed by and centered on the export sector, and acute economic instability. These five aspects added up to a peculiarly unfavorable situation for diversification or reinvestment of surplus, even where size would appear to have allowed it. At the same time, growth was very dynamic while the market was good.

Having attained independence from Spain, Cuba became a United States protectorate with the U.S. military occupation of 1898. It became a republic in 1902, but with its independence circumscribed, since the Platt Amendment to the Cuban Constitution obliged Cuban governments (among much else) to consent to U.S. intervention "for the preservation of Cuban independence" and the "maintenance of the government adequate for the protection of life, property and individual liberty."[71] The Treaty of Reciprocity with the United States (1902) gave tariff preference for sugar in the U.S. market in exchange for tariff preferences in Cuba for U.S. goods. A huge inflow of U.S. direct foreign investment, along with immigration (largely from Spain), facilitated tremendous expansion while fostering acute dependence on the United States. Eighty percent of Cuban sugar went to the U.S. in 1880; this rose to an annual average of over 98 percent from 1899 to 1912. By 1913, this amounted to 53 percent of U.S. sugar consumption. U.S. mills were producing more than 60 percent of Cuban sugar, while owning 22 percent of Cuban national territory. With the boom and bust of the early 1920s in world sugar markets, U.S. banks ended up owning mills. National City Bank of New York took possession of more than 50 sugar mills in the summer of 1921.

Thus it begins to emerge how product characteristics plus geography led to diversity of interests: the banks' involvement in mill ownership, resulting from instability and capital intensity; foreign and domestic ownership side by side in milling; and diverse refiners' interests (some buying from their own mills, some buying from many sources, some straddling several countries).[72] In addition, the cane was actually produced by large and small *colonos* who displayed varying types of dependence on the mills.

To the instability of the sugar market itself was added the instability brought on when beet sugar producers recovered and expanded in Europe after the First

---

[71] Pollitt, 1984: 4.
[72] This diversity is pointed out and documented by Pollitt, 1984.

World War. For example, the U.K.'s demand for Cuban sugar now became highly unstable, since its supplies came first from domestic beet and then colonial cane sugar. Any shortfall was then made good by residual purchases on the so-called world sugar market–i.e., overwhelmingly by purchases from Cuba.

The capital-intensive nature of sugar at its milling stage opened it naturally to foreign investment, and generated the possibility of a microeconomic response to fluctuations which could be particularly perverse. In the 1920s, producers who had invested heavily in response to the wartime boom needed to keep on expanding despite collapsing prices, so aggravating the instability.[73]

A further element in instability was employment, since the dead season lasted up to nine months. Since sugar production and associated activities penetrated geographically throughout the country, and the industrial side of sugar production was seasonal as well, the social consequences of this instability were devastating.

The nature of sugar as a commodity, with its high financial and transport needs, perhaps exaggerated what is seen everywhere with export economy stories: institutions constructed around the commodity, which then effectively ties the country to that commodity. Thus roads and railways were completely geared to sugar, with discriminatory freight rates in its favor. So were credit and marketing systems, and what technological development there was. At a more intangible level, sugar and instability together dominated the culture; investors were hesitant to invest elsewhere because sugar grew too easily and gave too good a return. Such patterns of thought and behavior were to continue even after sugar was less strong a growth engine.[74]

These characteristics together brought a peculiarly binding kind of dependency as well as a low propensity for diversification, or indeed for any kind of spread effects from sugar. By the time of the Revolution of 1933, even given poor primary product prospects, Cuba's best option appeared to be to secure continuing and improved access to the U.S. market. The diversity of interests in the sugar sector itself militated against exploring other possibilities.

These patterns, typical of plantation economies, were repeated elsewhere with variations that change the story but not the analysis. *Puerto Rico*, for example, was

---

[73] Santamaría, 1995.

[74] IBRD, 1951.

occupied by the United States in 1898 and became a U.S. possession. Under the Foraker Act of 1900, Puerto Rico was prohibited from determining its own tariffs, all trade had to be carried on U.S. ships, and the territory was made part of the U.S. monetary system. The Puerto Ricans generally welcomed the invading force, since it promised "a democratic alternative to the oppressiveness and backwardness of the Spanish domination."[75] Growth was extremely rapid, and by 1920, about 75 percent of the population depended on sugar. Puerto Rico's three main exports—coffee, sugar and tobacco—were dominated by U.S. corporations. By 1928, U.S. corporations controlled approximately 80 percent of the sugar land and processed over 60 percent of sugar exported.[76]

The *Dominican Republic* is a variation in a different direction. It experienced very rapid growth based on sugar and cacao, as well as a flood of U.S. capital, yet maintained its political independence, subject to a succession of U.S. military and other interventions (the last invasion being in 1965). *Haiti*, on the other hand, experienced virtually no growth. By the end of the 19th century, the country had gained the doubtful distinction of being the poorest in the Americas, and there it stayed, beset with instability and racial and other conflicts that were unresolved by a period of U.S. occupation starting in 1915.

The English and Dutch-speaking Caribbean islands tended to grow more slowly, though equally blessed initially with good sugar land. They had had a period of strong sugar growth earlier, in the 17th and 18th centuries, but were severely affected by the end of slavery. Despite indentured labor schemes, they had not resolved labor shortage problems when U.S. investment in sugar in the larger islands boomed and provided intense competition and exclusion from the growing major U.S. market. Labor shortages were aggravated by competition from the building of the Panama Canal, development of the oil sectors in Venezuela and Trinidad, and development of the Cuban sugar industry. The shortages also led to policy choices not to promote other sectors of the economy in order not to compete away labor. The West India Royal Commission appointed by British Colonial Secretary Joseph Chamberlain in 1897 made the following analysis: "What

---

[75] Dietz, 1986
[76] Silvestrini, 1989.

suits them [the sugar estates] best is a large supply of laborers, entirely dependent on being able to find work on the estates and, consequently, subject to their control and willing to work at low rates of wages."[77]

Small Economies of Latin America

The final group of countries reinforces the initial theme of the significance of size. Small internal markets, worsened by lack of national integration and limited resource endowment, and without the peculiar advantages of the Caribbean, made it difficult for these countries to profit from international expansion as much as better positioned neighbors. The two partial exceptions are Costa Rica and Uruguay.

Argentina's neighbors, *Uruguay* and *Paraguay*, lacked her rich resource endowment as well as her size. The poor soil used for ranching in both countries severely limited the alternative uses of land. The Pampas, with rich potential for pasture improvement and for wheat and maize as alternatives to livestock, stops at the Argentine border. Better production in Uruguay and Paraguay was possible only through better breeding and through wire fencing. But in Uruguay, the wire fencing released labor that had no alternative employment in the rural sector. The turn of the century in Uruguay saw a dispossessed rural population drawn into the armies of the Blanco *caudillo* Aparicio Saravia in the civil wars of 1897 and 1904.[78] Under these conditions, urbanization was rapid, providing a base in turn for precocious industrialization and the welfare state that was fostered in a unique fashion by Batlle, twice President of Uruguay and long-time leader of the Colorado Party. As long as ranchers could increase output by improving breeds—possible up to 1930—the export economy could provide the resources for this model, if with increasing antagonism on the part of the livestock sector. But its limits would be exposed increasingly thereafter, made more binding by the small size of Uruguay. The foreign-owned *frigoríficos* were not particularly interested in solving the problem of

---

[77] Page 18 of the report as cited by Mandle, 1989. By recommending the continued existence of peasant agriculture and plantation agriculture side by side, the report did not really face up to the logic of its own analysis, Mandle argues. Colonial governments generally favored peasant or smallholder production as stabilizing and good for the tax base.

[78] The Blancos and Colorados are the two political parties that have dominated Uruguayan political life for more than a century. *Caudillo* is the Spanish term for a regional or national warlord.

inadequate raw material supplies, having easier and more rewarding options next door in Argentina. The limited internal market also restricted the profitability of urban and industrial growth. In the large coffee economies, low levels of investment needed in the principal export sector could drive a move to diversification, if the export elites had sufficient political access to give them confidence to invest in other sectors. In Uruguay, however, there was a move to diversify, but the internal market was too small and the ranchers had neither sufficient access to nor much influence over the Batllista state. So no sense of partnership grew up around solving the imminent problem of rural stagnation.

An interesting contrast is with Denmark, very similar in size and resource endowment to Uruguay.[79] In the course of the 18th and 19th centuries, the feudal system of large estates in Denmark was transformed into a model of medium-sized holdings, with cooperatives rendering economies of scale and political influence. This favored development of intensive agricultural processing and an internal market for industry by the early 20th century. All this was lacking in Uruguay, where export elites were absorbed into the pattern of domination of British capital and the export trade. Processing of leather, for instance, occurred not in Uruguay but in Europe.

If Uruguay both gained and lost by its proximity to Argentina, Paraguay lived completely in the shadow of its neighbor.[80] With half of Uruguay's population, landlocked and devoid of precious metals, strategic importance and population, Paraguay existed by selling yerba mate, tobacco, tannin extract and hides, principally to Argentina, which controlled Paraguay's only access to the world market by river. Argentine shipping companies exercised control of this route and the Argentine government frequently imposed arbitrary import duties and quotas on Paraguayan exports in transit. The effect of these measures was often devastating and sufficient to change governments in Asunción.

The Triple Alliance War (1864-70) devastated an already poor economy, and led to the state withdrawing as far as possible from the economy.[81] Out of economic necessity and ideology alike, the government sold the enormous tracts of land that

---

[79] For the development of this contrast, see Senghaas, 1985.
[80] This section was written with the collaboration of Andrew Nickson.
[81] Abente, 1991: 69.

covered most of the country and privatized public utilities. Foreigners—Argentines, British, Germans and North Americans—bought up both. By the 1930s, 19 companies owned over half the country.[82] A conspicuous case was *La Industria Paraguaya*, which owned 8,400 square miles, including much of the best *yerbales*. It was bought by the U.S. Farquhar Syndicate, then purchased by Argentine-British interests. Argentina succeeded in restricting Paraguayan exports to raw yerba, processed in Argentine mills. In the case of quebracho, an Argentine company, Carlos Casado, dominated Paraguayan production of tannin. Paraguayan quebracho extract was shipped to Argentina where it was re-exported as Argentine tannin.[83] Up to 80 percent of Paraguayan exports went to Argentina in the early 20th century.[84] Under such conditions, there was no room for development of a significant independent local business elite.

Ecuador is similar to Peru in its regional complexity and diversity, but in this period it lacked Peru's mineral resources to tempt foreign investors. And it was smaller: Ecuador had a population of only 1 million in 1900, and its exports of $16 million in 1913 compared with Peru's $44 million. In the 19th century, each of Ecuador's regions had a strong life of its own: textiles in the Northern Sierra were exported, principally to Colombia; Panama hats principally from the Southern Sierra were a successful artisan export; and in the coastal region, cocoa, coffee, sugar, rice and cotton were grown. In both coast and sierra, land concentration and the expulsion of Indians from communal lands continued in the 19th century.[85] The process was accelerated on the coast by the strong surge of European demand for cocoa: its consumption per capita in center countries rose from 1.7 ounces in 1870 to 9.4 ounces by 1897.[86] By the end of the 19th century, 20 families owned 70 percent of the land in the cocoa-growing regions.[87] Labor migrated from the sierra to work in cocoa, since the sierra was growing more slowly, with artisan industry affected by imports and by legislation and campaigns against the Indians. Along the coast, by contrast, a strong export elite was forming, establishing banks and insur-

---

[82] Roett and Sacks, 1991

[83] Abente, 1991: 69.

[84] Erico, 1975: 133.

[85] Chiriboga, 1980: 136-78.

[86] Ibid.: 59.

[87] Ibid.: 64.

ance companies as well as export houses, while a separate group formed around importing and its finance. But it was natural, given the absence of railways and traversable roads and the lack of dynamism of the sierra, that the links from this expansion should run outwards. "Plantation stores entered into agreements with Guayaquil importers, and highland produce was replaced with goods from California, Baltimore, Chile, Panama and Peru."[88] Cocoa planters, immigrants themselves, set up offices abroad, and "five of the most important cocoa families set up limited liability companies in Hamburg and London."[89]

The planters of Guayaquil did not even engage in Peruvian-style shifting of surplus between mining and sugar. Their surplus went to Europe. For all its regional diversity and early industrialization around textiles and hats, with cocoa exports at 64 percent of total exports in 1913 (Table 3.3), Ecuador looked remarkably like a mono-export economy.

Domestic opportunities widened in the 1910s, as the sugar industry became an attractive field of investment and the Quito-Guayaquil railway linked the northern highlands with the coast.[90] But like Chile, Ecuador's crisis came early, with the collapse of cocoa, also in the 1910s, resulting from a combination of problems: World War I, increasing production in West Africa, decreasing productivity with declining quality of new land, and problems with fungus infections. Unlike wool in the south of Peru, cocoa was important enough that the crisis had major national implications. A producers' association was formed and Congress granted tax revenue to cover the association's expenses. Efforts were made to create a producers' cartel. But between further price falls and disease, the association could not prevail, and came to an end in 1920.

The example shows the problems of a mono-export economy and lack of regional integration at their most serious level: disease hit the plantations at a time when producers were already devastated by price falls and could not take action. When prices recovered in 1924, the supply response was weak. The lack of diversification internally and the external links meant that there was no offsetting force, and the recession was deep.

---

[88] Maiguashca, 1996: 73.

[89] Ibid.: 73.

[90] Ibid.: 83.

In *Central America*, the principal initial force for expansion was the international coffee market. Coffee cultivation began as early as the 1830s in the highlands of Costa Rica, but needed the political consolidation that came with the so-called Liberal reforms of the late 19th century throughout the isthmus. With political consolidation, British loans were sought for railways, ports and other infrastructure.

Already, the exceptionality of Costa Rica was obvious: small producers expanding into largely uncultivated land developed a coffee culture closer to Colombia's than to that of other coffee producers, and thus sustained a political system with more egalitarian characteristics than elsewhere (here diverging from Colombia). In Guatemala, it was necessary to dominate indigenous groups "with a combination of paternalism and violence" embodied in a state-led system of *enganche*.[91] The takeoff of coffee dated from 1880, as in El Salvador, where large estates were more prevalent and as a result there were more landless workers. In Nicaragua, there is less terrain suitable for coffee, so more products coexisted. But more importantly, the fragmented elites did not achieve reforms. Civil war and U.S. intervention followed. In Honduras, coffee did poorly for reasons of land quality, and economic expansion only happened with banana production in the 1880s.

Bananas brought U.S. multinationals (conspicuously the United Fruit Company), enclave development, the holding of idle land in the hands of the TNCs, and perhaps the most abusive crop of all in terms of the land. Banana production in Central America developed as an export sector from the 1870s onwards, but emerged on a larger scale in the 1920s and 1930s, when United Fruit came to own about 4 percent of the total land area in Honduras, Guatemala, Panama and Costa Rica.[92] The company dominated Honduran economy and society, while Costa Rican society and government, already more complex, were less dependent on bananas and able to bargain on more equal terms.

Banana production needs flat, lowland soils with a high nutrient content and balanced humidity. In other words, bananas compete for the best soils, and their expansion is thus likely to have a particularly significant crowding-out effect on local food crops, in combination with the TNCs' practice of holding land idle. The foreign companies monopolized idle land because the only way to deal with prob-

---

[91] Pérez Brignoli in Companion Volume 1. See also McCreery, 1994.
[92] Hernández and Witter, 1996.

lems of disease seemed to be to move to new land. However, the competing Standard Fruit Company developed the new Valery banana clone, which was resistant to the Panama disease. But the new variety was intensive in its use of fertilizers, pesticides, fungicides and herbicides. As these inputs were applied in quantities that could not be absorbed by the plantations, they caused significant problems for surface water systems and human health. By the middle of the 20th century, growing problems with the Panama disease led United Fruit to abandon most of the original plantations on the Atlantic coast, which were transferred to the Pacific lowlands.

Internationally, coffee was never a particularly dynamic market. Modest growth was hardly the problem, however, in that the existing surplus was not reinvested in Central America. The needs of coffee for technological improvement were minimal, as elsewhere, and the limits of the domestic market such that importing consumer goods or exporting profits were the logical alternatives. The fruit companies likewise took their money elsewhere. Military governments or governments with strong military links invested heavily in arms. Once more, we identify the Costa Rican exception: already in the first decades of the century, Costa Rica was spending more on education, health and development than its Central American neighbors.[93]

Modest growth and extreme fluctuations led to constant debt defaults, even in Costa Rica. Nevertheless, the period saw significant gains. Institutional developments were substantial throughout Central America. National monetary systems were unified, the gold standard adopted, first by Costa Rica in 1896. Banking and credit were developed. Railways and then roads linked the Atlantic and Pacific by 1910 in Costa Rica and Guatemala.

In Panama, the link was the canal, opened in 1914. Its geographical position was practically the country's only comparative advantage: it lived principally from the canal revenues, though also from bananas, with reasonable prosperity but with a particularly close relationship to the United States. Once independence from Colombia was achieved in 1903, Panama was described along the same lines as Cuba, as a "virtual protectorate."[94]

---

[93] Pérez Brignoli in Companion Volume 1.

[94] Ibid.

As always, the exceptions to the general rule are informative. The example demonstrates the importance of the early settlement patterns of free land and the evolution of an unusually egalitarian social structure. These two factors together led to unusually broad based and responsive policymaking and an early and remarkable commitment to investment in education. Uruguay was also something of an exception, with substantial growth and prosperity within this period, but with less promising characteristics for the long run. Uruguay lacked the prosperity and vitality of Costa Rica's small-holder coffee sector to sustain growth, and its political economy was not equipped to deal well with the resource limitations to its ranching economy.

Export-led Growth as a Development Tool

Examining export-led growth of the early part of the century helps us to understand what works for and against preparation of the economy for the long run, both in terms of policymaking capacity as well as more conventional elements. We have emphasized direct and indirect linkages, including the stimulus to infrastructure creation and broader institution building. The latter in a very intangible sense affects savings and investment propensities, a core aspect of resilience. Building state institutions and developing functional relations between the public and private sectors also affect policy design and implementation, as well as savings and investment behavior. We have also examined the downside of export-led growth—vulnerability to external shocks. Export economy experiences often increase this vulnerability by making countries more dependent on food imports and foreign savings, making public revenue more dependent on trade, and increasing commodity concentration or the dominance of a single trading partner.

The final section of this chapter draws out more explicitly from the national experiences what determined favorable and unfavorable situations for long-run development, including mechanisms of economic growth, how the engine worked, and the political, social and institutional dimensions.

The "Engine" of Export-led Growth

At first sight, the obvious conclusion is that these export-led decades brought growth and that growth was important. Much of the institution building—mining codes, legal codes, central banks, producer associations—would not have happened without growth. Growth was at the heart of the stimulus to infrastructure and urban development that gradually began to build a national market. But there were also examples of fast growth with little institution building and no diversification, as in small sugar economies. And growth was resource-consuming, particularly agricultural growth, which sometimes simply "mined" the topsoil. Frontier expansion was often associated with destruction of both soil and forest.

In the decades that followed, growth would become important if only because through it came technical progress. But in these early decades, investment was not the crucial transmitter of technology that it would be later. For substantial periods of time, growth was "extensive:" economies could grow simply by incorporating more land and labor. In fact, extensive growth by its very ease, as in Uruguay, disincentivated the search for solutions to natural constraints.

Size was also important, and in more ways and more deeply than might be thought at first. In the extreme case of Brazil, size provided market power, even enough to pass on the cost of protection, as well as an internal market that made local reinvestment of the export sector surplus profitable, as was the case as well in Colombia. On the other hand, small size and fragmentation doomed Ecuador to losing many of the benefits of its export boom. In Uruguay, size limited the interest of foreign investors in solving the problems affecting the livestock and manufacturing industries.

Size also limited the particularly favorable effect of regional elites negotiating and collaborating with one another. This phenomenon furthered institution building and problem solving in both Brazil and Colombia, but its absence in some other countries may have in part been due to the size of the economies and societies.

The development literature has stressed product diversity or its absence as key to growth during this period. But while export diversity reduced national vulnerability to the collapse of particular markets (such as wool in Peru), it was perhaps less important than one might think. Specifically, diversity sometimes impeded the building of national cohesion among business elites, particularly if combined with a lack of need for state support, as in Peru. It is true that the combination of market and commodity concentration often tied a country strongly into an external relationship, for better or worse. This happened with sugar in Cuba and with meat in Argentina. In the short term, this usually increased growth through access to capital and skills and more rapid institution building. In the longer term, however, the consequences of tariff preference schemes and other aspects of the relationship were sometimes less favorable.

In all countries, prior conditions turned out to be highly significant,[95] and provided the core of the notion of "path dependence." The entrenching of sugar throughout Cuba's institutions and structures was an extreme form of what was prone to happen everywhere. The nature of preceding booms was key–for example, the relevance of skills learned in exporting precious metals to the new mineral exports of the 20th century (as in Peru and Mexico).

The degree of previously existing state formation and national integration was also critical: lack of both explained late arrivals on the scene. This was particularly important where foreign investors played a large role in the next phase (colonial or semi-colonial control could substitute, of course). Mexico was in a far weaker position than, say, Brazil or Chile. The need for foreign capital in conditions of weakness might strongly condition governmental policies, as in the case of Mexico.

Another important prior condition was the extent to which the resources needed for the export economy expansion were already in the hands of local indigenous populations, which required wresting those resources away by some degree of force. This had consequences for conflict and attitudes on ethnicity and race for the long run and became significant in income inequality.

The product itself also affected the results of export expansion.[96] Mining had less land and labor needs than agricultural production, so it generally involved less conflict than exports for which large indigenous populations had prior possession of arable resources. The greater capital and technological intensity of mining gave foreign capital a significant advantage in owning resources, not just marketing

---

[95] The first analysis in the Latin American development literature to develop this point systematically was that of Sunkel and Paz, 1970.

[96] This builds on the taxonomies developed in Sunkel and Paz, 1970; Cortés Conde and Hunt, 1985; and Cardoso and Faletto, 1971.

them. (The notable exception was Simón Patiño, the Bolivian entrepreneur.) Mining production was associated with channeling returned value through the government: Venezuela was virtually a "pure" case of the resulting rentier economy, which interacted with prior conditions of underdevelopment and a culture of mixing the personal and the political, to the point of producing a "booty" state.

Agricultural production, on the other hand, by its nature raises the issue of the land frontier. Reaching a frontier at a given point in time had strong implications, even if the static notion of a frontier is misleading, since its limits and impact can shift as a result of technological changes or market developments. Also, some products can be produced in varying terrain. The altitude suitable for coffee, for instance, included the steep hillsides of Colombia and the relatively flatlands of Brazil. The prior existence of indigenous populations was also a variable. Coffee was produced by farms of extremely different sizes and with varying types of productive arrangements, from the large *hacienda* with dependent labor (Guatemala, El Salvador, Brazil) to the independent small farms covering many hillsides in Colombia and Costa Rica.

Different products also had different marketing needs. Some could be stored, others not. Some traveled well, others not. Some products could be processed easily and with economic advantage close to the point of production (mineral ores), though it does not always follow that they were. Others needed final processing close to markets (coffee before vacuum packing). Products varied in their possibilities for processing, hence in their potential for value added and the extent of possible linkages, bananas being about the least promising in both regards.

Different products had different significance for vulnerability. Internationally, products faced varying threats of substitution by other products. Domestically, tropical or semitropical export agriculture lessened the pressure on production of food for the local market only when both the type of coffee and small holding, for example, together gave high returns to shade and the intermingling of other crops. Mineral products did not directly damage agriculture (except for very specific local contamination, such as in Peru with copper mining, and Venezuelan oil at Lake Maracaibo[97]), but might do so indirectly via the exchange rate and cheap food imports. Oil licensed from the state produced the greatest dependence on revenue from trade, but this was typically high in all export economy experiences. Depen-

[97] Sullivan, 1976: 259.

dence on foreign savings was again generally high, but particularly so where foreign capital played an important role, which was primarily a function of the product.

Different products and their varying locations also had different transport needs, which affected how development of transport helped or hindered the generation of a national market. The tendency of many railway systems to focus on integrating the different hinterlands with the principal port could in the long run become a negative factor for national market integration (Argentina, for example). Clearly, export economy expansion shaped a country's infrastructure and institutions quite profoundly, for good or ill.

The interaction of products and preconditions helped determine the type of capital, labor and capital/labor relations (e.g., large or small scale, foreign or domestic, wage labor or some form of sharecropping or independent production). Out of such relations came varying linkage effects. Coffee had good local linkage effects, though an important precondition was reasonable size of the local economy, and size was not adequate to provide an internal market in this period in the Central American cases. The positive effects probably differed most strongly by reason of geographical spread. Coffee's regional diffusion tended to make the effect stronger in market integration, especially in Colombia, where geography gave natural protection.

The positive score of coffee in diversification was further helped by its relative lack of susceptibility to the macro characteristics of the typical export economy. First, export economies based on primary products were—and are—typically characterized by rent, and therefore attractive to foreign lenders and investors. One result of an export economy boom was that it made a country eligible for foreign borrowing, provided it had made at least a nod in the direction of redeeming any past bad behavior. A negative dimension of this, however, was that a boom might weaken the development of an internal tax system, bias technological characteristics in the direction of imported technology, and distort subsequent exchange rate policy, since overvaluation reduced the burden of external debt payments in local currency.

Second, export economies were typically associated with cycles of boom and bust and also prone to what today is called Dutch Disease: the effect of a revaluation of the exchange rate coming from a foreign exchange influx based on temporary factors. Such a bonanza carried the inherent danger of damaging export and im-

port-substituting capacity, and discouraging necessary new investment in that direction that would be badly needed when external conditions changed. It all too
often increased the vulnerability of the economy to future shocks, though of course
it provided funds which if appropriately used could have strengthened capacities
and increased flexibility. But the incentives went in the opposite direction. (The
different uses made of export booms would turn out to be crucial in shaping response capacity to the shocks of the mid-20th century, the subject of the next chapter.)

Peru is a classic case where early import-substituting industrialization was
eroded by the strength of the export boom, not because protection was opposed but
because it would have had to have been actively defended in the face of rising international prices and specific tariffs.[98] And no group existed to do this. Chile is the
one remarkable exception in avoiding revaluation and maintaining protection: the
high price paid for nitrates (war) and an awareness of their vulnerability to substitutes produced an exceptional instance of successful management, unrivaled by any
of the Dutch Disease problems that occurred later in the 20th century. Colombia,
by contrast, depended on a product—coffee—whose sales grew relatively slowly
internationally, compared with mining products. In the Colombian case this was
helped by an inability to borrow lavishly abroad, unfortunately overcome in the
1920s,[99] and a longstanding reluctance to invite foreign capital in large quantities.
In Brazil, the country's exceptional market power was such that tariffs were paid by
the foreign coffee buyer, hence the coffee sector felt no incentive to mobilize against
protection. In Colombia, wealthy businessmen involved in coffee were interested in
investing elsewhere, given the limited needs of coffee for reinvestment, so again
there was little general opposition to tariffs. Colombia and Brazil were protectionist from the 19th century, and this was significant for the degree of diversification—
perhaps the most significant factor of all.[100]

Other macro aspects varied not by product but according to wider international economic and political trends. For instance, the increase in foreign borrow-

---

[98] A "specific" tariff is levied on the physical quantity of a good, so its protective effect is automatically reduced
if prices rise; that is, it requires a deliberate act to maintain the real level of protection.

[99] On Colombia's 19th century difficulty in borrowing, and, in some cases, aversion to borrowing, see Deas,
1982; Junguito, 1996.

[100] As argued by Ocampo and Botero in Companion Volume 1.

ing was matched by an increasing tendency at the international level for lending not necessarily related to the specific conditions of the export economy. Such lending played a part in the 1912 recession in Argentina, principally caused by a draining of loan capital as a consequence of the Balkan War.

Also, while being attractive to direct foreign investment had micro consequences related to diversification, there was also a macro consequence, which applied to lending as well. The positive effect of the interest of both foreign lenders and investors, and the governments behind them, came in the form of institution building. For example, foreign bankers insisted on the strength of the Bolivian Fiscal Commission, and foreign financiers required the Brazilian government's presence in the coffee valorization scheme.[101] The negative effect, depending on the vulnerability given by geography, took the form of political interference, though the extreme of invasion was not typical of this period.

Social and Political Consequences and Institutional Feedback

The interaction of the type of product and the prior conditions also influenced the social consequences of export expansion and its propensity for conflict.[102] Where the nature of the product made land and labor important resources, and where indigenous populations controlled both, then resources tended to be forcibly taken from them, sometimes with repercussions that might not appear for years. Non-Indians also lost their land, but the thirst for land and labor, coupled with state-building and continued conquest, meant that Indian peasants suffered a double exploitation, reinforced both by racial attitudes inherited from the Colonial period and now by pseudo-scientific Darwinian ideas from Europe. In Guatemala, Mexico and through much of the Andes, exploitation could take extreme forms. While Indian populations sometimes successfully resisted for a time, resistance tended to retard, rather than reverse, the processes of capitalist penetration and state-building.

Where the nature of the exporting sector and its insertion in the domestic economy were such that external shocks were accommodated by the squeezing of wages, then labor organization, strikes and associated violence and repression were

---

[101] Topik, 1996.

[102] This section draws on a consultancy paper written for this book by Alan Knight.

frequent (oil, bananas, mines). Where the frontier was the focus of expansion, in some coffee cases and in temperate zones, then violence of a frontier type, related to land acquisition and lack of the rule of law, was typical. This type of violence was usually seen as a threat to investment, unlike the violence of the mine or the plantation. It was therefore less likely to generate repressive actions. More generally, weak institutions meant that, especially in remote areas, labor discipline would be summary and without appeal.

In political terms, export expansion usually strengthened rather than undermined the position of land-based elites. The single exception, by an indirect route, was Mexico. During the Porfiriato, the landed elite was greatly fortified. The strength of this process generated the special coalition of interests and extreme social pressure that produced the Mexican Revolution. Generally, peasant protest was repressed, helped by ethnic and other divisions among the peasant communities themselves, and by the fact that peasants had to return to their homes for the harvest.[103] And foreign investors did not attempt to disrupt the land monopoly of local elites. Though direct foreign investment went heavily into land-based export economies (Table 3.2), it rarely went into land (Cuba was an exception). When it did, it was sometimes as a result of bad debts, and the companies concerned were usually extremely unhappy, as was Duncan Fox in Peru. Land in the public domain was sold to foreigners, but this rarely resulted in direct production by them, and in any case was no challenge to the elite's position. This was the case with bananas, where the United Fruit Company did in fact produce directly: this was presumably because with bananas the only way to control disease was to move continually to new land. The reasons for the foreign investors' disinclination to invest in land were, first, that there was an existing system of land rights and existing claims, unlike Australia; second, they did not like becoming involved with complex labor systems fraught with ethnic aspects (Duncan Fox in Peru expressed this clearly); and third, they preferred to buy from small producers because it enabled them to distribute the burden of the bad times.

Where this entrenching of the landed elite model was strong, a further intangible shaping of institutions in the broad sense of the word took place, with conse-

---

[103] Knight in Companion Volume 1. This is the reason given for the failure of Yucatán's Mayan rebels when they seemed to have the state in their grasp during the Caste War of the 1840s.

quences for the longer run. Growth usually disrupts nonmodernizing forces and rewards enterprise. This it did in many instances, notably in mining, sugar, and examples of early industrialization. But where growth in fact led to a strengthening of traditional elites and a confirming of certain kinds of institutions, then it did not drive technical progress. The need to develop institutional arrangements to secure a labor supply further embedded many export enterprises in systems where profits turned on securing a cheap and docile labor force by whatever means, principally repression and political access, rather than on receptivity to innovations.[104] These systems were sustained by ethnic prejudice which legitimated brutality. Inequality was internalized at a deep level; see, for example, the attitudes expressed by Maria in Chapter Six (Box 6.3). The more institutions evolved to sustain these micro systems, the more change required a radical stimulus, since inequality was functional, served to increase growth, and was consolidated into complex institutional arrangements. The stimulus arrived in the case of mining in the form of rapid growth of demand for a permanent labor force with some element of skill, and *enganche* was abandoned. There was no equivalent stimulus in the agrarian economies.

As landholding became more solidly entrenched as a source of wealth, political power and access to other inputs such as credit and water, the peculiarity of land as an asset became increasingly important. While held and used by many dynamic business people in Latin America, land also yielded profits just by being held—particularly if inflation or an urbanization boom, frequent by the 1920s, happened to benefit its holder. Thus developed another kind of "institution:" the custom of holding land for other than directly productive reasons, a habit that clearly had an impact on agricultural productivity.

Implicit in all this analysis is the notion that the varying experiences of export-led growth can explain in some measure the different experiences in the periods that followed. In particular, the analysis can help us understand varying responses and results, as policymakers struggled with the shocks of the 20th century.

---

[104] Bulmer-Thomas, 1994, develops this theme in his account of the period.

CHAPTER 4

DISLOCATION AND EXPERIMENT: 1914-45

THE TITLE OF THIS CHAPTER COMES FROM W. Arthur Lewis,[1] who characterizes the period (actually the years 1913 to 1939) as "an age of dislocation and an age of experiment" in the world economy—a description reasonably extended to 1945. The long period of relative world peace and expansion ended with the First World War, and an equivalent expansion would not come again until the 1950s. However, two world wars and the Great Depression of 1929 provided Latin America with opportunities as well as threats: it is no accident that this is the only period of the 20th century when Latin America grew significantly more rapidly than the world average. Like any period of transition, it is a time difficult to characterize and extremely important. Structures shifted, new forces and coalitions emerged, experience accumulated, and attitudes and strategic thinking were reshaped. Incipient capacities for change were tested, forged in the fire of crisis, and sometimes distorted or destroyed.

Wars, of course, provide a different balance of threats and opportunities compared to world depressions. Both wars increased demand for Latin America's exports, though again the commodity lottery was important, since strategic minerals boomed while commodities dependent on European consumption (such as cacao

---

[1] Lewis, 1949.

Photo: Coffee Inspection in Colombia, 1940.

and coffee) fared quite badly, as did highly perishable nonessentials (such as bananas). The threat (which was also an opportunity) was felt most keenly on the import side in both world wars, though geography also mattered. Countries nearer to the United States could more readily turn to U.S. supplies, as war disrupted European sources. Japan was beginning to replace Europe as a supplier on the west coast of Latin America even before the First World War, with positive and negative effects. Capital inflows were also interrupted in an uneven fashion. The 1920s, in their way also a disruption, brought foreign loans on a scale and of a nature only to be paralleled in the 1970s. By contrast, the international depression of the 1930s produced a demand-side shock as well as a reversal of capital inflows. The Depression brought falling world prices; the two world wars imported large doses of world inflation.

An important phenomenon of the period is the shift in hegemony from the United Kingdom to the United States. Before 1913, the U.K. was still dominant in world trade and capital markets (although on the west coast of Latin America, in particular, the shift was already in evidence from the turn of the century). World War I changed the role of the United States, which quite abruptly emerged as the major world creditor. By 1945, the shape of things was fundamentally different, with the U.S. clearly established as the major world power and the dollar set to underpin world expansion for the next 25 years, just as sterling had done in the 19th century. The shift in global hegemony generated threats and opportunities; by World War II, the United States was playing a major role, entering the war in 1941 and drawing Latin America along with it as a raw material supplier of considerable importance. This had many consequences for institutions, the role of the state, and for political developments and economic structures.

A common message runs through these diverse experiences of external shock: it was risky to rely for growth on traditional primary commodity exports and on the importing of most goods vital for expansion. Sometimes it was supply-side vulnerability that was underlined, as in war, and sometimes it was demand. But either way, vulnerability was the common theme. This message interacted with internal forces—early signs of accelerated population growth, expansion of urban populations, growth of nationalism, and the beginnings in some cases of mass politics—and by the 1940s generated a swelling consensus around the need for deliberate industrialization.

The acceleration in population growth was documented in Chapter Two.

Whereas in the early years of the century the higher rates belonged to the countries with high immigration, pulling up the regional average, by now the acceleration was occurring everywhere. The continent's average population growth was 2.2 percent from 1930-50; in Mexico, for example, population growth accelerated to 2.6 percent during that period. With a birth rate of 44 per thousand and a death rate still at 27 per thousand, it was clear that population growth was set to rise as improvements in public health conditions, primary health care and infrastructure began to produce effects. In all but the smallest countries, urban populations were growing at faster rates, as rural-urban migration, temporarily halted by the Great Depression, took off again in the course of the 1930s and 1940s. In Paraguay and in Central America, this process would not occur until the 1950s. Growing middle and working classes were reflected in political trends, particularly in the Southern Cone.

This chapter first describes global disruptions and dislocations and their implications for Latin America. It then considers the response to these disruptions, or more specifically, to three principal shocks: the Great Depression of 1929, undoubtedly the most severe disruption faced by Latin America in this century until the debt crisis of the 1980s, and the two world wars. The final section considers an important consequence of the dislocations: the significant growth in institutions during these decades, a product of both long-run trends and the events of the period. The chapter thus overlaps chronologically with the previous one, since the traditional export-led growth period clearly lasted until 1929—and indeed beyond in a number of cases, such as Venezuela—while the shocks started with the First World War.

INTERNATIONAL SHOCKS

As the 20th century advanced, the expansion of the world economy that characterized the early years was marred by increasing instability and disruption. The first major dislocation was World War I, but in fact forces making for change had been gathering strength since well before 1914.

First, there was a shift in trade and investment. Britain's initiating role in trade in manufactures implied that as other countries industrialized, her share would have to fall; this was aggravated by her decline in competitiveness. Increasingly, her declining industries lost ground, although the pound's continuing role as a key currency and the corresponding role of sterling liabilities held abroad meant that the loss of competitiveness on the export side was initially concealed. But though Britain remained predominant, the role of the United States in trade and investment was increasing rapidly from the turn of the century: by 1913, Mexico, all the republics of Central America and the Hispanic Caribbean, Venezuela, Colombia, Ecuador and, marginally, Peru were already importing more from the United States than from the United Kingdom. This represented a major switch compared with the 1890s. U.S. investment was making rapid headway in Mexican mining, oil and railways, Peruvian copper, Chilean nitrates, Colombian bananas, and in a number of Central American economies. The United States' ever-increasing dominance in Cuban sugar was already well established by the 1890s.

Secondly, changes were already leading to a growing oversupply of primary products, and to increasing market instability. These trends affected both demand and supply. On the demand side, population growth in some developed countries was slowing, and rising income was leading to proportionately slower growth in demand for foodstuffs such as grain, as basic needs were satisfied. On the supply side, technical change and modernization were leading to greater productivity, and also in certain cases to increased short-run rigidity in supply as production became more capital-intensive. These trends were only offset by technical change in the case of a few primary products (oil, copper), which led to new demands—a factor that would be of greater importance in the 1920s.

During the First World War, the shift in trade and investment structures sharply accelerated. Britain's position in world trade declined, never to recover fully, while opportunities for exports by the United States were correspondingly transformed. The U.S. payments surplus swelled: by the end of 1919, the country was a net long-term creditor of over $3.3 billion, as compared with a similar net debtor status in the prewar period.[2] U.S. private foreign investment overseas rose from $3.5 billion in 1914 to $6.4 billion in 1919.[3] Determined pursuit of the export opportunities offered by the war was reflected in the huge growth of trade with Latin

---

[2] Aldcroft, 1977: 239.
[3] Lewis, 1938: 449.

America and in the infrastructure which began to grow around it, as U.S. banks sought to establish themselves abroad and as flows of information deepened.[4] Handbooks of advice for exporters appeared, with Latin America as the key focus of interest.[5] In 1914, U.S. federal regulations were changed so as to permit the expansion of U.S. branch banking overseas; between 1914 and 1918, the First National City Bank alone set up a dozen branches in Latin America. Trade was also stimulated by completion of the Panama Canal in 1914.

The war also stimulated an increase in productive capacity in many primary products where there was already danger of excess supply. Sugar was perhaps the outstanding example, but the same was true of many foodstuffs and raw materials where European domestic production was temporarily disrupted.

The war also had more specific effects. Germany's trading and investment links abruptly ended, providing a gap the U.S. was quick to fill. In the very short term, the whole system of banking, credit and money markets was suspended, producing for Latin America an acute crisis of liquidity and financial panic. "In August of 1914 there was virtually a total collapse of the financial and commercial infrastructure which underpinned world trade and upon which Latin America relied so heavily…Shipping and insurance became scarce and expensive, banks shut their doors, capital and credit completely dried up and sterling bills disappeared."[6]

Meanwhile, throughout Europe there were changes in the role of the state resulting from the sudden need to regulate war economies. The politics of war fueled nationalist movements in many countries, and wartime inflation and hardship resulted in a strengthening of working class organizations.

With the old system in disarray, and new forces such as state intervention emerging, there was an opportunity for fresh thinking and for an attempt to appraise and manage underlying problems. But the problems were not clearly perceived. The accepted wisdom of the postwar period, at least in the United States

---

[4] Stallings, 1987; Marichal, 1988.

[5] A good (and amusing) example is *Exporting to Latin America*, published by the U.S. Department of Commerce in 1916. The manual contains 369 pages of detailed instructions on every aspect of business, including advice on "the value of moving pictures" in advertising, and covering such practical details as the need for proper saddles when venturing into the Andes, and for "a liberal quantity of a preparation with which to anoint the body against insects."

[6] Albert, 1988: 37.

and the United Kingdom, was the need to return to the old system—particularly the gold standard and, as far as possible, to prewar exchange rate parities. From the United States came a strong move to reduce the role of the government to prewar levels, to drop price controls and any interference with trade or exchange rates, and to return as nearly as possible to "healthy" and "'free" competition. The U.S. Treasury argued in 1920: "...The Governments of the world must now get out of banking and trade...The Treasury is opposed to governmental control over foreign trade and even more opposed to private control...They look towards the removal of governmental controls and interferences, and the restoration of individual initiative and free competition in business...strict economy in public expenditure..."[7] The haste to return to market forces was particularly imprudent given pent-up wartime demand: the result was the badly mismanaged boom and crash of 1919-22.[8] The boom further worsened the problem of excess supply of agricultural goods.

From 1922 on, there was sustained economic expansion in the United States and many European countries, though Britain was struggling with deflation in an attempt to restore and maintain the prewar parity. But the international system was basically unsound, with capital movements only temporarily papering over the cracks. The reinstated gold exchange system never worked well: there were too many centers, the U.S. lacked experience in its new role, and neither France nor the United States was committed to making the new system work. The increased volume of short-term and volatile funds generated instability, and parities for the major currencies were seriously misjudged. Further, the size of the U.S. trade surplus was such that it urgently required policies for promoting imports and capital exports which would ease the payment problems of the deficit countries.

But trade was not as crucial for the United States as it had been for the U.K.; policies, in fact, were exactly the reverse of what was needed. The U.S. continued its protectionist policies, dating back to the Civil War, and its capital export policies created major problems for the recipient countries. The 1920s saw a bonanza of private foreign lending on the part of the United States.[9] Salesmen pressed loans on

---

[7] Annual Report of the Secretary of the Treasury on Finance for the fiscal year ended June 30, 1920.

[8] See Lewis, 1949, for a detailed account.

[9] Marichal, 1988; Stallings, 1987.

unwary governments, and borrowers were positively encouraged to overextend themselves. The money tended often to go either to unproductive uses or to increase further the supply of already dangerously surplus agricultural commodities. The role of the banks became increasingly important: by 1926, there were 61 branches of U.S. banks in Latin America[10] (in addition to many of other nationalities). U.S. construction companies frequently worked in close association with groups of bankers, as for example the U.S. Foundation Company did in Peru. By these and other means, the 1920s saw an extraordinary expansion of external financing of Latin American governments. It was the age of aggressive salesmanship, with few holds barred. A U.S. Senate investigating committee found 29 representatives of U.S. financial houses in Colombia alone, trying to negotiate loans for national and departmental governments.

With the rise in investment went a rise in U.S. trade with the region. The gains made by the United States in wartime were consolidated in the 1920s, as her competitive advantage strengthened thanks to the new dynamic products of the period (automobiles, above all). This resulted in shifts in relationships and a new potential for disequilibrium, vividly illustrated by the case of Argentina. In 1913, Argentina, like Brazil, had few trade and investment links with the United States, in contrast to Peru and Ecuador, for example, which were already importing both goods and capital from their northern neighbor. During the 1920s, Argentina increased its purchases of modern agricultural and other machinery from the United States, but the country's trading and investment relations with the U.K. constrained the rate at which this trade could grow.[11] Uruguay, too, was constrained by a growing trade dependence on Britain, as chilled beef exports became a large proportion of exports.

Aided by expanding flows of credit, the volume of primary production continued to grow. Meanwhile, the forces operating on supply and demand strengthened: worldwide, the 1920s were years of particularly rapid technical progress in agriculture, with the mechanization of farming and the introduction of new plant strains and fertilizers, all of which increased supply. There were also major struc-

---

[10] Phelps, 1927: 211.
[11] Fodor and O'Connell, 1973: 13-65.

tural changes in primary product markets, as substitutes supplanted nitrates and plantation rubber eliminated the Amazon's natural rubber industry. Price behavior in the decade is complicated to review, since the sudden boom of 1920 was followed by as sudden a crash, to be followed by continuing uneven movements. But underlying this was an unfavorable long-run trend; by 1926-29, the terms of trade for all primary products had fallen significantly below their 1913 level.[12]

The 1920s therefore emerge with hindsight as a period very similar to the 1970s: a period of irregular growth and rising debt presaging a decade of depression. As in the 1970s, Latin America could hardly have been expected to interpret the signals of coming disaster. Money was arriving in large quantities and price movements were very volatile, making the reading of the longer term trend difficult. But the elements of fragility were real: the major new creditor country was inexperienced, and the loans coming in were neither accounted for nor monitored. Nor were they matched by investments guaranteeing capacity to repay, a capacity further impaired by the overvalued exchange rates sustained by the inflow of cash. Corruption was rife, and trade was growing in response to an unsustainable expansion in the United States.

The international economic events of the 1930s can be told more briefly, since they were sudden and straightforward in their disastrous impact. The breakdown was signaled before the New York stock market crash of October 1929, as capital outflows from Latin America began in response to high interest rates in the U.S., and a number of primary product prices reached their peak well before: Argentine wheat in May 1927, Cuban sugar in March 1928 and Brazilian coffee in March 1929.[13] The subsequent fall in primary product prices was extreme. Every country was affected, and for nine of the countries included in Table 4.1, the unit value of exports between 1928 and 1932 fell by more than 50 percent. Those that suffered most severely were the mineral exporters (Chile, Bolivia and Mexico) and Cuba. The latter suffered a severe reduction in its share of the U.S. market, hit first by the Smoot-Hawley Tariff of 1930 and then by the Chadbourne Agreement of 1931, both of which affected Cuba but not Puerto Rico, the Philippines or Ha-

---

[12] Rowe, 1965: 83.
[13] Bulmer-Thomas, 1994: 196.

TABLE 4.1
PRICE AND QUANTITY CHANGES FOR EXPORTS, NET BARTER TERMS OF TRADE, 1932
(1928=100)

Country	Export prices	Export volumes	Net barter terms of trade
Argentina	37	88	68
Bolivia	79[a]	48[a]	na
Brazil	43	86	65
Chile	47	31	57
Colombia	48	102	63
Costa Rica	54	81	78
Dominican Rep.	55[b]	106[b]	81[b]
Ecuador	51	83	74
El Salvador	30	75	52
Guatemala	37	101	54
Haiti	49[b]	104[b]	na
Honduras	91	101	130
Mexico	49	58	64
Nicaragua	50	78	71
Peru	39	76	62
Venezuela	81	100	101
Latin America	36	78	56

[a] 1929 = 100
[b] 1930 = 100
Sources: ECLAC, 1976; Bulmer-Thomas, 1994.

waii.[14] The commodity lottery and the misfortunes of others brought some relief to a few countries. Gold and silver prices were raised by U.S. monetary policy; droughts in North America favored exporters of temperate foodstuffs; and the Dominican Republic gained sugar sales at Cuba's expense.

While prices fell, interest rates did not, and most countries suffered a fiscal crisis as public revenue from trade taxes fell and debt service rose in real terms. However, the greatest shock to Latin American economies lay not in interest rates,

[14] This group, known as the "U.S. insular producers," were able to significantly displace Cuba from the U.S. market in the 1930s.

but in "the emergence of a protectionist and nationalistic Centre."[15] Multilateralism effectively broke down in this decade. "Already during the 1920s imperial preferences were advocated in Britain by influential groups, and the 1928 presidential election in the United States was accompanied by a protectionist wave. That ferment was followed by passage of the Smoot-Hawley tariff in 1930 and the British Abnormal Importations Act of 1931...As the Depression deepened, protectionism gained ground: British Commonwealth Preferences were adopted in Ottawa in 1932, while France, Germany and Japan also reinforced their protectionism and discriminatory trade arrangements for areas under their political hegemony."[16] Protection in developed countries was accompanied by little foreign investment: indeed, the main capital flow was toward the United States, which once more became a debtor.

The following years were overwhelmingly shadowed by political events, culminating in the outbreak of war in 1939. Once again, Latin American sources of supply, export markets, shipping services and credit facilities were threatened. As in the previous war, import supplies began to dry up, the impact varying with the strength of trading connections with Europe. The new element was the strength of the United States, and its awareness of the importance of both strategic sources of supplies and Pan-American solidarity. The Export-Import Bank was strengthened with an injection of capital and became a major instrument of U.S. control over raw material sources in the region. In September 1940, the Export-Import Bank concluded an agreement with Brazil for a credit of $20 million to construct a steel mill at Volta Redonda. In the same year, the Metals Reserve Company contracted to buy for five years almost the entire output of Bolivian tin (other than that of Simón Patiño, which was sold to Britain). The United States also bought Chilean copper and nitrates on a grand scale.

As the United States was drawn more deeply into the war following the attack on Pearl Harbor, so Latin America was more profoundly affected. First, the U.S. demanded that Latin America commit itself to the Allied cause. In 1942, the U.S. Treasury called an Inter-American Economic and Financial Conference in Washington to urge Latin American countries to adopt legislation and measures to control "enemy assets" such as investments and bank accounts. Secondly, in return for solidarity and support, and in response to sharply increased strategic needs, the

---

[15] Díaz-Alejandro, 1984a: 21.

[16] Ibid.

possibilities of increased economic aid opened up in the form of purchase agreements and credits from the Export-Import Bank and numerous U.S. trade and technical missions. U.S. investment in Latin America rose, and extraordinarily close government-to-government relations followed. In Mexico, for example, the transformation of U.S.-Mexican relations was so complete that as early as 1942 the Mexican Foreign Minister described the frontier as "a uniting not a dividing line." Remarks like these were remarkable in light of the bitter clash over oil between the two countries only four years earlier.[17] Only Argentina and Chile held out, and suffered for it: Chile did not break with the Axis powers till 1943, and Argentina finally declared war in March 1945.

Among the striking paradoxes of the war years, and one of the major consequences of the war itself, was the growing U.S. economic involvement in Latin America alongside the expanding role of national governments, which included the use of direct controls, made politically acceptable by war. Throughout much of Latin America, private sector interests were becoming more closely tied to government in much the same way that in the U.S., business leaders were co-opted by the government to plan and execute a whole range of new projects. These developments were to be fundamental to the new model of growth in the postwar period.

RESPONSES, EXPERIMENTS AND RESULTS

Writing on the response to the shock of the 1930s, Díaz-Alejandro argued for a distinction between reactive and passive countries.[18] Those that could depreciate their exchange rate and thereby speed the relative price adjustment recovered faster, while others (typically small countries dependent on the United States), which stayed tied to the dollar and had no effective policy autonomy,[19] suffered severely and recovered slowly, if at all. The argument correlates being small with being passive, as well as passivity and slow growth.

---

[17] Niblo, 1988: 7ff.

[18] Díaz-Alejandro, 1984a, Chapter 2.

[19] Cuba, for example, could not even raise tariffs.

The classification has since been questioned on two fronts. Experts on Cuba have insisted that that country is not well placed in such a framework, since its policymakers did what was best by paying the needed price to renegotiate the terms of Cuba's sugar agreement with the United States. In fact, Cuba's growth in the 1930s was rather rapid. And Bulmer-Thomas has pointed out that many small countries pursued reactive policies, and that there is no correlation between a country's size and speed of recovery in the 1930s.[20]

If we extend the analysis beyond the Depression to include the two world wars, the forces at work are rather different. The most basic point is that we are no longer dealing with an export collapse, but the significance of size and degree of freedom of maneuver remain. In war, and particularly in the 1940s, the analysis is dominated by strategic considerations, resource endowment, prior industrial base and geography.

While the basic insight of Díaz-Alejandro into the importance of policy autonomy remains valid, it is usefully complemented by the arguments of the previous chapter, relating to product characteristics, size, geography and evolving political economy (policy capabilities, coherence of interest groups), as well as by other aspects of institution building.

The First World War, it has been argued, provided a stimulus to demand but also grave supply-side constraints. The nature of the response to these conditions has provoked an unusual concentration of literature, its proliferation aided by unclear data. The early view, stemming from the writings of Celso Furtado and ECLAC, was that the war stimulated industrial growth in Latin America. This argument was first challenged for Brazil by Warren Dean, followed by a number of other writers.[21] Dean actually suggested that the war interrupted a rather impressive growth process. Later work has concluded that there was accelerated growth of output during the war in the Brazilian case (the earlier arguments arising partly from differences in the weight given to export processing in the figures), but that it was based on fuller utilization of existing capacity. In other words, the war simply built on an expansion already under way.

---

[20] Bulmer-Thomas, 1994: 212.

[21] Dean, 1969. For the subsequent debate on Brazilian industrialization, see *Cambridge History of Latin America*, 1986, Vol. IV, Bibliographical Essay 2.

The war was also important, it is suggested, because small repair shops were induced to broaden their activities and thus provide a base for an incipient capital goods sector. One plausible view stresses the long-run tendency for periods of increase in capacity (when imports are cheap and available) to alternate with periods of rapid increase in output (when imports are expensive or unavailable). Thus, in economies such as Brazil, with a prior industrial base and preexisting capacity, it seems now to be agreed that the war led to an acceleration of output of some 8 or 9 percent a year. This view is accepted also for Chile.

However, other countries were already more closely tied into other import sources—the United States and Japan. West coast economies such as Peru and Colombia already had significant trading links with the U.S., and during the war were able rapidly to build on them with correspondingly less stimulus to import substitution than in Brazil. The same factor might have been true for Mexico, but here internal disturbances overrode all other considerations. Despite the fact that even in the short run the revolution was not such an economic disaster as was earlier claimed,[22] manufacturing had only just regained its 1910 level by 1920. The surprising case, perhaps, is Argentina, given its size, previous industrial base and relatively few links with the United States. The fact that by 1918 production was only 9 percent above the 1914 level appears to be explained by bad harvests in three of the four years of the war and the ending of a long cycle of railway investment. The extremely severe fall in imports was due to the strength of Argentine trade links with Europe (including Germany) and rising transport costs. The fall in trade reduced government revenue substantially and depressed the commerce sector.[23]

The smaller economies, such as those of Central America, were in no position to take advantage of wartime opportunities, and their elites are usually described as only waiting for the end of disruption to return wholeheartedly to the export model. There were, however, some small-scale effects: in Ecuador, for example, local enterprise in forestry was stimulated by the cutting off of supplies of Australian coal for lack of shipping.[24]

---

[22] Knight in Companion Volume 1; Womack, 1978.

[23] Cortés Conde in Companion Volume 1.

[24] See Restrepo, 1958, for an account, and Box 3.1.

The 1920s were a hiatus in the adjustment process, since the prosperity of these years generally suggested that the export-led growth phase was still surviving. Cuban sugar producers became worried about over-production, and backed a state-sponsored effort at modest industrialization, beginning in 1926, though this would not survive the coming shock. Three economies suffered the collapse of their major export sector: Chile, as nitrates lost their market, Cuba with sugar, and Ecuador with cocoa.[25] There were patchy increases in protection responding to particular circumstances, but they did not usually compensate for the effect of overvaluation generated by the inflow of loans.

Given this analysis, it is no surprise to find the industrial growth of the war years tailing off during the 1920s, despite some growth in capacity. The textile sector in Brazil, for example, suffered severely from relative price trends, and in Chile, the growth rate of industry in real terms was 2 percent a year between 1918 and 1929, compared with 9 percent between 1913 and 1918.[26] In Peru, stagnation of returned value from exports combined with a modest improvement in relative price trends and worsening income distribution to produce little or no growth in the industrial sector. The exception was Argentina, where the industrial sector did some "catching up" after not having grown at all during the war period. Colombia also grew swiftly, partly reflecting the previous underdevelopment of industry.

Even the larger Latin American economies during this period still lacked systematic policies promoting industry, a tendency entirely consistent with the region's stage of development. There was simply no basis yet for such policies. The surprise is how countries with dominant export elites managed to secure the degree of protection for the manufacturing sector that they did. It has been argued that in both Brazil and Chile, exporters quite often preferred tariffs on imports to taxes on their own sources of income, even though in the long run such an attitude might threaten their own position. And in fact industry was not always seen as such a threat: in Chile, traditional agrarian groups found their export markets weakening and looked increasingly to the domestic market. In Brazil, industry could make use of agricul-

---

[25] Palma, in Companion Volume 2, argues that all the processes in Latin America in the 1930s occurred in Chile a decade earlier. Maiguashca, 1996, describes the Ecuadorean case, and Santamaria, in Companion Volume 1, the Cuban case.

[26] Palma in Companion Volume 1.

tural products that did not have a major market abroad, and the blending of interests was aided by intermarriage and interlocking directorates. The piecemeal nature of tariff changes also helped. These factors combined, on the one hand, to
encourage a degree of protection, and, on the other, to inhibit the clear emergence
of an entrepreneurial group committed specifically to industry.

On the eve of the Great Depression, even the larger economies in Latin
America were still extremely dependent on exports, which made up large proportions of their national product. The dependence of the public sector on foreign
trade taxes was also high—over 50 percent in Chile in the 1920s, for example. Exports were comprised almost exclusively of primary products, and in most countries
two or three products accounted for some two-thirds of total export revenues (see
Statistical Appendix VII). Politically, export elites were still dominant, with one or
two complex exceptions such as Mexico and the Batllista government in Uruguay.
This already signaled the paradox of the 1930s: the role of import-substituting industrialization was large, yet the recovery process was centered on exports.

The initial Latin American response to the collapse of 1929 was universally
the orthodox gold standard reaction. As gold and foreign exchange flowed out, internal deflation added to the impact of the collapse of exports, and incomes and
employment fell heavily. Release only came with the U.K.'s abandonment of convertibility in 1931; once it was acceptable to abandon gold standard rules, Latin
America did so with alacrity. Defaults followed, since depreciation of the exchange
rate made the burden of the debt on the budget intolerable. By 1934, only Argentina, Honduras, Haiti and the Dominican Republic had not defaulted. (Venezuela
did not need to, having already paid off its debt; Colombia continued to service
central government debt until 1934.) The international financial markets of the
1930s simply allowed and even condoned nonpayment in a manner unthinkable in
the 1980s, given the numerical importance of individual bond holders with little
bargaining power (unlike the 1980s, when institutions predominated). Nonpayment
gave breathing space: often the effect of not paying increased foreign exchange availability by as much as 20 percent. As early as 1930, some countries were beginning
actively to support their export sectors. In Brazil, this took the form of purchasing
and burning surplus coffee stocks. In Colombia, the export sector's need for continued infrastructure development led municipal governments to react early on. In
October 1930, for example, the municipality of Cartagena raised a loan to begin

work on an aqueduct,[27] and by 1931 the national government was using deficit financing to expand.[28] Early in the decade, military spending was often added to public investment, as in the cases of the Chaco and Leticia Wars.[29] In Guatemala, the massive road building program of General Ubico essentially used forced labor, so it had more impact in terms of increasing access to new territory than for its multiplier effect on incomes.[30, 31]

The initial expansion was further facilitated by import quotas and tariffs in Brazil and Chile, and by moderate tariff increases in Colombia. However, Argentina gave tariff concessions to the UK under the Roca Runciman Treaty of 1933, and Cuba lowered tariffs in 1934 as part of the renegotiation of its reciprocity agreements with the United States. Multiple exchange rates were increasingly used, principally as a way of taxing the export sector without recourse to legislators, but they were also an element of further protection.[32]

Gradually, more "structural" elements were added to policy in the largest countries. The government of Getúlio Vargas in Brazil moved with increasing coherence to a broad policy of state expansion and intervention, particularly after 1937. Mexico did likewise, with a program of public works beginning in the 1920s. The Cárdenas government expanded the program and introduced an agrarian reform which, while in the long run it stimulated investment in agriculture, in this period probably helped move funds to industry.[33] The size of the government budget increased, a six-year plan was introduced, and the state oil company, PEMEX, was created in 1938. In Chile, CORFO, a state industrial development agency, was created in 1939.

---

[27] Thorp and Londoño in Companion Volume 2.

[28] Ocampo and Montenegro, 1982.

[29] These two events were different in scale. The Chaco War was fought between Paraguay and Bolivia from 1932-35; Paraguay was the victor but both sides suffered appalling losses. Some 50,000 persons died. The Leticia "War" was closer to a border incident, beginning in 1932, but Colombian fears of an invasion by Peru led to significant military spending.

[30] Bulmer-Thomas in Companion Volume 2.

[31] Uruguay's use of the World Cup in Montevideo in 1930 to revive national morale, and the government's building of the Centenario Stadium, can only be registered as a modest Keynesian policy. It was principally a substitution of psychological benefits for material ones in the face of heavy recession. Hancox, 1997.

[32] Contreras, in Companion Volume 1, provides an account of the Bolivian development of multiple exchange rates.

[33] Cárdenas in Companion Volume 2.

The resulting recovery is documented in Tables 4.2 and 4.3. It is notable that the two economies that reacted earliest and most vigorously in support of their export sectors, Brazil and Colombia, actually saw GDP recover in 1932, before any export recovery began. By 1933, Chile, Mexico and Argentina had all begun to grow again with the turn in export revenues. Costa Rica experienced a small downturn and an early recovery. With very conservative policies, Peru recovered as cotton exports improved by 1933. The recovery was more significant for domestic income than appears from Table 4.2, as cotton with high returned value took over from mineral exports, although small-scale mining benefited from the lack of interest of the multinationals given the conditions of the 1930s. Venezuela's oil sector faltered only slightly with the Depression.

In all cases, industry recovered very early and grew faster than GDP. However, the depth of the recession in the cases of Chile and Cuba meant that pre-Depression levels of GDP were regained only towards the end of the decade. In smaller economies, if the land frontier was open and accessible, and if labor and entrepreneurs were available, expansion of import substitution in agriculture provided a spur to recovery. Ecuador expanded coffee and rice production with the incorporation of new land, and renewed expansion of textiles and exports of Panama hats.[34] This kind of expansion was impossible, however, in countries like Honduras, where the United Fruit Company's control of land impeded alternatives to bananas. Nicaragua, Uruguay, Panama and Paraguay barely recovered, with weak export performance and severe limitations due to size and poor possibilities of diversification. Uruguay was the only one of this group with an industrial base, but it was not enough to compensate for the stagnation of livestock exports.

The reasonably early export recovery was important in sustaining industrial expansion and the general recuperation in economic activity. The export recovery was a function of several factors. The net barter terms of trade recovered between 1933 and 1937, based as much on weakness of import prices as on export price recovery. By 1939, the net barter terms of trade for all Latin America had recovered to their 1930 level, and were 36 percent above the 1933 level.[35] Stronger forces in most cases were volume increases responding partially to international events and

---

[34] Maiguashca, 1996.
[35] Bulmer-Thomas, 1994: 210.

TABLE 4.2

LATIN AMERICA: PURCHASING POWER OF EXPORTS,
GDP AND MANUFACTURING, 1927-38

(Indices 1928=100)

	Argentina			Brazil			Chile			Colombia		
	PPE	GDP	Manuf.	PPE	GDP	Manuf.	PPE	GDP	Manuf.	PPE	GDP	Manuf.
1927	85	99	100	89	90	97	91	80	103	84	93	99
1928	100	100	100	100	100	100	100	100	100	100	100	100
1929	91	101	98	102	101	97	110	110	122	103	104	103
1930	60	93	93	69	99	94	69	99	123	107	103	98
1931	62	95	86	71	96	95	44	82	91	112	101	96
1932	59	92	86	61	100	94	18	60	104	96	108	110
1933	68	94	91	68	109	98	35	70	115	87	115	129
1934	101	102	100	78	119	108	74	84	125	131	123	136
1935	108	115	114	79	122	120	80	90	144	113	126	151
1936	119	115	120	94	137	136	92	91	147	127	133	164
1937	177	124	128	109	143	141	140	107	154	140	135	192
1938	105	124	135	73	150	146	86	102	139	117	144	195

	Mexico			Peru		Uruguay		Venezuela	
	PPE	GDP	Manuf.	PPE	GDP	PPE	Manuf.	PPE	GDP
1927	111	99	103	95	94	97	na	71	87
1928	100	100	100	100	100	100	100	100	100
1929	95	96	106	108	110	90	102	130	112
1930	72	90	105	79	98	95	115	133	113
1931	65	93	100	59	90	61	na	105	96
1932	47	79	73	48	86	44	na	96	100
1933	51	88	97	75	96	51	na	135	98
1934	79	94	106	129	109	43	na	300	105
1935	92	101	123	140	119	57	na	232	116
1936	91	109	139	145	125	61	125	232	122
1937	100	113	143	147	127	80	na	246	136
1938	78	115	149	126	129	81	na	282	144

Note: GDP and manufacturing value added are in constant values at 1970 prices. Purchasing power of exports (PPE): current values have been deflated by each country's import price index, with the exception of Uruguay, where the U.S. export price index is used.
Source: Statistical Appendix.

ever, that the real value of total industrial production in 1930 was not regained until 1941.[39] The debate over Cuba is somewhat parallel to that concerning Argentina: was there, realistically, any other option than renegotiation of the sugar agreement, virtually at any cost, with the United States? The price, of course, was access to the Cuban market for U.S. manufacturers, and on a preferential basis. The reward was some growth, at least in the 1930s, and the effective subversion of the 1933 Revolution. Cuba was distinctive, however, in that sugar penetrated so deeply into every aspect of Cuban institutions and economic and political life. The diversification project embarked on in 1926 failed, both because of the New Deal trade agreements with the U.S., and because of the entrenched dependence on sugar. Credit, transport, the whole working of the bureaucracy, trading networks—all favored sugar.[40] There was hardly an urban or rural community in the land that did not depend wholly or partly on the local sugar factory and the cane growing that supplied it. The hold on Cuba was so deep that the issue went beyond the rational choices of policymakers.

The importance of primary exports in generating recovery and the support they received from governments come as no surprise, given the data presented at the start of this section. Even the largest economies were still heavily trade dependent in the 1930s, and had relatively small industrial sectors. Trade dependence changed, however, even in the course of the decade. By 1945, the situation would become more fluid.

The Second World War in one sense enabled the continuation of a healthy diversification process for Latin America. The subcontinent became an important source of raw materials and experienced even stronger growth of some exports, while at the same time import constraints created an independent stimulus to continued import substitution. But other exports lost European markets. The process acquired a regional dimension, as trade in manufactures between Latin American

---

[39] The GDP estimates of Brundenius, 1984, show that the levels of per capita GDP from 1910-20 were not regained by the time of Castro's Revolution, though there was growth in the 1930s, as sugar recovered: some 24 percent comparing 1928 and 1937. He takes the estimates of Alienes 1950, which deflated by U.S. prices, and deflates instead with the Cuban food price index. The Cuban GDP data for this period are not strong and have been the subject of much controversy, so the findings reported here should be taken only as a rough guide.

[40] This is well documented in IBRD, 1951.

countries opened up, and countries' ability to benefit from this opportunity varied. Thus the country experience was very diverse: for example, in the case of minerals, price controls in the consumer countries and delayed payments meant that little extra revenue was received. This explains the relatively limited growth of export revenues of mineral exporters like Chile, Bolivia and Peru. But even where revenues were available, there was little to spend them on; hence there was a substantial accumulation of reserves. Contradictory forces operated on industry. Scarcity of imports certainly encouraged new efforts at substitution, but these same efforts were limited in turn by scarcity of imported inputs and capital goods. The net result was a continuation of the industrial growth of the 1930s (Table 4.4), but at varying rates among countries, and with a new bias towards capital goods and basic inputs. For example, a number of the firms later to be important in the Brazilian capital goods industry evolved from workshop to factory in this period.[41]

These developments were aided, unusually, by the role of the United States: the war was accompanied by an overwhelming increase in U.S. influence in the Latin American economies, as the U.S. sought to safeguard existing supplies and to push for the development of new strategic resources. The expansion of the U.S. role was aided by the disappearance of Japan and Europe as sources of finance and imports, and the wartime disruption of the remaining export trade to Europe. With this increase in the U.S. presence, an impetus was given to expand the role of the state and to the use of direct controls, promoted paradoxically by the U.S. government, as the various U.S.-sponsored missions pushed for development of basic industries. At the same time, there was a definite expansion of private sector involvement in government, as businessmen responding to patriotic appeals became involved in a range of committees set up to push forward these new projects.

The emphasis of foreign missions and advisors on iron and steel and other basic inputs contributed to pushing the pattern of industrialization in a new direction, which had the potential to make the manufacturing sector more autonomous and open to important sources of technical change.[42] In addition, exports of manufactures began within the continent: Brazilian and Mexican textile exports rose from

---

[41] Gupta, 1989: 19.

[42] This tendency would by the 1950s be swamped by a renewed emphasis on consumer goods.

TABLE 4.4
GROWTH OF EXPORTS, GDP AND MANUFACTURING, 1938-45
(Indices 1938=100, value for 1944-45)

	Export values	Quantum[1]	GDP	Manuf.
Argentina	161	141	122	131
Brazil	220	93	123	144
Chile	150	108	126	184
Colombia	148	109	123	162
Cuba	295	146	137	138
Mexico	252	84	141	177
Peru	123	80	113	...
Uruguay	177	109	108	114
Venezuela	195	155	142	141
Central America:				
Costa Rica	110	77	96	86
El Salvador	202	118	124	133
Guatemala	149	107	89	109
Honduras	145	141	114	127
Nicaragua	250	89	157	286

Note: GDP and manufacturing value added are in constant values at 1970 prices. Exports are in current U.S. dollars.
[1] Export quantum for Cuba includes sugar exports only.
Source: Statistical Appendix.

almost nothing to 20 percent of exports by the last year of the war. Most of these sales were to other Latin American countries.

The results in terms of growth of income are shown in Table 4.4. Unusually, during the war there is no correlation between growth and export performance. This is intelligible in terms of the factors we have noted: the variable extent to which export revenues actually accrued to the producing countries, and the limits on using foreign exchange in conditions of war.

In many cases, the demand impetus coming from expansion of export income and the supply difficulties on the import side inevitably meant inflation, over and above that originating in rising world prices. But the pressures were worsened by the push to increase export supplies, as land was diverted from production for the home market. Demand pressures from the monetary side, deriving from the accumulation of large export balances, worsened the problem: only Colombia appeared to have learned to put in place appropriate containment measures.[43]

One serious consequence of these inflationary pressures was overvaluation. Many countries could perceive no short-run gains from devaluing, since their exports were being sold at fixed prices in direct purchase agreements with the United States. The resulting strong deviations from a "reasonable" exchange rate were to prove one of the most disastrous aspects of the wartime period.

A more positive effect of such rising reserves was that the defaulted foreign debt of the 1930s could now be paid. In the early 1940s, several countries, such as Brazil and Mexico, settled all their outstanding debt, thus clearing the way for renewed integration with international capital markets, which was to be an important element of the postwar model of growth.

INSTITUTIONS AND CAPABILITIES

Partially influenced by world events, social movements stressing the importance of community and collective interest gained impetus in the 1920s and 1930s. These movements arose from both elite and popular bases. Movements such as *indigenismo* throughout the Andes looked to Indian roots. Socialist and Communist parties developed, and governments sought the votes of the emerging working class.

Such developments produced new approaches to welfare and the social question. But generally, the major institutional developments of this period were more driven by economic modernization needs and by crisis than by social goals. International trends also favored the move towards a stronger role for government. The Soviet Union and its post-revolution industrialization drive, as well as the Fascist experience in Italy and Germany, had a clear influence on Vargas in Brazil, Cárdenas in Mexico and Perón in Argentina. U.S. New Deal policies of the 1930s and the increased role of planning and controls in wartime were added influences. These

---

[43] Triffin, 1944.

decades thus saw a number of developmentally-minded governments, some influenced by military thinking, such as Vargas in Brazil from 1937, and others building on social movements, notably Mexico. The role of the military in economic development increased and would remain important into the postwar period. Generally, traditional agrarian elites remained powerful. Institutions such as CORFO, the Chilean development bank, could be created precisely because of a tradeoff with the agricultural sector: if CORFO were permitted, land tenure would be left alone.[44]

The most notable developments were in economic institutions. The monetary side of institution building received an impetus from the wave of foreign money in the 1920s. External interests advocated more solid institutions, which led to the widespread creation of central banks and tax collection agencies. The "money doctor," Edwin Kemmerer, played an important role in a number of countries. Kemmerer, an expert on currency and banking and an authority on the U.S. Federal Reserve System, acted as financial adviser to Mexico and Guatemala and headed financial missions to Colombia, Chile, Ecuador and Bolivia in the 1920s, and to Peru in 1931.[45] He was responsible for the creation of central banks and other institutions of a modern monetary system, as well as elements of a modern taxation system. Although these institutions were constructed entirely around restoration of the gold standard (an article of faith for Kemmerer) that was shortly to disappear, his innovations produced financial institutions that would nevertheless serve for the long run, laying the foundation for an increased role for government.[46] Only in Colombia, however, did they serve adequately to control the monetary consequences of rising foreign exchange reserves by the 1940s,[47] and this was due not to Kemmerer but to Colombia's antipathy to inflation deriving from the collective memory of the Thousand Days' War,[48] a memory that appears to have become an institution in itself.

---

[44] Ortega, 1989.

[45] Seidel, 1972; Drake, 1989.

[46] What Kemmerer referred to as "his" countries were slower to come off the gold standard in the 1930s, which might be argued not to have been productive in the circumstances. But thereafter, "his" institutions survived to benefit successive governments with varying outlooks. See Drake, 1989.

[47] Triffin, 1944.

[48] Or so Colombian scholars insist.

The negative side of this same inflow of money was the growth in corruption. The fierce competition among banks to sell their loans was the starting point for trouble. Rivalry was unscrupulous and bribery widespread: one of the more innocent ploys was giving the son-in-law of the Cuban president a well-paid position in the Cuban branch of a U.S. bank while it successfully competed against other banks.[49] The fortune made by the son of the Peruvian President Augusto Leguia (1919-30) is a well-known story. Juan Leguia's best-known coup was the collection of $520,000 in commissions in 1927 from Seligmans, the New York investment bankers, as payment for his assistance in brokering two large foreign loan contracts.[50]

The countries most active in defending their export sectors and counteracting recession—Brazil, Colombia and Mexico—increased state functions and reinforced earlier learning experiences. By contrast, countries like Peru, which waited out the recession, did not increase their "learning by doing." In Brazil, the imperative of recession interacted fruitfully with the interventionist characteristics of the Vargas regime—still more so following the 1937 coup and the inauguration of the *Estado Novo.*[51] Institution building in Chile focused on diversification began in the 1920s, consistent with the fact that Chile's Depression began with the collapse of nitrates during the same decade. From 1927-29, with Pablo Ramírez as Minister of Finance, the role of engineers in the public sector greatly expanded. Two of these, Desiderio García and Guillermo del Pedregal, were, respectively, the architect and first Vice President of CORFO, founded in 1939.[52] Crisis also served to break bottlenecks, such as the Mexican prejudice against paper money.[53]

The need to replace taxes on foreign trade with other revenue sources also forced innovation: unfortunately, this usually took the form of differential exchange rates, which, while they increased the expertise of central banks and treasuries, were popular with governments precisely because they bypassed Congress and therefore obviated the need to "persuade" elites of the value of state spending. Government expenditure could thus grow more rapidly. However, it would have been healthier

[49] Lewis, 1938: 377.
[50] Thorp and Bertram, 1978.
[51] Ibid.: 66.
[52] Ffrench-Davis, et al. in Companion Volume 3.
[53] Cárdenas in Companion Volume 2.

for the fiscal system and for policymaking in general in the long run had governments been required by necessity to build the political base behind tax and expenditure policies.

Public enterprises received a particular stimulus from the Second World War, notably in Brazil and Mexico but also more widely, reflecting U.S. strategic interest in minerals.[54] Thus both Peru and Bolivia received an unusual stimulus to public sector growth. The role of the United States can also be seen in its wartime encouragement of the direct controls that had already become common in the 1930s in Latin America.

An important part of the expansion of the state is knowledge: it is significant that Brazil's *Conselho Nacional de Geografia* was created in 1937 and the *Instituto Brasileiro de Geografia e Estatística* in 1939. Other countries had a more mixed record, though Venezuela is notable for an expansion of state functions to distribute oil rent.[55]

The fact that population pressure, though mounting in urban areas, was still not intense during this period, helped public sector institution building. Expansion of the state could occur without the pressure to create jobs, a tendency that would dominate the postwar period. ECLAC estimates public sector employment at 0.8 percent of the labor force for all Latin America in 1925, and only 1.1 percent by 1950. Uruguay was the exception, with a public sector representing 3 percent of the labor force already in 1932 and rising.[56]

The welfare functions of government also expanded. This responded to the international demonstration effect felt in the 1910s and 1920s, with growing worldwide pressure for the eight-hour day and other social demands. Labor codes were developed and widely adopted. The pioneers in social security were Uruguay, Argentina and Chile, all before 1930. By the end of the 1930s, the Brazilian, Chilean and Uruguayan systems were all well developed, while the Mexican system took shape in the 1940s.[57]

---

[54] Humphreys, 1982.
[55] Whitehead, 1994: 53-54.
[56] ECLAC, 1965: 167.
[57] Whitehead, 1994: 76, 80.

CONCLUSION

The dislocations of the 30 years between 1914 and 1945 provided a powerful signal of the need for change. What can be concluded so far about the ability of Latin America to change? The analysis is complicated by the fact that only in the 1930s did the dislocation take the form of a strong imperative for change; the two wars provided opportunities but took away much of the urgency, and this ambiguity weakened if not cancelled the signal.

Nevertheless, the general record of capacity for change was impressive. Industry expanded, there was diversification in agriculture, and in the midst of the Great Depression, some countries even recovered before their export sectors did. Policy was innovative and pragmatic, and new institutions appeared. With a lesser presence of foreign capital in the 1930s, small and medium-sized enterprises expanded, particularly in mining. The foreign debt was not paid when that made sense, and repaid once it was possible. Literacy and basic health indicators improved and growth was better than in the center countries. By World War Two, exports of manufactures had begun and old dreams of Latin American integration were being revived.

The 1930s were the testing time, when the signals for change were unambiguous. There was an impressive and rapid recovery. However, the recovery was possible in large part only because of extraordinary circumstances of limited duration. In particular, many opportunities existed for import substitution, land and labor were available to expand and diversify in agriculture, and default on the debt was possible without sanctions or foregone benefits, since no loans and little direct investment were forthcoming anyway. The flexible if unkind world of the 1930s allowed "recovery" through bankruptcies, squeezing of margins, and even hunger in the form of reduced wages. Downward price flexibility meant that inflation did not eliminate the benefits of exchange rate devaluation, so exports could be stimulated without further drastic stabilization eroding investors' confidence. All this foreshadows in mirror image the telling of a very different tale 50 years later.

The response capacity may have been impressive in general, but it varied greatly across countries. At one extreme was Cuba, where the level of education and the relatively high per capita income before 1929 would suggest a reasonable response capacity. However, despite quite innovative policy and a diversification program, the consequences of the entrenching of sugar in institutions and structures were so deep that the economy remained completely tied to that good, even using wartime reserves to purchase U.S. sugar firms.[58] Lacking a central bank, Cuba had no autonomous monetary or fiscal policy.

At the other extreme, cases of strong response and significant diversification were Brazil, Colombia and, with its own special characteristics, Mexico. Recovery in Brazil and Colombia was in response to and driven by exports. The special characteristics of coffee, however, facilitated diversification, probably aided on balance by the relatively undistinguished performance of coffee prices. Mexico's positive response was part of a deeper phenomenon: the building on the revolution by the Cárdenas administration.

After the 1914-45 period, Latin America would move to the next stage of industrialization. However, there is a great difference between industrialization that reflects export sector interests and industrialization that leads the economy, backed by a state taking on new functions. The first is what principally occurred in the 1930s. The second is a reasonable description of the larger Latin American economies by the 1950s. The Second World War already marked a shift, helped by the change in attitude on the part of the United States, which during the war saw the promotion of industry in Latin America as helpful to its strategic interests. Even in the 1930s, the military's promotion of industry in Brazil under Vargas, as well as the new instruments of state promotion and intervention seen in Brazil and Chile, foreshadowed a shift in focus, instruments and priorities.

---

[58] See Pollitt, 1984, for the withdrawal of U.S. capital in the 1930s and 1940s.

CHAPTER 5

INDUSTRIALIZATION AND THE GROWING ROLE OF THE STATE: 1945-73

By MID-CENTURY, LATIN AMERICA WAS looking very different from how it looked when the century began, and strong processes of change were under way. The restructuring of the 1930s continued during the war and would now progress much further. The state had acquired a number of policy instruments, such as monetary discretion and a more diverse tax base, while the abandonment of the gold standard had left financial authorities free to adjust the exchange rate. During the middle years of the century, at least some national governments shouldered the responsibility of promoting economic development, though timing and commitment varied. They enlarged economic infrastructure or established state enterprises, either for defense, as in Argentina under Perón, or to assure domestic supplies of certain strategic inputs, as in Brazil and Mexico. The role of the state was also extended to promoting new entrepreneurs, often actually "creating" them under the umbrella of large government contracts for the construction of roads, public utilities and dams.

This chapter first reviews the new context of internal and external growth in the postwar period and then traces the evolution of the political economy of industrialization in the countries that led the process. The third section considers the strengths and weaknesses of the institutional evolution that supported and was in

Photo: Venezuelan oil worker, 1968.

turn supported by the growth process. The fourth and fifth sections address two important policy innovations of the period: economic integration and agrarian reform.

CHANGING ECONOMIC AND SOCIAL CONTEXT

The new role of government was a response to growing institutional capacities and to a social context in which the middle classes were now a significant and visible feature of the larger countries. Urbanization was increasing dramatically and rising literacy rates and the spread of newspapers and radio were changing the face of political and social life. The population trends of the previous period were now strengthened, above all the decline in death rates, which fell by half or more in half of the countries between the 1930s and the 1960s. The birth rate typically remained the same or even rose, with improving health, declining infant mortality and increased marriage rates. As a result, the average annual rate of growth of population rose from 2.2 percent from 1930-50 to 2.7 percent from 1950-70. Only Argentina, Uruguay, Cuba and Panama experienced falling birth rates and slower population increases. Migration to cities affected even the smallest countries: urban growth from 1950-80 was over 5 percent for the Dominican Republic and Honduras, and the average rate for Latin America was 4.1 percent. The population explosion brought with it a rise in the dependency ratio: that is, the proportion of those assumed only to consume to the total of consumers and producers.[1] The average by 1960 was 46 percent, with Costa Rica, Nicaragua and Panama over 50 percent.

These figures indicate how far jobs had to be on every policymaker's mind—the more so because of growing social tensions (for instance, rural violence in the 1940s and 1950s in Colombia and in the 1950s in Peru, and increasing tension throughout Latin America triggered by the Cuban Revolution). These tensions both accelerated migration and increased the sense of urgency to push forward a development strategy that would create jobs.

---

[1] This much-used concept, which designates as "productive" the 15-65 year-old age group, does not fit well with the realities of the Latin American labor market or with the survival strategies of poor households.

These trends interacted with the postwar international environment. Here the single outstanding change was the new dominance of the United States. While European countries had suffered terrible destruction, U.S. productive capacity had increased 50 percent during the war. In 1945, the United States produced more than half of all manufactured goods worldwide, and was capable of quickly converting its productive capacity from war to peacetime production. Further, the United States now owned half the world supply of shipping, compared with only 14 percent in 1939, and supplied one-third of world exports while taking only one-tenth of world imports.[2]

The U.S. government also knew clearly how it wanted to use its new role. Whereas signals pointing to the need for change in the international system in the inter-war years were weak and conflicting, as the Second World War drew to a close the international system was clearly perceived to have broken down and to require major institutional change. The United States led talks at many levels during the war itself to prepare to build the peace. The agenda covered institutional developments to ensure expanding trade and capital flows, the use of those institutions to reduce discriminatory controls and limit the increased role of government (though commodity agreements would remain important), and a sufficiently rapid recovery of the main trading nations to complement institutional renewal of the international system. This agenda shaped the Bretton Woods agreements of 1944, which created the International Monetary Fund and the World Bank, building on earlier ideas. The agreements specifically aimed at a return to stable exchange rates and an assured supply of long-term capital, with progressive liberalization of the European economies.[3] As it became clear that this action alone would not be enough to kickstart the European economies, and as the Cold War became the dominant political context, a more radical U.S. role was invented with the Marshall Plan in 1947. Lengthy negotiations eventually added the General Agreement on Tariffs and Trade (GATT), signed in 1947 in Geneva by 23 nations (including Argentina, Chile and Cuba). The participants failed to agree, however, on creation of the International Trade Organization.

---

[2] Ashworth, 1987: 266.

[3] It is important to note that the return to free markets was expected to take time—certainly until the mid-1950s. It was not anticipated that capital accounts would be liberalized. The practice turned out to be far more interventionist than the theory.

What would only become clear with time was how low a priority Latin America was on the U.S. agenda. Latin America was thought to be relatively "secure," though requiring assistance in controlling labor movements. The worldwide ideological battle was as important in Latin America as it was elsewhere during this period, and "Communist subversion" had to be watched carefully. But material aid was not a necessary part of the strategy, given needs elsewhere, particularly in Europe and Asia.

This low priority would become clear at the series of international conferences under the leadership of the United States, which began with the Eighth Inter-American Conference in Chapultepec, Mexico in 1945, before the war ended.[4] Chapultepec was a disappointment for Latin America: working out specific details of economic issues was mostly postponed until a later conference. On the issue of most concern to the United States—conditions for direct foreign investment—the Latin Americans were interested in responding. But the economic conference was postponed so often that it was christened the "elusive" conference.[5] The disillusionment grew, fostered by realities such as inconvertibility.[6] At the Rio Conference in 1947, there was an audacious suggestion from the Ecuadorian Foreign Minister that the time was ripe for a Marshall Plan for Latin America.[7] But by the time of the Ninth Inter-American Conference in Bogota in 1948, General Marshall's chief preoccupation was persuading the Latin American nations that the U.S. had too much on its shoulders as reconstructor of world peace and security to be considered a major source of finance for Latin America.[8] The corollary was that what was

---

[4] Besides Chapultepec, there was the Defense Conference in Rio, August 1947; the UN Conference on Trade and Employment (that tried to set up the International Trade Organization) in Havana, 1947-48; and the Ninth Inter-American Conference (at which the Organization of American States was founded) in Bogota, March 1948.

[5] By one of its analysts, Rabe, 1978.

[6] This was important for Argentina: once Perón had used his modest dollar reserves, his incentives to stay part of a free-trade world were not very great when Argentina's exports could earn only sterling and the country needed dollars for imported machinery. See Fodor, 1986.

[7] Willner, 1949: 38, quoting *The New York Times*, August 1947.

[8] U.S. Department of State Bulletin, April 11, 1948. General Marshall finished his speech with extemporary remarks, ending with something brought to mind, he claimed, by the mural of Simón Bolívar in the meeting room: that the U.S. Commander who led the attack on Okinawa was named Simon Bolívar Bucknell. He died in the fight, the last big battle for the peace and security of the Pacific. That is, Marshall implied, be grateful to your saviors.

more essential was to put in place solid guarantees so that private capital could do the job. The clashes over the "Calvo Doctrine"—which rejected resident aliens' right of appeal to their home governments—were such that thereafter the private sector strongly counseled abandonment of the planned conference and concentration on bilateral negotiations on direct foreign investment (DFI) legislation.[9] This was the route followed.

A further marked characteristic of the postwar world was a new stronger role for government and closer relations between business and government—both a heritage of close collaboration on wartime committees. This relationship between the public and private sectors was especially strong in the case of the large U.S. companies that looked internationally for investment opportunities.[10] Those new interests were already reflected in the conference negotiations we have described. The war left many such companies concerned about excess stocks of wartime production of machinery, a concern which reinforced the emerging consensus that the industrialization of developing countries provided both investment opportunities and good sales of machinery and equipment. The smaller firms whose principal interest in Latin America had been the sale of consumer goods were losing out as U.S. policymakers increasingly worried more about conditions for investors than about tariffs.

No one even considered the possibility that Latin America's new industries might begin to export to the United States: the region's industrialization focused on the domestic Latin American market. This may well have been the best development path at the time for the region, but it was also politically convenient for the United States, even more so once Eisenhower replaced Truman in office in 1953.[11] In practice, the new international financial institutions began quietly to favor protection in specific instances.[12]

These trends coalesced with others important to the boom of the 1950s and 1960s, as well as to the specific way Latin America would take advantage of world

---

[9] Rabe, 1978: 289.

[10] Maxfield and Nolt, 1990.

[11] Ibid.

[12] Webb in Companion Volume 3. He reports that the International Finance Corporation, a subsidiary of the World Bank, actually argued for protection of "its" industries.

expansion. In terms of technological development, the depressed conditions of the 1930s followed by the wartime stimulus to innovation had left a backlog of technology waiting to be applied internationally. The direction of technological change meant growth in the optimum size of firms. Increased spending on research and development (R&D), greater internationalization, more marketing efforts and development of patent protection combined to produce massive growth in trade and investment, since DFI in developing countries provided an ideal way of earning quasi rents from technology already developed for the home market. Meanwhile, on the Latin American side, the foreign exchange reserves in place as the war ended vanished sooner than anyone thought possible, provoking an abrupt resort to import quotas (the inconvertibility of sterling reserves was a problem for Argentina). When foreign firms found they were completely excluded from markets, they had a strong incentive to move to local production, which now became the only option. So the exceptional boom conditions of 1950-73 and the new form of Latin America's insertion into world markets went hand in hand. The development of financial institutions and international financial instruments, as well as the application of technology in transport, supported the insertion with efficient travel and communications that facilitated international operations.

The growing consensus on the importance of industrialization found theoretical and institutional support in the United Nations Economic Commission for Latin America (ECLA). After it came into existence in 1948, ECLA had to prove itself in a short space of time if it was to stay alive at all.[13] The group of young economists gathered together under the leadership of Raúl Prebisch had to show that there was a valid "Latin American viewpoint." Out of this came, by 1949, the "Prebisch thesis."[14] Initially lacking in coherence, its basic argument

---

[13] ECLA—CEPAL in Spanish—changed its English name in 1984 to reflect the growing number of member states from the non-Spanish-speaking Caribbean. We shall refer throughout to ECLAC, except in this chapter, where we are dealing in part with the history of the organization itself and it seems more appropriate to use its contemporaneous title. For an insightful account of the origins of ECLA and development of its ideas by a principal actor, see Furtado, 1985.

[14] The key original document is ECLA, 1951. See Fitzgerald in Companion Volume 3 and Love, 1994, for a full discussion and bibliography and for an account of ECLA's early history. See Furtado, 1985, for the opposition provoked by ECLA and Prebisch. See Pollock, 1978, for the conflict between Prebisch and the United States.

was that productivity gains from technical progress in industry at the center were not reflected in lower prices but retained there, while at the periphery, productivity gains in the primary sector were less significant, and wages were held down by surplus labor. Later versions emphasized more strongly the demand side of the model: the asymmetry produced by the income elasticities of demand for imports in the center and the periphery, with consequent implications for the behavior of the terms of trade. At the core of this approach was the reason why Latin American economies would not respond "automatically" to the price signal of the terms of trade: structural rigidities, that is, market imperfections rooted in infrastructural deficiencies, institutions, and social and political systems and values. The Latin American economies therefore required deliberate government promotion of industrialization.[15] The growth of industry was to provide independence from unstable and undynamic primary exports. (Oddly, there was little emphasis on more extensive transformation of primary exports.) Foreign capital inflows were seen as helpful to ease the overcoming of rigidities, but the ECLA of the 1950s envisaged such inflows as coming largely in the form of loans to the public sector. No contradiction was seen in using foreign capital, channeled through government, to achieve structural change. No one focused directly on issues such as whether depending on outside sources for finance might constrain governments' freedom in policymaking.

More was required than the theory provided by ECLA, however, for development based on import-substituting industrialization to settle into place in a stable manner. Two political desiderata were also important. The first concerned necessary preconditions for the required flow of foreign finance. The original ECLA thesis emphasized public foreign capital, which had played a role during the Second World War and was now envisaged as part of the new money that would flow in as the United States looked toward postwar reconstruction in Europe, and, it was hoped, elsewhere. However, with hindsight we now know that the model as it actually developed depended crucially not on public money but on direct foreign investment. For foreign investment to come in quantity, further development of the rela-

---

[15] At its heart, as Fitzgerald shows in Companion Volume 3, this was a dynamic theory of capital accumulation and growth, based on modifying key assumptions of the standard neoclassical trade model, whereas many of its critics have attacked it on grounds of static inefficiency.

tions between state, domestic and foreign capital was required. Only when this relationship was more fully resolved than in 1945 would a clear route to industrialization become evident. The second political requirement was a consequence of the first: if private foreign capital was to enter Latin America in quantity and feel secure, then the role of labor had to be "managed." The militant tendencies emerging during and immediately after the war had to be controlled in order to maintain adequate business confidence, though such control had as much to do with the political context of the Cold War and the anti-Communist crusade.

Evolution of the political economy of industrialization along these lines was particularly important in those countries that would go most wholeheartedly for a state-led industrialization strategy with significant TNC participation during these decades: principally, Brazil, Mexico, Argentina, Colombia and Chile.

Evolving Political Economy of State-led Industrialization

The evolution of the political economy of the new strategies can best be studied in Brazil, where tensions were most developed (and have been most fully documented). Already at their inception, ECLA's ideas found their echo in Brazil's industrial bourgeoisie. ECLA articulated the views of the group of industrialists led by Roberto Simonsen.[16] There was a complete agreement even concerning the role of foreign capital from public sources rather than private. Initial differences of emphasis quickly vanished: for example, the ambition of industrialists immediately after the war focused on maintaining and expanding export markets, but, at least in Brazil, the experience of the GATT negotiations of 1947 showed national entrepreneurs all too vividly how solid was the center countries' unwillingness to allow any market penetration, an unwillingness based on their shortage of dollars and their desire to be more self-sufficient in food.

During the 1940s, the new interest in industrialization did not yet amount to a "hegemonic" project, even in Brazil. The lack of consensus is seen most vividly over the issue of government intervention. The swing away from wartime

---

[16] Leopoldi, 1984: 138-40.

controls, which was strong in the United States, also responded to internal forces in Latin America. This was sharply evidenced in Brazil by the famous polemic between Roberto Simonsen and Eugenio Gudin at the end of the war.[17] Gudin headed a strong liberal faction which, while not opposed to industrialization per se, was firmly opposed to protection, and indeed to state intervention of any kind. The strength of the liberal reaction was evidenced by the fact that it supplied the rationale for Brazil's first postwar administration, that of Eurico Dutra (1946-50). The complexity of the reality underscores the contradictory elements in play, just as contradictions were in evidence at the international level. While the rhetoric and some actions were liberal, strong elements of interventionism were retained.[18] The brief experiment with tariff reductions had to end by 1947, when import controls were reintroduced, owing to the size of the deficit. But the forces behind Gudin were strong enough that industrialists in Brazil seemed to have realized that to pin all their hopes on a subsequent major tariff reform was unrealistic. Instead, they secured piecemeal but substantial protection via import controls (and later via multiple exchange rates). Only in 1957 was the first systematic tariff introduced and ratified by Congress.

Elsewhere in Latin America, the role of tariffs was more readily accepted. But the issue not so easily accepted was the direct entrepreneurial role of the state. In Brazil, Petrobrás faced constant opposition as it emerged in the early 1950s. In Mexico, the Mexican-American Commission for Economic Co-operation proposed a *Comisión Federal de Fomento Industrial* to expand industry with direct state ownership. Even though the state role was intended to be temporary, it aroused deep concern and opposition in the business community, and failed to gain acceptance.[19] In Chile, as in all economies with a high-productivity mining sector, state intervention was particularly essential, since without it the exchange rate would achieve levels at which new (or indeed any) exports would be unprofitable. Of course, this still meant conflict, in Chile's case focused upon the role of CORFO, the state industrial development agency, founded in 1939. The industrial sector welcomed

---

[17] IPEA *(Instituto de Planejamento Econômico e Social)*, 1978: 21-40.

[18] See, in particular, Draibe, 1985: 138-76. She argues against the interpretation of Ianni, 1971.

[19] Mosk, 1950: 95-97.

CORFO, but more for its provision of subsidized credit than for its direct entrepreneurial role, which they naturally feared. Nevertheless, this role accounted for the greater part of the agency's resources in its early years.[20]

The acceptance of protection and the proliferation of controls in all the industrializing economies of Latin America in the immediate postwar years led to rapid growth of state-business relations in order to reconcile the private sector's need for and fear of the state. In Mexico, for example, it is clear that the network of relationships grew by leaps and bounds during the war and the years immediately after. The links were mostly due to business initiative, but often with considerable encouragement from government.[21] The delicacy of the relationship has been well described by Sanford Mosk: "Businessmen assign the government a prominent role, it is true, but they want the government to arrive at its decisions on the basis of information and advice supplied by the interested industrialist groups. What they propose is business intervention in government rather than government intervention in business."[22]

The same expanded relations between the public and private sectors occurred elsewhere,[23] partly in legally-required participation on boards and other institutions, partly in informal contacts. The system was clearly one where the best way to increase profits often was to play politics rather than concentrate on the conventional technical variables determining productivity. In Brazil by the mid-1950s, the echoes of the Simonsen-Gudin debate had died away and the new role of the state was so well accepted that Juscelino Kubitschek's *Plano de Metas* (1956) aroused no opposition.

Conflicting forces were also at work in the 1950s with regard to the role of foreign capital. Again, the Simonsen-Gudin debate is illuminating. Simonsen wanted "selective" access for foreign capital, and saw public capital as the major solution. He argued for a Marshall Plan for Latin America. Gudin, of course,

---

[20] Ortega, et al., 1989: 112.

[21] Shafer, 1973: 126.

[22] Mosk, 1950: 29. He is here writing of the "New Group" of industrialists which emerged with the war, the importance of which later writers claim he exaggerated. But they would agree that the description fits the general attitude that was now to develop widely across Latin America.

[23] In Chile, see Muñoz, 1986: 210; in Brazil, see Leopoldi, 1984: 245-92.

wanted total liberalization. However, as protection encouraged the entry of foreign capital into Brazilian manufacturing, so the relative weight of different interests shifted. The industrial bourgeoisie became more fragmented. New groups emerged in the late 1940s and early 1950s that were increasingly associated with foreign capital, thus nullifying potential resistance to the eventual legislation embodied in instruction 113 of the *Superintendência da Moeda e do Crédito (SUMOC)* of 1955, which effectively gave preferential treatment to foreign capital.[24] The issue was further confused by the "carrot and stick" policy pursued by successive administrations, which offered bonuses for exports, favorable exchange rates and eventually tariff reform.

The evolution of a successful industrialization model eventually led to rapid growth in the coming decade. It was based on a three-way alliance between state, multinationals and domestic bourgeoisie, where the latter was definitely the junior partner, and its paradox was best summed up in a quote from a Brazilian businessman: "In the end we won, but we did not get the prize."[25]

Gradually, despite these tensions, the main features of economic policy for the postwar decades were consolidated country by country. The consolidation typically comprised measures that settled the issue of foreign capital, usually by strong promotional legislation and on favorable terms. There was also typically some reduction in the use of direct controls, particularly on imports and foreign exchange, and in the degree of overvaluation of the exchange rate, usually combined with simplification of the previous multiple exchange rate system. High protection stayed, as Table 5.1 shows, with very little rationalization, forming the heart of the strategy to attract TNCs. The core of protection was the combination of high tariffs on final goods, exemption from tariffs for many capital goods and intermediate products, and an overvalued exchange rate,[26] which meant that goods not subject to tariffs were extremely cheap.

---

[24] SUMOC was created in 1945 with a view to gradually developing a genuine central bank.

[25] João Paulo de Almeida Magalhães, interviewed in 1981 by Leopoldi, 1984: 337.

[26] Jorgensen and Paldam (1987) argue from data for eight countries for 1946-85 that real exchange rate overvaluation has been overemphasized. As a trend over time it appears only in Peru (prior to 1970). But if account is taken of the overvaluation in existence in 1946, the effect was still powerful. Brazil's exchange rate, for instance, was estimated to be 70 percent overvalued in 1946. Fishlow, 1972.

TABLE 5.1

NOMINAL PROTECTION IN LATIN AMERICA, CIRCA 1960
(In percent)

	Nondurable consumer goods	Durable consumer goods	Semi-manufactured goods	Industrial raw materials	Capital goods	Overall average
Argentina	176	266	95	55	98	131
Brazil	260	328	80	106	82	168
Chile	328	90	98	111	45	138
Colombia	247	108	28	57	18	112
Mexico	114	147	28	38	14	61
Uruguay	23	24	23	14	27	21
EEC	17	19	7	1	13	13

Note: Nominal protection has been calculated as the simple arithmetic mean of approximate incidence (in ad valorem terms) of duties and charges. In the case of Uruguay, it has been calculated as the simple arithmetic mean of theoretical incidence (excluding surcharges and prior deposits) on the CIF value of imports.
Source: Bulmer-Thomas, 1994, Table 9.1.

The price differential biased choices of production methods in the direction of imported capital goods, and with that, imported technology. The increasing pessimism with respect to new exports, given the protectionist tendencies in the center, led to neglect of factors unfavorable to exports. An example is the practice of many multinational subsidiaries of signing contracts with their parent companies not to export to third countries.[27] There was still a blind spot, it seems, over the extent to which new exports were penalized by existing policies, which was coherent with the TNCs' lack of interest in exporting and the extent to which the private sector could benefit from the actual set of policies. Even Prebisch did not see that generalized protection was a tax on exports.[28] Prebisch and others also tended to

---

[27] Bitar, 1971. The point was that the parent company did not wish to upset its present trading arrangements.
[28] Interviews with Joseph Ramos, Santiago, October 23, 1996; Hector Assael, Santiago, October 24, 1996; and Enrique Iglesias, Brussels, 1997. Assael, who worked in CORFO from 1968-70, recounts how it was only thanks to a lecture on industrial planning given by Ignacy Sachs in Santiago in the late 1960s that he himself was made to understand the relationship between protection, the exchange rate and new exports.

underestimate the degree of effort and institutional innovation that were required to begin exporting.[29]

In Brazil, the new focus was embodied in the foreign exchange law of 1953 and SUMOC instruction 113 in 1955. Similarly, in Chile the crucial legislation on foreign capital came in 1955, though Chile was further ahead in the process of consolidating the attitudes and institutions needed for ISI to flourish, given the country's early start and the strength and breadth of state involvement. By the early 1950s, a crisis in copper, inflation and balance of payments problems were already generating fear that ISI was nearing its limit. Chile's reorientation of 1955 was more fundamental than elsewhere, involving major stabilization and a commitment to more market-oriented policies.[30] In Argentina, 1955 was the critical year when Perón's reappraisal of the role of foreign capital helped spark growing opposition to him. However, a fuller move to a pro-foreign capital and noninterventionist stance did not occur until Frondizi assumed power in 1958.

We have described the evolution of the political economy of industrialization policies, namely tariffs, exchange rates and foreign capital legislation. But a further potential instrument has not been mentioned: taxation (other than the important taxation implicit in the above policies). The omission reflects the fact that tax reforms were conspicuous by their absence in this period. The single taxation policy that evolved was taxation of exporting multinationals: in both Chile and Venezuela this appeared an obvious way to finance industrialization.[31]

In Chile, as in other countries where there was strong foreign control, efforts to increase taxation prompted resistance. In Chile's case, there was an investment strike in the copper sector. The exchange rate was indeed the only remaining means of taxing the sector (hence the economic and political logic of eventual nationalization and why it has not been reversed). Where control was in national hands, the exception proves the rule: it took the strong multisectoral character of the Colombian Coffee Federation and its interest in diversification to achieve (eventually and after considerable effort) an agreement to tax coffee. Modest rates of taxation were

---

[29] Interview with Albert Fishlow, Washington, D.C., 1997. Furtado (1985: 106) was more perceptive, emphasizing the inadequacy of the financial system to allow restructuring.

[30] Ortega, et al., 1989: 132-38; Muñoz, 1986: 125-45.

[31] Behrman, 1976: 105; Rabe, 1982: 80-93.

negotiable in cases of export diversity: for example, Mexico instituted an export tax on oil, other minerals and some other exports in 1938, legitimatized as a device to absorb the windfall profits from devaluation. The tax evolved into a de facto differential exchange rate.[32] Despite these examples of taxation, however, the norm was that good arrangements could not be worked out.

Behind the lack of progressive tax policies lay the political reality of unequal distribution of wealth, particularly in land holding. Against this structure, agrarian reform could do little. But what is relevant here is that this power structure severely limited *other* areas of policymaking, especially the extraction of surplus for investment elsewhere in the economy. In contrast, Korea and Taiwan had carried out land reforms, with the United States playing an important role, since it saw reform as a means to weaken a reactionary political class to release resources for growth. Economic expansion was seen as crucial given the position of Korea and Taiwan in the front line of the Cold War in Asia.[33] As a result of the political change in which land reform was central, both countries had degrees of freedom that most countries of Latin America did not have. The result in Korea was a massive extraction of surplus from the agricultural sector, implemented through pricing policies.[34]

These serious constraints on policy continued to shape the evolving political economy into the 1960s in a number of different ways. The very weight of landed elites in the body politic, while it constituted an obstacle to land reform, also gave impetus to a move for reform, since it held out the promise of modifying the resource base of powerful and reactionary groups. The difficulties of redistribution lent force to the interest in regional integration as a solution to, among other things, the problem of market size.

---

[32] It was a concealed differential exchange rate system implemented through the use of official values, *aforos*, for exports. The *aforo* could be varied.

[33] These points come from a discussion with Brian Pollitt.

[34] The government was the only buyer of grains and was responsible for setting the price of fertilizer. The key point here is that the government had the flexibility to reverse these policies in the 1970s, once the harm to the supply side was perceived. In the Mexican case, where there had been a relatively serious agrarian reform, the same process was at work in much the same manner, using differential pricing, but was not reversed until the debt crisis (see Cárdenas in Companion Volume 3).

After the Korean War boom, policymakers became more concerned with the need to export, while retaining their blind spot in relation to the needs of a dynamic export sector. Resolving the political economy of direct foreign investment and getting legislation on the statute book that favored foreign capital was seen as an important advance (disillusion would only set in later, as the manufacturing TNCs' lack of interest in exporting became evident). But other lines of action were needed. The need to export and perceptions of the costs of excessive intervention led in only a few cases to an evolution of trade policies in the 1960s towards significantly fewer distortions. Colombia and Chile were the leaders here, with some similar elements in Argentina and Brazil (see the national analyses of the next chapter).

A second concern of policymakers was the issue of market size. These twin concerns of exporting and limited national markets gradually led to serious interest in economic integration, which appeared to solve both problems at a stroke. The market size issue also became a reason for interest in agrarian reform, despite the opposition we have already touched on. These new lines of policy were taken forward by institutional developments at the continental level, pushed partly by national and international responses to the Cuban Revolution of 1959. The challenge posed by Fidel Castro accelerated interest in expanding reforms to the social sector.

INSTITUTIONAL EVOLUTION

At the national level, the adoption of a strategy of inward-looking industrialization encouraged the development of many functions and instruments of the public sector.[35] A new class of technocrats appeared, with skills in economics, planning, management and engineering. In most countries they were instrumental in drawing up strategic plans for infrastructure development, and for setting up developmental agencies and financial institutions. Beginning in the late 1930s, numerous development banks were created. By the 1960s, a variety of public sector agencies to promote development were established.[36] Some of these would later lose their original

---

[35] For documentation of the expansion of different aspects of the state's role, see Whitehead, 1994.
[36] ECLA, 1971: 145.

rationale, as we see below in the case of Argentina, but others remained strong and acquired expertise, as with the National Economic Development Bank (BNDE) in Brazil. Industrial promotion instruments in place by the 1960s began to push non-traditional exports.

Institutional evolution was extremely varied. In Brazil, Kubitschek, who assumed the presidency in 1956, was able to build on the continuity with Vargas, who had expanded the role of the state and set up the BNDE in 1956. Kubitschek was seen as "a Vargas man,"[37] but both the quality and continuity of the bureaucracy helped. BNDE staff, for example, were mostly appointed on merit, and there was substantial continuity between administrations. There was no interest group representation in the BNDE directorate, but it had the confidence of the private sector. Executive groups with representatives of ministries and the private sector were formed around sectoral targets. The country's leading industrial organizations were behind development of tariff regulations and the tariff law of 1957.

In Argentina, Frondizi, who became president in 1958, was in principle anxious to implement similar policies, but what happened was very different. Continuity was a problem. The Peronist years had so deeply divided society that every issue was treated around the pro/anti-Perón axis, virtually to the exclusion of all else. President Frondizi's efforts, particularly to please foreign capital, did not receive support from the business sector. Frondizi's view was that he did not need to work on building support, because business would naturally support what was in its own interest.[38] The reality was that business was so frightened by Frondizi's pact with Perón that it was not prepared to support him. Institutional deficiencies aggravated business' lack of confidence in government: for example, the Industrial Promotion Law was never implemented, which was interpreted by the SME sectors as "evidence of bias in favor of international investors." The title of a 1960 article in *La Razón* asked, "Is It Worth It to Be Industrialized?"[39] On the private sector side, where Brazil's industrial associations had research teams and solid organization, ACIEL in Argentina, for example, had no organizational structure and "mainly ex-

---

[37] Sikkink, 1991: 64.

[38] Ibid.: 107.

[39] Ortega, et al., 1989: 2. La Razón, December 13, 1960.

isted as a vehicle for the expression of the shared liberal world view of the group members and as an opposition front to the CGE," the industrialist organization set up under Perón.[40] The Argentine version of a development bank, the *Banco Industrial* founded in 1944, was by the 1960s a distortion of what it was meant to be, operating as a commercial bank in the short-term credit market.

In Chile, both industry and agriculture were assisted by a wave of institutional development, particularly in regard to the processing of natural resources. Technological institutes were created and support given to universities.[41] CORFO, especially in its early stages, played a strong promotional role.[42] It was technically strong and viewed as highly professional. In 1958, CORFO was reformed to give more emphasis to its role as provider of credit and less to its entrepreneurial function.[43]

Throughout Latin America during this period, the state played the leading role in expanding the economic infrastructure that facilitated both industrialization and overall growth. Construction of roads, telephone networks, energy supply at reasonable costs (often subsidized), and other public utilities allowed, in turn, the consolidation of an effective domestic market. In addition, the state created a number of other agencies to promote specific sectors such as industry, forestry, agriculture and mining, depending on the country in question, as well as science and technology and skill-specific human resource development. The story told in Box 5.1 of the role of the Argentine Atomic Energy Commission and Jorge Sabato shows how crucial relationships were pushed ahead between the public and private sectors, and between education, knowledge and its application.

Institutional development was aided by developments at the continental and international levels, though less powerfully than was initially envisaged by supporters of the Alliance for Progress. By the mid-1950s, awareness was growing of the need for action on fronts not sufficiently addressed by the World Bank: education, housing, health, water and agriculture. From its 1954 meeting onward, the Inter-American Economic and Social Council made proposals for regional initiatives.

---

[40] Ortega, et al., 1989: 106
[41] Ffrench-Davis, et al. in Companion Volume 3.
[42] Ibid.
[43] Ortega, et al., 1989.

Box 5.1

ENDOGENOUS TECHNOLOGY: JORGE SABATO

Born in 1924 in Rojas in the Province of Buenos Aires, Jorge Sabato went on to have a distinguished career as an applied physicist and institution builder. He became head of the Argentine National Commission of Atomic Energy, created by Perón in 1950. He was a major influence throughout Latin America in the 1960s, particularly in Brazil, where he was a close friend of today's Minister of Technology, Israel Vargas. The minister considers Sabato to have originated the idea of the "technology factory," later used so effectively by the Koreans. The technology factory consists of a laboratory and team with a mandate to generate, adapt and transmit technology in a specific area. Sabato's key insight in terms of technology generation was the "triangle." He argued that sustainable development in any society depended on creating tight and permanent interconnections between the education system, the technical and scientific community, and the productive system. He fought for the creation and institutionalization of such links through his work at the commission and later as technical adviser to the Andean Pact. He was also determined to promote collaboration between the limited scientific communities of Latin America, and was active in the formation of a network of such communities that flourished in the 1960s. His contribution to Argentine industrial development was significant—the country's nuclear reactor was built with a high percentage of national components, and there were many spinoffs and externalities, independent of the nuclear industry itself. The work he promoted made significant headway up to the mid-1970s, when Argentina changed course.

Source: Interview with Aldo Ferrer, Washington, D.C., February 21, 1997; Wionczek, 1987; Sercovitch, 1987.

The United States showed little enthusiasm until the 1958 meeting of the council in Bogota, when it announced the U.S. would support a regional development bank. A joint initiative was developed by Kubitschek and Lleras Camargo, known as the *operación panamericana*, which contained the seeds of a regional initiative for long-run development. Prebisch was influential in lobbying in these areas.[44] A new urgency was given to the idea by the Cuban Revolution. An agreement was signed in 1960 to establish the Inter-American Development Bank, and within it the Social Progress Trust Fund, specifically designed to lend to those areas neglected by existing organizations. On his election in 1960, U.S. President Kennedy moved swiftly to follow up on these ideas and establish a hemispheric Alliance for Progress, brought formally into existence by the Charter of Punta del Este in August 1961. The core idea was that countries would be supported in their reform efforts by additional money, with the proposal from the U.S. side at $20 billion over 10 years.[45] The key themes were integration, planning, tax reform, agrarian reform and modernization, and investment in the social sector. A country review process was set up in 1963, conducted by the Inter-American Committee for the Alliance for Progress, known by its Spanish acronym, CIAP. Prebisch was influential in setting up the system whereby a "Committee of Experts" would come to work with a national planning team. The committee's approval of the process was important for securing Alliance money.

Despite the gains, momentum was soon lost in the process of regional structural reform with outside aid.[46] The flow of funds was not what had been promised, and much of the money had to be spent on U.S. goods, transported on U.S. ships, and spent on goods "additional" to what would have been bought anyway. This additionality clause led to much friction, and was eventually abandoned after

---

[44] Yale Ferguson, private communication; Albert Fishlow, interview, Washington, D.C., 1997. Both stressed the contribution of ECLA, and specifically Prebisch, to the direction of the Alliance for Progress, particularly its enthusiasm for economic integration. See also Dell, 1972; Levinson and Onis, 1970.

[45] Frei, 1967. The funds were to come from U.S. aid sources, with the rest from international and European sources.

[46] This summary is based on the testimonies recorded in the Oral History Project on the Alliance for Progress, as well as the secondary literature. The Oral History Project is led by Enrique Lerdau and Theodore Mesmer, who gave me access to the unpublished interviews and to their draft summary documents. Lerdau and Mesmer, 1997; Baskind and Mesmer, 1997.

Lleras Restrepo complained directly to President Nixon in 1969.[47] The flow of funds under the various frameworks is shown in Table 5.2. The IDB pursued its vocation of lending to the neglected sectors; from 1961 to 1972, 46 percent of its lending was allocated to agriculture, sanitation, urban development and education. Between 1961 and 1968, the IDB lent $643 million for agriculture, while the World Bank provided $350 million and USAID, $297 million.[48]

The World Bank, meanwhile, moved only slowly into development funding, as Webb shows. Because of its limited funding and its need to raise money on Wall Street, it lent with a heavy bias toward the kind of projects that looked solid, with visible returns. This meant in practice transport and energy, which comprised by far the greater part of its lending to Latin America, which was in any case small. In 1960, the Bank formed a subsidiary, the International Development Association, to lend on softer terms and to meet social needs, though the move into the social sector was so controversial that early discussions could not progress beyond "not excluding" social projects and "preferring to avoid any reference to health and education projects."[49] Nevertheless, new territories for lending were being opened up.

Innovations such as Committees of Experts, even when backed by funding promises, generally had little success in regard to the direct goal of creating national planning machinery, since there was neither sufficient technical capacity nor political backing. If national plans were produced, they bore little relation to political and sometimes economic reality. But the outside push complemented internal progress in human resource development, and in information gathering and awareness of national realities. In these areas lay the real gains from planning. An illuminating example comes from Uruguay, where a planning team used the opportunity provided by the Alliance for Progress in 1963 to develop a ten-year development plan to address long-term issues. Fully aware that the institutional capacity and political backing to respond to their recommendations were lacking,

---

[47] See Oral History Project, contributions of Rodrigo Botero and Abdón Espinosa Valderrama. The latter noted "...we had no trouble reaching understandings with USAID on overall objectives but serious disagreements arose when the Johnson administration began to use USAID as an instrument of U.S. foreign trade."

[48] Webb in Companion Volume 3.

[49] Based on comments of the Staff Loan Committee, quoted in Kapur, Lewis and Webb, 1997, Vol. I: 156.

TABLE 5.2

LATIN AMERICA: CREDITS AUTHORIZED BY SELECTED OFFICIAL SOURCES, 1961-69
(In millions of US$)

Source	1961	1962	1963	1964	1965	1966	1967	1968	1969
Development credit and grants	1,302.4	1,283.4	1,129.3	1,384.5	1,385.0	1,527.7	1,624.0	1,851.9	1,491.5
U.S. government	733.0	605.8	559.9	949.8	625.4	791.6	961.7	842.5	503.4
AID total	375.0	422.3	472.0	708.5	460.2	638.5	483.1	409.2	360.3
EXIMBANK	358.0	183.5	87.9	241.3	165.2	153.1	478.6	433.3	143.1
World Bank	276.5	348.8	307.3	135.4	384.0	342.1	166.5	578.5	385.1
IDB	292.9	328.8	260.1	299.3	375.6	394.0	495.8	430.9	637.1
SPTF	115.6	204.9	47.1	85.9	51.2	na	na	na	na
Food for Peace	102.4	222.8	215.4	263.3	145.6	139.4	141.1	156.3	137.0
Compensatory aid	1,048.2	348.9	352.6	312.1	476.1	467.9	391.4	428.8	219.4
U.S. Treasury	147.0	125.0	60.0	96.3	69.8	12.5	75.0	4.8	na
IMF	456.2	221.3	166.2	142.7	258.0	331.5	316.4	424.0	219.4
EXIMBANK	445.0	2.6	126.4	73.1	148.3	123.9	na	na	na
Total	2,452.0	1,855.1	1,697.3	1,959.9	2,006.7	2,135.0	2,156.5	2,437.0	1,882.0

Source: Dell, 1972.

the team purposefully used the plan to discuss Uruguay's development situation and collect census data and national accounts statistics. Looking back, although the team's specific recommendations on tax, investment, trade and public administration were largely ignored at the time, the plan laid the groundwork for subsequent constitutional and tax reforms and creation of a central bank and planning office.[50]

In addition to intangible results such as those achieved by the Uruguayan team, planning efforts helped channel resources into infrastructure and facilitated foreign borrowing, especially for transport and energy. Possibly the most positive

---

[50] Finch, 1981: 239-41; interview with Enrique Iglesias, Brussels, January 20, 1997.

results of the Alliance-led push for planning lay in the area of investment in human resources. Some came in the form of formal investments, as for instance the creation of ILPES in Chile.[51] Others came informally: the imminent arrival of a group of experts was an excellent discipline. As the Oral History Project reported, "it forced people to do their homework."[52] Encouragement for investment in human resources was complemented by expansion of programs of the various Foundations, such as Ford and Rockefeller, principally through funding of research in national universities.[53, 54]

In other words, where governments had solid reform agendas of their own, the Alliance was important in validating a moderate agenda for change. Where reform was not a serious possibility, however, and where externalities did not occur, the Alliance generated a waste of resources on "paper reforms" that became quite an industry. The Alliance also probably did harm by the gaps in its agenda: it ignored industry and export promotion, and it left stabilization issues to the IMF. It did not ignore inflation, since in practice USAID money was usually linked to the IMF's seal of approval, commonly via a Letter of Intent. But no one's agenda included an analysis of how short-term stabilization might be reconciled with longer term development.

In summary, institutional development was often vigorous, though with obvious limitations. We have mentioned the absence of tax reforms, and three other notable absences are worth noting, for their later significance. First was the lack of an institutional base to support the rapid expansion of state enterprises. Public enterprises grew in many varied forms under different regimes. Systems of control and accountability were typically underdeveloped, and central authority and control and organization were usually absent. This became apparent as the debt crisis erupted and it was found to be impossible to ascertain the indebtedness of some large public enterprises. Less sensational but still indicative were aspects like organizing the centralization of cash balances. A case in point was the National Housing

---

[51] *Instituto Latinoamericano de Planificación Económica*, a UN dependency with its seat in Santiago. Prebisch was its first director.

[52] As stated by Miguel Urrutia in the Colombian archive.

[53] Lerdau and Mesmer, 1997.

[54] Conversations with Juan Antonio Morales and Osvaldo Sunkel were helpful for this analysis.

Fund of Uruguay, which in one year accumulated nearly $10 million of unused reserves, which were left in various bank accounts.[55]

A second institutional shortcoming, common to many more developed countries as well, was lack of control over the financial system.[56] As foreign banking subsidiaries accompanied the expansion of TNCs, it became easy and efficient for TNCs to borrow on local capital markets, given low or negative real interest rates.[57] A third absence was the failure to develop a sense of stability around the rules of the game. To take technology policy as one example among many: "When a change in political regime occurs, not only do the individuals change, but so do the criteria for evaluation…and the relative weight given to industrial development and science and technology…[E]ntrepreneurs must rely on political 'tricks' to circumvent rules and regulations to get what they need or even to get information about current science and technology regulations…"[58] All these omissions would result in serious difficulties in the following decades, as Chapters Seven and Eight reveal.

ECONOMIC INTEGRATION [59]

Latin American integration was by no means a new theme, but interest was renewed with the increase in intraregional trade during the Second World War. Unfortunately, by the time the theme was widely taken up at the end of the 1950s by ECLA, Latin American political leaders, and in due course the United States and the Alliance for Progress, industrialization within national boundaries had gone too far for integration to be a simple matter. By the early 1960s, all large and medium-sized countries had an extensive range of industries, with strong and often excessive vertical integration. It was too late to achieve full rationalization across countries—or at least, to do so would have required negotiating machinery that compensated losers and reconciled conflicting interests, since reallocation would have had to take

---

[55] ECLA, 1971: 55.
[56] ECLA, 1971a: 142.
[57] Chudnovsky, 1974; Thorp and Bertram, 1978.
[58] Adler, 1987: 84.
[59] This section has been adapted from Ffrench-Davis, 1988.

place. This meant commitment to planning and intervention, when by the early 1960s the enthusiasts for integration in policymaking circles were looking to it to bring much-needed competition, not a greater role for government.[60]

A second related problem was that given existing levels of industrialization, less developed countries of the region feared they would lose out. Protection of their interests could have been built in, but again this would have required a different and more complex kind of institutionality, and a role for government. This was not the focus of those principally pushing the scheme.[61]

The three integration initiatives in the 1950s and 1960s were the Central American Common Market (CACM), the Latin American Free Trade Area (LAFTA) and the Andean Pact. The earliest and most successful integration experience was that of the least industrialized group in Latin America, the five countries of Central America, who also formed a more homogenous group in terms of GDP per capita than their southern neighbors.

The formation of the CACM can be traced to the creation by ECLA in 1951 of the Central American Economic Cooperation Committee, which drew up the Multilateral Treaty on Free Trade and Economic Integration, signed in 1958. This was followed by a more ambitious agreement between El Salvador, Guatemala, Honduras and Nicaragua—the General Treaty for Central American Integration, which took effect in 1960 and formed the basis of the Central American Common Market, which Costa Rica joined in 1963. The General Treaty of 1960 agreed on free trade in 95 percent of all goods considered, and called for the removal of remaining tariff barriers by 1966 and an agreement on a common external tariff. The Common Market also included provisions for Central American monetary union. Success on this front, however, was limited to coordination of multilateral payments.

---

[60] For Prebisch, regional integration had the dual purpose of enlarging the market to a viable size and restoring a minimum degree of "healthy" competition within ISI. For example, as early as 1959 he strongly criticized the excessively high tariffs in most countries of the region: "The return to the use of tariffs as a flexible instrument of protection (that is, not simply as an instrument to indiscriminately exclude imports), the lowering of intraregional duties in some cases, and their abolition in others, would do much to restore the spirit of competition, to the great advantage of industrialization." Prebisch, The Latin American Common Market (page 8), cited in Ffrench-Davis, Muñoz and Palma, 1994.

[61] Puyana, 1980.

The CACM achieved important successes during the 1960s, with the share of intra-CACM exports reaching 28 percent of total exports and 96 percent of total manufactured exports in 1970.[62] Since industrialization and integration occurred for the most part simultaneously, vested interests grew as a force in favor of intraregional trade. It was a case of integration-led ISI.

By contrast, intraregional trade actually declined in the rest of Latin America in the 1950s, from 11 percent of the region's trade from 1953-65 to 6 percent in 1961. Efforts to reverse this process culminated in the Treaty of Montevideo in 1960. Signed by seven Latin American countries (despite strong U.S. reservations), the treaty called for creation of a Latin American free trade area within 12 years. LAFTA members were gradually to eliminate tariffs and other trade restrictions in annual rounds of negotiations, working within the general rules regulating economic integration agreements for members of GATT. Considerable progress was made in eliminating trade barriers over the course of the first three annual rounds of negotiations, and by the mid-1960s, intra-LAFTA trade had already regained its postwar high. Following this brief period of success, however, negotiations stalled, as elimination of trade barriers reached the point where it hurt vested interests.[63]

Despite all the problems, some significant gains were made. Intraregional trade increased; exports within Latin America doubled as a share of exports over two decades, allowing for specialization and increased capacity utilization.

Although LAFTA's achievements fell far short of the goals set out in the original Montevideo Treaty, the agreement did in fact contribute significantly to the expansion of intraregional trade. The most outstanding gains were scored in the manufacturing sector, as LAFTA helped some producers secure markets and increase capacity utilization. An important feature of the growth of intra-LAFTA trade was the rapid increase of manufactures—from 10.6 percent of total Latin American trade in 1960 to 46.1 percent in 1980. The growth of manufactured exports to LAFTA partners was particularly strong in Argentina, Brazil and Mexico.[64]

---

[62] Figures from ECLA's International Trade Division.

[63] The original treaty was modified in 1968 with the signing of the Protocol of Caracas (Venezuela having joined LAFTA in 1966). The protocol extended the target for complete trade liberalization to 1980.

[64] Ffrench-Davis, 1988.

At the end of the 1960s, a group of countries attempted to learn from LAFTA's difficulties by establishing the Andean Pact. The Cartagena Agreement setting up the pact was signed in 1969 by Bolivia, Chile, Colombia, Ecuador and Peru, with Venezuela joining the group four years later. The Andean Pact was designed to work within LAFTA, rather than supersede it. In terms of levels of economic development, the Andean countries were relatively homogenous compared to the larger grouping. The multiple of largest-to-smallest country GDP among Andean countries was 19 in 1980, as opposed to nearly 50 among LAFTA members. By negotiating trade and tariff agreements with Argentina, Brazil and Mexico as a single economic unit, Andean countries hoped to make greater progress towards regional integration.

Moreover, with the LAFTA experience behind them, participants in the Cartagena Agreement were able to incorporate institutional arrangements they considered superior to those established under the Treaty of Montevideo. First, provision was made for an executive body (*Junta del Acuerdo de Cartagena - JUNAC*) with substantive powers. Second, the new treaty set out a clear schedule for trade liberalization, including the gradual establishment of common external tariffs. Third, a system was designed to achieve an equitable distribution of benefits, comprising both sectoral programs for industrial development and tariff preferences for the least developed members, Bolivia and Ecuador. Finally, the agreement sought to harmonize economic policies, beginning with rules pertaining to foreign direct investment. Industrial planning was to be facilitated by sectoral programs for industrial development. Under these schemes, the production of selected goods was assigned to member countries with a guarantee that the regional market would be free from internal import restrictions and covered by a common external tariff.

As in LAFTA, however, an initial period of optimism over the Cartagena Agreement was soon overtaken by events. The most significant setback was the 1973 coup in Chile. Chile withdrew completely from the Pact in 1976, and the remaining members never regained the group's early momentum.

LAND REFORM[65]

There were at least six reasons for the enthusiasm with which land reform was brought to the agenda in the early 1960s: growth, income distribution and poverty, inflation, market size, political arguments and external leverage. Various reasons motivated different people in government, ECLA, the Alliance for Progress or outside advisers. The first four reasons are interrelated: redistribution of land was seen as a route to modernization, thus easing, among other things, the inflationary bottleneck of food supplies as urban populations expanded, and as a way to increase the size of the market for industry by its effect on income distribution and poverty.[66] Some looked for a political effect via reducing the influence of landed elites, and many governments responded to the last element: access to Alliance for Progress money was in a broad way tied to evidence of reform efforts, including land reform.

Behind these motives lay a perception of the traditional *hacienda* as inefficient and inegalitarian. Large farms used land in an extensive manner, resulting in low land productivity, and much land remained uncultivated. Monoculture, which was generally adopted by plantations in areas of export agriculture, had deleterious effects on the environment. Extensive land use also limited employment opportunities and contributed to low labor productivity. The relative abundance of agricultural workers and the high degree of land concentration meant that landlords could continue to pay low wages even where labor productivity had increased through investments. It was also held that land concentration hampered adoption of modern technology; landlords could obtain high incomes without intensifying production, given the large amount of land they owned. Land was also considered a useful hedge against price rises in countries with endemic inflation. In addition, ownership of a large landed estate conferred high social status and political power. Thus farming effi-

---

[65] This section has been written in collaboration with Cristóbal Kay.

[66] In fact, the economic logic for radical redistribution to solve the problems of industry was weak. The consumer durable industries were those needing larger markets in the short term in order to achieve economies of scale; they would have been hurt by redistribution, which deprived their best potential customers of income. The actual measures necessary to implement significant redistribution in the short term would have affected investor confidence and therefore growth, as Allende was to find in Chile. And it became empirically obvious in the 1960s and 1970s that fast growth was completely compatible with high and rising inequality, notably in the case of Brazil.

ciency was not always a priority for landlords. Last, but not least, reformers blamed land concentration for the social inequality, marginalization and poor living conditions of the majority of the rural population in Latin America.

This view was given weight and exaggerated by new documentation, principally produced by the *Comité Interamericano de Desarrollo Agropecuario (CIDA)*. Its studies represent the most ambitious collective analysis to date of Latin America's land tenure.[67] The CIDA studies had a major influence on shaping a certain view of the Latin American agrarian question as well as on the design of agrarian reform policies.[68] They showed that Latin America had one of the most unequal agrarian structures in the world. At one extreme were *minifundios* (very small landholdings), and at the other were *latifundios* (very large landholdings) in the form of plantations, *haciendas* and *estancias*. By 1960, *latifundios* constituted roughly five percent of farm units and owned about four-fifths of the land; *minifundios* comprised four-fifths of farm units but had only 5 percent of the land.[69] In the CIDA data, the middle-sized farm sector appeared to be relatively insignificant. Subsequent studies have shown that tenants had a significant degree of control over resources within the estates, and medium-sized farms had access to better quality land and were more capitalized, thereby contributing more to agricultural output than originally estimated. However, despite this evidence of greater heterogeneity, Latin America still had one of the most polarized agrarian systems in the world. Not surprisingly, while labor productivity was much higher on *latifundios* than on *minifundios*, the reverse was the case regarding land productivity. Average production per agricultural worker was about five to ten times higher on *latifundios* than on *minifundios*, while production per hectare of agricultural land was roughly three to five times higher on *minifundios* relative to *latifundios*.[70]

---

[67] CIDA was set up in 1961 by the Organization of American States, the Inter-American Development Bank, the Inter-American Institute of Agricultural Sciences (known today as the Inter-American Institute for Cooperation on Agriculture—IICA), the UN Food and Agricultural Organization, and ECLA. In the mid-1960s, reports on seven countries were published: Argentina (1965), Brazil (1966), Colombia (1966), Chile (1966), Ecuador (1965), Guatemala (1965) and Peru (1966), followed subsequently by two or three other country reports.

[68] An excellent summary of these reports was edited by Barraclough, who, together with Domike, published a seminal article, 1966.

[69] Barraclough, 1973: 16.

[70] Ibid.: 25-27. The data reflects the situation during the 1950s and very early 1960s.

The reform movement met strong opposition. This came, of course, from those whose interests were directly threatened, but also in a more tacit fashion from urban business interests, who were often more closely linked to agricultural interests than reformers realized and unhappy with threats to property rights. The fact that it was relatively easy to design a "paper" reform meant that reforms now abounded, though they varied in nature from the highly collectivized and extensive reform of Cuba through to the paper reforms of countries looking for Alliance money with a minimum of pain. The most far-reaching agrarian reforms were outcomes of social revolutions: Mexico (1917), Bolivia (1952), Cuba (1959), and Nicaragua (1979). However, radical agrarian reforms were also undertaken by elected governments, as in Chile during the Frei (1964-69) and Allende (1970-73) administrations, or even by military regimes, as in Peru during the government of General Velasco Alvarado (1969-75). Less wide-ranging agrarian reforms in terms of the amount of land expropriated and the number of peasant beneficiaries were carried out largely by civilian governments in the remainder of Latin America. A major exception is Argentina, where to date agrarian reform has neither formed part of the political agenda nor been carried out. This is explained in part by Argentina's abundance of land, by the relative importance of family farming and medium-sized capitalist farms, and by the relatively high degree of urbanization. Brazil was a different kind of exception: strong opposition from landlords stalled any significant agrarian reform. Paraguay and Uruguay had colonization programs, but neither country achieved significant agrarian reform.

The scope of agrarian reform in Latin America varied greatly as regards both the amount of land expropriated and the number of beneficiaries. The agrarian reforms in Bolivia and Cuba were the most extensive in terms of land, with about four-fifths of the countries' agricultural land expropriated. In Mexico, Chile, Peru and Nicaragua, almost half the agricultural land was expropriated, while Colombia, Panama, El Salvador and the Dominican Republic expropriated between one-sixth and one-quarter of the total.[71] An even smaller proportion was affected by agrarian reform in Ecuador, Costa Rica, Honduras and Uruguay.[72] In Venezuela, about one-

---

[71] Cardoso and Helwege, 1992: 261.
[72] ECLAC and FAO, 1986: 22.

fifth of the land was affected by agrarian reform, but almost three-quarters of this had previously belonged to state and was largely in areas to be colonized.

Cuba, Bolivia and Mexico had the highest proportion of peasants and rural workers who became beneficiaries of agrarian reform. About three-quarters of agricultural households in Cuba and Bolivia were incorporated into the reformed sector, while in Mexico it was less than half. In Nicaragua, Peru and Venezuela, the proportion of beneficiaries was about one-third, in El Salvador, one-quarter, and in Chile, one-fifth. In Panama, Colombia, Ecuador, Honduras and Costa Rica, on average about 10 percent of agricultural families benefited from reform,[73] while in other countries the proportion was even lower.

The reforms varied greatly. Sometimes property was distributed on an individual basis, but frequently large estates were left undivided and some form of cooperative or collective system introduced. In both cases, the difficulties of the process were profound. Where individual plots were instituted, the key problem was lack of resources. Particularly where reforms were responding to leverage, the most straightforward way to render them meaningless was to allocate no budget to the land reform agency.[74] The task of enabling previously dependent peasants to manage their own plots was tougher, demanding more skilled and motivated extension agents than reformers had allowed for.

As a result of such problems, land frequently reverted to former or new landlords, under a variety of patterns but with the same result. Where the form was cooperative or collective, then to a lack of resources were added the well-known problems of uncertainty and management.[75] Agrarian reform policymakers throughout Latin America greatly underestimated the relative importance of peasant farming, such as sharecropping and labor-service tenancies, within large landed estates. National census data generally failed to record, or to record accurately, the number of peasant tenant enterprises within the *hacienda* system (the "internal peasant economy"). This led them to underestimate the difficulties of organizing collective farming and the pressure beneficiaries would exercise within the collective enter-

[73] Cardoso and Helwege, 1992: 261; Dorner, 1992: 34.

[74] See Hirschman, 1968, for the classic study of how to take evasive action against land reform in Colombia.

[75] Thiesenheusen, 1995.

prise for the expansion of their own family enterprise. The new managers of the collective reformed enterprises, generally appointed by the state, had far less authority over the beneficiaries than landlords had and were unable to prevent the gradual erosion of the collective enterprise from within.

For all its policy prominence in the 1960s, agrarian reform's role in modernization and growth was minor and indirect. "It is ironic that many agrarian reforms in Latin America resulted in the modernization of the *hacienda* system and its transformation into capitalist farms rather than its elimination from below by redistributing *hacienda* land to peasants."[76]

---

[76] Kay, consultancy document for this book; de Janvry, 1981; Kay, 1988.

CHAPTER 6

GROWTH AND EMERGING DISEQUILIBRIA: 1945-73

LATIN AMERICAN ECONOMIC PERFORMANCE during the three decades that followed the Second World War was outstanding. From 1945-73, continental GDP grew at 5.3 percent a year, while output per capita rose at nearly 3 percent. This was unprecedented for Latin America, just as the developed country growth record was the fastest ever. For the first time, the manufacturing sector became the engine of growth, growing at over 6 percent a year and reaching a sectoral peak of 26 percent of GDP in 1973, 8 percentage points more than in 1950. Sectoral behavior is vividly summarized in Figure 6.1, which shows how industry gained at the expense of primary production, as also occurred in most developing areas in the world. Along with growth came labor productivity gains, which translated into higher real wages, and stronger labor unions. Labor productivity increased at an annual rate of over 3 percent, which is not far below the 4.3 percent of the newly industrialized countries or the 4.5 percent of the developed market economies.[1] This reflected capital accumulation: gross investment grew from 16 percent of GDP in 1950 to 19 percent in 1973, reaching a growth rate of 9 percent in the 1960s.[2] Although growth was not particularly stable over time, the variability of growth rates tended to diminish in most countries.

---

[1] Maddison, 1995.
[2] Ffrench-Davis, Muñoz and Palma, 1994: 169.

Photo: Public Health Center, Uruguay, 1960.

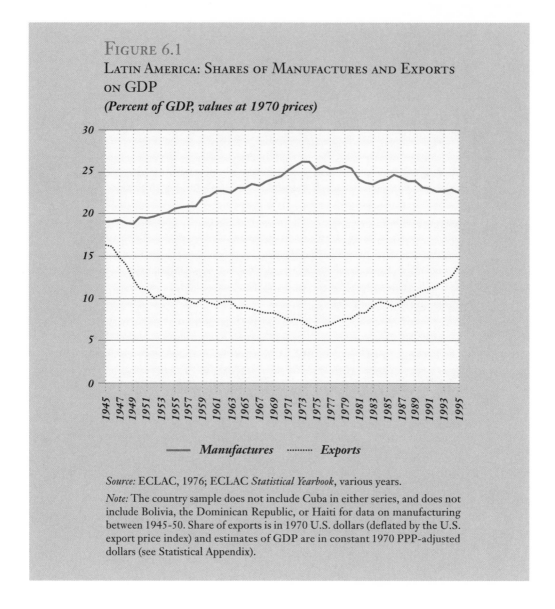

FIGURE 6.1

LATIN AMERICA: SHARES OF MANUFACTURES AND EXPORTS ON GDP

(Percent of GDP, values at 1970 prices)

—— *Manufactures* ········ *Exports*

Source: ECLAC, 1976; ECLAC *Statistical Yearbook*, various years.

Note: The country sample does not include Cuba in either series, and does not include Bolivia, the Dominican Republic, or Haiti for data on manufacturing between 1945-50. Share of exports is in 1970 U.S. dollars (deflated by the U.S. export price index) and estimates of GDP are in constant 1970 PPP-adjusted dollars (see Statistical Appendix).

Agriculture grew also, but less rapidly, reflecting the net outcome of discrimination against agriculture implicit in industrial protection, on the one hand, and on the other the benefits that agroindustry received from technological development.

This expansion was accompanied by growth in state enterprises, which increased their historical role in infrastructure, particularly electric power, while moving increasingly in some countries into industry. Of the countries for which there are data (not including Mexico), the role of public sector enterprises was greatest in Bolivia, where the share of public enterprises in total fixed investment reached 31 percent by 1960 and 39 percent by 1968. Next in terms of importance of public enterprises were Brazil, Argentina, Chile and Venezuela, where state enterprises represented some 15 percent of total investment by the late 1960s. Colombia, Costa Rica, Panama and Peru were around 6 to 10 percent.[3] The testimony of contemporaries is that in the 1960s some state enterprises were still functioning well. Inflation was increasingly making their management difficult, however, by concealing the real state of finances.[4]

Table 6.1 considers variations in the degree of industrialization between countries. Countries that in the 1940s and 1950s industrialized rapidly and whose governments were committed to industrialization included Brazil, Argentina, Mexico, Chile and Uruguay, with a high and rising share of industry in GDP, and Colombia, with a more moderate share but a significant rise. Peru joined this group in the 1960s with an accelerated industrial promotion policy.

Countries where the share was low in the first place and did not rise much include those of Central America, the Caribbean, Paraguay, Bolivia and Ecuador. In all these cases, a combination of relatively small size and reasonable or in some cases good (Ecuador, Peru) export prospects,[5] led to relatively open policies, often with exchange rates pegged to the dollar in countries geographically close to the United States. The 1960s brought an increase in the share of industry, particularly in Central America, where economic integration took off, and in the Caribbean under "industrialization by invitation," as described below. Venezuela falls between the two groups, with a low level of industry and strong export performance, but a considerable rise in the share of industry in nonoil GDP, from a low base.

The immediate driving force in this process was import substitution. ECLA estimated a 36 percent increase in industrial output attributable to import substitution for Argentina, Brazil, Chile, Colombia and Mexico between 1929 and 1960.

---

[3] ECLA, 1971: 6-7.

[4] Interviews with Ricardo Ffrench-Davis, October 1996, Santiago, and Enrique Iglesias, January 1997, Brussels.

[5] Peru enjoyed a mining boom in the 1950s, and Ecuador experienced a banana boom from 1948-65. Venezuela, of course, was benefiting (if that is the right word) from oil.

TABLE 6.1
SHARE OF MANUFACTURING IN GDP (1970 PRICES)
(In percent)

	Argentina	Brazil	Chile	Uruguay	Mexico	Peru	Colombia	Paraguay	Ecuador	Venezuela[1]	Bolivia
1940	22.6	15.2	19.7	17.5	16.6	na	9.1	16.0	16.9	7.8	na
1945	24.7	17.3	22.1	18.2	18.8	na	10.7	na	18.2	7.2	na
1950	23.8	20.8	23.3	20.3	18.6	14.1	13.1	15.9	17.1	6.3	12.3
1960	26.7	26.5	25.5	23.9	19.5	16.9	16.2	15.1	15.5	11.3	11.3
1970	30.6	28.3	28.0	24.2	23.3	20.7	17.5	17.3	17.6	13.7	12.8

	Nicaragua	El Salvador	Dominican Republic	Panama	Costa Rica	Guatemala	Honduras	Haiti
1940	na	na	na	na	na	na	6.8	na
1945	11.4	11.3	na	6.4	11.3	na	7.4	na
1950	10.8	12.9	12.4	8.2	11.6	11.1	9.1	8.2
1960	13.0	13.9	14.6	11.8	12.5	11.9	15.3	8.8
1970	19.2	17.6	16.7	15.8	15.1	14.6	14.0	9.8

Note: Figures are three-year averages (circa). Ranking according to 1970 manufacturing share in GDP figures.
[1] Venezuela: manufacturing without refining/nonoil GDP.
Sources: ECLA, 1978, except for Baptista, 1997, for Venezuela; Cortés Conde, 1984, for Argentina, 1900-35; and Bulmer-Thomas, 1994, for Honduras.

Excluding Brazil, the figure rises to 43 percent.[6] As ECLA recognizes, this is a minimum estimate, and in fact a significant underestimate, since it is based on the difference between what total imports actually were in 1960 and what they would have been if the relationship between GDP and imports had remained constant. Since imports in 1960 included new imports of intermediate and even capital goods necessary to the substitution process, the actual role of import substitution was considerably greater.[7]

The fall in imports of consumer goods was itself an indicator of the excessive diversification mentioned earlier. Firms both diversified horizontally and integrated vertically beyond the levels typical of more developed industrial structures. Horizontal diversification reflected the relatively undiscriminating tariff policy typically

---

[6] ECLA, 1966: 26-27.

[7] See Fishlow, 1972, for a more accurate measure for the case of Brazil.

applied.[8] Vertical integration reflected lack of domestic suppliers and uncertainty as to the regular supply of foreign exchange for importing.[9]

By the 1960s, the decline in the import coefficient was slowing in the more industrialized countries, and there were concerns over market size, which increased interest in integration. However, what was *not* slowing down was the rate of the sectoral increase in productivity, though in the early 1960s a slowdown in GDP growth in Argentina and Brazil had such an effect on the continental average that it had contemporary analysts worried.[10] Figure 6.2 for manufacturing and Appendix IV for the whole economy illustrate the reality that business was experiencing. Output per head[11] grew during the whole period in the countries we have been able to document, corresponding to the transformation in business organization and sophistication as well as to increased capital intensity. More strikingly, the figure shows that of the six countries covered, three actually experienced a spurt in the rate of growth of output per person in the 1960s. The largest country, Brazil, appears logically enough to have experienced such a discontinuity earlier, during the 1930s. Venezuela, pushing industrialization to absorb oil money, saw a slight weakening of productivity growth in the 1960s.[12,13]

Behind the growth in productivity were significant changes in organization and technology, which built on and reinforced the institutional evolution described in the preceding chapter. Public enterprises, particularly in strategic sectors, promoted by a number of military and nationalist-minded governments, led in research and deve-

---

[8] The usual comparison with Australia comes into play again here. See Kelly, 1965.

[9] This appears to have counterbalanced Hirschman's "stages" problem. Hirschman's classic and insightful article on the political economy of import substitution in Latin America was the first to conceptualize the process. He saw the dependence of consumer goods producers on imported inputs as posing a severe threat to the dynamics of import-substitution industrialization. These industries require that tariff structures evolve, since producers would resist local production because they would regard it as expensive and of unreliable quality. Hirschman, 1968.

[10] This was a normal cyclical aspect of a process led by import substitution. See Fishlow, 1972: 349.

[11] We explained in Chapter Two that since we have used economically active population, not numbers actually employed, we are not presenting a measure of productivity in the strict sense.

[12] Colombia appears to show an unchanged rate of progress, but this requires more work before a conclusion can be drawn.

[13] We have not cited total factor productivity data here, given the difficulty of the assumptions made by the methodology, but we can record that the two principal sources, Elias, 1992, and Hofman, 1997, show increases between their different subperiods over these years. See Solimano, 1996.

FIGURE 6.2
VALUE ADDED PER ECONOMICALLY ACTIVE PERSON IN MANUFACTURING
(In thousands of 1970 $PPP, log scale)

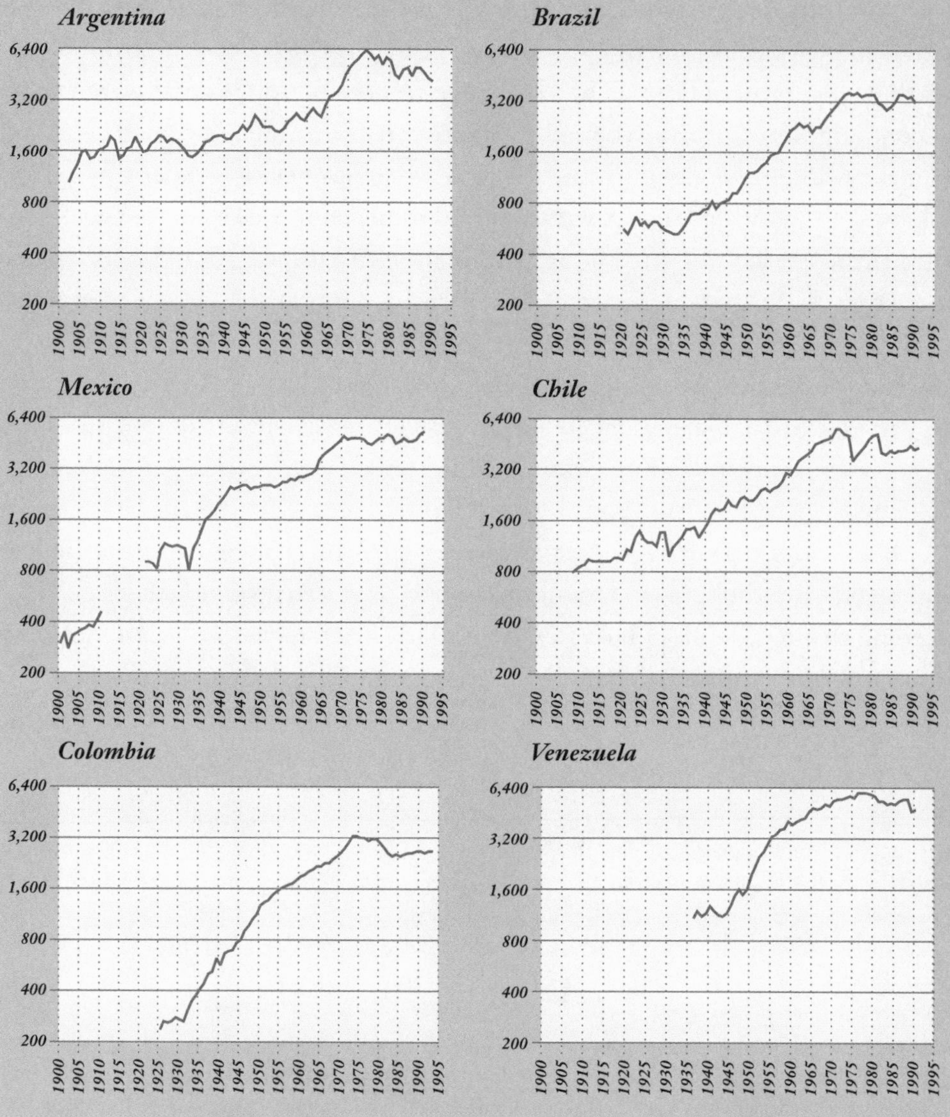

Argentina

Brazil

Mexico

Chile

Colombia

Venezuela

Source: Statistical Appendix.

lopment (R&D). The creation of technical know-how occurred in "...large R&D laboratories inside state enterprises, such as YPF and YCF in Argentina, Petrobrás in Brazil and Pemex in Mexico."[14] Around them grew a wide network of family and often immigrant-owned SMEs, which typically began by repairing and copying locally-available machines or product designs that were one or even two decades behind the world's technology frontier. Such firms were usually some 10 percent of the size of comparable facilities in more developed societies, and more immature in plant layout and the organization of production. They tended to be highly vertically integrated—more so than their developed country counterparts—since local suppliers did not exist. They usually carried a wide product mix coupled with small production runs. All this affected both static and dynamic efficiency, as it induced an excessive diversification of engineering activities within the plant and a learning process that did not benefit from specialization. Externalities and synergies were therefore less than they might have been. As Katz and Kosacoff conclude, in spite of their fragile beginning, many firms managed to proceed rapidly along their learning curve.[15] (Not all did, however. Box 6.1 tells the story of an immigrant entrepreneur forced into retirement by technical progress and the difficulties of coping with inflation.)

By the 1960s, problem solving and experience on the job brought many firms to the point where they began to think of export markets, both as a countercyclical strategy and in response to government incentives that by then were serious in all the five leading industrializers. Such firms began to export and compete despite the absence of the East Asian model, under which at this date an "exporting vocation" was being created by fierce authoritarian pressure and carefully tailored incentives.

With the change in model and consolidation of pro-foreign capital legislation in the mid-1950s, multinational subsidiaries arrived in large numbers. This provoked important changes in the organization of firms, bringing new product designs, new process technology and new forms of organization. The foreign firms displaced or absorbed many of the largest domestic firms, particularly in the consumer durable sector, in Argentina, Brazil and Mexico (Box 6.2).

---

[14] See Katz and Kosacoff in Companion Volume 3. The section that follows is taken from this source. The beginning of serious R&D varied. In Mexico, Pemex did not establish an R&D laboratory until the mid-1960s.
[15] Micro studies supporting this description are Katz, 1974, 1986 and 1987; Kosacoff, 1993; Lall, 1992; Teitel, 1984; Domínguez and Brown, 1995.

Box 6.1

The Immigrant Entrepreneur: Samuel

Samuel came to Argentina from Poland at the age of 18 in 1930. He came as many did, fleeing the threat of persecution in Europe. He was helped on his long overland journey through Brazil and the north of Argentina by a network of already-established family and friends. He joined the family wood business in Misiones and in 1938 was joined by his childhood sweetheart, getting married, as they had to, in the *"Hotel de inmigrantes"* at the port before his bride could legally enter the country.

They followed the family pattern: as their children reached the age when they had to be educated, the family moved to Buenos Aires to make it possible. And achieve education they did: all four completed their university education and postgraduate work, and they (and later the 10 grandchildren) entered a range of professional careers, from university professor to computer expert. Samuel, meanwhile, ran his wood business and built up a modest but comfortable middle-class life. In the 1940s, the family bought one of the first refrigerators made in the country. They also bought a sewing machine and in the 1960s a television—an enormous machine which to the amusement of the grandchildren was still functioning at the time of the interview. A telephone could not be legally obtained—the waiting list was infinite—but one was secured through a clandestine connection.

Despite these gains, Samuel's business gradually began to decline, primarily due to inflation and technical progress. Inflation ruined the informal credit system Samuel depended on, and the economic challenges it presented demanded financial skills he did not possess. It also ruined the pension fund to which he had assiduously contributed for many years. Technical progress replaced wood with plastic and metals—even for coffins, which Samuel had thought were his guaranteed source of income. He had to be gently but forcibly retired by his daughters, who closed down the business and supported him financially, to his eternal chagrin. In his retirement, Samuel's pride in his children's success battled with his resentment at having to depend on them.

Source: Interview with Samuel by Elizabeth Jelin.

The industrialization process of these decades, then, cannot be seen in the black and white terms in which it has often been presented. Its evolution depended heavily on factors of political economy, as the difference between the Frondizi and Kubitschek experiences showed (see Chapter 5). And it was evolving, even from its earliest days, on the basis of productivity growth and learning-by-doing. The quantitative evidence is considered in the next section. The anti-export bias and inefficiency were being fiercely criticized from the early 1950s, notably by Prebisch himself. Its distortions continued, but despite them there were new export successes.

The preceding account has emphasized supply-side responses, which built on the institutional developments described in Chapter Five. This emphasis contrasts with the approach of much of the existing literature on this period, which by focusing on the mechanism of import substitution has effectively looked primarily at the demand side. Where import substitution is the driving force of industrialization, production for an existing market behind tariff protection is like a free good, allowing very rapid growth, ahead of the rate of growth of the market. This was indeed an important mechanism stimulating growth in this period. But considering the industrialization of this period principally as import substitution has limited the analysis too heavily to the demand side.[16] The bias in the literature has not been helpful to the process of refining and maturing policies on a broad front, based on an understanding of the real forces at work increasing or restraining productivity growth.[17]

EMERGING DISEQUILIBRIA

The positive growth performance of these decades was, however, accompanied by the gradual emergence of disequilibria. Balance of payments and fiscal gaps eventually contributed to a weakening of growth in some countries, and turned the slowing down of import substitution into a more serious constraint.

---

[16] Fishlow, 1972: 54-55.

[17] Note that this was not an ECLA bias. ECLA's writing emphasized technology and productivity growth, and from 1962 the organization fiercely criticized policy for its supply-side effects. See Prebisch, 1962. The subsequent work by Fajnzylber, 1990 took up and developed the emphasis.

Box 6.2

A Local Firm Loses Out

The firm of Di Tella y Cia was established in 1910 to manufacture equipment for bakeries. By the 1950s, it was the most important metal goods producer in Latin America. Di Tella decided to enter the car market in the late 1950s, producing a design licensed by the British Motor Corporation. To produce some 12,000 cars a year, it employed nearly 3,500 people, with average labor productivity that was about one-third of the world's best practice at that time. Not having much experience in automobile production, the firm ran into major difficulties with production planning and organization, as well as in its access to working capital. It also faced large diseconomies of scale as a result of the small size of its plant and the high degree of vertical integration of its overall operation. The prevailing policy regime induced the domestic fabrication of parts and components instead of encouraging exports, as would have been the case had this been one of the newly-industrialized countries of East Asia. Such a policy regime was intended to capitalize on the accumulated learning experience of local autopart producers over the previous two decades.

While domestic demand expanded rapidly, Di Tella did quite well, benefiting from a seller's market. The 1962 recession plus entry into the market by Ford and GM—with clearly superior organizational, financial and engineering know-how—marked the end of Di Tella's success. The firm tried to enter into partnership with Kaiser Argentina, by then clearly the market leader, but this also failed. Kaiser ended up purchasing Di Tella's facilities and closing them down in 1968, taking a strong monopolistic stand in the domestic car market.

Source: Material supplied by Bernardo Kosacoff.

Exports of primary goods did not keep up with the growth of the economies, as Figure 6.1 shows, and grew less rapidly than world demand for such products. This reflected the discrimination implicit in protectionist policies, which made exporting less profitable than it would have been without protection. (This is because the restriction of demand for imports allowed the exchange rate to be more overvalued than it would have been without tariffs and restrictions, and because exporting sectors were made to buy high-cost domestic inputs.)

Exports of manufactures responded to the policy shifts of the 1960s; the rate of growth of such exports rose from 3.5 percent a year in the 1950s to 11.3 percent from 1960 to 1973, and as a proportion of exports they rose from 9 percent in 1952-53 to 12 percent in 1960 and 15 percent in 1970.[18] But as they rose they aggravated protectionist pressure in the developed countries, so the outlook on the external front as the 1960s ended was not promising. Imports remained high and rising, as agriculture for the domestic market did not keep pace with the rising demand for food that came with urbanization, and industry's need for imports was transformed rather than reduced. The high percentage of inputs and capital goods created a rigid structure of imports, with little room for economies in the face of crisis without damaging growth, and increased dependence on foreign investment for its financing of capital goods as well as for technology.

On the fiscal side, public investment was rising, representing between a third and a half of total capital formation. The public enterprises included in this total were rarely self-financing. A 1964 study of iron and steel, for instance, found that enterprises financed only 5 percent of their investment from internal sources.[19] In 1969, Brazil's public enterprises were on average in deficit.[20] Expenditure as a percent of GDP rose more rapidly than investment for three of the five largest countries, while fiscal income rose impressively only in Brazil. The public sector borrowing requirement rose in all five countries, and was on average for all Latin America 8.5 percent of GDP by 1970 (Table 6.2). Although still modest compared with what was to come, average inflation was over 20 percent a year in this period in all the larger countries except Mexico.[21]

---

[18] Movarec, 1982.

[19] ECLA, 1971: 14-15

[20] Ibid.

[21] See Statistical Appendix Table V.I.

TABLE 6.2
CENTRAL GOVERNMENT REVENUE AND EXPENDITURE
(Percent of GDP)

	Total government expenditure			Tax revenue			Tax revenue minus total government expenditure		
	1950	1960	1970	1950	1960	1970	1950	1960	1970
Argentina	22.5	21.4	25.2	17.0	14.2	15.0	-5.5	-7.2	-10.2
Brazil	17.5	25.3	33.3	16.0	20.1	27.0	-1.5	-5.2	-6.3
Chile	17.0	29.3	34.6	16.7	16.5	21.8	-0.3	-12.8	-12.8
Colombia	13.4	11.2	17.3	12.0	10.4	13.4	-1.4	-0.8	-5.6
Mexico	12.6	10.7	13.5	7.5	7.1	7.9	-5.1	-3.6	-5.6
Peru	13.9	14.6	21.5	14.0	14.9	18.9	0.1	0.3	-2.6
Latin America	na	20.7	25.7	na	14.4	17.2	na	-6.3	-8.5

Source: FitzGerald, 1978.

These disequilibria represented serious incipient problems. In the short term they signified an urgent need to stabilize the economy. More than the imperative of inflation, it was the balance of payments gap that took countries to the IMF, for lack of an alternative source of credit. This exposed them to the policy conditionality of the IMF. The practice of attaching economic policy conditions to the provision of Fund resources was gradually developed during the 1950s, mainly using Latin American economies as the testing ground for these techniques.[22]

The role of the Fund through the 1950s and 1960s was controversial, exacerbated by the fact that it would sometimes suit Ministries of the Economy engaged in internal battles to blame the Fund for insisting on unpalatable measures. But apart from such important political economy considerations, the most serious problem was that the whole pattern of development of these years made economies resistant to abrupt, orthodox stabilization. Yet no one had an alternative set of policies.

---

[22] The first incident of conditionality concerned Chile in 1947. Brazil in 1949 withdrew a request for credit because it was still not clear what conditions the Fund was entitled to demand. In 1952, the principles governing standby arrangements were defined (Horsefield and DeVries, 1969: 19).

The typical Fund-backed stabilization program of the 1950s and 1960s was based on an analysis that attributed inflation to excess demand, mediated through the budget deficit, rising money supply and a lax credit policy. The Fund's policies of this period were more extreme than they would be later. They required countries to eliminate both internal and external imbalances rapidly, usually in the space of a year, and recommended policies that tended to produce recession and perverse effects on price levels. This partly accounts for the relatively poorer growth performance of the countries with the more serious problems: Argentina, Uruguay and Chile. The underlying philosophy behind the programs was a belief in the power of the price system once it was restored to health, and skepticism as to the role of government. This philosophy led to advocacy of expenditure cuts (rather than tax increases) and to relative price adjustments to restore a dynamic economic system. The cuts were assumed to fall on consumption rather than investment. According to this theory, the temporary unemployment and "shake out" of prices could be expected to be brief. A crucial relative price adjustment was the exchange rate, and many of the clashes between the Fund and national governments occurred because of the IMF's insistence on devaluation. Wage and salary restraint was always a delicate issue, advocated behind the scenes, in particular for its role in cutting public expenditure, 80 percent of which was typically wages.

These programs aggravated inflation and generated social tensions that often led to their abandonment. The characteristics of semi-industrialized economies such as the larger Latin American countries made such measures particularly prone to resistance. The measures relied on relative price and income effects, but the relative price effects were weak. The high import content of industrial production and its concentrated nature led to sharp cost increases with devaluation, while traditional exports responded poorly in the short term. The balance of payments effect turned almost entirely on the income effect of recession on imports (though food exporters could increase export supply by cutting internal demand, but this still hit a market problem). Internally, as demand decreased and costs rose, various perverse effects operated. Fiscal revenue fell as sales and import taxes declined with the level of activity and falling imports. Costs rose further as interest rates rose, particularly as firms resorted to informal credit, and as the level of use of capacity in plants fell. The budget deficit did not decrease as planned. So further cuts in expenditure became necessary. Difficulties of management made fiscal discipline hard to secure, since central government control over spending of the public sector enterprises or even central government ministries was often weak, and ministers would quickly learn how to defend "their" budgets in the face of central cuts.[23] Further efforts at cuts increasingly affected investment, not consumption, so worsening long-run problems.

The exceptions to this gloomy scenario occurred when external conditions recovered simultaneously with the program. This was the case with Peru's stabilization in 1959, for instance, when long-run investments in copper plus a boom in fishmeal exports came on stream in the nick of time. The most interesting exception of a less orthodox kind was the program implemented in Colombia by Carlos Lleras Restrepo in 1967, involving a politically necessary and much dramatized break with the Fund, and a successful reduction of inflation with continued growth in a context of strong leadership and a broader program of institutional innovation.[24]

EMPLOYMENT, EQUITY AND WELFARE

A third emerging disequilibrium—that between formal sector jobs and the expansion of the labor force—takes us to our next topic. We have indicated that population, and above all the *urban* population, was growing very strongly from 1945-70. While industrial expansion created jobs, it also destroyed them by taking the market of artisan industry. Expansion increasingly was based on imported technology with rising capital intensity. The inevitable result[25] was the beginning of a trend that would later become far more extreme: the emergence of urban informal sectors. On average, the urban informal sector increased as a percentage of the economically active population by one-third between 1950 and 1970, according to the calculations of PREALC.[26]

---

[23] Angell and Thorp, 1986.

[24] Thorp, 1991. This experience was actually a clue to the later more extensive successes in controlling inflation, as we shall see in the next chapter, though this can only be recognized now.

[25] Inevitable in the sense that the poor cannot afford to be unemployed, and have to find ways to create work as a survival strategy.

[26] PREALC, 1982. PREALC is the ILO's office for Latin America, at that time based in Santiago. The calculation is based on census classifications and counts as "formal" wage and salary earners, proprietors and those self-employed with technical or professional qualifications. Domestic servants are tabulated separately.

TABLE 6.3

SHARE OF URBAN INFORMAL SECTOR IN THE ECONOMICALLY ACTIVE POPULATION, 1950 VS. 1970

(In percent)

	1950	1970	% change
Argentina	9.5	9.5	0.0
Bolivia	10.5	14.5	+38.1
Brazil	6.9	9.3	+34.8
Chile	13.8	11.5	-16.7
Colombia	8.5	11.5	+35.3
Costa Rica	6.3	7.3	+15.9
Dominican Republic	4.9	11.5	+106.1
Ecuador	7.7	13.7	+77.9
El Salvador	7.5	9.2	+22.7
Guatemala	11.0	12.9	+17.3
Honduras	4.5	9.8	+117.8
Mexico	9.7	14.5	+49.5
Nicaragua	6.5	12.6	+93.8
Panama	6.3	10.4	+65.1
Peru	9.8	17.0	+73.5
Uruguay	9.0	11.1	+23.3
Venezuela	11.4	16.0	+40.4
Latin America	8.7	11.5	+32.2

Source: PREALC, 1982.

The country experience is shown in Table 6.3: Peru and Ecuador stand out as extreme cases. With domestic service, these two sectors generally formed by 1970 nearly one-third of urban employment. The country variations in labor market structure by 1970 are shown in Table 6.4. Open urban unemployment was between 4 and 13 percent of the urban economically active labor force in the same year.[27]

---

[27] PREALC, 1982: 99. Unemployment is excluded from Table 6.4, since PREALC specifically warns against cross-country comparisons, given variations in census definitions.

TABLE 6.4
LABOR MARKET STRUCTURE IN 1970
(In percent)

	Urban formal	Modern agriculture and mining	Formal sector	Informal sector	Domestic service	Traditional agriculture
Peru	29.8	11.8	41.6	17.0	3.7	37.7
Venezuela	48.9	8.8	57.7	16.0	6.4	19.9
Mexico	33.9	23.0	56.9	14.5	3.7	24.9
Bolivia	15.4	11.5	26.9	14.5	5.1	53.5
Ecuador	17.2	17.9	35.1	13.7	10.0	41.2
Guatemala	22.5	23.2	45.7	12.9	4.4	37.0
Nicaragua	26.8	26.5	53.3	12.6	8.1	26.0
Colombia	38.7	21.3	60.0	11.5	6.2	22.3
Chile	53.1	20.9	74.0	11.5	5.2	9.3
Dominican Rep.	30.1	17.8	47.9	11.5	4.0	36.6
Uruguay	64.2	12.1	76.3	11.1	5.7	6.9
Panama	43.8	8.7	52.5	10.0	5.4	31.7
Honduras	21.8	24.1	45.9	9.8	4.0	40.3
Argentina	66.0	11.7	77.7	9.5	6.1	6.7
Brazil	38.6	13.1	51.7	9.3	5.6	33.4
El Salvador	25.4	30.0	55.4	9.2	7.4	28.0
Costa Rica	44.1	24.4	68.5	7.3	5.6	18.6

Note: Countries ranked by size of informal sector.
Source: PREALC, 1982.

At the same time as the increase in informality, formal sector wages rose.[28] We have no direct information on informal earnings, but it seems reasonable to assume they rose little if at all, given the increase in labor supply. With limited information on income distribution, we can only surmise that the tendency was adverse. Chapter Three described how inequality characterized the export economy model, particularly where labor needs constrained growth. This was perverse, since relative scarcity would suggest that relative returns to that factor would rise. Instead, institutions were developed to expand access to cheap labor, keep it cheap,

---

[28] Seven of the eight countries studied by Mikkelsen and Paldam, 1987, show an increase in real wages between 1948-70. The exception is Uruguay, for which the data are incomplete.

and exert nonmarket control over it. Once labor began to be abundant, as it was by the post-World War Two period, institutions to control labor were well established and the inequity of asset holding was a fact, especially in relation to land and water. The power of rural elites was thoroughly consolidated, especially as they were developing urban bases as well. It would have required strong forces indeed to change such institutions. In fact, far from challenging the structure of demand, inward-looking industrialization simply responded to the structure of demand emanating from such a social system, supplying urban demand for consumer durables and other goods and producing with relative capital intensity, which in turn reinforced inequality.

A graphic illustration of this institutional embeddedness is given in Box 6.3. People like Maria, who was mired in poverty and moved from sharecropping to labor gangs, understood all too well the core of the inequity they faced in Brazil: access to land. Her words reflect the tough resistance of the system to change: "[We] are like stray dogs."

The period saw some redistribution of land, though notably not in Brazil. But even where there was redistribution, the benefits for income distribution were not great.[29] With the notable exceptions of Cuba, Mexico and to some extent Bolivia, the poorest were typically excluded from the benefits of land reform. While standards of living usually improved for the direct beneficiaries of agrarian reform, beneficiaries were not generally the poorest of rural society. For example, the agrarian reforms rarely helped the *minifundistas*, seasonal wage laborers, or the *comuneros*, the members of the indigenous communities that accounted for the largest share of the rural poor and, particularly, the rural destitute. In Peru, it is estimated that Velasco's agrarian reform redistributed only 1 to 2 percent of national income through land transfers to about a third of peasant families.[30] Sugar workers on the coast, already the best paid rural workers, benefited most, while *comuneros* benefited least.[31]

Women were ignored in land reform legislation, which failed to include them explicitly as beneficiaries, to give them land titles, or to incorporate them into key administrative and decisionmaking processes in the cooperatives, state farms and

---

[29] These next two paragraphs are drawn from a consultancy report for this book by Cristóbel Kay.

[30] Figueroa, 1977: 60.

[31] Kay, 1983: 231-32

Box 6.3

The Landless Worker

Maria J. is a middle-aged black woman from Jaguariúna, near Campinas in Brazil. A former sharecropper, now a coffee worker, she became part of a labor gang once the *colonato*, or sharecropping system, ended. At the time she told her story in the early 1970s, she was living with her family in a comparatively well-equipped house of four rooms and a kitchen, which they owned, though still very poor. She had bought a refrigerator on hire purchase but usually kept only water in it. Maria was illiterate but particularly articulate, feared by the labor contractors for her militant defense of her rights. She felt that her neighbors were envious of her relative well-being, and relationships were often tense.

"I was born on the *fazenda* Estiva; my parents were *colonos*…When it was time to get married I bought my trousseau myself with what I earned. I worked three days and traded three days, bought old iron, chickens, and sold them. We were nine at home and the income was just not enough. I would knit little woolen shoes and sell them. To the poorest I would sell cheaper, and to those who I felt could afford it I would sell higher. Once I married, we stayed on the *fazenda* Santa Cruz in Amparo; we were *colonos* for four years. Later we moved to the *fazenda* Estiva as *colonos* for another six years…

"We have been living in the Roseira for seven years now. We were *colonos* for 22 years; we would move from one *fazenda* to another to improve our living conditions, but then the *patrão* would sell the *fazenda*…Little by little we saved some money and bought this little house…

"Those of us in the truck labor gangs are like stray dogs…But even so, before things were quite a bit worse; at least now we have a wage, everybody works…[Yet,] in the old days, everybody had a plot of land; now, the *fazendeiros* don't allow the use of a plot."

Source: Stolcke, 1988, and material supplied by the author.

other organizations emanating from the reform process. Even in Cuba, women made up only one-quarter of production cooperative members and were even fewer on state farms.[32] In Mexico, women comprised 15 percent of *ejido* members, and in Nicaragua and Peru, they made up only 6 and 5 percent of cooperative members, respectively. Women were excluded as beneficiaries due to legal, structural and ideological factors. The stipulation that only one household member could become an official beneficiary, i.e., a member of the cooperative or beneficiary of a land title, tended to discriminate against women, given the assumption that men were head of the household.[33] The agrarian reform in Chile reinforced the role of men as breadwinners and gave only limited opportunities for women to participate in running the reformed sector, despite some legislation to the contrary during the Allende government.[34]

In urban areas, women's participation in the labor force increased as urbanization and industrialization proceeded, but only within certain job categories. This was the result of several factors: job stereotyping, the fact that only certain jobs could be combined with family care, and women's relative lack of education. Women earned less than men within given occupations, and their employment tended to be in less well remunerated occupations. This evolving segmentation of the labor market became increasingly important as another tendency became apparent: an increase in female-headed households. Such households tended to be poorer than male-headed households, and more of the family members worked. These particularly vulnerable households would suffer disproportionately in the next period as recession hit.

Inequality was compounded, not surprisingly, by the nature of public policy. This had various aspects. First, those designing the admirable early investment in social security in the five pioneering countries noted in Chapter Two could never have anticipated this evolution of the labor market. By the 1960s, coverage of the informal sector was still extremely limited;[35] as informality grew, this became more serious. Secondly, health and education spending, though generally rising, was heavily

---

[32] Deere, 1987: 171.

[33] Deere, 1985.

[34] Tinsman, 1996.

[35] Mesa-Lago, 1994: 20.

biased towards urban provision. The bias in health care was aggravated by its curative character. The early public health interventions of the 1920s and 1930s, designed to control epidemics, by their very nature needed to reach the whole population in order to make vaccination campaigns effective. The next stage, unfortunately for equity, had no such logic, and facilities were biased towards the better off and the urban population. Money was spent on large hospitals in major urban centers, rather than on primary health schemes. Only Cuba took a different route and saw marked benefits in health indicators.[36]

Expenditure on the social sector also suffered various forms of pressure or crowding out. One was from the multilateral agencies. The World Bank, in particular, took a decision to fund preferentially "productive" investment, principally in physical infrastructure, a decision only modified in the 1970s.[37] Another pressure arose from competing needs such as defense. Table 6.5 shows central government expenditure by use. Costa Rica, having abolished its army in 1948, was able to spend "disproportionately" on the social sector.

National Experiences

The postwar decades saw extremely disparate country experiences and practices, within a common framework of received wisdom on development strategies, internal demographic pressures and external possibilities and threats. The disparate performances can be divided into four categories. First, there were countries that industrialized strongly on an inward-looking pattern, some moving in a significant way to modify that pattern by the 1960s, though in most cases there were serious incipient problems. This group includes Chile, Brazil, Colombia, Argentina, Mexico and Uruguay. Second were the countries that, either because of small size or their particular fortune in the commodity lottery, remained with the primary product exporting sector as the leading force, but nevertheless attempted inward-looking policies, particularly by the 1960s.

---

[36] See Statistical Appendix. Costa Rica in the 1960s launched a major effort for safe drinking water and provision of medical services, and reduced the differential in infant mortality, which in the 1960s was 4.5 times higher for the working class than for the more privileged. Merrick, 1994.

[37] See Webb in Companion Volume 3.

TABLE 6.5

CENTRAL GOVERNMENT EXPENDITURE ON DEFENSE AND THE SOCIAL SECTOR IN THE 1950S

(Percent of total)

	Argentina	Brazil	Chile	Costa Rica	Mexico
1950					
Defense	30.2	28.3	17.6	6.1	12.9
Social Sector	14.0	11.0	22.8	23.8	16.3
Education	8.6	na	14.4	9.4	11.4
Health	3.0	na	8.4	4.0	4.9
Social Security	2.4	na	8.4	10.4	4.9
1958					
Defense	21.1	27.6	21.9	3.8	11.3
Social Sector	19.0	10.7	26.8	24.2	26.0
Education	14.3	na	15.7	19.6	14.7
Health	3.2	na	11.1	2.3	11.3
Social Security	1.5	na	11.1	23.6	11.3

Source: United Nations, 1951: Table 166; Wilkie, 1968: Table 16.

These were Venezuela, Ecuador, Peru, Bolivia, Paraguay and the countries of Central America. Third, Cuba has to be considered separately, as the only case of a fully centrally planned economy. And fourth, the remaining islands of the Caribbean developed their own version of industrialization.[38]

Strong Industrializers

Chile and Colombia were the most serious examples of early modification of inward-looking industrialization, while Chile, as we have seen, was unusually advanced in its level of industrialization. The dominance of foreign capital in Chilean copper, to the exclusion of local groups, and the dominance of copper in Chile's exports,

---

[38] This section draws extensively from the case studies to be published as Companion Volume 3 and the associated workshop debates summarized in the introduction to that volume. Norman Girvan provided a consultancy paper on the Caribbean.

forced local elite groups at a relatively early date to look elsewhere—particularly to industry—for profit opportunities. The effect of buoyant copper revenues on the exchange rate was such that other tradables could survive only by means of fairly strong state action. Chile had developed mechanisms of intervention in favor of industry in the 1920s and 1930s to a degree unusual for a country its size,[39] culminating in the creation of CORFO. The postwar period saw considerable industrial growth, productivity increases and sustained institutional development.[40] Although the distortions were large and the degree of inwardness exaggerated, this did not prevent industry from growing at over 5 percent a year over three decades. The cumulative benefits for the long run were substantial, as would be demonstrated in the 1980s and 1990s. The success of Chilean nontraditional exports in those years came from solid beginnings in the 1960s in the forestry, fishing, mining and engineering sectors.

However, a viable pattern of accumulation did not result. Chilean investment and savings were low; the overall growth of GDP was 25 percent below the Latin American average. The reasons appear to lie deeper than the distortions of inward-looking development itself, and are to be found in the political and social structure.[41] A striking early analysis was that of Kaldor, who focused on income distribution and the patterns of luxury consumption of Chile's upper classes.[42] However, an insight from other Kaldorean writings is more helpful: if the willingness to invest is there, savings can usually be mobilized, given the extent to which, in underdeveloped capital markets, savers and investors are the same people. In Chile, the willingness to invest was lacking because successive political leaders were unable to overcome distrust of government by business leaders during the 1920s and 1930s. The governments were distrusted for their leftist tendencies, despite the fact that they initiated significant institutional development that helped build the productive sector. Overlaid on these elements of mistrust came the distortions of postwar policies, conflict with the mining companies over tax shares,[43]

---

[39] Muñoz, 1986: 101; Ortega, et al., 1989: 33-64.

[40] See Ffrench-Davis, et al. in Companion Volume 3.

[41] See Hirschman, 1968, for the way social discord translated into inflation.

[42] Kaldor, 1959.

[43] Reynolds and Mamalakis, 1976.

and inflation, a product of limited growth and distribution battles.[44] These factors together resulted in further disincentives to invest productively.

This was the all-too-pertinent context of the significant reform efforts, and partial reforms, of the 1960s. Chile was the first to introduce the crawling peg in 1965, combined with an extensive set of policies developed over the next few years, including tax rebates, tariff reductions and rationalization of the tariff structure. CORFO was active in these years with programs that laid the basis for subsequent exports in fishery and forestry. But the political context did not allow a coherent set of policies to develop. An illuminating instance is the decision in Alessandri's presidency in the early 1960s to push import substitution further in the automobile sector when, given the small Chilean market, it was clearly inappropriate. This presumably derived from the same passion for job creation seen elsewhere, as demographic and urban pressures increased. Another telling example was CORFO's initiative in 1968-69, led by Sergio Bitar, to negotiate with the private sector on a whole range of instruments to modify distortions in import substituting industrialization policies, and to move to serious promotion of exports and industrial investment. However, it needed a sustained political effort, which was lacking. The initiative collapsed with the 1970 elections.[45]

Hence, despite the growth of industry, the progressive institutional evolution of the 1950s and 1960s, and the healthy reforms of commercial policy in the 1960s, the reforming Christian Democratic government was caught in the middle between strong conservative forces and radicalizing tendencies. The *Unidad Popular*, to everyone's surprise, including its own, won the 1970 election. The rapid move to the left by the Allende government encountered fierce problems: lack of management skills, internal contradictions and enormous external pressures.

By contrast, Colombia's leading export sector, coffee, was nationally owned. Special institutional developments meant that even the commercialization of coffee stayed partly in local hands; the strength of the *Federación Nacional de Cafeteros Colombianos* was such that foreign trading houses preferred other easier terrain. In addition, the link between coffee and industry was harmonious and natural: regionally diffuse coffee activity led to local processing and related industrialization, and

---

[44] For the classic analysis in these terms, see Hirschman, 1968.

[45] The example is drawn from material provided by Oscar Muñoz and from workshop discussions for this book.

the surplus from the coffee trade needed an outlet.[46] This led to a strong dual focus on agriculture and industry. There was a relatively low level of industrialization by the 1940s, due to a very late start, and given problems of violence in the 1940s and 1950s, growth and investment were hardly likely to be spectacular. Still, the reconciling of diverse interests was not the problem, and neither was the need to "resolve" the issue of foreign capital: Colombia maintained its consistently subtle but discouraging attitude to a substantial penetration by direct foreign investment, and certainly enacted no law parallel to those we have noted in all other economies of any size.

Thus there was substantial institution building, based more in the rural sector than in industry.[47] The institutional development covered technology, irrigation and credit with the *Caja Agraria*, *Banco Cafetero* and *Banco Ganadero*. Producer organizations also expanded. From the 1940s, policies embraced the rural sector. Although agriculture's participation in GDP fell as it did everywhere, noncoffee agriculture grew at 4 percent a year. This provided in due course nontraditional exports out of the agricultural sector. Most important of all was commercial policy and the institution-building surrounding it. There was no exchange rate overvaluation over the long term; Colombian management of its interests in the International Coffee Organization was notably skillful, and even as early as the 1950s the explicit promotion of nontraditional exports was the earliest and most coherent on the continent. The promotion began with the *Plan Vallejo* in 1957, and in 1967 a range of institutions was created, led by the *Fondo de Promoción de Exportaciones* (PROEXPO). The crawling peg also was established. Colombia was perhaps the only country where "promotion" of nontraditional exports at an early date amounted to substantially more than just subsidies.

Industry was not free of the inefficiencies found elsewhere, and the degree of concentration was high; however, by the 1960s policies had shifted and neither inflation nor a looming fiscal crisis had appeared. Colombia even resisted the early temptations of the lending bonanza by deciding not to borrow in 1974 (it gave in later). While social problems loomed, drugs were threatening and in-

---

[46] Thorp, 1991: 6-11.

[47] See Ocampo and Tovar in Companion Volume 3. The rest of this paragraph draws on this source.

equality and violence would dog the next two decades, policymakers had never-theless managed the macro side of inward-looking industrialization relatively efficiently.

In Brazil, the pattern of industrialization was relatively solid.[48] The strong and early military push to build state enterprises, the sheer size of the country, and the elements of continuity, particularly between Vargas and Kubitschek, both pos-sessed of a powerful developmentalist mission, produced rather advanced institu-tions, a strong system of industrial promotion agencies, and close collaboration be-tween public and private sectors. The expansion of agriculture was adequate. Food imports were negligible and food production rose in line with the population, since the frontier still gave room for expansion.

The elements of collaboration were not strong enough, however, to prevent elements of the private sector from backing the military coup in 1964, principally for fear of land reform. The military regime, while highly repressive, did also push forward development. Brazil shifted to more openness, principally in the form of extensive incentives to manufacturing exports.[49] Subsidies in some years were equiva-lent to an exchange rate devaluation of more than 70 percent. The results were seen in a substantial growth of manufacturing exports, with a growth rate twice as fast as overall exports from 1965-75. The fastest expansion in exports originated from those sectors established or consolidated in postwar industrialization.[50]

Brazil's fragility lay in its extreme dependence on multinational corporations, in inflation and in fiscal imbalance. Behind this imbalance lay the problem of a large federal system that failed to generate consensus between states and the central gov-ernment on tax and expenditure burdens. The 1970s would prove irresistibly dam-aging to such a situation, despite relative health on the external account and grow-ing exports of manufactures.

Argentina also saw rapid industrial growth from 1945-70 with a strong rise in industrial productivity.[51] However, the country had an unimpressive overall perfor-

---

[48] See Abreu et al. in Companion Volume 3.

[49] Neves and Moreira, 1987.

[50] See Abreu et al. in Companion Volume 3. But the opening was limited due to pressures from vested interests, including multinational corporations.

[51] See Katz and Kosacoff in Companion Volume 3.

mance that was tailing off before the OPEC price rise or the debt crisis.[52] Investment as a percentage of GDP was 15 percent from 1945-49, low for an economy of Argentina's size and wealth.

Once again, the problem was the interaction of politics with economic policymaking. The divisions introduced by the first Peronist government seemed unresolvable and bedeviled coherent policymaking, as we saw in the account of the Frondizi years.[53] The early efforts to promote SMEs faded and the initial design of the *Banco Industrial* deteriorated. Although there was institutional development during the 1950s and 1960s—especially the creation of the *Instituto Nacional de Tecnología Agropecuaria* (INTA)—the institutional expansion did not amount to the "auge" or strong rise described for Chile.[54] By the 1960s and early 1970s, there was some rethinking of industrial and commercial policies,[55] but without the coherence and breadth of the late 1960s in Chile. Yet there was an accumulation of capacities and know-how, described by Katz and Kosacoff as a form of social capital. TNCs played an important role, at the expense of those elements of national capital that opted not to form alliances with foreign firms, while SMEs also remained a significant strand.

Although protection was relatively low in Mexico, the use of quotas and prohibitions developed extensively after the war.[56] Such protection was lobbied for by the *Cámara Nacional de la Industria de la Transformación* and other private sector pressure groups, and became the heart of the PRI's relationship with the private sector—as well as its instrument for political control of the private sector. The key actor in the urban labor movement—the *Confederación de Trabajadores Mexicanos* (CTM)—identified its interests with this process and gained concessions for its members. The growth strategy worked exceptionally well for Mexico up to 1960.

---

[52] Ibid.

[53] Aldo Ferrer records similar frustration as Minister of Finance in 1970-71, when, despite a positive experience with the private sector as Minister of Public Works, he found it impossible to negotiate with business interests. "It was as if they didn't exist." He quotes Furtado's analysis: the early development of unions before the consolidation of industrial groups, plus the environment created in the Perón period, produced a situation where unions pushed weak industrial organization into conservative and entrenched positions (Interview, Washington, D.C., 1997)

[54] See Ffrench-Davis et al. in Companion Volume 3.

[55] Principally in the form of sectoral and regional subsidies, and some reductions in tariffs. See O'Connell, 1994.

[56] These paragraphs are drawn from Cárdenas in Companion Volume 3.

Export revenues did not weaken as they did elsewhere in the 1950s, sustained by expanding tourism as well as cotton. Transfers from agriculture to industry (via price control) were an important part of expanding industrialization, but nevertheless the growth of agriculture was adequate at 3 percent a year, just keeping pace with population. Here the indirect effect of agrarian reform was powerful, driving a search for efficiency to avoid expropriation. The dynamic role of the public sector crowded in private investment, and the percentage of investment in GDP rose at a reasonable rate. Financial instruments were developed and channeled finance to the private sector.[57] Inflation was avoided, given the adequate performance of exports and agriculture, and possibly some effect of the long border with the United States. When others moved to reduce the distortions in the strategy in the 1960s, Mexico did not. There was every indication that a protectionist route could still yield dividends, and enormous pressure to continue growing, principally from the demographic side. Neither government nor the private sector was interested in liberalizing, the former because it would lose precious instruments of control and co-optation, the latter because it would lose privilege and market.[58] Now protection was accentuated, and increasingly conserved space for the national entrepreneur as much as for national products, lessening the contribution of DFI. Public sector expansion accelerated, and the resistance of business and other private sector interests repeatedly prevented much-needed tax reform, notably in 1972. Borrowing abroad was the solution, and by 1970, well before the borrowing bonanza, Mexico was paying 23 percent of its export revenues in debt service. Oil would arrive to compound a fragile situation, despite continued growth.

The final member of this group, Uruguay, is a curious and exceptional case. Uruguay was already highly industrialized for its size in 1945, with 18 percent of GDP in industry, a figure characteristic of Brazil and Mexico, which have GDPs six times the size. This was a result of the protectionist policies of the Batllista state. The growth of industry from 1945-55 was over 6 percent a year, based on high protection. The issue of controls that deterred foreign capital elsewhere was not a problem: there was little foreign investment, but in the short term, surplus was available from protected profits and from the rural sector, which benefited in price

---

[57] Brothers and Solis, 1966.

[58] See Cárdenas in Companion Volume 3.

terms from the Korean War boom. Fundamentally, however, the situation was anything but healthy: the long-run stagnation of the rural sector continued, with no growth in export volume during these years. This stagnation was clearly related to lack of investment in the sector, the explanation of which is the key controversy in Uruguayan economic history. The growth of industry was a product of trade and exchange controls, and elements of a long-run development policy were lacking. As Finch has written, "The structure of domestic production was in fact reshaped fundamentally by policy weapons operating on the external sector, rather than by domestic fiscal instruments, integrated industrial credit policies or an industrial development bank."[59] By the mid-1950s, industrial growth had slowed dramatically, as rural stagnation brought problems of raw material and foreign exchange supplies, and as the market limitation began to be reached. Uruguay thus prematurely reached the point of "exhaustion," which elsewhere was perceived as a problem only in the 1960s.

The account given in the previous chapter of the impotence of the Uruguayan planning team already signaled how little space there was for reform in the 1960s. Slow growth continued and inflation increased. Investment fell from 18 percent of GDP in 1955-57 to 11 percent in 1964-66.[60]

Primary Product Export Models

Countries in this category hold a particular interest in the narrative of inward-looking industrialization, given the emphasis in the standard Latin American economic literature on the role of the foreign exchange constraint in shaping policy choices and many of the distortions of inward-looking industrialization.[61] These countries did indeed promote industrialization, at least by the 1960s and sometimes earlier. But what is fascinating is that where the growth of the primary exporting sector was very strong, the problems and characteristics of the resulting industrial sector seem to have resembled remarkably closely those produced by the classic foreign exchange bottleneck.

---

[59] Finch, 1981: 177.

[60] Ibid.: 225.

[61] The seminal article on the broad phenomenon of import-substitution industrialization is Hirschman, 1971.

Venezuela, Ecuador, Peru, Bolivia and Paraguay were less prepared for in-dustrialization in the immediate postwar period in terms of their prior base. But whereas in Central America the strength of export-elite interests and the success of exports dictated a relatively clear-cut continued adherence to the old primary ex-port model, the developments in these medium-sized economies were less simple, since there was already a relatively greater internal diversity of interests. In each case, the share of imports in GDP rose, usually with a rise in the share of consumer goods, indicating little progress in industrialization. But this was associated with extreme differences in export performance. Bolivia and Paraguay lost ground radi-cally, while Venezuela and Ecuador, and to a lesser degree, Peru, appear as trans-parent cases of strong primary export growth permitting and pushing a fresh com-mitment to old-style, export-led growth.

Venezuela is the most exaggerated instance of the combination of the tradi-tional export economy model with state-led industrialization. It was only in the 1940s and 1950s that Venezuela actually developed the full version of the pure rentier economy described schematically in Chapter Three, where income is chan-neled through government, foreign companies play the entrepreneurial role, in-come from the booming export dominates GDP, and all this occurs in a context of low levels of development and a culture prone to confuse the political and the personal. The political necessity of "sowing the oil" produced an enthusiastic com-mitment to industrializing.[62] As Astorga points out, it is remarkable how far abun-dance produces the same problems as scarcity. Venezuelan industry was promoted with state enterprises, high protection, a revaluing exchange rate and cheap food and energy—and it grew. Inward-looking industrialization interacted with a rather long drawn-out version of Dutch Disease: Venezuela overcompensated for the effects of overvaluation on the nontradable sectors, and the medicine produced an inefficient industrial sector with strong rent-seeking characteristics that never-theless grew and even increased labor productivity. However, once the tempta-tions and subsequent chaos of the 1970s and 1980s arrived, the distortions would become extreme.

Ecuador shared some of Venezuela's strong export success. The economy had grown relatively slowly since the collapse of cocoa in the 1920s. As always in

---

[62] See Astorga in Companion Volume 3.

Ecuador, the regional aspects were crucial. The economy had survived the Depression by incorporating unused resources, expanding small-scale industry, and reviving textiles and exports of Panama hats. The heart of the expansion process had occurred in the Sierra.[63] The expansion had given rise to much social change, but not to the consolidation of anything approaching an industrial bourgeoisie. Now the banana sector began to grow rapidly, rising from 2 percent of exports in the 1930s to 6 percent in 1948 and to 42 percent by 1955. Not surprisingly, therefore, it was a time of reversion to the agro-export model, with bananas, coffee and cocoa accounting for 90 percent of exports in 1955. The new wealth was centered in the coastal lowlands; it was not surprising that industry fell from 17 percent of GDP in the 1940s to 16 percent by 1960, while imports rose as a percentage of GDP and exports of Panama hats fell from 9 percent of exports in 1948 to 1 percent by 1955. With this, the process of building a political economy that might sustain an alternative path was directly undermined. The element of fragmentation was emphasized by continued growth of autonomous public enterprises, many reflecting regional interests. With declining terms of trade in the early 1960s, the government moved to implement the standard policies adopted elsewhere much earlier. As industry initially grew very fast, the traditional elite groups profited from new opportunities provided by import-substituting industry, and there was no serious modification of the traditional political economy.[64]

Peru's immediate postwar experience was superficially rather similar to that of the larger economies, since a period of controls and intervention from 1945-48 was followed by strongly favorable foreign capital legislation in 1949.[65] But the similarity was more apparent than real. Peru's diverse and rich resource base had led to several decades of strong export growth, with a substantial presence of foreign capital. But unlike Chile, in Peru there was always room within the sector for an associated and profitable role for domestic elites, who therefore never had the incentive to push for protection of industry. The state had a considerable presence in the economy, employing large numbers of people, but lacked experience of in-

[63] Maiguashca, 1996.

[64] Larrea, 1992.

[65] This paragraph is based on Thorp and Bertram, 1978.

terventionist policies. The brief period of populist government (1945-48) led to such chaos in the use of such policies, as a result of inexperience and an incoherent political base, that they were deplored even by the industrialists whom they were meant to favor. The unfavorable attitude to intervention generated by this experience, plus the strong growth of mineral exports, led along with the right-wing coup of Odria in 1948 to an early swing back to market-oriented policies and to primary exports. Industry grew in the early 1950s, but the dynamic sectors were strongly related to primary exports. The export processing industry grew from 18 percent of industrial production in 1950 to 26 percent by 1960.[66] In the 1960s, more classic import substitution industrialization policies developed as unemployment and rural unrest became preoccupations. The policies, however, were exceptionally undiscriminating.

In Bolivia, the three major mine owners, Patiño, Hochschild and Aramayo, known as the *rosca*, dominated the main export sector. The economic and political power of the *rosca* was inversely matched by the weakness of the state. This meant that the capacity for administration and tax collection was underdeveloped even by Latin American standards.[67] The rest of the economy suffered from lack of investment as the power of the tin industry to act as an engine for growth was not harnessed, so that debt was used as a substitute for extracting revenue. Borrowing allowed the government to keep on good terms with the mining elite and to use borrowed money to pay off interest on previous loans and on railroad construction.

The 1940s were dominated by the confrontation between the old guard of the mining elite and new nationalist groups, led by the *Movimiento Nacionalista Revolucionario* (MNR), which wanted wider distribution of the gains from tin and an end to the power of the *rosca*. Bolivia was set apart by the dominance of tin, the strength of the elite group dominating it, and the strength of the corresponding political reaction. Following the Second World War, various elements crucial to Bolivia's survival were strongly modified. The United States now dominated the tin market, so that the former ability of the *rosca* to play UK and U.S. interests off each

---

[66] Thorp, 1991: 49.

[67] Contreras, 1990. The ability to rely on foreign borrowing is seen as one of the major reasons for the lack of fiscal efficiency of the Bolivian state. Taxation was improved during the 1930s because the country needed to fund the war effort and money was not forthcoming from abroad (p. 267).

other was weakened. Demand fell heavily, and Far Eastern producers returned to the market, while Bolivian costs were rising (there had been no new investment during the war).

Faced with falling profits and a combative miners' union, the *rosca* resorted to repression. The fall was only temporarily reversed by the Korean War boom. The MNR took power in the Revolution of 1952, intending to use the nationalized tin sector for "national autonomous development," but found it had taken over assets in poor condition, faced international recession following the Korean War, and needed to pay off political debts to the mine workers. The resulting inflation led in 1956 to drastic stabilization and a shift to the right. Bolivia's revolution failed to create the strong (if undemocratic) post-revolutionary political system of Mexico; political instability and conflict followed, and in due course immense difficulties in managing the state-owned sector. But in the 1960s, foreign investment flowed into the mining and petroleum sectors, the Alliance for Progress financed much public sector activity, and growth was high, reaching 6.6 percent from 1965 to 1969.[68]

Paraguay was dominated until the dictatorship of Alfredo Stroessner in 1954 by a small number of families closely tied to the primary export sectors (meat and tobacco), and there was a strong presence of foreign capital in land and infrastructure. So, as in Central America, the 1940s simply saw a strengthening of the traditional model, but after a brief wartime boom in meat exports the result was far less successful than in Central America. The geographically isolated and rather closed nature of the Paraguayan economy meant an absence of the "discipline of openness" much in evidence in Central America. Isolation was also in principle an opportunity, but there was no internal base, in either economic or political terms, to create something out of the possibility.

The coup that brought General Stroessner to power in 1954 set Paraguay's course for the next 34 years. His political skill and use of repression allowed him to build a series of alliances with military, economic and political power blocs in Paraguay, which became the means to demobilize and co-opt much of civil society. Loyalty to Stroessner and the Colorado Party became a matter of economic necessity. Lucrative public contracts and opportunities for corruption allowed senior party members to become successful businessmen. Unlike Somoza in Nicaragua, Stroessner took

---

[68] Morales and Sachs, 1990: 181.

care not to alienate the business sector. Paraguay in the 1960s was "a haven…provided, at a fee, for assorted bank-robbers, swindlers and fraudsters from around the world."[69] In the 1960s, with foreign aid under the Alliance for Progress and colonization of the eastern border region, there was slow growth based on agro-exports. U.S. aid as a share of GDP was 2.7 percent from 1953-61 and 4.9 percent from 1962-65, aided by $504 million from the World Bank and $619 million from the IDB.[70]

Bolivia, Ecuador and Paraguay all had GDPs comparable to the classic "small economies" of Central America. But the Central American economies remained far more clearly within the export-economy model in the immediate postwar period. There was simply no question of extending controls or other interventionist policies to permit the emergence of a more autonomous or nationalist model. The only partial exception to this was Guatemala, where the Arévalo government (1944-50) introduced a progressive constitution modeled on the Mexican 1917 charter, supported the labor movement, and attempted educational and other reforms. But even here there was no break with traditional export-led growth.

This outcome was a product of related phenomena: the strength of the elite and export-dominated political model in Central America, relative good fortune in the commodity lottery, and the continued existence of at least some spare capacity to permit the expansion of crops in response to buoyant conditions. A natural accompaniment of the model was the tying of currencies to the U.S. dollar. With abundant foreign exchange, easy importing soon abated wartime inflationary pressures and remarkable exchange rate stability ensued.

Exports grew vigorously in this period, with coffee particularly buoyant. Banana exports recovered quickly after the war, although there were severe problems with disease. The most striking characteristic of the period was the increase in the state's share of net benefits from banana production. This led to shifts in the role of the state, and in the balance of power between the state and foreign companies. This led to some increase in taxation of the sector. Outside of banana production, however, most foreign-owned companies remained largely untaxed. The most important example of export diversification in this period was the expansion of cotton production. This was of major importance in El Salvador, Guatemala and Nicaragua.

---

[69] Nickson, 1989: 24. These paragraphs draw heavily on his work.
[70] Nickson and Lambert, 1997: 608.

Cotton was a highly concentrated industry and cotton growers began to form a distinct social class and pressure group comparable to coffee growers (both coffee and cotton were largely in national hands). Their combined influence was strong enough to distort the fiscal system in their favor and to deny the state an equitable share in the expansion of the two industries.[71]

In the 1960s, more deliberate industrialization became a target of policymakers within the context of the Central American Common Market. Integration generated rapid industrial growth, but ran into political problems, in particular the war between El Salvador and Honduras. However, industrial growth and the wider forces of modernization in no way affected the traditional agrarian-elite domination characteristic of four of the five countries (Costa Rica is the exception), and this domination was helped by U.S. support.[72]

The Centrally Planned Option [73]

Until 1959, Cuba remained within the extreme export-dependent mode of development that had characterized the economy from the 1920s. Sugar still provided satisfactory growth based on strong international prices. The rate of growth of per capita income was 2.4 percent between 1946 and 1952. Mining and tourism grew, though in general there was little development of activities other than sugar. Non-sugar manufacturing is estimated to have grown at 6 percent a year from 1946-52, but from an extremely low base.[74] From 1953-56, sugar production was deliberately cut back in response to collapsing international prices associated partly with the end of the Korean War and partly with Cuba's own record production of 1952. However, the growth of oil refining and a buoyant construction sector accompanied the recovery of sugar markets in 1957.

The 1960s constitute one end of the spectrum in terms of reform options and capacities. Following the revolution, the Castro government made the diagnosis that dependence on sugar and on the United States were equivalent. The decision

---

[71] Bulmer-Thomas, 1987: 106.

[72] See Cohen in Companion Volume 3.

[73] This section draws on a consultancy report for this book by Brian Pollitt.

[74] Brundenius and Lundhal, 1982: 18.

was to foster agricultural diversification by cutting back sugar production and to adopt an ambitious and necessarily import-intensive industrialization program. Large-scale manufacturing, including the sugar industry, was taken into the state sector from 1960. Agrarian reform, decreed in 1959, was largely implemented in 1960, and by 1962, the state farm, with workers receiving wages, became the dominant agricultural organization, with the government determining sowing plans and prices. The private sector, which retained some 60 percent of farm land until October 1963, was cut to about 30 percent thereafter.[75] The early 1960s saw a move towards agricultural diversification in order to break the dominance of sugar. Corn, rice, cotton, tomatoes and soybeans were planted. Sugar production fell from 6.9 million tons in 1960 to just 3.9 million tons in 1963, partly because of the diversion of high-quality irrigated cane plantations to rice and other crops and partly because of growing labor shortages, particularly for cane harvesting. However, this loss was not accompanied by the expected success of other crops: rice, corn and millet production each fell by 25 percent. Explanations for this failure of diversification vary: agrarian reform disrupted planting and harvesting; there were labor shortages as workers left agriculture for more attractive opportunities elsewhere; new crops were unfamiliar; and there was bad weather. By 1963, Che Guevara had concluded that the "entire economic history of Cuba has demonstrated that no other agricultural activity would give such returns as those yielded by the cultivation of sugar cane. At the outset of the Revolution many of us were not aware of this basic economic fact, because a fetishistic idea connected sugar with our dependence on imperialism and with the misery in the rural areas, without analyzing the real causes: the relation to the unequal balance of trade."[76] Broad agricultural diversification was thus abandoned and emphasis was laid on sugar exports to the Soviet Bloc. The difficulties of the 1960s culminated in the unrealized goal of a 10 million ton sugar harvest by 1970. Despite a sacrifice of resources in other sectors, production reached only 8.5 million tons. Industrial growth, too, was hampered in the early stages by shortages of materials and lack of skilled technicians, even though new plants were installed by the Soviets and Eastern Europeans by 1962.[77]

---

[75] Pollitt, op. cit. The cane farms were initially organized as cooperatives.

[76] Cited by Pollitt, 1986: 200.

[77] Cardoso and Helwege, 1992.

The difficulties posed by lack of capacity in forcing the pace of industrialization have been vividly described by Boorstein.[78] More fundamentally, the historical analysis of Chapters Three and Four has emphasized repeatedly how deeply sugar shaped all elements of the economy and institutions. Given this inherited structure, it is not surprising that efforts at diversification led to huge balance of payments problems and the need to turn to the USSR to provide resources and a new market for sugar, which had to remain central to the development effort.[79]

Export Promotion and Industrializing by Invitation

The rest of the Caribbean had its own version of industrialization, which was fundamentally different from the inward-looking model, since it was centered on the paramount need of such small economies to export. In the immediate postwar period, the principal focus of policy was not industry but the search for primary exports other than sugar. In the English-speaking Caribbean, policy focused on citrus fruits and bananas, along with palliative social measures under the Colonial Development and Welfare Programme.

The impetus to a Caribbean-style industrialization effort, always strongly focused on exporting, came from Puerto Rico. More tightly tied to the United States than Cuba, Puerto Rico nevertheless developed a stronger national political movement than did Cuba in the 1930s and 1940s, with the leadership of Luis Muñoz Marín and his PPD, and helped from 1941 by an unusual governor, Rexford Guy Tugwell. The PPD's industrial project was initially soundly based on institutional reform, emphasizing credit to small firms and nationally based development.[80] It in fact became both the first and the most extreme version of what was to become the stereotype of import substitution industrialization, at least in regard to the role of foreigners. The shift had occurred by 1947, when Operation Bootstrap was put into effect, and seems to have responded to the lack of domestic supply response, given

---

[78] Boorstein, 1968.

[79] We cannot do justice here to the shifts in policy in Cuba in the 1960s. See Mesa-Lago, 1981, for a full account.

[80] It owed much to the Chardon Plan, developed in the mid-1930s on New Deal lines but never implemented. Its main author was Carlos Chardon, Chancellor of the University of Puerto Rico. Dietz, 1986: 150.

the way local capital was "locked into sugar-cane production, trade, and banking,"[81] an analysis which suggests a parallel with Cuba. The resulting program gave lavish concessions such as tax breaks to foreign firms, and the original incentives to domestic development disappeared. Its strength was that it produced a boom in manufactures and in new manufacturing exports. Its weaknesses were, first, that although part of the attraction was cheap labor, the other part consisted of tax breaks, which cheapened capital,[82] and as a result employment did not grow adequately. The lack of jobs became more marked by the 1960s, with a definite shift to capital intensity. Second, Puerto Rican entrepreneurship and technical effort were not stimulated. Third, by the 1960s, once tax holidays ended and real wages rose,[83] firms tended to leave. Fourth, agriculture was neglected, the more so as Puerto Rico was eligible for U.S. federal government benefits such as food stamps.

The 1960s and 1970s saw rapid economic growth, first doubling then tripling each decade.[84] By 1980, per capita income exceeded that of all Latin American countries except Venezuela. However, the economy remained very dependent on exports, though their nature had changed. Between 1950-80, the value of GDP exported increased from 34 percent to 64 percent.[85] Furthermore, by far the largest portion of manufacturing income was paid out to non-Puerto Rican owners; by 1978, non-Puerto Rican[86] ownership in core industries was 98 percent. And for all the growth in manufacturing, unemployment remained high.[87]

The incipient problems constituted a risk possibly worth taking when Puerto Ricans had rights in the U.S. federal system: the same model, copied as it began to be widely in the Caribbean under the label of industrialization by invitation, had no such safety net. Its Caribbean proponent was W.A. Lewis, whose seminal article in 1950 explained that "the islands cannot be industrialized to anything like the extent

---

[81] Dietz, 1986.

[82] Helped by the lack of an educated labor force to produce supervisors, important for a labor-intensive firm. See Strassman, 1968, for the importance of this factor in the Mexican case.

[83] The tax breaks granted in 1947 ended in 1959.

[84] Dietz, 1986: 244.

[85] Ibid.: 289.

[86] The clumsy phrasing reflects the fact that since Puerto Rico is part of the United States, the word "foreign" is inappropriate.

[87] Dietz, 1986: 278.

that is necessary without a considerable inflow of foreign capital and capitalists, and a period of wooing and fawning upon such people."[88] Lewis was insistent that agriculture and industry had to modernize and progress together (although in practice, agriculture was left behind), and that exporting manufactures was the key to the solution of small markets and surplus labor. For this, experienced firms with market access were needed, as was regional integration. However, the reality neglected both agriculture and exports of manufactures and did not promote integration. Nevertheless, it produced industrial growth (7 percent a year in Jamaica between 1950 and 1968, for instance), even with primary commodity booms (bauxite in Jamaica, 1952-1972, Suriname in the 1960s, the oil boom in Trinidad and Tobago from 1950 to 1962, and tourism and bananas in many of the smaller islands). Free trade zones were an important part of the strategy in Haiti, the Dominican Republic, Barbados and Jamaica.

The high levels of education characteristic of the English-speaking Caribbean, and the early recognition of trade unions, hampered a strategy based on supposed cheap labor, since labor costs were high relative to Latin America and East Asia, while the education in question was insufficiently tailored to labor market needs.[89] Thus the 1960s saw waning success in employment creation. In Jamaica, only 9,000 jobs were created between 1950 and 1963, while over the same period the labor force increased by 20,000 a year.[90] The failure to create jobs and the difficulty of attracting foreign investment, together with independence for several countries, consolidated the regional focus, which shaped the creation of the Caribbean Free Trade Area in 1969.

[88] Lewis, 1950: 38.
[89] McIntyre, et al., 1996.
[90] Thomas, 1988.

CONCLUSION: LIGHTS AND SHADOWS OF STATE-LED INDUSTRIALIZATION

The narrative of state-led and inward-looking industrialization has revealed that the *leyenda negra* in fact obscures a reality that is complex and contains both good and bad. Some of the negative perceptions came from false analyses at the time, such as the obsession with the exhaustion of import substitution and the link made between inward-looking policies and the move to authoritarian regimes in the 1960s and early 1970s. Subsequent events and academic analyses have shown both lines to be false.[91]

In conclusion, we would highlight six points. First, we have seen repeatedly that while there were distortions, inefficiencies and lost opportunities, there was also a radical transformation of infrastructure and institutions. The characteristics of the process in terms of growth and productivity have been summed up above. The less tangible aspects were no less important, and Chapter Five attempted to list some of them. The inward-looking strategy complemented other forces responsible for creating a considerable middle class, and both responded to and took further a strong process of urbanization. This entailed the provision of public utilities, such as running water and sewage systems. Industrialization brought with it enlargement and diversification of the service sector, and it created a corresponding "industrial class" of both workers and businessmen. Formal sector workers constituted an important segment of the growing domestic market for the newly produced goods and services; they also formed labor unions, which in some instances were strong enough to affect the balance of political power, above all in Argentina. A national business class appeared under the umbrella of industrialization policies, and in many instances under the auspices of direct government sponsorship or public contracts. Industrial entrepreneurs had to acquire fresh skills, including mastery of new forms of organization of production, adaptation of existing technology to their own conditions, and management of new technologies offered by the TNCs. The emerging working class also had to become accustomed to the discipline of factory work. The extent of these transformations is qualified, not negated, by the

---

[91] See Collier, 1979, especially the chapters by Serra and Hirschman, for perceptive analyses of the falsity of the original thesis put forward by Guillermo O'Donnell. On "exhaustion," see Fishlow, 1972.

aspects that were neglected, such as control and monitoring of the financial system and the public budget, and the need for more extensive and effective taxation systems as well as for rules of the game that survived changes of government.

Second, when costs became extreme by the 1960s and the path of inward-looking industrialization seemed to turn into a dead end, the problems often derived from political choices rather than ignorance on the technical side. Politicians saw further protection and industrial promotion as the most secure route to job creation, which was important given the rising urban population. After all, the policy of industrial protection was still delivering growth and higher productivity in the 1960s, and with higher productivity came higher wages for those fortunate enough to be employed in the formal sector. Neither business nor in many countries organized labor had reason to wish to change direction. The result was that well-qualified national teams often designed well-based reforms, only to see them watered down or overtaken by political events. The case of Chile, described earlier, is the clearest example.

There were many instances of divergence between technical teams and the politicians' choices. Examples abound where senior advisers recommended devaluation or tax reform, in circumstances where with hindsight we can see that the institutional conditions and macro/micro relations were favorable, but politicians rejected the option.[92] Fiscal reforms were also badly needed, given increasing pressures on the expenditure side. Growing deficits had to be covered by borrowing, often from foreign sources, which led to fiscal crisis with longlasting consequences in public indebtedness.[93] In addition, protection was pursued when it was already clear that market size could not sustain it.

---

[92] Examples included the individual efforts of several economists to persuade Mexico's President Echeverría into a 15 percent devaluation in 1971-72, blaming the collapse of Bretton Woods and the devaluation of the dollar rather than the peso's overvaluation; it was a real option, discarded by the president, that would have changed the character of Mexican development in the 1970s. Another example was the extensive work done on a recovery plan in 1962-63, with very modest foreign borrowing—and the fury of the Ministry of Finance when it emerged that a group of politicians had negotiated a considerably larger loan, quite unnecessarily.

[93] Also in Mexico in the 1960s, a viable tax reform was presented to the President, but not acted on (the same story was repeated in 1972-73). Instead, the financial system was used to tax the private sector, through marginal reserve requirements, inappropriately raising the cost of investment finance. (The increased reserve requirements had to be placed in special accounts. The government then drew on these accounts, issuing bonds in exchange.)

Third, in reappraising the original policy design, it does not condone poor policy but it does modulate our judgment to recognize the limits and constraints of the time, particularly given the pressure for urban employment in Latin America and the strong protectionist tendency developing already in the 1950s in the center countries.

Fourth, in appraising these three decades of industrialization, we have put relatively little stress on the mechanism of import substitution, which in the literature on the period features heavily, above all under the label "import-substituting industrialization." This has been a conscious decision, as indicated earlier, reflecting the consensus of the workshop for this book that earlier approaches that focused on industrialization principally from the angle of import substitution have directed the analysis too heavily to the demand side. In fact the supply side, and policies and institutions affecting the supply side, were every bit if not more important.

Fifth, the experience of particular countries varied greatly. The first group of countries had all made significant progress in industrialization. Of these, some were adjusting their economic strategies in quite promising ways before 1970. In Argentina and Chile, political problems, rather than inward-looking industrialization itself, were leading to crisis. Two members of the group, while different in their growth rate and most other respects, nevertheless were similar in that they were both locked into policies that were soon to prove inappropriate. The second group was typically the smaller countries, where a combination of continued primary export-led growth, and belated and accelerated industrialization with a limited internal market, led them into a very fragile situation by the end of the 1960s, often made worse by the fact that such a limited and brief period of diversification did little or nothing to modify existing power structures. The Caribbean in a sense is a subset of this group, but distinguished in the case of Cuba by the solution chosen and in the case of the rest by the lavish invitation to foreign capital.

Sixth, while the growth record overall was impressive and while the institutional story was one of radical change in many areas, industrialization and import substitution were inserted into and reinforced the existing extremely unequal economic and social system. Even brave efforts at land reform did not modify the essential picture of poverty and exclusion. Women and indigenous groups remained relatively dispossessed, and urban labor market trends tended to create new inequalities.

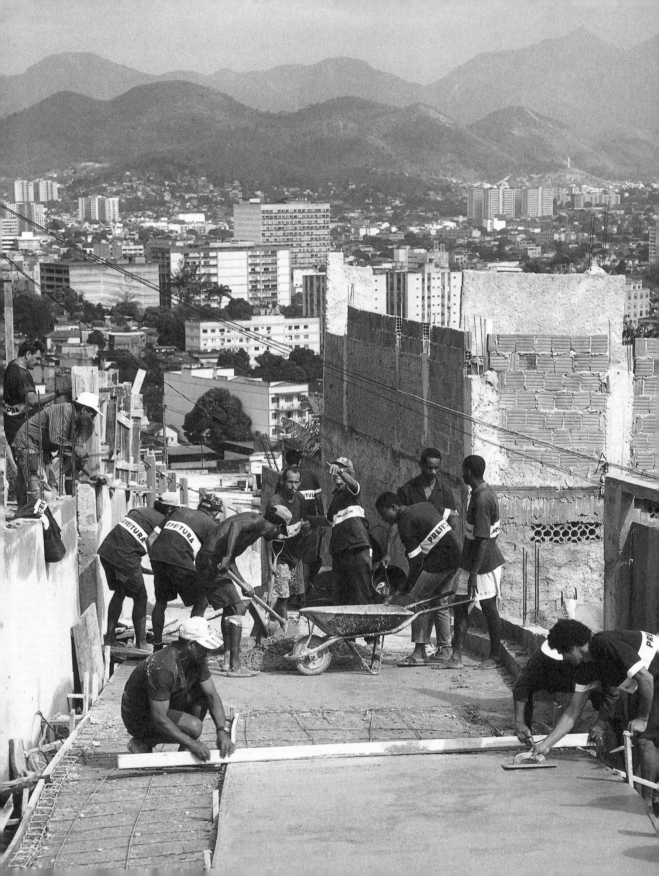

CHAPTER 7

DEBT-LED GROWTH, DISASTER AND REDIRECTION AFTER 1973

REVIEWING THE LAST QUARTER OF THE CENTURY poses complex and distinct problems: radical changes have occurred at both national and international levels, and it is far too soon to appraise the results. For instance, contemporary analysts talk of a historic shift in paradigm by the end of the 1980s and a move to "structural reform." But it is far from clear that historians of the mid-21st century will find it appropriate to dignify the process in such strong terms. The perspective is also complicated by the way different processes occurred in parallel, overlapping to varying degrees and at different dates in the different countries. The narrative needs to cover, first, the process of increasing financial integration, the buildup of debt, and the debt crisis itself. Second, we must relate how the international financial system responded to crisis, a story complex enough in its own right. Third, we need to look at the huge internal implications of Latin America's struggle to maintain debt payments through the 1980s. And fourth, we need to trace out how policies that were often adopted initially for reasons of short-term expediency developed into a new

Photo: Street paving in Rio de Janeiro, 1996.

long-term policy approach. The last topic is the most difficult, since the country stories are extremely varied. While the "shift in paradigm" is perceptible at some general level from the mid-1980s on, how and the extent to which the shift influenced national policies is difficult to delineate and evaluate. As we shall see, inflows of money in the 1990s, only partly related to the reforms, created conditions under which the sustainability of the process becomes an open question.

The chapter first outlines the important changes in the international context that conditioned all these processes. The second section describes the buildup to the debt crisis and the crisis itself. Third, we cover the 1980s by looking at both the creditors' responses over time and initial consequences of the debtors' burden incurred by Latin America. Fourth, we deal at a general level with the emergence of a corpus of neoliberal reforms. The chapter then looks at how two important lines of policy were reconceptualized and reshaped according to the new model. The actual functioning of the new policies and the preliminary assessment of their results are so country-specific and so affected by prior national conditions that we must resort to the national narratives in order to explore the policies, which will be done in the subsequent chapter.

INTERNATIONAL CONTEXT

Just as the period up to 1930 was dominated by increasing integration of world markets and expanding factors of production, so was the last part of the century. From the 1970s on, a technological revolution in communications and a corresponding growth in knowledge-intensive industries underpinned liberalization and expansion of world trade and a radical transformation of capital markets.

The process was accompanied by an ideological shift towards belief in free markets, which gathered force with the governments of Reagan and Thatcher and was strengthened by the fall of Communism and the general weakening of left-wing parties. The key achievement of postwar Europe—the welfare state—came increasingly under threat. By the 1980s, the shift in ideology and the absence of alternatives was a major influence in many areas, such as the formation of future policymakers and the spread of influence of the Chicago School, notably in the case of the Chilean "Chicago Boys."

From 1973 to 1994, world export volume rose 4.5 percent a year—no faster than in the previous decade, but with significant increases in intrafirm trade and in manufacturing exports from low-wage to high-wage economies. More significant still were international capital flows. The U.S. commercial banking industry underwent major structural changes in the postwar period, leading by the late 1960s to more aggressive international competition, with U.S. banks spearheading an international banking boom.[1] The OPEC price rise of 1973 and the international banks' need to recycle surplus oil country funds precipitated a massive expansion in the international movement of funds. Average daily trade in the global foreign exchange market rose from $15 billion in 1973 to over $1.3 trillion by 1995. Cross-border buying and selling of financial assets was less than 10 percent of GDP in the United States in 1980, and 135 percent by 1993.[2] Equity and portfolio investments boomed, sustained by financial innovation designed to reduce investors' risk.

The positive side of global expansion was that it brought gains in efficiency and competitiveness. The negative side was a huge increase in instability, as capital movements became increasingly detached from real investment and prone to the wild swings seen later in the 1990s. The increase in world growth that would go some way to justifying the credentials of the new order has not yet been seen. The world economy has seen growth in the last decade of around 3 percent a year—some two points lower than that achieved during 1950-73,[3] and too little to solve the North's employment problems, let alone the poverty problem of the South.

Perhaps the key consequence of these trends for Latin America has been the extent to which finance has become separated from trade and investment. Exit from financial markets is easy and that flexibility is highly prized, and is reflected in an increase in world profits without a concomitant rise in investment.[4] For individual Latin American countries, the new trend translates into high interest rates needed to retain liquid capital, but which deter productive investment. Even direct foreign investment can still involve instability. As a World Bank analysis notes: "A direct investor can borrow in order to export capital, and thereby generate rapid capital

---

[1] Devlin, 1989.
[2] UNCTAD, 1997: 70-71.
[3] Ibid.: 70
[4] Ibid.: 96.

outflows."[5] These developments represent a serious decline in the margin of maneuver of national policy.

Technological trends have also had powerful consequences for production and trade. The dynamic industries of today are in the service sector and in knowledge-intensive industries. Resources can be moved internationally with considerable ease. A country's human capital, above all, and efficient service provision are what now most strongly determine comparative advantage in trade, as well as attractiveness to foreign investment. And scale no longer matters as it used to. Small and medium-sized industries can be competitive in the new lines, benefiting from flexible specialization linked to electronics-based manufacturing systems.[6] Economies of scale can be substituted by networks of small firms, which collaborate and compete simultaneously: "social capital" in the form of trust and good social relations facilitates competitiveness, along with skills in the new technologies.[7]

Towards the end of the period, a further dimension of increased global integration—at first sight contradictory—has become regional integration. The United States has been seeking through regional trade agreements in Latin America to move towards a regional Free Trade Area of the Americas by 2005. Presented as the "Initiative of the Americas" in 1990, the stated objective of the plan was creation of a free trade zone stretching "from the Port of Anchorage to Patagonia." The first step was envisaged as a free trade zone including Canada, the United States and Mexico—the North American Free Trade Agreement (NAFTA). These developments have brought other actors onto the scene with new vigor: Canada, which joined the Organization of American States in 1990, and the European Union, interested in maintaining a European role in the new order.

A final aspect of the new global awareness has been environmental concern. As pollution and deforestation took their toll, there was at last by the 1980s an increased awareness on the part of the public and some politicians that action was needed. This led to the Brundtland Commission and subsequently to the first UN

---

[5] Claessens, Dooley and Warner, 1993: 22.

[6] Piore and Sabel, 1984; Brundenius and Göransson, 1993.

[7] We shall adopt the phrase "social capital," introduced into the literature by Putnam, based on Italian experience. Putnam uses it to express the wealth a given society has in the intangible form of traditions of trust, reciprocity and conventions of behaving, which all affect productivity, possibly in very indirect ways.

Conference on Environment and Development in 1992 in Rio de Janeiro. Five years on, however, there was little to show for it. From Latin America's point of view, the threats were more obvious than the benefits, as all too often environmental concern on the part of the developed world seemed to translate into the developing countries slowing much needed expansion, taking measures that increased costs, or accepting protection on the part of developed countries on the environmental pretext.

DEBT-LED GROWTH AND CRISIS

The first impact of this global expansion on Latin America came in the aftermath of the OPEC price rise of 1973. The role of the dollar as the key currency through the 1950s, which helped maintain a system of fixed exchange rates, was undermined during the 1960s as the pool of dollars held outside the United States increased. The process was accelerated as U.S. spending on the Vietnam War increased at the end of the decade. The outflow of dollars led to the development of the so-called Euro-dollar market, which grew from $9 billion in 1964 to $80 billion by 1972. In August 1971, the United States finally abandoned the Bretton Woods rules of fixed parities. Price movements immediately increased, and price fluctuations on world commodity markets were greater in the next four years than at any other time since the Second World War. At the heart of this was OPEC's decision to raise the price of oil fourfold in 1973.

The Latin American balance of payments was dramatically affected by the OPEC price rise, the resulting increase in the cost of oil imports, and the sudden need by the OPEC countries to deposit surplus dollars. Through the 1950s and 1960s, though direct foreign investment in manufacturing had been important in the larger countries, the total net flows had not been large, as shown in Table 7.1. Commercial bank credit came in even smaller quantities until the late 1960s. Both facts reflected in part borrowing by TNCs on Latin American credit markets. The creation of the Alliance for Progress and the IDB led to more official lending. But as the outflow of profits rose, net transfers became negative in the 1960s. In the late 1960s, increased bank lending at first principally took the form of trade credit, but increasingly banks began to look for customers of all kinds, as the developed coun-

TABLE 7.1

LATIN AMERICA: COMPOSITION OF CAPITAL MOVEMENTS
(Annual averages in millions of 1980 U.S. dollars)

Average:	Direct foreign investment (1)	Net loans (2)	Official unrequited transfers (3)	Net capital movements[1] (4)	Payments of interest and profits (5)	Net transfers[1] (6)	Change in reserves (7)
1950-60	2,067	1,451	231	3,673	3,562	111	75
1961-65	1,131	1,861	480	3,370	4,860	-1,480	101
1966-70	2,283	5,460	524	6,900	7,369	-469	1,367
1971-73	3,418	11,757	498	9,100	8,371	729	6,572
1974-77	3,495	20,355	348	25,048	10,237	14,811	6,394
1978-81	5,940	29,233	575	38,048	19,535	18,513	5,243
1982-89	4,599	5,549	1,428	14,513	35,863	-21,350	-3,327

Note: Figures in current U.S. dollars were deflated by the unit value index of developed market economies' exports of manufactures.
[1]Column (4) is the sum of (1) to (3) plus errors and omissions in the balance of payments. Column (6) is equal to (4) minus (5).
Source: Ffrench-Davis, Muñoz and Palma, 1994.

tries went into recession because of higher energy costs, and the banks' usual customers fell away.

The subsequent boom in lending combined with other international factors, first to aggravate the difficulties of macro management already present in the 1960s, and second, to obscure the real problems of development with a deceptive and dangerous veil of dollars. Countries varied in their degree of vulnerability, but none escaped entirely. Throughout Latin America, something of the atmosphere of the 1920s was recreated, even if not quite all the same sales techniques were used. Ironically, the borrowers were as much those Latin American countries benefiting from the OPEC price rise, with new or renewed oil booms, as those whose balance of payments worsened because of the rising cost of oil and falling primary product prices. Creditors saw good export revenues as a far better reason for lending than increased bills for oil, and the scarcity of cash in the preceding two decades had strengthened a culture where if an international body considered a country creditworthy, then it was safe to borrow.

Moreover, real interest rates in the mid-1970s were negative, so borrowing appeared rational at a time when countries were faced with unstable and deteriorating terms of trade, particularly since commodity price forecasts by organizations like the World Bank were optimistic at the end of the decade and exports were rising at some 8 percent a year in real terms.[8] Borrowing was also encouraged by a whole range of international actors, including the international financial institutions, which did not appear to perceive the dangers.[9] An evaluation by the IMF in 1981 stated that "the overall debt situation during the 1970s adapted itself to the sizable strains introduced in the international payments system...Though some countries experienced difficulties, a generalized debt management problem was avoided, and in the aggregate the outlook for the immediate future does not give cause for alarm."[10] International institutions and creditors in general ignored the danger of a "herd effect," even though it was likely to happen when banks were adjusting their level of activity upward in Latin America after 30 years of a small presence.[11]

The lack of sensitivity to the growing size of the problem was aggravated by lack of information, both in national governments and in the international financial institutions. There was no centralized control of borrowing, or even information gathering by governments. Public enterprises and local governments borrowed without anyone perceiving that while each individual decision was rational, the whole would be far more disastrous than the sum of its parts. Information systems had not kept up with the changing nature of debt, particularly the growth of short-term and private nonguaranteed debt.[12] By mid-1982, shortly before the crisis, Mexico was 12 to 18 months behind on supplying the World Bank with information.[13]

As commissions and corruption became a characteristic of highly profitable deals, the lack of information suited all sides. Imports rose strongly, and the military regimes of the 1970s took advantage of the availability of resources to build up

---

[8] An accepted rule of thumb was that borrowing was reasonable if the rate of growth of exports was expected to exceed the rate of interest.

[9] See Kapur, Lewis and Webb, 1997, Vol. I, Chapter 11, on the World Bank's lack of concern.

[10] Nowzad, et al., 1981.

[11] Devlin, 1989; Kindleberger, 1978.

[12] Devlin and Ffrench-Davis, 1995.

[13] Kapur, Lewis and Webb, 1997, Vol. I: 605.

defense equipment. International commercial banks and the arms trade together assisted Latin America in using its credit.[14] Foreign reserves still rose strongly, as Table 7.1 shows.

Demand pressures meant that inflation tended to rise, which created a further incentive to allow the exchange rate to overvalue, thus helping to reduce inflation by reducing dollar costs.[15] As exchange rates moved in the direction of overvaluation, expectations of eventual devaluation accelerated the export of Latin American capital: in Argentina, Mexico and Venezuela, domestic capital exports began to match if not exceed the inflow of new money, in a dance crazier than that of the 1920s, if that were possible. By the end of 1983, the stock of nonofficial Latin American assets in the United States reached around $160 billion, not far from the $209 billion owed to U.S. banks. The combination of incentives to export capital and the revolution in communications (telex, fax, etc.) led to new ways of behaving and transmitting information. The "propensity to move money internationally" increased rapidly as modest savers, who would never have thought internationally 10 years earlier, now began to do so.[16]

While foreign borrowing followed a common trend across Latin America, countries borrowed at different rates and put the money to different uses. Some countries had already been increasing their borrowing in the late 1960s, as the Eurocurrency market grew: debt service (interest plus amortization) as a proportion of exports was already as high as one-quarter by 1973 for the continent as a whole, with Mexico standing at 34 percent.[17] There were, however, four partial exceptions to the borrowing spree. The Sandinista regime in Nicaragua from 1979 and the Castro government in Cuba did not have the same access to international financial markets that other countries had, though both borrowed bilaterally from Europe and the Soviet Bloc, and Nicaragua had the continent's highest debt ratio when the crisis broke. Peru's access was restricted after the conflict with the banks

---

[14] Ugarteche, 1968.

[15] Among the eight countries for which data are reported by Jorgensen and Paldam, six (Argentina, Chile, Mexico, Peru, Uruguay and Colombia) tended toward more overvaluation in the course of the 1970s.

[16] This was confirmed in many interviews with finance managers in the early 1980s. See Devlin, 1989, for an illuminating account.

[17] Fishlow, 1991.

described below. The fourth case was Colombia. Here the economic team in 1974 took a strong decision not to increase foreign borrowing, on the grounds that it would damage national savings. The team opted instead for tax reform and measures to increase domestic savings. These were implemented against considerable resistance from the private sector, various elements of the public sector and the armed forces, and were achieved by means of bureaucratic obstacles to borrowing.[18] The pressures the policy encountered illuminate the forces behind the expansion elsewhere.

Both public and private sectors borrowed. The use of credit varied more than the scale of debt. Investment rose generally, though with a high imported component. Figure 7.1 shows the rise in investment made possible by the inflow of money. In most cases, much money went into imports and financing of capital flight. Brazil and Colombia retained controls on the capital account and benefited from this. Imports of military equipment were particularly significant in the countries ruled by military dictatorships. Financing of investment was most significant in Brazil, Colombia and Mexico,[19] though in the latter it was associated with huge and misdirected projects which became notorious white elephants.[20] The share of public sector enterprises in public expenditure typically rose.[21]

The multiple effects of the sudden easy availability of money were felt in the structure and nature of production. The potential benefits from the new technology described above were not reaped; on the contrary, the cheapening of capital worsened the existing bias toward excessively capital-intensive and large projects, both in the public sector and in industry. The cheapening dollar and negative real interest rates produced a boom in capital-intensive hydroelectric projects, which vastly overequipped this sector, particularly in Mexico, Argentina and Venezuela. The nontradables sector boomed, to the long-run detriment of exports. The combination of increased scale and worsening financial control was damaging for the

[18] Thorp, 1992: 166.

[19] Devlin and Ffrench-Davis, 1995. See Fishlow, 1989, for a critique of Brazilian public investment in this period.

[20] Ros, 1987.

[21] Fishlow, 1989: 95, gives data on Brazil. Inter-American Development Bank, 1984, Annex B, shows rises for five of the seven countries studied, and gives no data for Brazil.

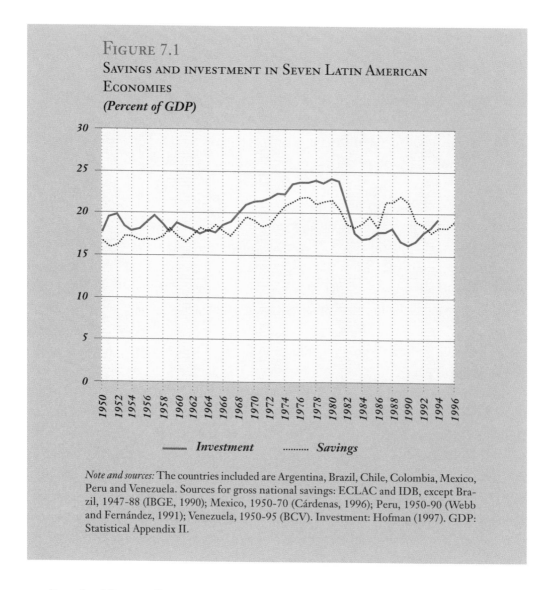

FIGURE 7.1
SAVINGS AND INVESTMENT IN SEVEN LATIN AMERICAN
ECONOMIES
(Percent of GDP)

——— Investment   ·········· Savings

Note and sources: The countries included are Argentina, Brazil, Chile, Colombia, Mexico, Peru and Venezuela. Sources for gross national savings: ECLAC and IDB, except Brazil, 1947-88 (IBGE, 1990); Mexico, 1950-70 (Cárdenas, 1996); Peru, 1950-90 (Webb and Fernández, 1991); Venezuela, 1950-95 (BCV). Investment: Hofman (1997). GDP: Statistical Appendix II.

quality of public spending. Large and poorly-conceived projects frequently had negative indirect and direct environmental and social consequences. Box 7.1 illustrates the point with the Grande Carajás Program in the Eastern Amazon, where project results were damaging despite the fact that the mining company had a good record for environmental safeguards. Increased capital intensity meant that industrial expansion and concentration continued in the 1970s, aggravating high concentration ratios and poor employment outcomes.

Box 7.1

The Grande Carajás Program in Brazil

The Grande Carajás Program in the Eastern Amazon was the largest mining project in a rainforest region, within Brazil's most ambitious development program, administering an area of 850,000 square kilometers. In the mid-1960s, rich minerals were discovered in this region, including iron ore, manganese, gold, bauxite and nickel. Investments in the Serra dos Carajás iron ore mine totaled approximately $3.4 billion, about one-third of which was provided by foreign capital (Japan, the World Bank and the European Community). For foreign investors, a main strategic interest was the provision of cheap and high-quality iron supplies: in 1991, 32.6 million tons of ore were produced. An environmental assessment of the program must distinguish between the direct effects related to pig iron production, and the derived impacts in the larger zone of influence. Regarding the direct component, the domestic mining company Companhia Vale do Rio Doce (CVRD), which contributed 45 percent of the total investment, had a good environmental record and developed a number of pioneering environmental safeguards (green belts, ecological zoning, etc.) for the mine and the workers' settlement zone. However, huge problems affected the surroundings: the building of a 890 km railway to the sea port of São Luis opened up the area for squatters and cattle ranchers. Native Amerindians were displaced despite a land demarcation project, which was mismanaged by FUNAI, the Brazilian Indian Administration Institute. Perhaps the greatest cause of concern was that energy for the large-scale pig iron production was initially supplied from charcoal produced by native forest felling. These forests were then by law gradually to be reforested with eucalyptus plantations that would take over the energy supply function—a scheme that was unrealistic in practice.

Sources: Treece, 1989; Romano, 1992; IUCN-NC, 1996; Wunder, 1997 (consultancy report for this book).

In various ways, these processes increased the structural weaknesses of the Latin American economies. First, the emerging problems produced out of the pattern of the previous 25 years were covered up. The beginnings of well-directed policy reform, which could be detected in at least four of the five largest economies, were aborted because of internal political events in some cases (Chile and Argentina), rather than because of the sudden availability of money. Generally, however, the inflow of money neutralized the messages being given to policymakers in the 1960s by the signs of emerging gaps and limited market size. Protection actually increased in Brazil.

In particular, fiscal reform and the quality of government expenditure now became unlikely candidates for policy agendas. Who wanted to push tax reforms through reluctant congresses when money could be readily borrowed at negative or very low real interest rates? Who wanted to battle with the quality of existing spending when new projects brought new money (and of course with that more commissions)? The bias toward "solving" problems with new projects rather than dealing with existing difficulties was most obvious in agriculture, where problems such as excessive salinity or poor maintenance of irrigation were much easier to address with new schemes rather than by confronting the difficulties, especially when maintenance was difficult to fund by borrowing. The quality of management and financial control in large state companies tended to deteriorate in the general atmosphere of easy money and private gain.

Meanwhile, the expenditure side was burdened by increasing debt service, with larger fluctuations as the composition of the debt shifted from official credit to loans at free market rates of interest. These loans were preferred, as they became more available, since they avoided the problem of conditionality. Expenditure was also increased by the gradual takeover of private sector debt by the state.[22] This happened gradually, but was notable in Chile, where initial mismanagement by the military regime that took power in 1973, committed to radical trade and financial liberalization, produced a private sector crisis. Hence the move to free market economics actually resulted in an *increase* in the weight of the public sector in the economy between 1981 and 1984.[23]

---

[22] O'Connell, 1994: 7; Whitehead, 1979.
[23] Ibid.

The tax revenue component of public saving did not always fall, despite the erosion caused by rising inflation, since revenue based on foreign trade increased with rising imports and sales taxes were maintained by buoyant activity. But with the exception of Colombia, no major revenue-raising reforms occurred.[24] Nothing was done to encourage private savings, and real interest rates were very low in several countries. Financial liberalization, particularly in the Southern Cone, led to high financial savings but low national savings. Financial liberalization without other institutional reforms, however, tended to mean that domestic saving ended up as capital export.

The balance of payments deficit behaved in diametrically opposed ways for oil exporters and importers in response to the oil shocks, but whether the deficit disappeared or grew, the pressure to restructure was lessened, either by oil or by the option of borrowing. The inflow of money, demand pressures, and rising import prices all led to inflation and generated overvaluation, resulting in a particularly perverse process, whereby financial integration disastrously outran trade integration.[25] Although trade flows increased in the 1970s, important steps to develop exports for the future were not taken. Furthermore, the consequence of the pattern of increasing financial integration was *reduced* long-run trade integration. Although there was an immediate increase in imports, and in fact export volume rose in several of the larger countries, the environment of the 1970s did not encourage major efforts at export promotion, for several reasons. Surplus funds that were the source of the debt derived partly from recession in the developed countries, whose defensive protectionist moves deterred new efforts at exporting. Overvaluation compounded the problem.[26] So did the fact that the availability of money meant that there was no urgency to develop schemes to promote new exports.

Overvaluation was worsened in the Southern Cone by adoption of extreme monetarist policies in the second half of the 1970s. These policies were based on

---

[24] Colombia was an exception both in limiting borrowing and in putting through a tax reform, which raised revenue as a share of GDP from 19 percent in 1973 to 21.5 percent in 1975. Thorp, 1991: 166.

[25] Fishlow, 1991.

[26] Ibid.: 163. Fishlow explores the issue of exports and the real exchange rate, and shows that there is no clear short-term correlation. Existing productive structures, and a wide range of policies including nonmarket interventions, are more important.

the assumption that a sufficiently fierce holding of the exchange rate, combined with great trade openness, would allow the law of one price to operate. This assumption predicted that the internal rate of price inflation would approximate quite swiftly to the international rate. The extreme assumptions of well-functioning markets behind such policies did not hold, and the result was overvaluation. Parallel financial liberalization led to inflows of money with limited profit opportunities because of the combined effect of overvaluation and trade liberalization on the industrial sector, leading, notably in Chile, to speculative booms in real estate and durable consumption goods.

With the internationalization of capital movements, an increasing proportion of Latin American debt was held abroad by Latin American nationals, further reducing external flexibility. Internal debt also grew. Both phenomena limited the freedom to consider a moratorium on foreign debt as an option when the collapse came, since domestic creditors saw it as a threat to their own position.

Flexibility in relation to stabilization needs and policies also diminished. In the 1960s, orthodox responses to fiscal and balance of payments gaps tended to have perverse effects due to the structure of costs, the degree of monopoly, and the difficulty of fiscal discipline. As debt service rose, so its impact on the public sector accounts increased, which meant more vulnerability of the fiscal balance to interest rate increases. As private sector debt rose, interest costs had a heavier impact on business costs.[27] As public sector enterprises increasingly used foreign funding, and as lack of control allowed interesting possibilities of associated commissions, so centralized management of fiscal discipline became, if anything, more difficult. Growth of the informal sector removed more of the economy from the reach of the usual instruments of policy, and the culture of tax evasion became pervasive.

These problems mattered less in the 1970s than in the 1960s for many countries, since with easier commercial borrowing both the need for drastic action and the role of the IMF were reduced. But some countries had severe adjustment problems—notably Peru, which, encouraged by the World Bank,[28] borrowed on the

---

[27] In Peru in the 1970s, some manufacturing firms dedicated 70 percent of their running costs to interest charges. Thorp and Whitehead, 1979.

[28] Thorp and Whitehead, 1979.

expectation of oil. It faced the need for adjustment when in 1977 those expectations were not realized, and the terms of trade turned unfavorable. In Peru's case, these problems came on top of the extended use of price controls on food and public enterprise prices by the Velasco regime. The controls were extended because of the possibility of external credit and oil, but the result was a huge deficit, as other prices rose and the necessary subsidy increased. Peru's case was unique in that in 1977 the commercial banks for the first time agreed to refinance without the seal of approval of the IMF. However, the banks found it impossible to monitor the agreement. This led to a confirmation of the rule whereby the banks lent only with the seal of approval of the multilateral agencies.[29]

As oil prices weakened in 1981, Mexico, by then the largest oil producer in Latin America, ran out of foreign exchange. Devaluation began at the end of 1981 and continued into 1982. On August 13, 1982, the Mexican government announced a 90-day moratorium on repayment of the principal due on its external public debt. On September 1, all banks were nationalized and exchange control imposed without warning. Soon the moratorium was extended into 1983, and an emergency agreement signed with the IMF.

Mexico's crisis was certainly the most dramatic event of 1982, but the financial crisis of that year extended far beyond one country. Latin America as a whole was severely affected, as was the U.S. banking system (Mexican debt alone accounted for 44 percent of the capital of the nine largest U.S. banks) and the prosperity of many U.S. exporters. Even before the Mexican crisis, Argentina was already in severe difficulties because of a domestic banking crisis, aggravated by the South Atlantic conflict of April-June 1982. By the end of the year, Brazil was far advanced down a path similar to that of Mexico: its exports were hampered by the international recession, and its large external debt implied a heavy balance of payments cost when interest rates rose. Venezuela, Chile and Cuba were soon all engaged in negotiations with their creditors, together with many of the smaller Latin American countries. Indeed, virtually every nation in the region was soon either openly negotiating or on the brink of such action.

---

[29] Stallings, 1987; Thorp, 1979.

The origins of "the debt crisis" were older, however. The weakening of commodity prices from 1976-78 had been offset by fresh loans. Given weak financial institutions and inadequate supervision, the extreme openness of Latin America on capital account allowed a sharp accentuation of the degree of exposure at the end of the decade, with debt denominated at floating rates and in dollars. As President Reagan failed to cut the U.S. deficit, so real interest rates were driven up. While the tightening of U.S. credit was meant to cut demand for credit in the United States by weak domestic borrowers, the end result of the policy hit the weakest borrowers outside the country—and particularly Latin American nations, whose interest payments were, of course, not tax deductible, in contrast to those of most U.S. debtors. If LDC export prices are used to calculate real interest rates, then the discontinuity is startling: the average real rate of interest on LDC debt rose from -6 percent in 1981 to +14.6 percent in 1982.[30] An increase in international interest rates of one point meant for Brazil, for example, that exports had to increase by 3 percent simply to cover the increased interest burden.

Echoes of the 1920s resound. Both the 1920s and the 1970s witnessed debt booms subject to the classic overshooting that follows from the tendency in such situations to underestimate risks. The rash lending of the 1970s was again led initially by U.S. banks, the lessons of 50 years before having been forgotten. Just as in the 1920s, the rapid expansion and the way loans were used in the 1970s had much to do with the nature and the difficulties of the adjustment crisis. Curiously, common to both shocks was the outflow of capital from Latin America, which preceded the main shock. In the 1920s, the outflow occurred in 1928; in the 1980s, there was a significant increase in capital flight from several countries as early as 1981. In both crises, too, there was a precise date—September 1929 and August 1982, respectively—when a sea change occurred. In 1929, it was a precipitous collapse of the U.S. stock market; and in both 1929 and 1982, it was a sudden reversal of both capital flows and creditors' attitudes.

---

[30] Reisen, 1992.

THE CRISIS OF "ADJUSTMENT"

The impact of the shock was felt in four ways: import and export prices, interest rates, the recession in developed country markets, and the abrupt turnaround in the supply of finance from abroad. The continent's heavy borrowing at free market rates in the 1970s made Latin America particularly vulnerable to changes in interest rates and the supply of funds. By contrast, East Asia, characterized by greater trade integration and exports of manufactures, suffered more from price movements and the developed country recession. This had the further consequence that financial markets remained open to East Asia, which compensated for the trade shock and facilitated adjustment.[31] Latin American countries lacked credit entirely.

As a result, the direction and manner of adjustment in the first instance were dictated by the creditors, who acted in a coordinated manner from an early date.[32] Unlike the anonymous bondholders of the 1930s, commercial banks were easily identifiable, since they had granted a significant share of their loans through publicly organized credit syndicates. Following Mexico's announcement, an informal arrangement was rapidly made, constituting in effect a "lender of last resort." The initial understanding of the banks was that the crisis was temporary, one of liquidity not insolvency, and that debtors could and should retrench in order to keep paying, aided by rescheduling. The mindset of many in international financial circles was that the crisis represented a unique opportunity to force Latin American governments out of old bad habits, so rescheduling was usually tightly tied to reducing protection and the role of the state. The early reschedulings took place on terms extremely unfavorable to the debtor countries. An index of the cost of debt renegotiation, taking into account the fees paid, the maturity term and the spread over LIBOR, and comparing the cost with the same costs paid in 1980-81, taken as 100, found that in the first round of reschedulings, Argentina paid 319, Mexico, 280 and Brazil, 144.[33] The banks' profits were high: dividends declared by the large U.S. money-center banks in 1984, just two years into the crisis, were double those of 1980.[34]

---

[31] Fishlow, 1991.

[32] This paragraph draws on Devlin and Ffrench-Davis, 1995.

[33] Devlin and Ffrench-Davis, 1995, Table 3.

[34] Kapur, Lewis and Webb, 1997, Vol. I: 610, citing Lissakers, 1991.

Early efforts by debtors to act in unison, such as the Cartagena Meeting of 1984, were weak. Policymakers had different agendas and the major economies reached their crisis points at different times. But the creditor banks moved to forestall a buildup of momentum. "Whether by design or happenstance…the choice of the cooperative debtor, Mexico, as the first country to be granted a MYRA [multiyear rescheduling arrangement] both demonstrated the rewards of cooperative behavior and ensured that Mexico did not defect."[35]

The consequences for the Latin American debtors were extreme. Figure 7.2 shows how external transfers moved in the space of a year from significantly positive to minus 30 percent or so. The typical situation was one of immediate and severe balance of payments and fiscal crises, since debt service impinged heavily on the national budget. Countries devalued and adopted varieties of sharply orthodox policies, seeking to cut imports by cutting demand. In the first months, only Bolivia followed a more heterodox route.

Table 7.2 traces how in the first two years of the crisis, demand had to be radically cut in order to free up resources to pay this external transfer. Investment crashed immediately in 1983: in per capita terms it was 40 percent below its 1981 value. Per capita consumption was also squeezed and imports fell to nearly half their precrisis level. The benefit of the small increase in exports was wiped out by the continuing unfavorable terms of trade effect. The decline in imports offered the means to pay the increase in the external transfer. The burden continued through the 1980s: GDP per capita did not regain its precrisis level, and investment per capita was far below the figure for 1980-81.

The so-called adjustment was a misnomer, therefore.[36] Countries were forced from one disequilibrium position to another: that of balance of payments surplus, with huge social costs. This is seen in the internal dynamics that matched the external transfer. The principal internal transfer instrument was recession, which generated cuts in consumption, investment and growth, as Table 7.2 shows. The result was extreme short- and long-term social costs. There was also a huge fiscal problem implied in the debt and in the effect of devaluation on the debt burden in local

---

[35] Kapur, Lewis and Webb, 1997, Vol. I: 620. On debtors' cartels and how countries did not exploit their bargaining position, see Griffith-Jones, 1988; Tussie, 1988.

[36] This point was made to me by Osvaldo Sunkel.

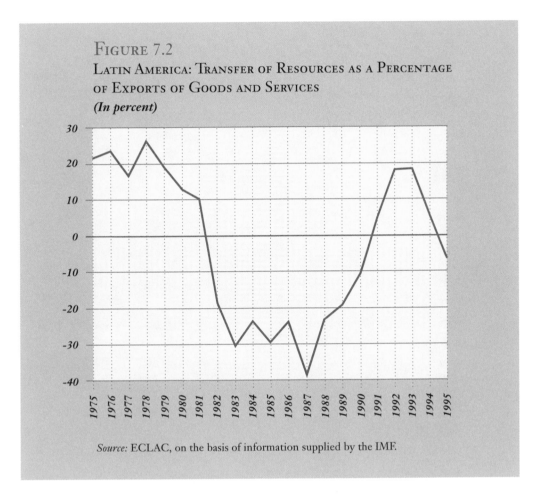

Figure 7.2

Latin America: Transfer of Resources as a Percentage of Exports of Goods and Services

(In percent)

Source: ECLAC, on the basis of information supplied by the IMF.

currency. The fiscal problem was made worse by recession and compounded in some cases by the need to extract foreign exchange from the private sector, if the government did not directly control exports. If it was difficult to tax the export sector before, it was doubly so now. The result was often an acceleration of inflation, which was a further burden on the poor, who were less able to protect themselves against the falling value of money. The worst case was Bolivia, where despite the government's control of tin revenues, the collapse of the tin market on top of the debt crisis created a disastrous situation, which by 1984-85 included hyperinflation.[37]

---

[37] Hyperinflation represents the complete loss of confidence in money, which had undoubtedly occurred at that point in Bolivia.

TABLE 7.2
LATIN AMERICAN GDP PER CAPITA AND THE EXTERNAL SECTOR
(Percent of 1980-81 GDP)

	1980-81	1982	1983	1984	1985	1986-90 avg.	1991-93 avg.	1994-95 avg.
GDP	100.0	95.6	91.3	92.2	92.7	94.1	94.7	95.8
Consumption	77.0	74.0	70.3	70.4	69.9	71.6	72.8	75.5
Investment	24.4	19.6	14.9	15.2	16.1	15.9	16.6	21.1
Nonfinancial current account								
Goods								
Exports	12.5	12.6	13.6	14.5	14.2	15.2	18.0	15.4
Imports	-12.3	-9.7	-7.5	-8.0	-7.9	-9.2	-13.0	-17.1
Services								
Exports	2.0	2.1	2.0	2.0	2.1	2.5	2.7	3.0
Imports	-3.6	-2.9	-2.0	-1.8	-1.7	-1.9	-2.4	-3.9
Terms of trade effect	-0.4	-2.3	-2.5	-2.1	-2.5	-4.3	-5.9	0.3
Net transfers								
Capital	4.7	2.5	0.3	1.3	0.4	1.2	4.9	1.2
Net profit, interest	-3.2	-4.9	-4.5	-4.8	-4.5	3.8	2.9	3.9
Change in reserves	-0.1	-2.5	-0.5	1.2	-0.1	0.1	2.0	1.0

Source: Devlin and Ffrench-Davis, 1995; updated for 1994-95 based on ECLAC, *Preliminary Overview*, 1996.

Social indicators for the continent show that GDP per capita (Table 7.2) in aggregate for the continent fell 8 percent in the first two years. Real wages fell 17 percent in aggregate for the continent in the first two years. At the country level and over the whole decade, they fell in all but five cases, often by 20 percent or more.

The fiscal crisis resulted in severe cuts in social spending (Table 7.3). Per capita social spending fell 10 percent in real terms between 1982 and 1986, to recover somewhat by 1990, though it remained 6 percent below the level of 1980-81.[38] Poverty grew, with the proportion of households below the poverty line in-

---

[38] IDB, 1997: 47.

TABLE 7.3
LATIN AMERICA: SOCIAL INDICATORS
(Annual rates of growth and index)

Indicator	1980	1985	1990	1995
Rate of open unemployment (%)	6.7	10.1	8.0	7.8
Urban informality (%)	40.2	47.0	52.1	55.7
Real wages in manufacturing (index)	100.0	93.1	86.8	96.3
Minimum real wages (index)	100.0	86.4	68.9	70.1
Social spending per capita (index)	100.0	90.0	94.0	
Poor as % of all households	35.0	37.0	41.0	39.0

Source: Tokman, 1997; ECLAC, *Social Panorama of Latin America*, 1995,1996.

TABLE 7.4
LATIN AMERICA: NONAGRICULTURAL EMPLOYMENT STRUCTURE
(In percent)

	Informal sector[1]				Formal sector		
	Total	Own-account workers	Domestic service	Small business	Total	Public sector	Large private firms
1980	40.2	19.2	6.4	14.6	59.8	15.7	44.1
1985	47.0	22.6	7.8	16.6	53.1	16.6	36.5
1990	51.6	24.7	6.7	20.2	48.4	15.3	33.0
1995	56.1	26.5	7.1	22.5	43.9	13.2	30.8

Source: PREALC, based on household surveys and other official sources.
[1] Includes small businesses, defined as those that have five or 10 workers, depending on the available information.

creasing from 35 percent in 1980 to 41 percent in 1990 for the region as a whole (Table 7.3). Income distribution also worsened, with Uruguay the only country going against the trend and actually showing an improvement.

Adjustment occurred principally through wages and the labor market. The urban labor market is described in Table 7.4. The outstanding fact is the increased role of the urban informal sector, which responded to three factors: medium-sized and large firms reorganized, reduced their labor forces, and restructured to make more use of subcontracting; survival strategies meant that more family members sought employment; and the cutting back of the public sector reduced jobs. New work patterns meant greater precariousness, because of lack of contracts, regulation and health protection. The new trends affected women more than men, since there were more women in the informal sector. If domestic service is included in the urban informal sector, then women's share of urban informal employment was over 70 percent in most cases. The share of Indians and migrants was also disproportionately high.[39] Youth also suffered: data for 12 Latin American countries show that rates of unemployment were higher for young people than overall almost by a factor of two and within that, higher for young women than young men.[40] A further consequence of the crisis was in education: women and girls dropped out of education in order to pursue survival strategies in larger numbers than men.[41]

Initial efforts to respond to the apparently inevitable short-run dislocation took the form of various kinds of emergency funds. Chile had been the pioneer in the 1970s with PAIT, a fund which financed short-term employment creation. Bolivia now followed with a Social Emergency Fund in 1986, and the model was rapidly imitated in many countries.[42] These funds did ease the short-term burden. But because they operated outside the mainstream social sector ministries precisely in order to be effective,[43] they also exposed and even aggravated the institutional weaknesses of the core systems of service delivery. Further, the creation of employment at any cost did not touch the underlying need to reshape structures to provide for the marginalized population in the long term. For instance, the use of a program's resources was typically by demand, which guarded against paternalism and helped identify some needs. But this overlooked the depth of the privation implied in poverty: a poor man or woman may well be incapable of putting forward his or her demand.

---

[39] This paragraph is based on Arriagada, 1994.

[40] The exceptions were Chile and Paraguay, both growing quite fast in the 1980s.

[41] Based on United Nations, 1989, a world study including data on Argentina, Brazil, Chile, Colombia, Jamaica, Mexico and Peru.

[42] See Graham, 1994, for an authoritative review.

[43] In fact, they were often directly under the Presidency, as in Peru and Mexico. The "effectiveness" was a matter both of rapid disbursement and of political control.

The rest of the 1980s was a time of huge adjustment efforts with a heavy focus on the short term, continual debt renegotiations, and generally ineffective stabilization, with the notable exception of Bolivia. (Chile had already achieved some success). By mid-decade, new elements in policies were in evidence, principally responding to the desperate need to stabilize. Some policies took countries in the direction of the neoliberal package described below; others took them (briefly) in the opposite direction.

The neoliberal elements that gradually became common were principally trade liberalization and privatization. Both appeared as lifelines to governments desperate to stabilize and to gain access to foreign credit. Trade liberalization was typically set as a condition for rescheduling. Mexico, a long-time adherent of protection, opted for trade liberalization in 1984 in the hope of moderating inflation, but also as a response to creditor pressure. In the following year, Mexico joined GATT, a momentous decision given previous policy stands.[44] Privatization now began to emerge as a rather attractive policy option, since it offered a simultaneous solution to various problems. It became clear that the selling of assets was very attractive to foreign interests. Such sales helped both the fiscal and the balance of payments sides of the adjustment problem. However, what dawned more slowly and to varying degrees was the extent to which such help was short-term and therefore had to be accompanied by other measures to raise tax revenues and exports, as well as the extent of the challenge implied in proper regulation of crucial public utilities once in private hands. Chile had already led the way in the 1970s, with a strong neoliberal orientation, divesting the state of over 550 enterprises, with more privatizations in the mid-1980s. The short-term value to the budget now increased interest among policymakers, and programs began to get under way in Argentina and Mexico.

It was unfortunate, if inevitable, that policy innovations were driven by expediency and by lack of options, given the collapse of alternatives and the straitjacket of the international environment. These characteristics enhanced what became the key weakness of such policies: the lack of supporting measures on the micro side, i.e., sectoral policies. The revenue effect of privatization was also a hazard, since it risked dampening ardor for measures essential for long-run fiscal health, such as tax reform.

---

[44] See Urzua, 1997: 80-81.

The element of policy that went in the opposite direction from the general neoliberal groundswell concerned stabilization programs more directly. Orthodox anti-inflation programs had been running into difficulties because they frequently resulted in stagnation and increased inflation. It was disillusion with such policies that pushed Brazil, Argentina and Peru into experiments with what came to be called "heterodox" stabilization policies. These policies, however, had no greater success. Heterodox shock policies combined price control across the board with varying degrees of orthodox demand restriction. They were premised on the importance of inertial inflation. With continuing inflation, a large part of the rise in prices in any one year can usually be explained simply by "inertia," i.e., the effect of past price rises.[45] As inertial inflation becomes entrenched, so inflation becomes less responsive to demand, and therefore to adjustment packages dependent on demand deflation for their effect. However, the argument that radical price control could annihilate the expectations sustaining inflation was reasonable if—and only if—first, aggregate demand was appropriately managed, and second, there was sufficient administrative capacity, and public confidence in that capacity, to secure an effective price freeze. In fact, neither Brazil nor Peru even tried to restrain demand, since in Brazil the preceding fiscal adjustment was thought to be enough, while in Peru the economic team considered that recession was actually aggravating inflation.[46] Policymakers also found it impossible to restrain prices across the board, so that those prices they could hold down fell in real terms, contributing to overvaluation and worsening deficits of state enterprises. Nevertheless, Argentina and Brazil persisted with versions of these policies throughout the 1980s. Mexico at the end of 1987 actually implemented the most successful version of all, using the PRI's ability to co-opt both business and the top echelons of the labor movement to manage and fine-tune the price and wage control.

---

[45] This is the result of formal indexation, but also stems from policy responses and private sector expectations revolving around four crucial "prices:" the exchange rate, the interest rate, public utility prices and wage rates. Certain other controlled prices—typically food prices—may also play a strategic role.

[46] By increasing unit costs as output fell and by reducing tax revenue.

The fiscal crisis was extraordinarily severe in Bolivia. Internal borrowing was impossible, given the limited bond market, so when external credit disappeared the recourse was to print money, which rapidly produced hyperinflation. By mid-1985, prices were rising at an annual rate of 20,000 percent and the effects on the real side were extremely serious. A dramatic stabilization program with a strong wage policy and drastic cuts in public sector employment turned the situation around. The perversity of arriving at such a serious situation was that stabilization brought positive supply-side effects, which helped sustain the anti-inflation program. In addition, external funding and the nonpayment of debt were important in reducing the kinds of negative feedback that derailed other programs.

Alongside the crisis-imposed, short-term focus, there was also a growing internalization of the line pushed by external financiers and others: that at least part of the problem lay in overextended public sectors. Gradually, the forced abandonment of sectoral policies, for example, became consciously justified as a radical and necessary rethinking of the role of the state. Interventionism became a discredited term and finance ministries consolidated their position at the expense of sectoral and planning ministries.

Increasingly, thinking began to shift towards free market policies. The traditional approach to economic integration was a casualty of the new spirit of free trade, since the emphasis was now on integration into the world economy.[47] Deregulation was pursued, apart from the ventures into heterodox policies. The resulting rises in food and some public utility prices had serious short-term consequences on social welfare. Financial and labor markets began to be liberalized, and the removal of restrictions on land markets heralded a new variety of land reform.

---

[47] Integration was also a casualty of the manner of external adjustment, which involved cutting imports. Thus, the debt shock of 1982 led to a drastic fall in trade among Latin American countries. For example, in real terms, the 1985-86 level of intra-Latin American exports was less than two-thirds of the 1981 level ($7.5 billion and $11.9 billion, respectively).

The Neoliberal Policy Package

By the 1990s, events and policymaking had clearly moved on. Gradually, both a learning process and the consolidation of a new policy approach became perceptible, helped on the international front by various factors which went to lessen short-term pressures. First, in March 1989, the United States launched the Brady Plan to put the rescheduling of debt on a better footing. This followed previous unsuccessful plans and included important new instruments for debt renegotiation backed by significant funding from the United States and Japan.[48] In addition, the commercial banks began to get their own houses in order, writing off or rescheduling debt. Second, interest rates finally began to come down again. Third, privatization programs and attractive interest rates began to draw capital into the larger economies, and Argentina, Brazil and Mexico even began to issue their own bonds on the international market. By 1992, the net external transfer at last turned in Latin America's favor, for the first time since 1981 (Figure 7.2). The snowball effect was strong, as "newly emerging markets" and "globalization" became fashionable. The crucial factor sustaining the expansion of equity financing from the end of the 1980s was international institutional development, as regulatory changes allowed pension funds and insurance companies to diversify their portfolios internationally as mutual funds grew. Financial liberalization became almost universal.[49] "Eurobonds" boomed, and European direct investment in Latin America grew, supported by institutional innovations within the European Union in the form of the European Investment Bank, European Commission Investment Partners, and AL-INVEST.

Whereas in the mid-1980s the emerging "Washington Consensus"[50] was focused on fiscal orthodoxy, liberalization and reducing the role of the state, by the 1990s a major shift of language had occurred. Now the talk was all not of

---

[48] Devlin and Ffrench-Davis, 1995.

[49] Eichengreen and Fishlow, 1996: 30. See Ffrench-Davis, 1989, and Griffith-Jones, 1988, for a detailed discussion of U.S., EU and Japanese markets.

[50] So named by John Williamson, a label which became a focus of criticism and much misunderstanding. He wrote in 1997: "My reason for compiling the Washington consensus was simply to document or report on the change in policy attitudes that I sensed was occurring in Latin America but of which Washington seemed largely unaware at the time" (Emmerij, 1997: 48). The name was resented as suggesting implicitly that policy consensus comes or is imposed from Washington.

liberalization but of reform, and structural reform at that. The IDB's evaluation of the new policies in 1996 was almost entirely phrased in such terms. Its documentation of the reform process, shown in Table 7.5, reveals the spread of the new policies through the entire continent, accelerating in the 1990s. As the IDB report recognizes, policies were a mix, varying by country and by time period, and ranging all the way from dogmatic liberalization to serious efforts at institutional reform.

In the 1980s, for example, policymakers had attempted financial liberalization, with weak institutions and frequently with destabilizing results. Now in the 1990s, they attempted financial reform. Legislation was passed to make central banks more independent and regulations covering capital markets and banks were strengthened. Peru and Nicaragua, for instance, two countries with historically serious institutional weaknesses, now undertook reforms of commercial bank supervision and in support of central bank independence. By mid-decade there was still, needless to say, a long way to go, and a few countries had not embarked on reform at all. How far the new reforms will make the necessary difference remains to be seen. One observer comments wryly on the Mexican 1994 crisis that "…foreign observers may have overestimated the independence of the Central Bank, perhaps taking too seriously the fact that the *Banco de México* became nominally autonomous in April 1994."[51]

Privatization now became widespread. Very few countries stood apart from the process, as will be seen in the next chapter: Uruguay was a notable example, but Costa Rica and Paraguay also moved slowly. Along with the former Eastern Bloc countries, Latin America in the 1990s became a leader in privatization. It is striking how far the process was allowed to affect sectors hitherto considered sacred to the state. Suddenly, electric power and even oil could be offered up to the private sector. In the course of 10 years, the shape of the Latin American economy was profoundly changed.

Privatization is the example par excellence of a reform that is both a threat and an opportunity. Table 7.6 shows the revenue from privatization as a percentage of central government revenue, a figure that captures elements of both promise and danger. Inflows of money were large and advantageous, but such a dramatic "so-

---

[51] Urzua, 1997: 106.

TABLE 7.5
STRUCTURAL REFORM POLICIES

	Stabili-zation	Trade liberali-zation	Tax reform	Financial reform	Privati-zation	Labor reform	Pension reform
1985 (or before)	Argentina (1978 and 1985); Bolivia, Chile (1975 and 1985); Costa Rica, Peru, Uruguay (1978)	Argentina (1978); Chile (1975 and 1985); Mexico, Uruguay (1978)		Argentina (1978); Chile (1975); Uruguay (1974 and 1985)	Chile (1974-78)	Chile (1979)	Chile (1981)
1986	Brazil Dom. Rep.	Bolivia Costa Rica		Mexico			
1987	Guatemala Jamaica	Jamaica			Jamaica		
1988	Mexico	Guatemala Guyana		Costa Rica Brazil Paraguay Guyana	Chile (circa 1988)		
1989	Venezuela	Argentina Paraguay El Salvador Trinidad and Tobago Venezuela		Chile Venezuela			
1990	Dom. Rep. Peru	Brazil Dom. Rep. Ecuador Honduras Peru		Bolivia Colombia El Salvador Nicaragua Peru Trinidad and Tobago	Argentina	Colombia Guatemala	

TABLE 7.5
STRUCTURAL REFORM POLICIES *(continued)*

	Stabili-zation	Trade liberali-zation	Tax reform	Financial reform	Privati-zation	Labor reform	Pension reform
1991	Argentina Colombia Guatemala Nicaragua Uruguay	Colombia Nicaragua Uruguay	Argentina	Dom. Rep. Honduras Guatemala	Belize Jamaica Guyana Venezuela	Argentina Peru	
1992	Ecuador Guyana Honduras Jamaica	Barbados	Nicaragua Peru	Argentina Jamaica	Barbados Mexico		
1993			El Salvador	Ecuador Bahamas	Nicaragua		Peru
1994	Brazil	Belize Haiti Suriname	Ecuador Guatemala Honduras Jamaica Paraguay Venezuela	Barbados Belize Haiti	Chile Peru Trinidad and Tobago		Argentina Colombia
1995	Suriname	Panama	Belize Bolivia		Bolivia	Panama	
1996		Bahamas					Uruguay Mexico

Source: Inter-American Development Bank, 1997.

TABLE 7.6
PUBLIC SECTOR PRIVATIZATION REVENUE AS A PERCENTAGE OF
CENTRAL GOVERNMENT EXPENDITURE

	1990	1991	1992	1993	1994	1995	1990-95
Belize	8	22	5	9	0	na	8
Bolivia	0	0	1	1	0	0	0
Mexico	2	16	13	3	2	na	11
Guyana	1	13	0	0	4	3	3
Trinidad and Tobago	0	0	0	14	19	2	6
Peru	0	0	4	2	35	13	12
Nicaragua	0	7	2	14	3	na	5
Jamaica	4	7	3	6	6	na	5
Argentina	12	5	12	10	2	3	7
Barbados	0	1	6	0	4	na	2
Venezuela	0	14	1	0	0	0	3
Chile	1	3	0	1	5	na	2
Honduras	0	1	3	3	1	na	2
Panama	0	0	1	2	4	na	2
Brazil	0	1	2	na	na	na	1
Colombia	0	2	0	4	2	na	2
Bahamas	0	0	0	0	2	1	1
Ecuador	0	0	0	0	4	na	1
Costa Rica	0	0	0	1	2	na	1
Paraguay	0	0	0	0	2	na	0
Uruguay	1	0	0	0	0	na	0
Dominican Republic	0	0	0	0	0	0	0
Guatemala	0	0	0	0	0	0	0
Haiti	0	0	0	0	0	0	0
Suriname	0	0	0	0	0	0	0
Latin America	2	6	5	7	5	5	5

Source: IDB, 1997: 175.

lution" to a fiscal problem—as seen in the large percentage of central government expenditure in Peru and Mexico coming from privatizations—requires considerable discipline if governments are to persevere with fiscal reform against the day when such revenues have been used up.[52] (One country, Bolivia, invented an ingenious "capitalization" scheme under which privatization revenues did not benefit the public treasury.) The other area of experimentation and experience was regulation: it is early to assess progress in this field, even in countries such as Britain with a longer tradition of regulation, but it is one of the most important areas for future evaluation and research.

A major opportunity was the gain in productivity from certain public services that worked, such as telephones, after years of deteriorating quality. This was both a continuing gain and a one-time boost of some magnitude, and it was important to establishing new strategies, since the efficiency gain was attractive to foreign and domestic investors. The attendant threat was that governments might be tempted to slow down the more tedious work of improving productivity through sectoral support policies to innovation and restructuring, given the one-time and conspicuous improvement.

Trade liberalization was also widely implemented, as Table 7.5 reveals. Figure 7.3 shows the shift in the openness of the continent, using trade as a percent of GDP as the measure. The average level of tariffs fell from 45 percent before the debt crisis to 13 percent by 1995. The maximum tariff fell from its precrisis level of 84 percent to 41 percent. Only Brazil, Mexico and El Salvador had restrictions affecting over 5 percent of imports. By mid-decade, only seven countries had an average tariff greater than 15 percent: the Bahamas, the Dominican Republic, Honduras, Nicaragua, Panama, Peru and Suriname.[53]

---

[52] The full costs and benefits of privatization depend on many empirical issues, such as the relative efficiency of enterprises in the public and private sector, and the effect on growth and thereby on revenue collection. See Inter-American Development Bank, 1997, for an excellent review and further references.

[53] The data of this paragraph are from the Inter-American Development Bank, 1997: 72.

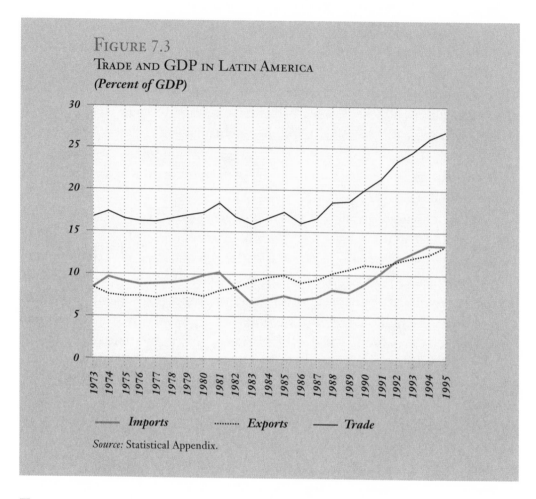

FIGURE 7.3
TRADE AND GDP IN LATIN AMERICA
(Percent of GDP)

——— *Imports*   ·········· *Exports*   ——— *Trade*

Source: Statistical Appendix.

ECONOMIC INTEGRATION IN THE NEW PARADIGM[54]

The traditional approach to economic integration was also a casualty of the debt crisis, having already fallen into disrepute in the 1970s. Growing obstacles to the integration process had included conflicts of interests, economic policy instability within the countries of the region, external pressures (particularly from the U.S. private sector and government), and short-sighted domestic industrial groups (which often preferred the monopolistic control of their own small national markets to the discipline of a regional market). For governments embarking on the neoliberal ex-

---

[54] These paragraphs have been adapted, with permission, from Ffrench-Davis, 1988.

periments of the 1970s and 1980s, particularly in the Southern Cone, integration came to be seen as another form of protectionism, and was therefore rejected from an ideological point of view.

Around the middle of the 1980s, however, integration began to come back on the agenda, pushed by ECLAC, as a kind of "steppingstone" to a more open international order. The European Community took fresh interest in supporting integration, which it saw as its particular mission given its comparative advantage in this field. The EC signed accords with the Andean Pact and with the CACM and increased aid to integration projects. Such support benefited from the increased interest in Latin America on the part of the EC following the entry of Spain and Portugal.

A number of informal bilateral agreements among Latin American countries were created. Integration of infrastructure became a concern, particularly in the energy sector.[55] The outstanding bilateral agreement of the 1980s was the Argentina-Brazil accord of July 1986, which was to form the basis of the Southern Cone Common Market, MERCOSUR. The agreement covered issues as varied as the renegotiation of tariff preferences, binational firms, investment funds, biotechnology, economic research and nuclear coordination. Of the 16 protocols signed, the most significant was the first, which dealt with the production, trade and technological development of capital goods. The stated goal was to establish a customs union covering half of all capital goods.

The Andean Pact also experienced a resurgence, with bilateral trade links flourishing (Colombia-Venezuela, Ecuador-Colombia). Soon, however, worldwide interest in trading blocs had further repercussions. In 1990, the Free Trade Area of the Americas was proposed by the United States, building on the concept (already in play and initially proposed by Mexico) of a free trade zone including Canada, the United States and Mexico, the North American Free Trade Agreement, NAFTA. The irony of the Bush administration's proposal was that it represented a reversal of the initial motivation for integration in the 1950s. Economic integration was then envisaged both as an essential stimulus to import substituting industrialization and as a creative defense against U.S. economic superiority, and was therefore opposed by the United States (with the exception of the Alliance for Progress period). Ad-

---

[55] Olade, 1996.

herence to a supranational integration agreement now became a way of locking a country into a new set of rules, and of expressing a commitment to those rules in the eyes of investors. The interest of the United States in a free trade area with Mexico and Canada was also more explicitly a byproduct of the enthusiasm for the market, since at the heart of the project was leveling the playing field, that is, the harmonization of rules so that U.S. investment might flow smoothly into Mexico and facilitate trade and growth. The negotiations produced the agreement shaping NAFTA. Other countries immediately began to make moves to be considered for NAFTA membership.

In newly democratic Brazil and Argentina, the longstanding idea of a common market had been revived with the Argentina-Brazil Accord of 1986. This was already a breakthrough in integration, since it recognized the need for negotiations at the firm level and appropriate institutional support, if fears were to be allayed and proper channels of communication constructed. This had been lacking in LAFTA, even in the sectoral agreements scheme. Now MERCOSUR received new impetus from the northern moves. The treaty was signed in 1991 by Argentina, Brazil, Paraguay and Uruguay. Chile in 1996 and Bolivia in 1997 became associates of the group.

Even in Central America, where continued political tension made it particularly difficult to reinvigorate integration, a presidential summit in 1990 launched a new integration agreement, the *Comunidad Económica Centroamericana*. The main objectives of this new scheme were to preserve earlier gains and to proceed via bilateral agreements.

These moves prompted a response in Europe, where policymakers were concerned at falling trade shares with Mexico and could only assume that the FTAA would continue what NAFTA had begun.[56] Their preoccupation led to major policy initiatives in relations with MERCOSUR and attention to mechanisms to increase trade and investment. New agreements were signed between the European Union and both the Andean Pact and CACM in 1993, and the first agreement with MERCOSUR was signed in 1992. There followed the new institutional developments described earlier: the extension of the European Investment Bank's operations to Latin America and the development of AL-INVEST.

---

[56] The EU share of trade with Mexico between 1990 and 1996 fell from 17 percent to 8.6 percent. Andrew Crawley, 1997, consultancy report for this book.

Another experiment in trade relations was the Caribbean Basin Initiative, conceived by the Reagan administration as a further way of isolating Nicaragua and Cuba. It consisted of Costa Rica, Honduras, El Salvador, Guatemala, Panama and the Caribbean region (except Guyana and Cuba). This agreement provided for duty-free access to the American market (with some exceptions) for 12 years. Sugar, however, a major commodity export from the Caribbean, remained subject to import quotas. And since 80 percent of the region's exports were already covered by special agreements, the new facility increased the list by only 15 percent.

AGRARIAN REFORM UNDER THE NEW PARADIGM

Just as integration was rethought in the 1980s and found its niche in the emerging neoliberal consensus, so with agrarian reform.[57] From the 1970s, the approach to rural development shifted away from expropriation and redistribution toward favoring individual property rights over collective or communal systems. International agencies such as the World Bank, as well as nongovernmental organizations, financed programs of land registration and titling throughout Latin America. It was argued that secure and transparent property rights would facilitate land transactions and give producers access to credit in the formal financial market, since they would be able to use their property as collateral. Governments were encouraged to introduce measures to facilitate privatization of communal land held by indigenous communities, as well as to break up the collective sector. In some cases, these measures formalized an ongoing unraveling of the earlier collectivist reform, and of communal arrangements within peasant communities.

Mismanagement and inadequate state support led beneficiaries to look for individual solutions to the collectives' problems. This generally meant expanding their own peasant economy within the reformed sector. With these reforms and the parcelization of collectively held land, the former peasants from the *hacienda* who had become land reform beneficiaries now became the new owners of a plot of land. The growth of this new group, known as *parceleros* after the plot of land or *parcela*, has greatly expanded the peasant farm sector in many Latin American countries.

---

[57] This section was written in collaboration with Cristóbal Kay.

Chile was the first to initiate this process in late 1973, Peru followed in a more gradual manner since 1980, Nicaragua since 1990 and Mexico and El Salvador since 1992 (in Mexico, few *ejidos* were in fact collectives). Some expropriated land was returned to former owners (particularly in Chile), but most was distributed as *parcelas* in private property to members of the collectives or cooperatives. In some countries, a significant proportion of the beneficiaries of the earlier reform were now unable to secure a parcel and joined the ranks of the rural proletariat. This process of parcelization doubled or even tripled the land area under ownership of the peasant farm sector.

Under the counter-reform of Pinochet's military government in Chile, about 30 percent of expropriated land was returned to former owners, almost 20 percent was sold to private individuals or institutional investors, and about half remained in the cooperative sector.[58] The latter was itself subdivided into family units. Less than half of the original beneficiaries were able to obtain a *parcela* because the size of the reformed sector was reduced by half through the counter-reform and because the plots were relatively generous in size. *Parceleros* had to pay for the land, which was sold to them by the state for about half its market value. In subsequent years, about half of the *parceleros* in Chile lost their land as they were unable to repay their debts (incurred to purchase the plot), or lacked capital, management or market experience.

Agrarian reform and its subsequent unraveling thus gave rise to a more complex agrarian structure. In some countries the process reduced and transformed the *latifundia* system, and enlarged the peasant sector and the commercial medium-to-large farm sector. Decollectivization also increased heterogeneity among the peasantry, as the leveling tendencies of collectivist agriculture were removed. Capitalist farmers benefited from the liberalization of land, labor and financial markets, the further opening of the economy to international competition, the new drive to exports, and the withdrawal of supportive measures for the peasant sector. Their greater land, capital and technical resources, their superior links with national and especially international markets, and their greater influence on agricultural policy ensured that they were more able to exploit the new market opportunities than peasant farmers.

---

[58] Jarvis, 1992: 192.

PROBLEMS AND POSSIBILITIES FOR THE 1990S

A rounded conclusion on the shift in the development paradigm in Latin America and the results of structural reform awaits the evaluation of the varied country experiences in the next chapter. However, some preliminary reflections here may provide the context in which to appraise national variations and responses to the new environment.

Perhaps the outstanding problem with the reform process is the size and instability of capital flows. This has become the core of macroeconomic instability on the continent, and requires that close attention be directed to all the institutions governing the financial sector. With flows assuming such dimensions, and with such unstable characteristics, policy autonomy has become more limited; specifically, the need for high interest rates conflicts with the need to promote investment. The tendency to overvaluation associated with inflows threatened to undermine the results of the new commitment to promoting exports in the 1980s and still more in the 1990s. Overvaluation helps relative price stability in the short term, with the danger that the degree of that stability might be deceptive.

Another problem arises from the fact that much of the export growth in the 1980s and 1990s has been based on natural resources yet again: products such as shrimp and salmon, for example, or processed minerals and related products. The challenge here concerns the need for sufficient value-added and product diversity to make such products less vulnerable to exhaustion of resources or the market problems that have historically beset primary product-dependent economies. There is also a renewed threat to the environment, from pollution, contamination and the exploitation of resources.

Two serious deficiencies of the new policy package are the absence both of sectoral policies and of a sufficiently deep attack on social problems and inequity. Policies that might support, for example, the rapidly-expanding microenterprise sector, encouraging those businesses to play an Italian-style[59] dynamic role, have progressed little if at all. Such policies could help answer the challenge of new primary export dependence by encouraging industrialization of primary products as

---

[59] Recent literature on Italian growth emphasizes the contribution of networks of small firms, with beneficial effects on employment.

well as other microenterprise products with export potential, and by giving support to small firms in the activity of exporting itself. Such policies could also be important on the social side, since employment and productivity in the small-scale sector are central to greater equality of opportunity.

The lack of sectoral policies in the new policy package is an indication that on the equity front, the learning process has been slow, reflecting the complexity of the issue in both political and economic terms. The politics behind the neoliberal shift basically reflected an increase in the weight of private sector business interests. But during the 1990s, there was certainly a growing preoccupation with social issues across much of the political spectrum, assisted by the move to democratic government, itself a partial product of the debt crisis. There was also growing skepticism that growth alone would solve social problems. The collapse of options on the left served to concentrate the minds of progressively-minded people on the challenge of combining market-centered growth with equity. Skepticism about growth led to an emerging consensus on the continued importance of the role of the state as "partner, catalyst and facilitator of the whole of society, rather than provider."[60] Policymakers and outside advisers therefore began to pay more attention to the relationship between economic and social reform, and to look elsewhere, such as Europe and Canada, for helpful examples of mixed economies with progressive social policies. History had already shown that in Latin America, inequality could be perfectly compatible with growth, and even functional to growth.[61] The new approach began to be: if we do not wish to accept inequality, are there ways of reducing or softening the tradeoff between growth and equity?

Whereas some policymakers and international advisers still concentrated on growth as the answer to welfare problems, thus marginalizing politics and (almost) social policy, others began to look in two complementary directions. Both lines indicate interesting possibilities. The first was developed by ECLAC, led by the late Fernando Fajnzylber's analysis of the "empty box," which illustrated that in Latin America the category of countries experiencing both fast growth and increased

---

[60] World Bank, 1996.

[61] Recent literature has argued that in worldwide cross-section studies, increased growth correlates with increased equity in a democratic context (Alesina and Rodrik, 1994; Persson and Tabellini, 1994). The explanation given is the cost of maintaining stability in the face of inequality in a democratic context. Fishlow, 1991, has shown that for Latin America specifically, the data do not support the argument.

equity had indeed been empty in the postwar period.[62] The box diagram showed a four-way relationship between growth and equity. Latin America provides cases of no growth and more equity, and of less equity with both growth and no growth, but there is no case of fast growth and more equity. The ECLAC line of analysis (so-called neostructuralism) sought a solution to the emptiness of the box by developing the potential complementarity between widespread productivity growth, growth itself, and equity. The approach explored the institution-building needed to obtain such complementarities in terms of technology, finance and support to information flows and networks.

The second direction was to look at innovative ways of linking the new policies to the creation of a political constituency. If people feel a sense of ownership of institutions or policies, then this leads to better monitoring and compliance and unleashes sources of energy and innovations that might allow a fruitful combination of economic and social development. Decentralization, by providing opportunities to link local tax-raising efforts to local needs, was one such area of innovation.

To appreciate more deeply the different strands of this learning process, and the areas where the jury is still out, the next chapter evaluates performance and policymaking under the auspices of the "new paradigm" by exploring and comparing national experiences.

---

[62] Fajnzylber, 1990. The work on a second version of the study was led by Joseph Ramos and published in 1992. The 1995 document, "Policies to Improve Linkages with the Global Economy," is a further important step. See Sunkel, 1993, for an important collection of essays in this line.

CHAPTER 8

PERFORMANCE AND POLICYMAKING UNDER THE NEW PARADIGM

EVALUATING THE CONSEQUENCES OF the tumultuous events and changes in Latin America over the past quarter century is a difficult and premature task. At the international level, a sea change in institutions, technology and factor movements brought opportunities and threats. Within the region, increasing international flows of capital, the debt crisis and the costly adjustment period that followed gradually brought a radical shift in paradigm, which in turn consolidated the globalization of the Latin American economies. The phrase "new model," however, may not necessarily be the appropriate description: it will be argued in this chapter that reform processes have taken different shapes in different contexts.

The bare facts of performance up to the mid-1990s appear in the tables and figures of Chapter Seven. Exports increased despite overvaluation, but the terms of trade worsened. Foreign exchange revenues were aided in a few countries by increased remittances (Mexico, Colombia, El Salvador, Jamaica).[1] The chief source of

---

[1] Income from remittances was equivalent to 10 percent of merchandise exports in 1989 in Mexico, 21 percent in Jamaica and 8 percent in Colombia. No figure was available for 1989 for El Salvador, but in 1984 the figure was 22 percent. Russell and Teitelbaum, 1992: 54.

Photo: Buenos Aires Stock Exchange, 1997.

the improved balance of payments was the inflow of capital. Growth recovered in the 1990s, but only modestly. Investment began to rise again as a percent of GDP (Figure 7.1) and national savings also at last began to rise, but both were still far below the level required to sustain a serious development effort. Savings and investment only regained the share in GDP they had in the 1950s. Inflation came down, but not enough. Income distribution, having worsened everywhere except Uruguay, Costa Rica and possibly Colombia, showed only slight indications of recovery in the 1990s. The poverty headcount likewise worsened in the 1980s and barely began to improve again in the 1990s. Formal sector employment rose only slightly in the private sector and stagnated in the public sector due to government cutbacks and privatization. The result was a huge expansion of the informal sector, much of it in microenterprise.

Attributing of any of these results either to globalization or to policy shifts is difficult.[2] A number of recent studies have attempted to relate performance to policy by cross-country assessments of "before and after" the reform process.[3] As the various authors are the first to admit, the analysis can only be tentative, since the time elapsed is very short, other forces are at work (such as slow growth of the world economy), and it is difficult to work with a method which perforce has to decide how to pinpoint the onset at a single point in time. The reality has, of course, been that policy shifts often occur slowly, and hopefully mature and deepen, though they sometimes decay. This book uses a different approach: we shall look at policies in their historical and evolving institutional context, and explore individual country experiences to derive some initial conclusions about the significance of globalization and the shift in paradigm, in terms of both growth and social welfare.

This approach has its own dangers. Apart from being premature, there is the appearance of ranking and evaluating different economic teams, if not governments. We cannot stress too heavily that this is not the point. The purpose is to seek out the interplay between long-run structural factors and what can be made of the short-

---

[2] For a study which finds that the reforms have worsened inequality, see Berry, 1997.

[3] Notably a number of studies by the IDB Office of the Chief Economist. See Fernández Arias and Montiel, 1997; Lora and Barrera, 1997; and Inter-American Development Bank, 1997. Our analysis is consistent with theirs, in particular with the finding of Fernández Arias and Montiel that the reforms need to be supplemented with other measures on the micro and sectoral side.

run threats and opportunities of the period under consideration. Over decades, un-equal distribution of income and wealth was embedded in institutions, attitudes and vested interests that deeply conditioned the process of industrialization and efforts at rural development. External economic dependence simply changed its form as financial vulnerability took over from heavy dependence on primary products. Arguably, the degree of external exposure actually increased. Over the long run, different economic, political and social structures gave rise not only to varying trade or industrial structures, but also to varying kinds of policy traditions, experiences, and interactions between the public and private sectors. These are in their turn part of the underlying conditions. Of course, there can always be surprises; we are not talking of determining factors. And even individuals can make a huge difference, for good or bad, intentionally or unintentionally.

For individual countries, certain sets of prior conditions enabled the paradigm shift to be used in an effective and creative way, not always related to the direct goals of the conventional wisdom, whereas in other cases, results were far less positive. Sometimes this was because particular prior conditions and structural problems exposed countries dramatically to the perils of globalization. Sometimes the story was less dramatic, but basically marked the continuation of deep developmental or political problems that prevented countries from taking advantage of opportunities. Finally, in some countries, the new policies were important and progress was made, but the shift in paradigm was far from the most important force at work, and indeed in itself created problems.

USING THE PARADIGM SHIFT

The most celebrated application of the new policies occurred in Chile, where the democratically elected government of President Aylwin was able eventually to use the new paradigm to achieve results over and above those which followed from the individual reforms. This achievement built on the specific trajectory of the Chilean economy, as well as on the exceptional preconditions that we have followed over time: the developmental role of the state was unusually large, and promotion of investment and of an investment-export nexus had made headway in the 1960s in a quite atypical manner. The trajectory is well known. The military government that took power in 1973 took advantage of the general reaction to the difficulties of the Socialist experiment to impose its rules with extreme force. There followed a lengthy learning process in terms of economic policy. Chapter Seven described how the military regime committed serious errors, combining financial with trade liberalization in a way that produced a private sector crisis and a consumption boom, then implementing an extreme monetarist model which produced serious overvaluation. With declining terms of trade in the early 1980s and capital withdrawal in 1982, the ensuing crisis led to serious rethinking. For the remaining years of military rule, maintaining the exchange rate needed for long-run competitiveness took precedence over the market and an undue faith in the law of one price. Some restriction of capital movements and modest agricultural protection discreetly became part of Chilean policy.[4] Privatization practice improved and priority was given to fiscal reform and the development of a pension scheme that was to have powerful effects on the capital market, and possibly on savings.[5]

As recovery gained momentum in the 1980s, the "new-style" natural resource-based exports[6] led the improvement, based on investments in research and institutional support for forestry, fishing and other natural resource sector programs that had begun under the Frei government in the 1960s. Responses to market forces certainly did not emerge from a vacuum; this must stand as an important qualification to the widespread belief of the early 1980s in the instant and automatic response of the market.

The timing of the transition to democracy also helped consolidate the new growth model.[7] In the 1988 plebiscite, the Chilean people repudiated Pinochet and in 1990 the democratically elected government of President Aylwin took power. The years since the crisis of 1982 had allowed for consolidation of the model now perceived as successful in restoring stable rules of the game. Furthermore, by 1990 the Berlin Wall had collapsed and several Latin American governments of which there had been high expectations had failed, notably that of President Alfonsín in

---

[4] Scott, 1996.

[5] Agosin, Crespi and Letelier, 1996, argue that any increase in the savings rate was in fact cancelled out by the fiscal cost of the change.

[6] Examples are manufacturing activity with a high primary product content, such as shrimp or salmon farming and the processing and marketing of shrimp and salmon and related products.

[7] Andrés Bianchi made this point in an interview, Santiago, April 1997.

Argentina. Given the weakness of any alternative, democratic governments were more disposed to build selectively on foundations laid by military governments. Thus, when the Aylwin government took office in 1990, it openly endorsed elements of the military project, especially a new commitment to the rules of the free market game. This was extraordinarily important in maintaining investors' confidence throughout the transition.

While Chile's record of investment and growth in the 1990s is one of the most promising in Latin America, however, its record on income distribution and poverty is less impressive. In that sense, Chile is similar to the general Latin American story, though targeting has produced a much better record than the average in regard to certain basic needs, notably reducing infant mortality. But at a more intangible level, there is perhaps a more hopeful story. Equity and quality of development had to be part of the platform of the incoming Aylwin government in 1990, given the high social cost of the preceding years. So did coherent thinking about the role of the democratic process, within the limits of a still basically elitist system. The government worked on developing consensus politics in order to increase the legitimacy, efficiency and efficacy of policy. The theory was that, in principle at least, a process of consultation early on would identify policies that were poorly designed, technically or politically. People would monitor institutions and policies they felt were of their own making; the effective supply of knowledge could even be increased. Consultation and communication could make policies that might appear threatening to investors more acceptable for their long-run benefits—this was important for tax reform, for instance.[8] While Chile did not become a utopia in terms of basic needs, and many received little benefit from the model, a degree of consensus politics began to function in areas like tax reform, social spending and even labor relations, raising hopes of reconciling the tradeoff between growth and equity.

All these quite subtle aspects of the new policies and approaches to policymaking were possible because the Chilean project was rooted in historically stronger

---

[8] Based on a discussion with Alejandro Foxley, Minister of Finance in the Aylwin administration, in London, May 1995. In a seminar on the occasion of that visit, Foxley quoted Putnam, whose 1993 seminal book on trust and institution-building in Italy is renowned in the academic world. In the interview, he described in detail how elements of trust, built out of years of relationships while in opposition, could condition and facilitate negotiations with the unions without vitiating the genuine healthy role of opposition and conflict.

institutions than elsewhere in Latin America, and embodied deeper understanding of the need to build political consensus behind the economic model. Nevertheless, questions remain about the Chilean experience, the strength of which has also been its limit: it is highly centralized and still highly elitist, despite some progress in democracy. "Decentralization" in Chile, heralded as the key to deepening the democratic process, has been closer to "deconcentration,"[9] and authoritarian enclaves continue to limit the progress of democratization. Other questions concerning the model are its viability as a growth strategy given underinvestment in capabilities, and its concentration in natural resource-based exports.[10]

Two cases that can usefully be explored by direct comparison with Chile are Argentina and Uruguay. In both cases, military dictatorship played a prominent role, but the learning process observed in Chile was absent. The institutional base for policymaking was also far less developed.

Chapter Six emphasized that Argentina's economic management was continually compromised by political problems, particularly the instability and bitterness characterizing the political process from the 1940s.[11] Political instability and regime changes continued into the 1970s, when the second Perón administration from 1973-76 was ended by military coup. In this context, the move to right-wing monetarism took an extreme and ideological form, and the learning process in Chile had no parallel in Argentina.

Democracy returned in 1983 after the disaster of the South Atlantic conflict, and in the middle of the debt crisis. The following years saw both orthodox and heterodox efforts to control inflation, each of which became self-defeating, with prices exploding again in an increasingly exaggerated version of a process under way since the 1950s.[12] In 1990, the new Peronist government of President Menem decided to tie the Argentine currency to the dollar through the constitution, so making it impossible for the government to finance itself by issuing money without a further revision of the constitution. This decision, however, was not the only focus of

---

[9] "Decentralization" transfers decisionmaking powers to the local level; "deconcentration" keeps control at the center while it transfers execution and administration to the region.

[10] Sunkel, 1997, Pietrobelli, 1995.

[11] Though the form Peronism itself took derived from the difficulty of challenging the dominant political elites in more democratic ways. See the discussion of the elites' entrenched position in Chapter Three.

[12] Di Tella, 1987.

the policy: convertibility was the keystone of a radical option for insertion into the international system, with a dynamic privatization program and trade openness.

Here we see yet another version of the role such reforms can play: Menem and Domingo Cavallo, his Finance Minister, used them to consecrate a new set of rules around stability and openness, which was indeed effective in attracting external finance, and allowed exporting despite a high degree of overvaluation. This helped keep inflation low. The secret appears to have been that, in contrast to the earlier episode of the *tablita*, or pegged exchange rate, the economic team was well aware that a peg to the dollar would mean rising peso costs for domestic manufacturers, and they implemented a wide range of measures designed to compensate. These included cutting payroll taxes, for instance, while introducing programs to develop supplier networks, a national system of standards and quality controls, technological support, and employment and training schemes. Meanwhile, stability reduced uncertainty and expanding demand helped reduce unit costs.[13] Privatization also began to help, given that some public services had been chronically inefficient.[14] Years of inefficiency at least now meant that the economy could benefit from a fall in transaction costs.

Although more efficient tax collection affected profits, the fall in certain costs, while slow, allowed the more dynamic firms to continue to reorganize, expand, build networks, invest and export, helped by MERCOSUR. This learning process had been developing in the 1980s and now allowed a response to MERCOSUR and to the cost-side measures, as well as to the new stability. The more dynamic firms—numbering some 20 to 25 businesses[15] and responsible for 40 percent of industrial output—pursued an "offensive" strategy,[16] all helped in some way by explicit government policies. The remaining 60 percent of output—25,000 firms—reacted defensively, reducing vertical integration and importing a larger share of their inputs

---

[13] Canavese, 1992; Bouzas, 1993.

[14] Azpiazu, 1993.

[15] Kosacoff, 1996: 4. They were to be found in four sectors: basic inputs (iron, steel, petrochemicals); processing of natural resources (oilseeds, fish); automobiles; and mass consumption goods on a strongly differentiated basis, ranging from sweets to mobile phones.

[16] The phrase is that of Jorge Katz and Bernardo Kosacoff, whose numerous works exploring the micro side of response to the new policies give us a richness of material for Argentina as yet unavailable for other countries. See Katz and Kosacoff, 1989; Kosacoff, 1996.

as a rationalization measure to lower costs, with few organizational changes or investment.[17] This sector lacked the skills and financial support to restructure. As industrial concentration grew and firms increased their reliance on imports, the victims in this process were the unemployed. The rate of unemployment climbed from 6 percent in October 1991 to 16.4 percent in October 1995 before leveling off.[18]

The question marks are numerous, but two are paramount. The first concerns whether, given Argentina's past, enough change can occur in traditions of policy management, political behavior and party structures to allow a Chilean-style continuity and maturity of policymaking to develop through another democratic change of government, given the damage done to any process of building a political base with such increases in unemployment and industrial concentration. The second concerns whether the cost decreases that apparently made overvaluation compatible with exporting can convert into dynamic productivity increases, even given limited support for restructuring from the financial sector. A further concern is the dependence of success on the continued health of MERCOSUR.

Like Chile, Uruguay's 1973 military dictatorship coincided with the OPEC price rise, which hit Uruguay hard on the heels of a fall in meat exports the previous year, and the military implemented a form of economic liberalism that increased the role of the state. More so than Chile, however, Uruguay achieved success through financial liberalization, which brought inflows of money into a weak institutional setting, and through subsidies to nontraditional exports, which rose strongly. Unlike Chile, the Uruguayan military-led model did not survive to learn by its mistakes, ending in 1985 after three years of vicious recession with the debt crisis, leaving neoliberalism discredited and having failed to benefit from the timing factor that helped Chile's transition. The transition government had to differentiate its economic model from the military's with no real alternative to offer, and ended amid accelerating inflation and falling growth rates.

The new government of 1990 was committed to stabilization but had to make a pact with the unions, which made income policy impossible. The result was an

---

[17] Kosacoff, 1996: 5. This group of firms is small in scale, some 5 to 10 percent of the optimum scale observed at the international frontier.
[18] Ibid.: 10; *Financial Times*, December 13, 1996.

option for exchange rate-based stabilization, which reduced inflation but favored consumption at the expense of industry. Industry was also threatened by the 1990 decision by Brazil and Argentina to form MERCOSUR. Uruguay had no option but to join, though the benefits of the common market for the country were not clear.[19] Since then, however, growth has been strong, with nontraditional exports benefiting from the growth of MERCOSUR, but underpinned by overvaluation and capital inflow, and subject to the economic cycle in Brazil and Argentina. Meanwhile, efforts at privatization have encountered resistance, since the general public sees the state as its shelter and is less willing than in the rest of Latin America to accept the loss of public sector jobs. The considerable power of the referendum—which can be secured on any issue by a minimum number of signatures and has been strengthened by concentration of the population in Montevideo—has been used to limit privatization. The growing popularity of the new left-wing group *Frente Amplio* reflects the lack of a solid political base for neoliberal policies. With the return to democracy, "Uruguay's distinctive political culture—conservative, middle class, representative, seeking consensus—emerged from the dictatorship remarkably unscathed."[20] This political culture, along with the weak executive and an electoral system which fragments voting, inhibits changes that might challenge such values. Uruguay is left with the best welfare record during reform, third in the HDI index for Latin America, and is the only country to improve its income distribution since the debt crisis. But it also remains reliant on capital inflows and overvaluation, and limited in possibilities for state reform. Its growth prospects are heavily dependent on a common market in which it is a very small player. The increased use of the referendum casts doubt on whether traditional politics can evolve to handle change in this vulnerable situation.

Mexico also used the paradigm shift as an opportunity, with a particularly strong international orientation, a function of the country's geographical position. As is well known, Mexico's case was complicated by its oil bonanza, which encour-

---

[19] Uruguay's tariffs are much lower than Brazil's, particularly on capital goods, which are relatively protected in Brazil and by the Common External Tariff. The trade patterns within MERCOSUR lock Uruguay into concentrating particular types of exports on a single market, so vulnerability on that score is not reduced. New agroindustrial exports go to Brazil, manufactures to Argentina, and traditional exports to the rest of the world.

[20] Finch, 1981: 7.

aged further heavy borrowing and continued avoidance of tax reforms. The 1970s also saw a disruption of business/government relations; the Echeverría government was perceived as too radical and nonconsultative. Relations with the private sector were further disrupted by nationalization of the banks in the course of Mexico's collapse, when oil prices fell further. What followed was, on the one hand, a strong version of market reforms, with radical trade liberalization, complete freeing of the capital account, and an extensive privatization program. On the other, after unsuccessful efforts at orthodox stabilization, the next oil collapse of 1985-86 precipitated an innovative heterodox stabilization, which had considerable success compared with others. Both these results owed something to Mexico's particular political system. The radical nature of the neoliberal model implemented is tentatively attributed to the weakness of technical economic debate and of opposition in Mexico, a product of the authoritarian system that discourages dissent. A revealing parallel is that between CIEPLAN in Chile, which struggled on through the military dictatorship providing a source of sophisticated analysis to help mediate the transition, and CIDE in Mexico, which in the 1980s saw its team of anti-neoliberals dispersed.[21] Fine-tuning of policy was further complicated by continual problems in relations between the government and the private sector. These problems did not prevent, however, institutionalization of weekly negotiations between the business sector and trade union leaders, which gave flexibility to the heterodox stabilization policies from 1987 on. For lack of such flexibility the policies collapsed elsewhere. The union leaders' ability to deliver wage restraint was also a unique Mexican characteristic.

The policy still turned on the exchange rate anchor, however. Privatization and the prospect of NAFTA substantially increased foreign direct investment, mainly from the United States, and, due to high interest rates and yields in the stock exchange, large inflows of short-term speculative capital, even from supposedly cautious U.S. pension funds.[22] By the 1990s, the result was overvaluation, slow growth, and difficulties for the manufacturing sector in particular. The political tensions were softened by the import boom and by profitable speculation. Interest rate increases in the United States affected capital inflows, however, and there were politi-

---

[21] Whitehead, 1997: 29.
[22] Folkerts-Landau and Ito, 1995: 53.

cal disruptions in Mexico,[23] leading to capital flight. As the presidential election drew near, President Salinas chose not to raise interest rates or adjust the exchange rate, preferring to sustain the situation by using reserves to finance private sector acquisition of short-term liabilities in dollars in huge amounts. The situation collapsed in December 1994, resulting in a massive devaluation and a record-breaking rescue operation mounted by the United States, with the help of the international financial institutions.

Where the Brazilian government used the opportunity of globalization for the ends of a strongly defined national project, for Mexico globalization—in its particular manifestation of NAFTA—seems to have *become* the national project, to a degree that permitted the dangers to be neglected. In this outcome, Mexico's size and proximity to the United States were both an advantage and disadvantage. And its peculiar political economy—the stability deriving from what has effectively been a single dominant party since the revolution—may also have hindered flexibility. By the 1980s, there were new social forces looking for participation, and the system found it difficult to accommodate them. The political and policymaking system also allowed a huge disequilibrium in 1994, in part because of the temptations of NAFTA.

OTHER RADICAL STABILIZERS

Peru and Bolivia provide lessons in how crisis can be cathartic. In both countries, in fact, catharsis was probably more important than the direction of reform, though the reforms had the enormous benefit, as with Argentina, of providing a clear signal to the international community that the tide had turned. Earlier discussion of Peru emphasized its institutional weakness in policy management and lack of experience in various policy areas important for development. This had already resulted in the 1970s in an unhappy adjustment story, so it is hardly surprising that come the 1980s, the reversal of capital supply and the rise in interest rates caused severe problems, on top of which the El Niño phenomenon caused widespread natural disasters in

---

[23] The peasant revolt in Chiapas at the beginning of 1994, and the assassination of the PRI presidential candidate in March 1994.

1983. The rest of the 1980s went from bad to worse, as the APRA government attempted to grow out of inflation by using price controls. Soaring inflation plus the revolutionary movement *Sendero Luminoso* led to a sense of ungovernability by the end of the decade.[24] The new government of President Fujimori clearly "used" the neoliberal package. President Fujimori actually had two strategies prepared by different teams before the election, one a moderate left plan and the other neoliberal; his approach was in part to consider which would bring him most foreign finance. The answer was clear, hence the "Fujishock," a massive devaluation and relative price adjustment accompanied by monetary and fiscal tightness. The shock was accompanied by a wider commitment to a pro-market strategy, which rapidly brought foreign finance. The capture of the *Sendero* leader by intelligence forces, in addition to the abrupt control of inflation, brought the government enough popularity and credibility to sustain the policies. Distinct successes followed, thanks to a reform strategy that involved high-quality task forces of committed professionals bypassing or separating themselves from the mainstream bureaucracy.[25] This enabled quality reform of the tax administration and an impressively well-managed privatization process. The harder part was social policy, where the mainstream bureaucracy was an insurmountable obstacle. What was lacking was any attempt to use the democratic process to sustain reforms; in fact, the president closed down Congress and discouraged grassroots organizations, even more so after the guerrilla takeover of the Japanese embassy in December 1996. (Congress was subsequently reinstated on a different electoral basis.)

The Peruvian economy grew, but with a reliance on inflows of foreign money, overvaluation and high interest rates—the usual phenomena. Exports rose, partly because privatization improved service infrastructure, and mineral export projects matured. Some of the benefits from reform that sustained the economy in the 1990s, however, were one-time gains, such as the 10 percent of fiscal revenue coming from privatization (Table 7.6) and the initial efficiency gains from having telephones and

---

[24] The "Shining Path" movement originated in Ayacucho in the early 1980s, led by university teachers with Maoist inclinations and creating its base from peasants' despair and lack of political alternatives. By the early 1990s, the movement was a serious threat to civil order in the country's major cities, and millions of peasants had been displaced by rural violence. Much of the country was inaccessible.

[25] Silva, 1996, Chapter 2.

other public services that worked.[26] The reform of the tax administration, having helped raise revenue from 4 percent of GDP to 12 percent, reached its limits; it then required political support for a serious tax reform, and, above all, reforms on the expenditure side to build enough credibility to sustain taxation.

The 1970s saw no resolution of Bolivia's development problem, either; rather there was a succession of military governments, great instability and external loans increasingly propping up the government budget. The culmination of a bad political era was the narco-related military government of General García Meza in 1980-82. When the debt crisis hit, the government could only print money, and hyperinflation followed swiftly. Ironically, it was left to the same party that implemented the Revolution of 1952, the MNR, to implement the next revolution, this time an economic one. There seemed only one option: the new government implemented radical orthodox stabilization, with massive devaluation, relative price adjustment and an income squeeze imposed on miners (and others) with force and bloodshed. The important unorthodox element was the nonpayment of Bolivia's huge external debt, and indeed the reverse occurred: considerable foreign money poured in and this allowed the stabilized system to survive. Financial and trade liberalization were all implemented in radical form. The innovative element was the creation of the Social Employment Fund. But growth did not follow, the tin market collapsed shortly after the program was introduced, exports fell for three years, and growth was only 1 percent a year up to 1993—hence per capita income in the 1990s was still below its level in 1980.[27]

The MNR again returned to power in 1993, determined to innovate further and find a way to build a socially progressive element into the market model and thereby a broader political base. The result was the "Plan for All," a novel scheme incorporating education reform, maternity health care, a strong decentralization program, and its particular innovation, the capitalization program. This offered the six largest public enterprises for tender to buyers who had to commit specified and substantial investment funds and in return would receive half the equity and management control. The other half of the equity was formally owned by all Bolivians

---

[26] Of course, there are continuing gains from efficient public services, but there is also a one-time gain given the virtually complete absence of a service in some instances.

[27] IRELA, 1996: 20.

of voting age, and was held in new collective pension funds, with the legal obligation to provide a universal and equal annual pension, a "bonosol," to all Bolivians of 65 and over. It is too soon to evaluate this experiment at reconciling a very market-friendly model with social development. Its limits are clear: it could only attempt such a reconciliation by going for the one element of egalitarian social policy consistent with generating a satisfactory surplus in the six enterprises—i.e., pensions, most of which were not yet due. This leaves untouched many areas of deep social need and may not prove enough to build a social base for the model.[28] It also avoids at a stroke the key problem of privatization, that it provides a perilously illusory answer to the fiscal problem, and as a result leaves the country with a serious fiscal imbalance, since not only does the government get no revenue but it loses the revenue from the state-owned mining company. Next and perhaps most importantly, the "Plan for All" is no magical solution for Bolivia's basic problem: employment. By the late 1990s, the economy was creating 70,000 jobs a year, 90 percent in the informal sector, while there were over 200,000 new entrants a year to the labor market.[29] Finally, the plan also can work no miracles on debilitated institutions. Some important institutional reforms have been put on paper, and a financial reform carried out, but it was noticeable that by the end of the MNR government's term of office in May 1997 nothing had been done to implement judicial reforms, probably the most crucial.

Both Peru and Bolivia, then, enable us to elaborate the preliminary conclusion suggested by Argentina. The battle against inflation is enormously difficult—probably impossible without severe repression—when external transfers are negative. Peru, like Argentina, was able to use the reforms to signal to investors, and particularly to the international community, that a new era had begun. The resulting inflow of money, whatever its other consequences, was important in reducing inflationary feedbacks, especially by limiting depreciation of the exchange rate, and attention was successfully diverted from watching prices and betting on future price

---

[28] Only 272,933 of 6.4 million Bolivians enumerated in the 1992 census were classified as 65 or older. Writes Whitehead: "Pensions at 65 may seem an odd priority for those with a life expectancy at birth of only 60.5 years, or with an infant mortality rate of 86 per 1,000 (in 1992), or with only four mean years of schooling…" Whitehead, 1997: 202.

[29] Ibid.: 45.

movements. Bolivia had the further "advantage" that the trauma of hyperinflation typically forces through previously impossible radical action, and the decline of the economy with the collapse of confidence in money so totally halts productive activity that stabilization per se brings a recovery in output. A further crucial factor was the international support the program received.

RELUCTANT CONVERTS

The previous section described countries where there was an abrupt, almost violent conversion to the new paradigm. There were some major players who were more reluctant, such as Brazil, Colombia and Costa Rica, and their cases yield considerable and quite different insights.

Chapter Six described the fiscal problem as Brazil's Achilles' heel, which in turn related to the federal structure of a huge and diverse country. Borrowing in the 1970s allowed a rapid funding increase at many levels of both the public and private sectors, with MNCs increasing their presence. Growth was brisk; inflation remained high[30] but indexing was by now well established and there was no politically powerful group being hurt by inflation. The central government was outstanding among Latin American governments for borrowing in order to carry out investment to break bottlenecks, particularly in the energy sector.[31] Nevertheless, during the early 1980s, Brazil's fragility was rapidly exposed. The internal debt was also large, producing a taxable income that generated a healthy symbiosis with growth while all was well.[32] But once growth faltered and capital was withdrawn, high inflation could no longer be ignored. The initial heterodox effort failed to curb it, but this was only after a miracle year of stability which, if nothing else, revealed the size of the anti-inflation vote. Still, however, Brazil did not opt for structural reform; it remained a maverick, an adherent of capital controls and trade restrictions, and a stumbling block to the international financial community until the 1990s, when the Collor government finally introduced trade reforms and initiated privatization. Even then,

---

[30] The average for 1980-89 was 260 percent.
[31] Carneiro, 1987.
[32] Because the assets generated income which could be taxed. Carneiro, 1987: 62.

the program moved slowly and retained strong elements of financial and trade controls. Under the leadership of President Cardoso from January 1995, this was made into a virtue and another advantage of size: "Brazil is so large and so diverse it is impossible to be radical."[33] The rhetoric dwelled on self-confidence: Brazil could integrate into the global market on its own terms, because foreigners wanted access to its market badly enough. And Brazil could choose at what speed to liberalize. By getting direct foreign investment to build infrastructure, resources could be freed to take care of social expenditure.

The shift in model, then, for Brazil as for Mexico, was deeply related to globalization and to access to foreign investment, in particular. Brazil was at the other end of the spectrum from cases where macroeconomic chaos had produced a virtual collapse of the state and state intervention. Brazil's historical institutional and policymaking strength was still in evidence, despite the difficulties at the end of the 1980s. An example of that strength was the government's clarity on the need to get foreign investors into specific projects within an overall vision. The inflow of money then made possible the stabilization which had earlier been impossible. Cardoso decided to fight for ending inflation abruptly, against the advice of his advisers and the international financial institutions. His *Plan Real*, initiated when he was Finance Minister, brought down inflation by judicious use of an exchange rate commitment plus restraint of demand, principally by means of high interest rates. Its political popularity was an important element in his successful presidential campaign, and the fact that the anti-inflation program was rapidly subsumed in a wider development project was important to its sustainability. But industrial firms then had to face restructuring while paying high interest rates on the credit they needed for the task. This epitomized the conflict between inflation and growth, and cost some sectors of industry dearly.[34]

The battle for reform of the state was seen by policymakers as the key to both finessing the opposition between growth and inflation by allowing lower interest rates, and achieving effective social expenditure.[35] However, reform en-

---

[33] Interview with President Cardoso, Brasília, April 1997.

[34] Kosacoff, 1996: 10.

[35] Vitally necessary as the abuses mounted, particularly in the area of land claims. Disputes over land were responsible for a number of deaths in the mid-1990s, as police and peasants clashed.

countered the opposition of right and left, both fearing they would lose patron-age. It remained to be seen by the mid-1990s whether the mobilization of "the people's vote" in favor of reform of the state could win through, and whether financial and corporate structures could survive the swings and roundabouts of international financial flows.

The discussion of Colombia in Chapter Six detailed the strong elements of institutional development and political coherence that, like Chile, were in place to help face the temptations of the 1970s and the perils of the 1980s. But where in Chile the lack of consensus concerning the rules of the game undermined investors' confi-dence up to the late 1960s, Colombia had developed its own distinctive and unusual set of rules. It was a tacit system, which in dualistic fashion allowed for coexistence of competent and honest professional macro management at the top, with corruption[36] and violence lower down, especially in regions where old-style party barons often ruled. The coexistence was helped by the political pact known as the National Front, which from 1958 on guaranteed the alternation of the two principal parties in power for 16 years. The second element of Colombia's duality was the way an elite-domi-nated system allowed enough social control for moderate growth, and for unequal income distribution to be compatible with formal democracy.

Where the new structural reform policies and the commitment to the market that went with them could partially answer Chile's need, they had little to offer Colombia. After 1973, Colombia's peculiar system continued to function well, pro-viding the basis for an exceptionally mature response ("no") to the offering of loans, only giving way later in the Turbay government of 1978-82. Management of the coffee boom in 1975-78 and the adjustment in 1982-86 were carried out with skill and pragmatism, continuing the blend of conservatism, prudence and willingness to intervene that characterized Colombia's dealings with the IMF. Meanwhile, mari-juana gave way to cocaine, responding to the market, and the new Dutch Disease of the 1980s came from drugs. While dollars from drugs were an asset, the increased smuggling associated with the need to repatriate illegal dollars (money laundering)[37]

---

[36] Corruption in general was no worse than in most other countries of the continent. Drugs produced specific and serious problems, as they did in other countries with a heavy presence of drug trafficking.

[37] One method of money laundering is to buy goods abroad and smuggle them in for resale in the domestic market. This undermines tariff protection to local industry.

undermined one of Colombia's traditional abilities, the discreet and successful use of protection. Illegal dollars also distorted urban and rural land markets and limited the functioning of monetary and capital controls. As drugs and violence came more conspicuously onto the scene, it became more difficult to finesse the traditional separation between Colombia's quality macro management and the political and social problems associated with high levels of violence and corruption. A further complication was growing U.S. pressure to deal with the drug problem. Also, mounting population pressures made the second balancing act—elite control and the need for human development—more difficult to sustain. The economic difficulties of the 1980s came on top of these problems. In addition, from the mid-1980s it was clear that the new primary exports for Colombia were to be oil and coal, which required foreign participation. This raised the issues of local violence in new ways, since foreign oil companies needed to know they could depend on some level of local security for personnel and pipelines.

The response to the international enthusiasm for economic liberalization was typically Colombian. Only in 1990 were free market policies adopted in a broad way. Even then, and increasingly with the next administration, institutional renovation, particularly in the area of judicial reform, was an important part of the policy. Liberalization measures were also more moderate than elsewhere, and tempered with prudence; machinery was left in place to limit and control where necessary, particularly capital movements. Concern for equity led to a new emphasis on targeted social spending. The new constitution of 1991 also sought political renewal, based on increased participation. Colombia is the only case in Latin America where liberalization coincided with a growing state, a fact reflected in the rapid growth of social spending from 8 to 10 percent of GDP in the early 1990s, and to 16 percent in 1996.

It remains to be seen if Colombia's traditional effective economic management can withstand the strong tradition of local clientelist politics, the effect of the oil and coal bonanza, the threat to fiscal management from the level of fiscal transfers to local governments, and the continuing problems posed by drugs and guerrillas.

Costa Rica has also been another frequent exception to Latin American trends, notably for its democratic values and high scores on education. But in the last quarter of the century, Costa Rica's traditional emphasis on consensus was threatened by the new policies. In the 1970s, the economy had followed a quite unhappy route, using the opportunity to borrow in a surprising fashion, deepening import substituting industrialization with a range of state enterprises under the umbrella of CODESA, which was set up as a publicly-owned nonbank financial intermediary. The result was a large debt and an extreme crisis in 1982. After an initially difficult period of conflict with the IMF,[38] the government moved decisively toward export-led development while preserving social policies. Although the 1980s were as bad in trade and financial terms for Costa Rica as for the rest of Central America, exports grew strongly and social spending was unusually well protected. As the external context radicalized in a neoliberal direction in the 1990s, consensus was temporarily disrupted. The strongly orthodox program of the 1990-94 government, which called for extensive privatization and cuts of state expenditure, was never ratified by the Legislative Assembly. The incoming PLN government of President Figueres did not accept a number of elements of the program, and Figueres persuaded the World Bank and the IDB to accept modifications[39]—only to have the modifications rejected internally by the neoliberal groups, with an ensuing six-month battle over tax reform.[40] Eventually compromise was reached. Although growth and investment were not impressive through the mid-1990s, some major direct foreign investment began to arrive, responding to the strategy of investing in technical education to attract high-tech software industries. Privatization, however, made little progress.

Costa Rica thus differed from many of the other countries in that the benefits from wholesale adoption of "the package" were unclear, and the danger to political consensus great. Existing public services functioned better than in many other countries, so the "catch up" effect from privatization would have been less pronounced. Foreign investment could be attracted, anyway. The slower process of reform was a necessity but also very probably a virtue—it meant slower economic progress in the 1990s, but welfare indicators were maintained, and public debate allowed the beginning of a consensus on the necessary role of the state behind privatization.[41]

---

[38] The president at the time, Rodrigo Carazo, described the breakdown thus: "The IMF representative arrived in my office for a private meeting, proceeded to take out his bit of paper and tell me we had to cut public services, sacrifice education, nutrition standards, shut hospital services…My reply was, "The only things shutting around here are going to be the doors of this country, against you, for lack of respect to national sovereignty. You have 48 hours to leave.'" (Quoted in Cerdas, 1997, consultancy report for this book.)

[39] In the form of a "waiver" in a private letter.

[40] Economist Intelligence Unit, 1997/98: 42.

[41] Cerdas, 1997, consultancy report for this book.

Small-scale coffee producers played an important role in the histories of both Costa Rica and Colombia, though their coffee economies actually had quite different consequences. In Costa Rica, the small-holder economy was significant in creating and sustaining a democratic tradition important in producing a commitment to investment in education and health, and facilitating elimination of the army and the release of resources from defense to the social sector. In Colombia, the coffee sector was deeply embedded in a strong oligarchic and paternalistic system, so that its significance lay not in fostering democracy but in maintaining a strong tradition of policy management and institutions. This was sustained by strong regional elites, who needed such mechanisms to do business with one another.

These two distinct traditions led in quite different ways to marginalization of the paradigm shift that dominated policymaking in many other countries. Subject to problems characteristic of Central America in the preceding decades, and without Colombia's exceptional institutional strengths, Costa Rica went too far in its policy shift and was pulled back by its traditional emphasis on consensus and the social sector. Colombia had already unobtrusively absorbed the learning that Chile had to do in the 1980s; policymakers knew quite well that financial controls were important and that liberalization needed to be prudent, while monetary stability and fiscal conservatism had always been prized. In the 1990s, policymakers were able to take the best of the new policies—their emphasis was on institutional renovation—without discarding the discreet pragmatism that had served Colombia well. But much deeper political and social problems were meanwhile emerging, related to exclusion and growing violence and illegality. The shift in the development model could not cope with such problems.

PAIN WITHOUT GAIN?

The remaining medium-sized and small countries of Latin America had little in their history or prior institution-building that equipped them to pursue opportunities or neutralize threats. The worst placed, it seems, were those where the "gifts of the devil" seemed to become quite overwhelming. Discussion of the Mexican case has already foreshadowed the exceptional difficulties of maintaining policy coherence and good decisionmaking under the influence, especially, of petroleum (though not all Mexico's difficulties were attributable to oil).

In one sense, no country was better qualified than Venezuela to benefit from the package of market-oriented reforms—and in no other country did the package collapse so spectacularly. The example underlines the importance of interaction between politics and economics, and the increasingly obvious need to integrate social issues centrally in a development strategy.

As Venezuela's oil income rose to dizzying heights in the 1970s, accounting for over 90 percent of exports and 80 percent of public revenue by 1975,[42] labor productivity in industry actually fell. The state borrowed abroad and channeled money to industry, which borrowed and put its own money in liquid assets, and as the crisis broke, overseas. With weakening oil prices, political management became extremely incoherent in its interventionism and capital exports increased. Private domestic investment, having averaged 23 percent of GDP over 1975-78, was 7 percent in 1984, 6 percent in 1985 and 7 percent in 1986.[43] The political system operated as an effective way of siphoning off rent. The two traditional parties colonized the state and incorporated the main unions.[44] Public employment seemed to have no limit, and Venezuela spent more on health and education than any other country in Latin America, yet achieved worse results.[45]

When mismanagement reached a peak in 1988, the economic team of President Pérez pushed for full liberalization. They were so focused on the magnitude of the benefits available from introducing economic rationality that they gave little thought to political support. The degree of economic irrationality was indeed so overwhelming that they may well have been dazzled. As a result, they were taken aback first by the political reaction within Congress, which failed to pass important elements of the program, and second by the public reaction: riots, and eventually enough unrest to produce two attempted military coups.

---

[42] Data from CORDIPLAN quoted in the report prepared for the Social Agenda Group of the IDB: Thorp, Angell and Lowden, 1995.

[43] World Bank, 1990: 2.

[44] Inter-American Development Bank, 1993.

[45] Ibid.: 12.

Why, if the case was so overwhelming, did the policies prove so unpopular? First, what was missing was any effort to build political support[46] or to communicate the logic of what was being done.[47] The fact that the parties had ceased to be effective communicators had left a vacuum which was simply not seen to matter. Second, the program made no effort to alleviate social costs, initially even by compensatory measures[48] and throughout by any more fundamental efforts at integration of economic and social elements. Again, the culture of oil did not help, since Venezuela's apparent wealth left it poor in NGOs, important agents in improving social service delivery.

The measures did not lead to economic collapse, especially as the Gulf War (1990-91) brought higher oil prices once more. But mismanagement of the boom brought a serious banking crisis. And the government failed to deliver on social issues. Important initiatives occurred at the local level: one of the most encouraging was a vigorous decentralization program allowing local election of mayors and governors, which produced micro instances of the power of market mechanisms and local community initiatives to complement each other. But political coherence and leadership at the center were needed to make something of these isolated micro successes. In 1994, the new government reversed the measures, reintroducing exchange and other controls. The privatization program begun in 1991 had made little headway and was now suspended.

However, the results of the return to interventionism were no better, accompanied by inflation and no growth. After two years, the political base for a return to market reforms had been created. The fundamental step was the opening of the oil sector to foreign investment. But improving oil prices meant that pressure for long overdue institutional reforms once more dissipated.[49]

In Ecuador, economic management had remained very much subject to the interests of the traditional exporting groups, and as in Peru and Venezuela, import substituting industrialization had come late and in distorted form. It was a misfor-

---

[46] Ibid.: 19.

[47] A member of the cabinet wrote later: "The language was new, almost incomprehensible to most producers. It sounded strange and threatening. It made them feel inadequate, dumb. They felt insulted." Coles, 1993.

[48] The *Plan de Enfrentamiento de la Pobreza* came out eventually, but had a weak institutional base.

[49] *Financial Times*, March 14, 1997.

tune that the commodity lottery then gave Ecuador oil in the 1970s, so that a classic oil boom was added to an already fragile situation, increasing the bias towards capital-intensive, import-intensive and noncompetitive industry and weak agriculture, and tempting the government to increase its debt. It is no surprise that the 1980s were a decade of "muddling through adjustment," and "highly conflictive in political terms, with frequent and chaotic reversals."[50] The first effort to deal with the crisis using public sector measures failed, and was seen as the collapse of statism. This paved the way for a succession of governments attempting to impose neoliberal solutions, against much opposition, including that of the business classes, for whom devaluation and high interest rates were acceptable, as was squeezing wages, but trade liberalization or the removal of subsidies were not. Even President Cordero, a conservative businessman, was forced by popular unrest to reverse his reforms in 1986, opting for economic deterioration in order to save democracy.[51]

Reform efforts constantly bogged down because of extreme regional diversity, weak and fragmented parties, and a Congress that only worked three days a week and spent its time trying to impeach ministers rather than improve legislation. The new government of 1992, pledged to all the necessary legal and institutional reforms, made singularly little headway. The collapse of party politics in 1996 produced the unhelpful parallel to the kind of election result that seemed to be common in Latin America in the 1990s: a populist president deposed via popular protest in February 1997. This undermined what beginnings of credibility there had been under the previous government.

Despite the difficulties of making policy, there were successes. In particular, the Export Promotion Law contributed to the diversification of exports. Oil exports fell from 52 percent of the total in 1990 to 36 percent in 1996, and nontraditional exports rose from 7 to 23 percent, based on increasing incorporation of modern technology in agricultural and fish-based activities.[52] But with bananas and oil between them amounting to 67 percent of exports in 1990, economic prosperity remained dependent on the fortunes of these two products. In the case of oil, asso-

---

[50] Larrea, 1992: 295.

[51] His own analysis, quoted by Conaghan and Malloy, 1994.

[52] Maiguashca, personal communication, December 1997.

ciated environmental problems were huge.[53] The special oil factor was probably fairly marginal: the underlying political and economic problems were huge, and only compounded by the push into excess spending and eventual debt which came via oil. But the free market model did not address growing problems of poverty and exclusion. As a result, popular and ethnic movements expanded and became militant.

Like Venezuela and Ecuador, Paraguay suffered an embarrassment of riches. Perhaps more clearly than in either of the two previous cases, its bonanza was not the heart of the problem.[54] For several years in the 1970s, an economic boom gave the country the highest growth in Latin America. This was centered on opening up the eastern border region, which drew direct foreign investment into the expansion of cotton and soybean production, and a construction boom associated with the Itaipú dam on the border with Brazil. Completion of Itaipú in 1981 coincided with a drop in world prices for soybeans and cotton. The result was stagnation and rising inflation, fueled by the gross mismanagement of a multiple exchange rate system. Through the 1980s and 1990s the country lived increasingly from contraband. The overthrow of Stroessner in February 1989 came not from popular mobilization but from internal divisions within the Colorado Party and the military, and was supported by a mixed group, many motivated by a desire to protect their own economic empires. It is hardly surprising that after 34 years of a dictatorship that demobilized and co-opted so much of civil society, no efficient system of government could develop in Paraguay in the 1990s.

A start was made on tax and financial reform,[55] but much more was needed. Economic areas that needed urgent attention included the agrarian sector, where land issues needed action, and diversification away from cotton was essential; reform of the state and the judiciary; drugs and contraband, now to become pressing as contraband was seen as a grave obstacle to the development of MERCOSUR; and restructuring of an extremely weak industrial sector, which would only get special treatment within MERCOSUR for a limited period of time. Neither the transition government nor the first freely-elected government was prepared to tackle any of these problems in a serious manner. The transition government declared "a

---

[53] Pichón, 1997; Thomson and Dudley, 1989: 219-24; Southgate and Whitaker, 1992: 115.

[54] This section has been written in collaboration with Andrew Nickson.

[55] Economist Intelligence Unit, 1996/97.

free market economy," which basically meant freeing the exchange rate, although the government did also reduce the overall level of tariffs and abolish the remaining quotas. With the first freely-elected government, the executive actually opposed judicial reform. The degree of success achieved "was the work of an opposition-dominated Congress, whose dogged determination succeeded in overcoming backsliding by the executive."[56] Diversification in agriculture hit the resistance of the cotton ginners' organization, to which the president was connected. Contraband continued to account for one-third to one-half of Paraguay's imports.[57]

The Central American version of import substitution was embedded in its integration process. By the 1970s, this process was increasing its medium-term dependency on capital goods and intermediate goods from outside the region, paradoxically requiring stronger growth of traditional exports,[58] squeezing domestic use agriculture, and opening the way to avid borrowing as trade deficits grew. The region's current account deficit rose from 3.8 percent of GDP in 1977 to 9.3 percent in 1984, reflecting a 50 percent decline in external terms of trade, the sharp rise in interest rates, and private capital flight variously estimated at $2.5 billion to $4.5 billion.[59] The crisis hit hard, and in all countries except Costa Rica, interacted with the culmination of decades of oppression and corrupt military and civilian regimes. Political tensions exploded in the 1970s and grew worse in the 1980s, aggravated by the way Cold War tensions played out in the region.[60] Nicaragua saw the victory of the Sandinistas in 1979 over the corrupt and longstanding Somoza dictatorship, only to have their attempts at Socialist policies, with a major literacy campaign and basic health care, undermined by the horrendous costs of war. This came to an end after the defeat of the Sandinistas in the 1990 elections. In Guatemala and El Salvador, conflict with guerrilla forces produced tragic consequences.

Only by the 1990s were peace accords gradually put into place, following the Peace Plan devised by Costa Rican President Oscar Arias and signed in 1987. Rather conservative governments moved cautiously, aware of unresolved social problems, military presence and ex-guerrillas. The Central American Common Market

---

[56] Nickson, 1997: 199.

[57] Borda, 1997: 138.

[58] Irvin, 1995.

[59] Ibid.: 8.

[60] See Cohen in Companion Volume 3.

(CACM) all but collapsed, with intraregional exports falling from a peak of $1.1 billion in 1980 to only $406 million in 1986.[61] This was one instance among many of the way external political agendas intervened. U.S. policy throughout the 1980s was conditioned by the need to fight off what was seen as the threat represented by the Sandinista government in Nicaragua. Thus, for example, there was little enthusiasm for revitalization of the CACM, since strong regional growth could strengthen the Sandinista government.[62] Aid was spent heavily on military needs.

This was not a context for innovative economic and social development, and the region struggled desperately with the structural adjustment packages that caused enough difficulties elsewhere. As with Mexico, it was the prospect of trade deals and fringe benefits that dominated, though the region had a weaker base from which to negotiate or restructure. Affecting all the countries was the new lease on life given to the Central American Common Market by NAFTA and the prospect of association. In 1991, the Mexican government committed itself to negotiating free trade agreements with each of the Central American countries. El Salvador, Honduras and Guatemala formed the so-called Northern Triangle in 1993, taking the lead in eliminating all trade barriers. Nicaragua subsequently joined. Even Costa Rica, which had gone its own way in its efforts to increase exports outside the region to surmount the crisis of the 1980s, now took a new interest. Panama opted for membership in the *Sistema de Integración Centroamericana* (SICA), the new executive organization for the integration system, while remaining outside the Common Market itself. In 1992, Honduras was formally readmitted (having withdrawn in 1970 following the strain on its balance of payments, tensions with El Salvador and even a brief war with the latter). By 1995, intraregional exports were back to $1.5 billion.[63] But the focus had shifted for all: the importance of integration was seen increasingly as a stepping stone to the U.S. market.[64] By the late 1980s, motivated in part by the importance of being seen as good partners, all the countries were attempting market reforms. But continued economic and political fragility meant that the immediate short-term benefits seen elsewhere were negligible.

---

[61] Economist Intelligence Unit, 1997/98: 6.
[62] Bulmer-Thomas, 1987: 263.
[63] Economist Intelligence Unit, 1997/98: 8. Excludes Panama.
[64] Cerdas, 1997, consultancy report for this book.

The Caribbean: Greatest Vulnerability?

The Caribbean is the outstanding case where the historical experience and the resulting vulnerability exposed all countries quite dramatically to the perils of globalization. Cuba is, of course, a special case, but its vulnerability was at base very similar to that of its Caribbean neighbors.

The Caribbean was even more severely affected by the adverse trends of the 1970s and 1980s than was Latin America. As Table 8.1 shows, while performance was varied, GDP on average grew 0.1 percent a year from 1981 to 1990, while the average for the whole of Latin America and the Caribbean was 1.1 percent. From 1990-96, the Caribbean's 1.5 percent growth still compared unfavorably with the regional total of 3.1 percent. This reflected the fact that whereas Latin America had at least moved beyond the worst elements of trade vulnerability before it was hit by the new forms of financial vulnerability, the Caribbean had not. In 19 of the 26 Caribbean states (using the widest definition), the ratio to GDP of the sum of exports and imports of goods and services in the 1990s was over 100 percent—often far over. The larger island states—the Dominican Republic, Haiti and Trinidad and Tobago—still had ratios ranging from 50 to 72 percent.[65] Exports remained concentrated in a very small number of primary commodities: 78 percent of exports for Jamaica, and 76 percent for Trinidad and Tobago (and this was oil, so the boom and bust characteristics were particularly pronounced).[66]

Preferential arrangements, principally with Europe under the Lomé Convention, provided support. By the 1990s, these arrangements were under threat, as the Lomé convention was reviewed and the United States challenged banana preferences at the World Trade Organization. Cuba, of course, was the most extreme example, as the collapse of COMECOM damaged its sugar market and the problems and eventual collapse of the Soviet Union ended the financing of Cuba's trade deficit. In addition, Cuba's import dependency had risen with mechanization and the effort to increase the productivity of sugar through increased use of fertilizer and irrigation.[67]

---

[65] Girvan, 1997, Table A2.
[66] Harker, El Hadj and Vinhas de Souza, 1996.
[67] Pollitt, 1997: 11-13.

TABLE 8.1

THE CARIBBEAN: GDP ANNUAL GROWTH RATES (1990 PRICES)

(In percent)

Country	1981-90	1991-96
Guyana	-2.9	8.4
Belize	4.5	4.2
Dominican Republic	2.4	4.3
St. Lucia	6.8	3.4
St. Vincent and the Grenadines	6.5	3.0
Grenada	4.9	1.8
Trinidad and Tobago	-2.6	1.7
Jamaica	2.2	1.0
Antigua and Barbuda	6.4	0.9
Barbados	1.1	0.5
Haiti	-0.5	-2.1
Cuba	3.7	-4.9
Caribbean (English-speaking countries)	0.1	1.5
Latin America and the Caribbean	1.1	3.1

Source: ECLAC, *Preliminary Overview*, 1996.

In general, the commodity lottery did not favor the Caribbean in the last quarter of the century. Oil was produced in Trinidad and Tobago, and in Barbados from 1974. The rest of the countries were heavily dependent on tourism, sugar, bananas and bauxite-alumina, the latter facing a weakening market because of its energy intensity and reduced input per unit of final output in consumer countries.[68] Public revenue was also dependent on trade in the manner which characterized Latin America some 40 years earlier. Only in Jamaica, Trinidad and Tobago and Barbados did trade taxes account for less than 40 percent of fiscal revenues; in Antigua it was 66 percent, and in Anguilla, 77 percent. In addition, agriculture performed so badly through the 1970s and 1980s that the region became a net food importer.[69] Vulnerability to natural disasters made matters worse, as the Caribbean suffered hurricane and volcano damage.

[68] Harker, 1989: 18. To process bauxite into aluminum requires large amounts of electricity.
[69] Ibid.: 13.

On top of this traditional vulnerability came the new vulnerabilities of the late 20th century, with increased availability of finance and a new era of international capital mobility. While one or two countries could benefit by developing financial services (the Bahamas, for example), most acquired debt and vulnerability to capital flight and international interest rate changes. By the end of the 1970s, Guyana and Jamaica had debt service-to-export ratios of 17 and 18.5 percent, respectively. By 1985, Jamaica was at 41 percent, Cuba came next at 32 percent, followed by Grenada at 20 percent.[70] For the region as a whole, the debt service ratio climbed from 11 percent in 1980 to 17 percent in 1988.[71] Unlike most of Latin America, this debt was owed to the multilateral institutions, not to the private banks, and was therefore ineligible for the relief gradually provided through rescheduling in the commercial field.

In addition, integration fared badly in the 1980s.[72] The Caribbean Basin Initiative, a U.S. program that began in 1984, was designed to facilitate U.S. trade and investment in the region.[73] The trade balance moved from surplus in favor of the Caribbean to balance, however, in the next six years, principally because of declining raw material prices. The balance of payments also suffered as tourism, having grown initially very rapidly, began to slow, though not in time to prevent severe environmental damage.[74] The international market for tourism began to demand less "sun, sand and surf" and to favor special interest holidays. Major tourism infrastructure investments of a particular kind had already been made, however, and adaptation was neither easy nor favored by the resource endowment of most islands.

Faced with the depth of these development problems, the region could make little of the opportunities of the "new orthodoxy" of the 1980s and 1990s. In addition, CARICOM began in the 1960s in a protectionist spirit and firms were not ready for liberalization. The country that tried most obviously to jump on the bandwagon was the Dominican Republic. After decades of variations on the theme of personalist politics and policies, President Balaguer in 1990 opted for market poli-

---

[70] Girvan and Beckford, 1989: 45.

[71] Girvan, 1993: 108.

[72] Wendell, 1993: 166.

[73] Some 87 percent of U.S. imports from the Caribbean already entered duty-free. The main point of the scheme was to attract U.S. business. Harker, 1989: 26-27.

[74] Tourism in the Caribbean has seriously damaged the barrier reefs and caused severe pollution problems.

cies, without consulting business interests and in a context of exceptionally weak institutions and a pervasive and near-bankrupt state sector. The policy switch caused a sharp divide among business groups and the free trade/protectionist battle was fierce. The result was a set of policies, which while nominally market-oriented, still contained many elements of control and intervention. A budget could not be passed, and a fiscal crisis erupted.[75]

Equity and human development fared badly, too. Until the end of the 1980s, with notable exceptions such as Haiti, most of the Caribbean performed well in human development relative to per capita income, including gender-related development. Good performance related mainly to high levels of life expectancy and educational attainment. Recent economic changes, however, have had their impact on human development. Between 1991 and 1997, half of the independent states declined in the global human development ranking, including all the larger islands: Haiti lost 31 places, and Cuba and Jamaica, 24.[76]

Privatization did flourish in a number of countries, however, with particular success in placing state telecommunications and electricity companies on the market. The ratio of privatization revenue to GDP for 1990-95 was 1.15 percent for the Caribbean, compared to only 0.8 percent for Latin America as a whole.[77]

As with Central America, and also in part in reaction to NAFTA, the 1990s saw a new effort to reinvigorate CARICOM, with Haiti, the Dominican Republic and Cuba all seeking some form of association. The focus was on using CARICOM to "promote international competitiveness, greater self-reliance and Caribbean identity."[78]

Within this general context, Cuba's problems were in part those typical of the Caribbean, in part the product of an unusual history.[79] The 1970s saw strong growth. World sugar prices more than tripled over 1970-75, Soviet aid poured in, and Cuba joined the COMECOM in 1972. The value of gross investment nearly tripled, according to one estimate,[80] and new sugar mills and terminals and cement

---

[75] Durand, 1997, consultancy report for this book; Caribbean and Central America Report, January 14, 1997.
[76] Girvan, 1997: 15.
[77] Inter-American Development Bank, 1996: 173.
[78] Demas, 1997: xiii.
[79] This section draws on a consultancy report for this book by Brian Pollitt.
[80] Brundenius and Zimbalist, 1989.

and textile plants were built. Social welfare gains were even more impressive. Infant mortality and illiteracy became the lowest in Latin America in the late 1980s. Medical advances were outstanding.[81] Achievements were also made in racial integration and women's rights. But the crisis of the early 1980s hit Cuba with the rest of the Caribbean. The first reaction was to take Cuba further from the market with the "Rectification Process," which backed away from decentralization and from the limited use of the market that had been allowed at the end of the 1970s in an effort to solve food problems.

The problem was that by this date Cuba was as dependent on the Soviet Union as it had been on the United States in the 1950s. In 1990, Soviet aid was cut drastically. Eastern European supplies of butter, buses, medicines, grains and fertilizers almost came to a standstill. The desperate need for foreign exchange led to production practices in sugar that were disastrous for the long term, such as cutting immature cane and extending the harvest season (so that the following year's planting was disrupted). The lack of imports of fertilizer and spare parts contributed to a massive fall in productivity.[82] Cuban trade fell by some 25 percent between the first half of 1990 and the same period of 1991. GDP fell 3 percent in 1990, 25 percent in 1991, 25 percent in 1992 and 10 percent in 1993, with export earnings shrinking by two-thirds and no access to international finance. The extraordinary burden of adjustment reflected in these figures would in most other countries have led to a breakdown of the social order. The fact that it did not in Cuba suggests the strength of the "social capital" represented by commitment to rationing and the minimum provision of basic necessities.[83]

Nevertheless, by 1993 the government began a series of reforms that effectively legalized widespread survival strategies. These included decriminalization of use of the dollar in internal transactions, and legalization of self-employment. The reforms also converted state farms into cooperatives, decentralized economic decisions, allowed the emergence of profit-driven trading companies, reintroduced free

---

[81] By 1986, Cuba's life expectancy equaled that of the United States and the United Kingdom. The population per doctor fell from 1,217 in the early 1970s to 532 in the early 1980s and 274 in the early 1990s. The average for the same income group among Latin American countries was 3,277. World Bank, 1995. At a different level, advances in biotechnology were notable.

[82] Pollitt, 1997: 182-88.

[83] Ferriol, 1997.

markets for agricultural products (subsequently for industrial products), and eliminated a range of state subsidies. With this degree of liberalization, tourism and foreign investment both picked up. The next step was two free trade zones. Although rapid results could hardly be expected from such radical changes on the production side in terms of labor and management systems,[84] there was some immediate recovery. However, it was at the cost of equity—principally the inequity between those with access to the dollar economy and those without. It remains to be seen whether the new culture of globalization and competitiveness can survive alongside the continued desire to maintain the socialist paradigm and the social capital it produced.[85] Although tourism replaced sugar as the largest foreign exchange earner in 1997, Cuba also remains dependent on sugar as a source of hard currency and as its leading employer.[86]

CONCLUSION

Perhaps the most notable characteristic of the 1990s for Latin America has been the variety of experiences. For some countries there has been a clear learning process. There has been increased pragmatism, and more focus on institutional reform, the social sectors, and on the potential for interrelating political and economic issues, most notably in Chile but also in most of the larger economies. Other countries are still traumatized by the disasters of the 1980s, and given their histories and the resulting limitations of their institutions, remain vulnerable to the perils of globalization and unable to avail themselves of the benefits.

The benefit of continuity has been clear: Brazil and Colombia are instances where historical continuity and acquired experience brought a prudence that prevented them from buying into the new fashion in too radical a way.

But clearly, continuity and stability alone cannot work miracles: Bolivia and Peru have at last acquired a considerable measure of both, but each economy has other problems to face and has had difficulty building the "investment-export nexus."

---

[84] Ibid.: 199-204.
[85] Girvan, 1997.
[86] Caribbean and Central American Report, February 29, 1996.

The issue goes deeper than whether the present emphasis on the market is appropriate. It turns on the fact that there is no substitute for the long haul of building or rebuilding institutional frameworks.

This takes us directly to the importance of politics: transforming newly found stability and continuity into something more profound is very much a matter of a mature political system. There is reason to doubt both Argentina and Peru on this score. The consequences of lacking a political base have hobbled many countries, Venezuela being the most dramatic illustration, though Ecuador and the Dominican Republic also have had problems.

The temptations and perils of globalization came out most vividly in Mexico. But the problem is widespread in a less acute form, since many countries have found it difficult to raise investment and develop an investment-export nexus, given a dependence on inflows of money that generates overvaluation and makes policy teams reluctant to lower interest rates for fear of outflows. National savings remains volatile and difficult to tempt into productive investment. National financial systems lack sufficient depth and sophistication to survive the huge swings in international finance.

The potential benefits from globalization lie particularly in technology, developing small-scale industry, and returns to education. Many benefits could ensue if this could be brought together with the burst of expansion of microenterprises, and sustained by vigorous micro policies to support and enable such firms to prosper. This is the area par excellence where growth and equity-friendly policies coalesce. So far there are a few indicators of possibilities developing, though the issue needs more documentation. Recent work on Argentina suggests a growing dynamic role for microenterprise. But micro policies—basically a new concept of "sectoral policy"—need far more emphasis than they have had.

It is hardly a striking conclusion, in relation to the new policies, that "it all depends." But of course it does—on prior institutions and capacities, acquired experience and the political base. While the macro reforms that constituted the initial push of the new paradigm were important, much remains to be done on the micro and institutional side to move toward growth with equity.

REFLECTIONS ON A CENTURY OF LIGHT AND SHADOW

LATIN AMERICA HAS SEEN TWO WAVES OF expansion in the course of the century, each of which led to significant growth. The first, ending in 1929, saw strong growth led by exports. Brazil was the only country already growing faster than its export sector. There was an impressive buildup of infrastructure such as railways and ports, and of basic institutions such as central banks and tax collection agencies. In some instances, there were the beginnings of progress in the long haul of human development, with increased literacy and a reduction in mortality rates, particularly as epidemics began to be controlled.

The second wave of growth began between the 1930s and the 1950s and ended in the early 1980s. This period saw the fastest growth of the century and remarkable progress in both production and the productivity of labor, supported by a surge of infrastructure and service provision. It also saw human development indicators transformed. By the 1960s, the percentage of people in poverty was falling and there were some indications in a few countries that worsening income distribution had been halted and even reversed.

Despite these gains, each wave of expansion was marked by the continuation of extreme inequality of wealth, which had consequences for institution-build-

Photo: Computer class in Honduras, 1996.

ing and policymaking. In the first wave, institutions were consolidated to provide land and labor to the new model: that is, inequality was functional to the growth model. The dislocations of the early and mid-century did not disrupt those structures, despite increased political and social diversity. The second wave of expansion was similarly embedded within the same distribution of wealth, which shaped its form.

While there was a variety of national experiences during these expansion periods, what really differentiated countries in regard to outcomes was how they handled subsequent crises. This was even more marked in the second crisis period of the century than the first. Managing change is both a challenge and an opportunity, and it is crucial to ask why countries responded so differently and had such different outcomes. The answer lies principally in what had gone before.

In the period of export-led expansion up to 1929, growth varied principally according to the commodity lottery and a number of preconditions. Political stability in a basic sense was important: countries still torn by internal strife by the end of the 19th century, whatever their resource endowment, did not appear attractive to the foreign capital that was the motor of development in this early period. The degree of diversification was also important as a precondition for later expansion. The extent of diversification varied with the nature of the commodity as well as with the size of the internal market. Given a certain minimum market size, coffee appeared to be an export commodity particularly conducive to diversification: it spread over large areas, tended to be nationally controlled, and its own need for reinvestment of the surplus it generated was low. The degree of social tension and repression also varied with the commodity and with prior conditions, with consequences for the future. A sure recipe for social tension and severe inequality was an export crop with large labor needs, combined with a substantial indigenous population whom newcomers believed had to be controlled or displaced in order to secure access to land and labor.

In terms of political economy, tension and continuing political instability required expenditure on the military and the police, rather than on institutional and human development. A unique path was that of Mexico, where extreme tensions provoked the catharsis and terrible costs of the 1910 Revolution, but also as a result a subsequent surge in institution-building. In Costa Rica, particularly egalitarian conditions in regard to landholding and social structure led to a distinctive political economy that from an early date was conducive to human development. It also laid the foundation for future collaboration and consensus in policymaking.

A push to early egalitarianism, however, did not always imply a successful political economy. In Uruguay, where the egalitarian push came principally from a remarkable political leader, the policies followed were excellent for human development. But policymaking failed to address effectively some underlying economic problems, leading to slow growth of investment and lack of productivity growth in agriculture.

Policy competence and institutional development also seemed to advance if export expansion was less based on foreign capital. If overly dominant, foreign capital would play many of the roles which government might otherwise be pushed to perform. An illuminating contrast was that between Peru and Colombia. In Peru, a strong presence of foreign capital and its symbiotic relationship with local business groups resulted in laissez faire government, since foreign capital could be depended upon to perform such basic tasks as building infrastructure. Colombia had substantial foreign capital only in certain areas, so it needed government and institutions at all levels to advance the incipient coffee economy. This encouraged and supported a domestic institutional response, principally in the form of the Coffee Federation.

Institutional development and working relationships between the public and private sectors also progressed better in situations where diverse regional elites needed to learn to trade with each other in political terms, as in Brazil and Colombia.

Latin America's recovery after the Great Depression in 1929 was remarkably rapid. Most countries grew either through industrial expansion supported by import substitution, or through the growth of agriculture for the domestic market. Certain countries stood out for their skillful use of policy to take the recovery forward: Brazil and Colombia recovered early and saw rapid growth on the basis of precocious Keynesianism and well-managed controls. On the other hand, growth in the previous period was a poor predictor of relative success. Two countries that had grown particularly rapidly under export-led growth—Argentina and Cuba—now grew relatively slowly, constrained by the very factors that had led to previous success: their prominent position in "informal empires."[1]

---

[1] See Díaz-Alejandro in Companion Volume 2.

In terms of post-World War Two industrialization, Chile had many of the elements in place for a well-functioning political economy and rapid growth. It had well-developed state capacity, and prior high levels of industrial and institutional development that had been pushed forward as early as the 1920s. Yet it lacked the political coherence to pull all this together. The apprehension of business groups about socialist tendencies in successive governments seems to have undermined the investor confidence that is at the heart of a well-functioning political economy. However, institution-building continued, some investments were made in potential export sectors that would later bear fruit, and policy responded to the growing problems of inward-looking industrialization at an early date. In a somewhat similar instance, the obstacles to progress in Argentina were also those of political economy, though the level of institutional development was less advanced.

Where there were elements of continuity and competence in policymaking, and good relations between the public and private sectors, then cumulative processes were observable. In Brazil, where Kubitschek built on the policies of Vargas, a tradition of coherent and constructive public sector initiatives fostered trust and well-functioning relations with the private sector, which then survived some stormy seas. In Colombia, the political stability achieved by the *Frente Nacional* built confidence in the country's efficient, if closed and oligarchic, system. Only Colombia had the internal coherence and prudence to resist the temptations of the 1970s, when a panacea—borrowing—suddenly came available to deal with growing fiscal constraints.

Smaller countries with lesser institutional and policymaking capacities were often seduced into rash protectionist policies that went beyond the reasonable possibilities of the local market. This had the perverse effect of building up unproductive and uneconomical structures and encouraging rent-seeking. The "business dictatorships" of some Caribbean and Central American countries, along with Paraguay, were the countries that, despite growth, progressed least in terms of building the institutions, political structures and attitudes that would have prepared them for the longer run. In some cases external support for the regimes was important in cementing regressive structures and practices.

Recovering from the crisis triggered by the unsustainable borrowing of the 1970s was long and painful, and the process is far from complete for most. The easy opportunities of the 1930s for recovery—import substitution and default on debt—

were not available this time around. And there was a new vulnerability to international capital movements and interest rates, which more than offset reduced exposure as trade structures diversified. Further, the disruption to the political economy was greater, with major shocks to the whole structure of business interests. As industrial interests lost out, international trade and business interests gained strength and a wave of privatization rolled in.

Gradually, the initial swing of the pendulum in favor of market-friendly policies began to moderate into a more mature appreciation of the role of the state, public institutions and the political base for policies. It possibly needed the collapse of the Berlin Wall to generate serious commitment among progressives to seek ways to make the new market policies compatible with development. No equivalent process had taken place in the 1930s. Also, this time, with new democracies on all sides and sensitivities heightened by the appalling human development record of the 1980s, there was a renewed effort to integrate social and economic development. Again, initial solutions such as Emergency Social Funds began to evolve into a more complex search for lasting, home-grown solutions.

As happened earlier in the century, there were profound differences in how countries responded to the 1980s crisis. By the 1990s, some countries had moved in their own ways to take advantage of the opportunities presented by the new consensus on liberalization and privatization. The new democratic government in Chile used its commitment to the new rules of the game to sustain the confidence of business interests—the lack of which had constrained the country's development a generation earlier. Argentina employed a similar strategy to end inflation. Others jumped onto rather precarious seats on the privatization bandwagon, with questionable ability to make the most of its advantages and limit its dangers. Some countries viewed new social demands as opportunities for innovation and real change, while others saw them as a threat that required increased social control. How far the resulting repression will ultimately limit the viability and productivity of the new social and economic strategies is one of the many question marks for the future.

Balancing the historical record demands that much attention be given to political economy, as well as to the underlying structures that influenced it. Policies operate at different levels, with different outcomes depending on the time frame. On the one hand is the intention of those policies as seen at the time, often much disputed—the gold standard, protection, planning, liberalization. On the other is their significance over time, which is often quite different and not always what was originally envisaged. The Kemmerer reforms of the 1920s centered on reinstating the gold standard—but they ultimately were significant for creating monetary and fiscal institutions that would become a powerful asset for a quite different policy scenario. The "planning" of the 1960s was most significant not necessarily for what it accomplished of its explicit goals, but rather for encouraging better data collection, economic analysis and institutional development. Inward-looking development may have created inefficient industries behind walls of tariffs, but it also built a sense of national identity, institutions, new roles for the state, and sources of productivity growth for the long run. On the other hand, in countries without appropriate political economies, such development indeed resulted principally in high-cost industry. And in small countries with corrupt and often military-based or externally supported dictatorships, it brought "the booty state" and the "business dictatorship." The neoliberal paradigm's greatest significance over time may turn out to be not its specific content, but the opportunity it provided for countries—many at the point of collapse in terms of business confidence or even in some cases the state itself—to impose new clear rules with a strong signaling effect. This reflection is intended not to make us agnostic in regard to policy itself, but to encourage a deeper probing behind policies to the institutions and structures they depend on, generate, change or reinforce.

In terms of policies, this historical review points to perceptible progress in political economy in Latin America. Albert Hirschman over many years has pointed out the tendency of policymaking in Latin America to swing to extremes—the pendulum that goes from market to intervention and back. Hirschman insists, quite rightly, that the swing of the pendulum is a bad metaphor.[2] Since a pendulum is entirely mechanical, the metaphor excludes the role of feedback mechanisms in moderating (or failing to moderate) its swings and in generating continuity by building consensus. Hirschman's view is that in Latin America, such mechanisms historically have been weak; there is considerable evidence that today they are gaining strength. The extreme pro-free market views common in the early 1980s have moderated to an increasingly sophisticated view of the role of the state and of the potential in interaction between civil society and government. The narrowing of the de-

---

[2] Interview, Princeton, New Jersey, September 1996.

bate may itself be productive, as long as within the new territory opposition and criticism remain lively.

Balancing the progress and setbacks of the century is therefore a matter of combining such intangibles with a factual record itself full of good and bad, of light and shadow. The evidence shows poverty and exclusion remained extensive and deeply rooted, and inequality persisted. Slight signs of improvement in income distribution in one or two cases, and the wider reduction of poverty by the 1960s and 1970s, were aborted by the debt crisis and subsequent economic collapse. Damage to the environment was widespread in the export era, as forests were destroyed and fertility "mined" out of the land, and was exacerbated by industrialization and urbanization. In the last two decades the renewed importance of natural resource-based exports has revived the issue of the environmental threat from primary export growth. The ecological fragility of the Caribbean was compounded by continued trade and financial dependence and political vulnerability. In general, in the last decade of the century, the increased importance and instability of international financial flows has seriously threatened macro stability and policy autonomy. The machinery crucial for dispelling the shadows—effective relations between the public and private sectors and a well-trained bureaucracy—has in a number of respects and places deteriorated rather than improved.

Yet there has been progress, too: the significant growth in output and productivity, particularly through the middle part of the century, and the building of modern infrastructure. Despite the setbacks of recent years, the trade structures of the larger and even some of the smaller countries have been transformed over the century, away from dependence on a few primary exports. Skills and knowledge have accumulated and are there to be drawn on once expansion can be consolidated. The basic indicators of human development show a strong advance on average over the century. And a number of governments seem to be revealing a difference in kind in their capacity to ride the storms that no doubt lie ahead. There are signs in at least some countries and institutions that policymakers and others are beginning to recognize the potential for complementarity between growth and equity, along the twin paths of increased productivity and participation. If these complementarities can be developed, with the necessary institutions to support them, and if policymakers can identify and act on specific points of vulnerability to external shocks, then the "empty box" of growth with equity may yet be filled.

BIBLIOGRAPHY

Abel, C. 1996. *Health, Hygiene and Sanitation in Latin America c. 1870 to c. 1950.* Research Paper Series 42, Institute of Latin American Studies, University of London.

Abente, D. 1991. Foreign Capital, Economic Elites and the State in Paraguay during the Liberal Republic, 1870-1936. *Journal of Latin American Studies* 21: 61-88.

Adler, E. 1987. *The Power of Ideology: the Quest for Technological Autonomy in Argentina and Brazil.* Berkeley: University of California Press.

Agosin, M.R., G.T. Crespi, and L.S. Letelier. 1996. *Explicaciones del aumento del ahorro en Chile.* Red de Centros de Investigación Económica, IDB. Mimeo.

Agosin, M.R., and R. Ffrench-Davis. 1996. *Managing Capital Inflows in Latin America.* Discussion Paper Series No. 8, UNDP Office of Development Studies, United Nations Development Programme.

Albert, B. 1988. *South America and the First World War: the Impact of the War on Brazil, Argentina, Peru, and Chile.* Cambridge: Cambridge University Press.

Aldcroft, D. 1977. *From Versailles to Wall Street, 1919-1929.* London: Allen Lane.

Alesina, A., and D. Rodrik. 1994. Distributive Politics and Economic Growth. *Quarterly Journal of Economics* (May): 465-90.

Alienes, J. 1950. *Características fundamentales de la economía Cubana.* Havana: Banco Nacional de Cuba.

Altieri, M.A., and D. Masera. 1993. Sustainable Rural Development in Latin America: Building from the Bottom Up. *Ecological Economics* 7: 93-121.

Altimir, O. 1979. *La dimensión de la pobreza en América Latina.* Santiago: CEPAL.

_____. 1982. *The Extent of Poverty in Latin America.* World Bank Staff Working Paper No. 522, Washington, D.C.

_____. 1984. Poverty, Income Distribution and Child Welfare in Latin America: A Comparison of Pre- and Post-Recession Data. *World Development* 12(3): 261-82.

_____. 1994. Cambios en la desigualdad y la pobreza en la América Latina. *El Trimestre Económico* 62(241).

_____. 1997. Desigualdad, empleo y pobreza en América Latina: Efectos del ajuste y del cambio en el estilo de desarrollo. *Desarrollo Económico* 37(145). April-June.

_____. 1997a. The Long-term Evolution of Inequality and Poverty in Argentina, Colombia and Mexico. Consultancy paper for this book. Santiago.

American Petroleum Institute. 1958. *Petroleum Facts and Figures.* New York: API.

Angell, A., and R. Thorp. 1986. El efecto de la depresión de 1929 sobre América Latina. *Opciones* 6. May.

Anglade, C., and C. Fortin, eds. 1990. *The State and Capital Accumulation in Latin America.* Basingstoke: Macmillan.

Arriaga, E. 1968. *New Life Tables for Latin American Populations in the Nineteenth and Twentieth Centuries.* Berkeley: Institute of International Studies, University of California.

_____. 1970. *Mortality Decline and its Demographic Effects.* Population Monograph Series 6, Institute of International Studies, University of California, Berkeley.

Arriagada, I. 1994. Changes in the Urban Female Labour Market. *CEPAL Review* 53: 91-110.

Ashworth, W. 1987. *A Short History of the International Economy since 1850.* 4th ed. London: Longman.

Astorga, P., and V. FitzGerald. 1998. *The Standard of Living in Latin America During the Twentieth Century.* Development Studies Working Paper No. 117, Centro Studi Luca D'AGLIANO-QEH.

Azpiazu, D. 1993. *Desregulación, privatizaciones y apertura en la economía argentina: reflexiones preliminares sobre sus efectos en el sector industrial.* Buenos Aires: CEPAL.

Bairoch, P., T. Deldycke, H. Gelders and J.M. Limbor. 1975. *The Economic Development of the Third World since 1900.* London: Methuen.

Bairoch, P., et al. 1968. *The Working Population and its Structure.* Brussels: Institut de Sociologie Université Libre de Bruxelles.

Ballesteros, M.A., and T.E. Davis. 1963. The Growth of Output and Employment in Basic Sectors of the Chilean Economy, 1908-1957. *Economic Development and Cultural Change* 2: 152-76.

Banco Central de Venezuela (BCV). 1966. *La economía venezolana en los últimos veinticinco años,* Caracas: Banco Central de Venezuela .

——————. 1990. *Series estadísticas de Venezuela.* 50th anniversary edition. Caracas: Banco Central de Venezuela .

Banco de la República (BR). 1993. *Principales indicadores económicos: 1923-1992.* Bogotá: Banco de la República.

Banuri, T., ed. 1991. *Economic Liberalization: No Panacea: the Experiences of Latin America and Asia.* Oxford: Clarendon Press.

Banuri, T., and E. J Amadeo. Work Within the Third World: Labour Market Institutions in Asia and Latin America. In *Economic Liberalization: No Panacea: the Experiences of Latin America and Asia,* ed. T. Banuri. Oxford: Clarendon Press, Oxford.

Baptista, A. 1989. *Bases cuantitativas de la economía Venezolana, 1830-1989.* Caracas: Ediciones María di Mase.

——————. 1997. *Bases cuantitativas de la economía Venezolana, 1830-1995.* Caracas: Ediciones Fundación Polar.

Barraclough, S.L. 1973. *Agrarian Structure in Latin America.* Lexington, Mass.: D.C. Heath & Co.

Barraclough, S.L., and S. Domike. 1966. Agrarian Structure in Seven Latin American Countries. *Land Economics* 42(4).

Baskind, I., and T.C. Mesmer. 1997. Colombia and the Alliance for Progress. Mimeo.

Bates, R.H. 1997. *The Political Economy of the World Coffee Trade.* Princeton: Princeton University Press.

Behrman, J. 1976. *Foreign Trade Regimes and Economic Development: Chile.* New York: National Bureau of Economic Research.

Beneria, L. 1992. The Mexican Debt Crisis: Restructuring the Economy and the Household. In *Unequal Burden: Economic Crises, Persistent Poverty, and Women's Work,* eds. L. Beneria and S. Feldman. Boulder, CO: Westview Press.

Berry, A. 1997. The Income Distribution Threat in Latin America. *Latin American Research Review* 32(2).

Bethell, L., ed. 1994. *The Cambridge History of Latin America*. Vol. VI, Part II. Cambridge: Cambridge University Press.

Birdsall, N., and L. Londoño. 1997. Asset Inequality Matters: an Assessment of the World Bank's Approach to Poverty Reduction. *The American Economic Review* 87(2): 32-7.

Birdsall, N., T.C. Pinckney, and R.H. Sabot. 1990. Why Low Inequality Spurs Growth: Savings and Investment by the Poor. Inter-American Development Bank. Mimeo.

Bitar, S. 1971. La inversión extranjera en la industria chilena. *El trimestre económico* 33(4), No. 152: 995-1010.

Blakemore, H. 1974. *British Nitrates and Chilean Politics, 1886-1896*. London: Institute of Latin American Studies, University of London.

Blejer, M., A. Solimano, and O. Sunkel, eds. 1994. *Rebuilding Capitalism: Alternative Roads after Socialism and Dirgisme*. Ann Arbor: University of Michigan Press.

Blomstrom, M., and P. Meller, eds. 1991. *Diverging Paths: Comparing a Century of Scandinavian and Latin American Economic Development*. Washington, D.C.: Inter-American Development Bank.

Boorstein, E. 1968. *The Economic Transformation of Cuba*. New York and London: Monthly Review Press.

Borda, D. 1997. Economic Policy. In *The Transition to Democracy in Paraguay*, eds. P. Lambert and A. Nickson. Latin American Studies Series. Basingstoke: Macmillan; and New York: St. Martin.

Bouzas, R. 1993. Más allá de la estabilización y la reforma? Un ensayo de la economía argentina a comienzos de los '90s. *Desarrollo Económico* 33(129): 3-28.

Brandenburg, F.R. 1964. *The Development of Latin American Private Enterprise: a Report*. Planning Pamphlet No. 121, National Planning Association, Washington, D.C..

Brew, R. 1977. *El desarrollo económico de Antioquia desde la independencia hasta 1920*. Archivo de la Economía Nacional, No. 38. Banco de la República, Bogotá.

Brothers, D.S., and L. Solís. 1966. *Mexican Financial Development*. Austin: University of Texas Press.

Brown, K., and D.W. Pearce, eds. 1994. *The Causes of Tropical Deforestation: the Economic and Statistical Analysis of Factors Giving Rise to the Loss of the Tropical Forests*. London: UCL.

Brundenius, C. 1984. *Revolutionary Cuba: the Challenge of Economic Growth with Equity*. Boulder, CO: Westview Press.

Brundenius, C., and B. Göransson. 1993. *New Technologies and Global Restructuring: The Third World at a Crossroads*. London: Taylor-Graham.

Brundenius, C., and M. Lundhal, eds. 1982. *Development Strategies and Basic Needs in Latin America: Challenges for the 1980s*. Boulder, CO: Westview Press.

Brundenius, C., and A. Zimbalist. 1989. *The Cuban Economy: Measurement and Analysis of Socialist Performance*. Baltimore: Johns Hopkins University Press.

Bruton, H. 1967. Productivity Growth in Latin America. *American Economic Review*. December: 1099-166.

Bulmer-Thomas, V. 1987. *The Political Economy of Central America since 1920*. Cambridge: Cambridge University Press.

_____. 1994. *The Economic History of Latin America since Independence*. Cambridge: Cambridge University Press.

——————, ed. 1996. *The New Economic Model in Latin America and its Impact on Income Distribution and Poverty*. Basingstoke: Macmillan.

Buttari, J. J., ed. 1979. *Employment and Labour Force in Latin America: a Review at National and Regional Levels*. Washington, D.C.: ECIEL and Organization of American States.

Buttari, J. J. 1992. Economic Reform in Central American Countries: Patterns and Lessons Learned. *Journal of Interamerican Studies and World Affairs* 34(1), Spring: 179-214.

Cammack, P. 1980. State and Federal Politics in Minas Gerais, Brazil. Doctoral thesis, Oxford University.

Canavese, A. 1992. Hyperinflation and Convertibility-based Stabilization in Argentina. In *The Market and the State*, ed. A. Zini, Jr. Elsevier: North Holland.

Cárdenas, E. 1987. *La Industrialización mexicana durante la gran depresión*. Mexico City: El Colegio de México.

——————. 1994. *La hacienda pública y la política económica, 1929-1958*. Mexico City: El Colegio de México and the Fondo de Cultura Económica.

——————. 1996. *La política económica en México 1950-1994*. Mexico City: El Colegio de México and the Fondo de Cultura Económica.

Cárdenas, E., and C. Mann. 1987. Inflation and Monetary Stabilization in Mexico during the Revolution. *Journal of Development Economics* 27: 375-294.

Cárdenas, E., J.A. Ocampo, and R. Thorp, eds. (Companion Volume 1) *The Export Age: The Latin American Economies in the Late Nineteenth and Early Twentieth Century*. Macmillan. Forthcoming.

——————. (Companion Volume 3) *Industrialization and the State in Latin America: The Black Legend of the Post War Years*. Macmillan. Forthcoming.

Cardoso, E., and A. Helwege. 1992. *Latin America's Economy: Diversity, Trends and Conflicts*. Cambridge, Mass.: MIT Press.

——————. 1992a. *Cuba after Communism*. Cambridge, Mass.: MIT Press.

Cardoso, F.H. 1977. The Originality of a Copy: CEPAL and the Idea of Development. *CEPAL Review* 2: 7-40.

Cardoso, F.H., and E. Faletto. 1971. *Dependencia y desarrollo en América Latina*. Mexico City: Siglo XXI.

Caribbean and Central America Report. 29 February, 1996, 6 May, 1997, and 14 January, 1997. London.

Cariola, C., and O. Sunkel. 1982. *La historia económica de Chile, 1830 y 1930: dos ensayos y una bibliografía*. Madrid: Ediciones Cultura Hispánica del Instituto de Cooperación Iberoamericano.

Carneiro, D.D. 1987. Long-run Adjustment, the Debt Crisis and the Changing Role of Stabilisation Policies in the Recent Brazilian Experience. In *Latin American Debt and Adjustment Crisis*, eds. R. Thorp and L. Whitehead. Basingstoke: Macmillan and St. Antony's College.

Castaner, J. 1987. Recent Experience of the Puerto Rican Economy. In *Development in Suspense: Selected Papers and Proceedings of the First Conference of Caribbean Economists*, eds. N. Girvan and G.L. Beckford. Kingston, Jamaica: Friedrich Ebert Stiftung Foundation and the Association of Caribbean Economists.

CELADE. 1996. *Boletín Demográfico* 29(58), July: 55.

Chiriboga, M. 1983. Auge y crisis de una economía agroexportadora: el período cacaotero. In *Nueva historia del Ecuador, Vol. 9*, ed. E.A. Mora. Quito: Corporación Editora Nacional.

Chonchol, J. 1996. *Sistemas agrarios en América Latina: de la etapa prehispánica a la modernización conservadora*. Santiago: Fondo de Cultura Económica.

Chudnovsky, D. 1974. *Empresas multinacionales y ganancias monopólicas en una economía Latinoamericana*. Mexico, D.F.: Fondo de Cultura Económica.

Claessens, S., M. Dooley, and A. Warner. 1993. *Portfolio Capital Flows: Hot or Cool?* World Bank Discussion Paper No 228, Washington, D.C.

Cline, W. 1984. *International Debt: Systemic Risk and Policy Response*. Washington, D.C.: Institute for International Economics.

Coale, A. 1978. Population Growth and Economic Development: the Case of Mexico. *Foreign Affairs* 56.

Coale, A., and E.M. Hoover. 1959. *Population Growth and Economic Development in Low-income Countries: A Case Study of India's Prospects*. Princeton: Princeton University Press.

Coles, J. 1993. Reforming Agriculture: The Venezuelan Experience. Caracas. Mimeo.

Collier, D., ed. 1979. *The New Authoritarianism in Latin America*. Princeton: Princeton University Press.

Collier, R.B., and D. Collier. 1991. *Shaping the Political Arena: Critical Junctures, the Labour Movement, and Regime Dynamics in Latin America*. Princeton: Princeton University Press.

Collver, A.O. 1965. *Birth Rates in Latin America: New Estimates of Historical Trends and Fluctuations*. Berkeley: Institute of International Studies, University of California Press.

Companion Volume 1. E. Cárdenas, J.A. Ocampo, and R. Thorp, eds. *The Export Age: The Latin American Economies in the Late Nineteenth and Early Twentieth Century*. Macmillan and St. Antony's College. Forthcoming.

Companion Volume 2. R. Thorp, ed. *Latin America in the 1930s*. Macmillan and St. Antony's College. Forthcoming.

Companion Volume 3. E. Cárdenas, J.A. Ocampo, and R. Thorp, eds. *Industrialization and the State in Latin America: The Black Legend of the Post War Years*. Macmillan and St. Antony's College. Forthcoming.

Conaghan, C.M., and J.M. Malloy. 1994. *Unsettling Statecraft: Democracy and Neoliberalism in the Central Andes*. Pittsburgh: University of Pittsburgh Press.

Contreras, M.E. 1990. Debt, Taxes and War: the Political Economy of Bolivia, c. 1920-1935. *Journal of Latin American Studies* 22.

_____. 1990a. The Formation of a Technical Elite in Latin America: Mining Engineering and the Engineering Profession 1900-1954. Ph.D. Dissertation, Columbia University.

Corbo, V., S. Fischer and S.B. Webb. 1992. *Adjustment Lending Revisited: Policies to Restore Growth*. Washington, D.C.: World Bank.

Córdova, A., and H.S. Michelena. 1967. *Aspectos teóricos del subdesarrollo*. Caracas: Universidad Central de Venezuela.

Cortés Conde, R. 1994. *La economía Argentina en el largo plazo*. Buenos Aires: Universidad de San Andrés.

_____. 1996. *Estimaciones del producto interno bruto de la Argentina*. Working Paper, Universidad de San Andrés, Buenos Aires.

Cortés Conde, R., and S. Hunt. 1985. *The Latin American Economies: Growth and the Export Sector 1880-1930*. New York: Holmes and Meier.

Cuban Economic Research Project. 1965. *A Study on Cuba*. Coral Gables, FL: University of Miami Press.

Dean, W. 1969. *The Industrialization of São Paulo, 1880-1945*. Latin American Monograph No. 17, Institute of Latin American Studies, University of Texas Press, Austin.

_____. 1995. *With Broadax and Firebrand: the Destruction of the Brazilian Atlantic Forest*. Berkeley: University of California Press.

Deas, M. 1982. The Fiscal Problems of Nineteenth Century Colombia. *Journal of Latin American Studies* 14(2): 287-328.

Deere, C.D. 1985. Rural Women and State Policy: the Latin American Agrarian Reform Experience. *World Development* 13(9): 1037-53.

_____. 1987. The Latin American Agrarian Reform Experience. In *Rural Women and State Policy: Feminist Perspectives on Latin American Agricultural Development*, eds. C.D. Deere and M. Leon. Boulder, CO: Westview Press.

de Janvry, A. 1981. *The Agrarian Question and Reformism in Latin America*. Baltimore: Johns Hopkins University Press.

Dell, S. 1972. *The Inter-American Development Bank: a Study in Development Financing*. New York and London: Praeger.

Demas, W.G. 1997. West Indian Development and the Deepening and Widening of the Caribbean Community. *Critical Issues in Caribbean Development* 1, Ian Randle and Institute of Social and Economic Research, University of the West Indies, Kingston, Jamaica.

Devlin, R. 1989. *Debt and Crisis in Latin America: the Supply Side of the Story*. Princeton: Princeton University Press.

_____. 1990. *Latin America and the Caribbean: Options to Reduce the Debt Burden*. Santiago: United Nations Publications.

_____. 1992. *Equidad y transformación productiva: un enfoque integrado*. Santiago: United Nations Publications.

_____. 1994. *Políticas para mejorar la inserción en la economía mundial*. Santiago: United Nations Publications.

Devlin, V., and R. Ffrench-Davis. 1995. The Great Latin American Debt Crisis: a Decade of Asymmetric Adjustment. In *Poverty, Prosperity and the World Economy*, ed. G. Helleiner. Basingstoke: Macmillan.

Díaz-Alejandro, C. 1970. *Essays on the Economic History of the Argentine Republic*. New Haven: Yale University Press.

_____. 1984a. In *Latin America in the 1930s: The Role of the Periphery in World Crisis*, ed. R. Thorp. Basingstoke: Macmillan and St. Antony's College.

_____. 1984b. *Latin American Debt: I Don't Think We Are in Kansas Any More*. Brookings Paper on Economic Activity No. 2.

Diéguez, H.L. 1972. Crecimiento e inestabilidad del valor y el volumen físico de las exportaciones argentinas en el período 1864-1963. *Desarrollo Económico* 12: 333-44.

Dietz, J. 1986. *Economic History of Puerto Rico: Institutional Change and Capitalist Development*. Princeton: Princeton University Press.

Di Tella, G. 1987. Argentina's Most Recent Inflationary Cycles, 1975-85. In *Latin American Debt and the Adjustment Crisis*, eds. R. Thorp and L. Whitehead. Basingstoke: Macmillan and St. Antony's College.

Domínguez, L., and F. Brown. 1995. La naturaleza micro y macroeconómica del cambio técnico: un caso de la industria alimentaria. November. Mimeo.

Donghi, T.H. 1995. The Buenos Aires Landed Class and the Shape of Argentine Politics, 1820-1930. In *Agrarian Structure and Political Power: Landlord and Peasant in the Making of Latin America*, eds. E. Huber and F. Safford. Pittsburgh and London: University of Pittsburgh Press.

Dore, E. 1988. *The Peruvian Mining Industry*. Boulder, CO and London: Westview Press.

Dornbusch, R., and S. Edwards. 1991. *The Macroeconomics of Populism in Latin America*. Chicago: University of Chicago Press.

Dorner, P. 1992. Latin American Land Reforms in Theory and Practice. Madison, WI: University of Madison Press.

Draibe, S. 1985. *Rumos e metamorfoses: um estudo sobre a constituição do Estado e as alternativas da industrialização no Brasil:1930-1960*. Rio de Janeiro: Paz e Terra.

Drake, P. 1989. *The Money Doctor in the Andes: the Kemmerer Missions, 1923-33*. Durham, NC: Duke University Press.

Dyster, B. 1979. Argentine and Australian Development Compared. *Past and Present* 84: 91-110.

Easterley, W., N. Loayza, and P. Montiel. 1996. Has Latin America's Post-reform Growth Been Disappointing? World Bank, Washington, D.C. Mimeo.

Economic Commission for Europe (ECU). 1970. International Comparison of Real Incomes, Capital Formation, and Consumption. *Economic Survey of Europe, 1969.* Part I, United Nations, New York.

ECLA. 1951. *Economic Survey of Latin America, 1949*. New York: United Nations.

_____. 1951a. *Public Finance Developments in Latin America*. New York: United Nations.

_____. 1955. *Foreign Capital in Latin America*. New York: United Nations.

_____. 1964. *El financiamiento externo de América Latina*. New York: United Nations.

_____. 1964a. *Statistical Bulletin for Latin America*, Vol. 1. New York: United Nations.

_____. 1964b. The Growth and Decline of Import Substitution in Brazil. *Economic Bulletin for Latin America* 9(1). United Nations, New York..

_____. 1966. *The Process of Industrial Development in Latin America*. New York: United Nations.

_____. 1971. Public Sector Enterprises: Their Present Significance and Their Potential in Development. *Economic Bulletin for Latin America* 16(1), United Nations, New York.

_____. 1976. *America Latina: relación de precios del intercambio*. Santiago: United Nations.

_____. 1978. *Series históricas del crecimiento de América Latina*. Santiago: United Nations.

ECLAC. *Statistical Yearbook for Latin America*. United Nations, Santiago. Various years.

_____. 1990. *Los grandes cambios y la crisis. Impacto sobre la mujer en América Latina y el Caribe*. Santiago: United Nations.

_____. *Preliminary Overview of the Economy of Latin America and the Caribbean*. Santiago: ECLAC. Various years.

_____. *Social Panorama of Latin America*. Various years. Santiago: ECLAC.

ECLAC, and FAO. 1986. *El crecimiento productivo y la heterogeneidad agraria*. División Agrícola Conjunta CEPAL/FAO, Santiago.

Economist Intelligence Unit. 1996/97. *Country Profile: Paraguay*. EIU, London.

_____. 1997/98. *Country Profile: Central America*. EIU, London.

Edwards, S. 1992. Trade Orientation, Distortions and Growth in Developing Countries. *Journal of Development Economics* 39: 31-57.

——————. 1993. Openness, Trade Liberalization, and Growth in Developing Countries. *Journal of Economic Review* 31 (September): 1358-93.

——————. 1997. *Openness, Productivity and Growth: What Do We Really Know?* Working Paper Series No 5978, National Bureau of Economic Research, Cambridge, Mass.

Eichengreen, B., and A. Fishlow. 1996. *Contending with Capital Flows: What Is Different about the 1990s?* A Council on Foreign Relations Paper, New York.

Eichengreen, B., and P.H. Lindert. 1989. *The International Debt Crisis in Historical Perspective.* Cambridge, Mass.: MIT Press.

Elías, V. J. 1992. *Sources of Growth: a Study in Seven Latin American Countries.* San Francisco: ICS Press.

Emmerij, L., ed. 1997. *Economic and Social Development into the XXI Century.* Washington, D.C.: Inter-American Development Bank.

Erico, M.A. 1975. Estructura y desarrollo del comercio exterior del Paraguay: 1870-1918. *Revista Paraguaya de Sociología* 12(3): 125-55.

Fajnzylber, F. 1990. *Industrialization in Latin America: From the "Black Box" to the "Empty Box:" A Comparison of Contemporary Industrialization Patterns.* Santiago: ECLAC.

Fearnside, P.M. 1990. Deforestation in the Brazilian Amazon. In *The Future of Amazonia: Destruction or Sustainable Development?*, eds. D. Goodman and A. Hall. Basingstoke: Macmillan.

Feinber, R., and R. Ffrench-Davis, eds. 1988. *Development and Debt in Latin America.* South Bend, Indiana: University of Notre Dame Press.

Feinstein, C.H. 1972. *National Income, Expenditure and Output of the United Kingdom, 1855-1965.* Cambridge: Cambridge University Press.

Fernández-Arias, E., and P. Montiel. Reform and Growth in Latin America: All Pain and No Gain? Paper presented at the Annual Meeting of the Inter-American Development Bank, Barcelona, March, 1997.

Ferns, H. 1992. The Baring Crisis Revisited. *Journal of Latin American Studies* 24(2): 241-73.

Ferrer, A. 1963. *La economía Argentina.* Mexico City and Buenos Aires: Fondo de Cultura Económica.

Ferriol, A. 1997. Economic Reforms in Cuba in the 1990s. Paper presented to the Fifth Conference of Caribbean Economists, Havana.

Ffrench-Davis, R. 1988. Economic Integration in Latin America. In *Lessons in Development: A Comparative Study of Asia and Latin America*, eds. S. Naya, M. Urrutia, S. Mark, and A. Fuentes. San Francisco: International Center for Economic Growth.

——————. 1989. *El devenir de una ilusión: la industria argentina desde 1930 hasta nuestros días.* Buenos Aires: Editorial Sudamericana.

——————. 1996. Transformación productiva con equidad: algunos elementos de la propuesta de la CEPAL. In *La globalización de los desajustes*, ed. R. Urriola. Quito: ILDIS/Editorial Nueva Sociedad.

Ffrench-Davis, R., O. Muñoz, and G. Palma. 1994. The Latin American Economies, 1950-1990. In *Cambridge History of Latin America*, Vol. VI, Part I, ed. L. Bethell. Cambridge: Cambridge University Press.

Figueroa, A. 1977. Agrarian Reforms in Latin America: A Framework and an Instrument of Rural Development. *World Development*, Vol. 5: 155-68.

Filsinger, E. 1916. *Exporting to Latin America*. Washington, D.C.: United States Department of Commerce.

Finch, M.H.J. 1981. *A Political Economy of Uruguay since 1870*. London: Macmillan.

Findlay, R., and S. Wellisz, eds. 1993. *Five Small Open Economies*. New York: Oxford University Press for the World Bank.

Fishlow, A. 1972. Origins and Consequences of Import Substitution in Brazil. In *International Economics and Development: Essays in Honour of Raul Prebisch*, ed. L. Di Marco. New York: Academic Press.

_____. 1989. A Tale of Two Presidents: the Political Economy of Crisis Management. In *Democratizing Brazil*, ed. A. Stepan. Oxford: Oxford University Press.

_____. 1991. Some Reflections on Comparative Latin American Performance. In *Economic Liberalisation: No Panacea, the Experiences of Latin America and Asia*, ed. T. Banuri, Oxford: Clarendon Press.

_____. 1995. Future Sustainable Latin American Growth. *The Review of Black Political Economy* (Summer): 7-21.

FitzGerald, E.V.K. 1978. The Fiscal Crisis of the Latin American State. In *Taxation and Economic Development*, ed. J.F.J. Toye. London: Frank Cass.

Fodor, J. 1986. The Origins of Argentina's Sterling Balance, 1939-43. In *The Political Economy of Argentina, 1880-1946*, eds. G. Di Tella and D.C.M. Platt. Basingstoke: Macmillan and St. Antony's College.

Fodor, J., and A. O'Connell. 1973. La Argentina y la economía atlántica en la primera mitad del siglo XX. *Desarrollo Económico* 13(49).

Fogel, R.W. 1991. New Sources and New Techniques for the Study of Secular Trends in Nutritional States, Health, Mortality, and the Process of Aging. Working Paper No. 26, National Bureau of Economic Research, Cambridge, Mass.

Folkjerts-Landau, D.F.I., and T. Ito. 1995. International Capital Markets: Development Prospects and Policy Issues. World Economic and Financial Surveys, International Monetary Fund, Washington, D.C.

Font, M. 1990. *Coffee, Contention and Change in the Making of Modern Brazil*. Oxford: Basil Blackwell.

Fowler-Salamini, H., and M.K. Vaughan, eds. 1994. *Women of the Mexican Countryside, 1850-1990: Creating Spaces, Shaping Transitions*. Tucson: University of Arizona Press.

Frei Montalva, E. 1967. The Alliance that Lost its Way. *Foreign Affairs* 45 (April): 437-48.

Fritsch, W. 1993. The New International Setting: Challenges and Opportunities. In *Development from Within: Toward a Neostructuralist Approach for Latin America*, ed. O. Sunkel. Boulder, CO and London: Lynne Rienner.

Furtado, C. 1970. *Economic Development of Latin America: A Survey from Colonial Times to the Cuban Revolution*. Cambridge: Cambridge University Press.

_____. 1985. *A fantasia organizada*. Rio de Janeiro: Paz e Terra.

Gavin, M. 1997. A Decade of Reform in Latin America: Has it Delivered Lower Volatility? Paper presented at the Annual Meeting of the Inter-American Development Bank, Barcelona.

Geddes, C.F. 1972. *Patiño, the Tin King*. London: R. Hale.

Gerchunoff, A. 1936. *Los gauchos judíos*. M. Gleizer.

Girvan, N. 1993. The Debt Problem of the Caribbean and Central America: An Overview. In *Caribbean Economic Development: The First Generation*, eds. M. Freckleton and S. Lalta. Kingston: Ian Randall.

――――――. 1997. *Societies at Risk? The Caribbean and Global Change.* MOST Discussion Paper Series No. 17, UNESCO, Paris.

――――――. 1997a. Cuba: Structural Adjustment with a Human Face? Paper presented at the Fifth Conference of Caribbean Economists, Havana.

Girvan, N., and G. Beckford. 1989. *Development in Suspense: Selected Papers and Proceedings of the First Conference of Caribbean Economists (1987).* Kingston, Jamaica: Friedrich Ebert Stiftung.

Glade, W.P. 1969. *The Latin American Economies: A Study of Their Institutional Evolution.* New York: American Book.

――――――. 1981. Industrialization and the State in Latin America. *Hispanic American Historical Review* 61(2): 351-53.

Graham, C. 1994. *Safety Nets, Politics and the Poor: Transitions to Market Economy.* Washington, D.C.: Brookings Institution.

Grieshaber, E. 1980. Survival of the Indigenous Communities in 19th Century Bolivia: A Regional Comparison. *Journal of Latin American Studies* 12(2): 223-69.

Griffith-Jones, S., ed. 1988. *Managing World Debt.* London: Harvester Wheatsheaf.

Griffith-Jones, S., and O. Sunkel. 1986. *Debt and Development Crises in Latin America: The End of an Illusion.* Oxford: Clarendon Press.

Grindle, M.S. 1986. *State and Countryside: Development Policy and Agrarian Politics in Latin America.* Baltimore: Johns Hopkins University Press.

Ground, R.L. 1988. The Genesis of Import Substitution in Latin America. *CEPAL Review* 36: 179-204.

Grunwald, J., and P. Musgrove. 1970. *Natural Resources in Latin American Development.* Baltimore: Johns Hopkins University Press.

Gupta, B. 1989. Import Substitution in Capital Goods: The Case of Brazil, 1929-1979. Doctoral thesis, Oxford University.

Gurrieri, A., ed. 1982. *La obra de Prebisch en la CEPAL.* Mexico City: Fondo de Cultura Económica.

Haber, S.H. 1989. *Industry and Underdevelopment: The Industrialization of Mexico, 1890-1940.* Stanford: Stanford University Press.

――――――, ed. 1997. *How Latin America Fell Behind: Essays on the Economic History of Brazil and Mexico, 1800-1914.* Stanford: Stanford University Press.

Harker, T. 1989. The Caribbean in the Context of the Global Crisis. In *Development in Suspense*, eds. G. Beckford and N. Girvan. Kingston: Ebert Foundation and Association of Caribbean Economists.

――――――. 1993. A Brief Overview of Economic Performance in the Eighties. In *Caribbean Economic Development: The First Generation*, eds. S. Lalta and M. Freckleton. Jamaica: Ian Randle.

Harker, T., S.O. El Hadj, and L. Vinhas de Souza. 1996. The Caribbean Countries and the Free Trade Area of the Americas. *CEPAL Review* 59, ECLAC, Santiago .

Hausmann, R, and M. Gavin. 1995. Securing Stability and Growth in a Shock-prone Region: The Policy Challenge for Latin America. IDB Working Paper No. 315, January.

Hausmann, R., and G. Márquez. 1993. *La crisis económica de Venezuela.* Cuadernos del CENDES 1, Caracas.

Hecht, S.B. 1989. The Sacred Cow in the Green Hell. *The Ecologist* 19(6): 229-34.

Helleiner, G. 1995. *Poverty, Prosperity and the World Economy.* London: Macmillan.

Hernández, C.E., and S.G. Witter. 1996. Evaluating and Managing the Environmental Impact of Banana Production in Costa Rica: a Systems Approach. *Ambio* 25(3).

Heston, A, and R. Summers. 1991. The Penn World Table Mark 5. An Expanded Set of International Comparisons, 1950-1988. *Quarterly Journal of Economics* (May): 327-68.

Hirschman, A.O. 1968. *Journeys Toward Progress: Studies of Economic Policy-making in Latin America.* New York: Greenwood Press.

_____. 1971. *A Bias for Hope: Essays on Development and Latin America.* New Haven: Yale University Press.

_____. 1991. *The Rhetoric of Reaction.* Cambridge, Mass.: Harvard University Press.

_____. 1997. *Fifty Years after the Marshall Plan: Two Posthumous Memoirs and Some Personal Recollections.* Princeton: Institute for Advanced Study.

Hobsbawm, E. 1995. *Age of Extremes: the Short Twentieth Century, 1914-1991.* London: Abacus.

Hodara, J. 1987. *Prebisch y la CEPAL: sustancia, trayectoria y contexto institucional.* Mexico City: Colegio de México.

Hofman, A. 1997. Economic Performance in Latin America—A Comparative Quantitative Perspective. Consultancy paper for this book, Santiago.

Hora, R. 1997. Argentine Elites and Economic and Social Development in the Twentieth Century. Oxford University. Mimeo.

Horsefield, J.K., and DeVries, M.G. 1969. *The International Monetary Fund, 1945-1965: Twenty Years of International Monetary Cooperation.* Washington, D.C.: IMF.

Humphreys, R.A. 1981. *Latin America and the Second World War, 1939-1942.* London: Athlone Press.

_____. 1982. *Latin America and the Second World War, 1942-1945.* London: Athlone Press.

Hunt, S. 1973. *Prices and Quantum Estimates of Peruvian Exports, 1830-1962.* Discussion Paper 31, Woodrow Wilson School Research Program in Economic Development, Princeton University.

_____. 1997. The Human Condition in Latin America, 1900-95. Consultancy paper for this book.

Ianni, O. 1963. *Industrialização e desenvolvimento social no Brasil.* Rio de Janeiro: Editora Civilização Brasileira.

_____. 1971. Estado e planejamento econômico no Brasil, 1930-1970. Coleção Retratos do Brasil, Vol. 83. Editora Civilização Brasileira, Rio de Janeiro.

Iglesias, E., ed. 1994. *The Legacy of Raúl Prebisch.* Washington, D.C.: Inter-American Development Bank.

Instituto Brasileiro de Geografia e Estatística (IBGE). 1990. *Estatísticas históricas do Brasil.* Rio de Janeiro: IBGE.

Instituto de Planejamento Econômico e Social (IPEA). 1978. A *controvérsia de planejamento na economia brasileira: coletânea da polêmica Simonsen X Gudin.* Rio de Janeiro: IPEA.

Instituto de Relaciones Europeo-Latinoamericanas (IRELA). 1994. La cooperación europea hacia América Latina en los 90: una relación en transición. IRELA, Madrid.

_____. 1996. *Bolivia: The Difficult Process of Transformation.* Dossier No. 57. IRELA, Madrid.

Instituto Nacional de Estadística, Geografía e Informática (INEGI). 1990. *Estadísticas históricas de México*. Mexico City: INEGI.

Inter-American Development Bank. 1971. *The IDB's First Decade and Perspectives for the Future*. Washington, D.C.: Inter-American Development Bank.

————————. 1976. *Economic and Social Progress in Latin America: 1976 Report*. Washington, D.C.: Inter-American Development Bank.

————————. 1984. *External Debt and Economic Development in Latin America: Background and Prospects*. Washington, D.C.: Inter-American Development Bank.

————————. 1996. *Volatile Capital Flows: Taming Their Impact on Latin America*. Washington, D.C.: Inter-American Development Bank.

————————. 1997. *Economic and Social Progress in Latin America: 1996 Report*. Washington, D.C.: Inter-American Development Bank.

International Bank for Reconstruction and Development. 1951. *Report on Cuba*. Baltimore: Johns Hopkins University Press.

International Labour Organization (ILO). 1980-1996. *Yearbook of Labour Statistics*. Geneva: ILO.

International Monetary Fund (IMF). 1970. *Yearbook of International Financial Statistics*. Washington, D.C.: IMF.

————————. 1986. *Yearbook of International Financial Statistics*. Washington, D.C.: International Monetary Fund.

————————. 1996. *Yearbook of International Financial Statistics*. Washington, D.C.: International Monetary Fund.

————————. 1995. Evolution of the Mexican Peso Crisis. In *International Capital Markets, World Economic and Financial Surveys*. Washington, D.C.: International Monetary Fund.

International Union for the Conservation of Nature and Natural Resources - Netherlands Committee (IUCN-NC). 1996. Mining in Tropical Regions—Ecological Impact of Dutch Involvement. Amsterdam. December.

Irvin, G. 1995. ECLAC and the Political Economy of the CACM. *Latin American Research Review* 23(3): 7-29.

Izard, M. 1970. *Series estadísticas para la historia de Venezuela*. Mérida, Venezuela: Universidad de los Andes.

Jarvis, L.S. 1992. The Unravelling of the Agrarian Reform. In *Development and Social Change in the Chilean Countryside: From the Pre-Land Reform Period to the Democratic Transition*, eds. C. Kay and P. Silva, CEDLA Latin American Studies 62, Amsterdam.

Jefferson, O. 1972. *The Postwar Economic Development of Jamaica*. Mona, Jamaica: Institute of Social and Economic Research (ISER), University of the West Indies.

Jenkins, R. 1987. *Transnational Corporations and the Latin American Automobile Industry*. London: Macmillan.

Jorgensen, S.L., and M. Paldam. 1987. Exchange Rates and Domestic Inflation: A Study of Price/Wage Inflation in Eight Latin American Countries, 1946-85. World Bank Development Research Department Report 233, Washington, D.C.

Junguito, R. 1995. *La deuda externa en el siglo XIX: Cien años de incumplimiento*. Bogota: Tercer Mundo Ed., Banco de la República.

Kaldor, N. 1959. Economic Problems of Chile. *El Trimestre Económico* (April-June).

Kapur, D., J.P. Lewis, and R.C. Webb, eds. 1997. *The World Bank: Its First Half Century, Vols. 1 and 2*. Washington, D.C.: Brookings Institution Press.

Karlsson, W. 1975. *Manufacturing in Venezuela: Studies on Development and Location.* Stockholm: Institute of Latin American Studies.

Katz, J. 1976. *Importación de tecnología, aprendizaje e industrialización dependiente.* Mexico City: Fondo de Cultura Económica.

_____. 1986. *Desarrollo y crisis de la capacidad tecnológica Latinoamericana. El caso de la industria metalmecánica.* Buenos Aires: CEPAL.

_____. 1987. *Technology Generation in Latin American Manufacturing Industries.* Hong Kong: The Macmillan Press, Ltd.

Katz, J., and B. Kosacoff. 1989. *El proceso de industrialización en la Argentina: evolución, retroceso y prospectiva.* Buenos Aires: CEPAL.

Kay, C. 1983. The Agrarian Reform in Peru: An Assessment. In *Agrarian Reform in Contemporary Developing Countries,* ed. A.K. Ghose. London and New York: Croom Helm & St. Martin's.

_____. 1988. Cuban Economic Reforms and Collectivization. *Third World Quarterly* 10(3): 1239-66.

_____. 1997. Latin America's Agrarian Reform: Promises and Fulfilment. Consultancy paper for this book.

Kelly, R. 1965. Foreign Trade of Argentina and Australia, 1930-1960. *Economic Bulletin of Latin America* 10(1): 49-70.

Kemmerer, E.W. 1927. Economic Advisory Role for Governments. *The American Economic Review* 17: 1-12.

Kessing, D. 1977. Employment and Lack of Employment in Mexico: 1900-1970. In *Quantitative Latin American Studies: Methods and Findings.* SALA Supplement Series 6, eds. J.W. Wilkie and K. Ruddle. Los Angeles: UCLA.

Kindleberger, C. 1978. *Manias, Panics and Crashes.* New York: Basic Books.

Kirsch, H.W. 1977. *Industrial Development in a Traditional Society: The Conflict of Entrepreneurship and Modernization in Chile:* Gainesville, FL: University of Florida Press.

Klein, H. 1993. *Haciendas and Ayllus, Rural Society in the Bolivian Andes in the 18th and 19th Centuries.* Stanford: Stanford University Press.

Knight, A. 1986. *The Mexican Revolution.* Cambridge: Cambridge University Press.

Knight, F.W. 1978. *The Caribbean: The Genesis of a Fragmented Nationalism.* New York: Oxford University Press.

Kornblith, M., and L. Quintana. 1984. Gestión fiscal y centralización del poder político en los gobiernos de Cipriano Castro y de Juan Vicente Gómez. *Politeia* 10: 143-219.

Kosacoff, B. 1993. La industria argentina: un proceso de reestructuración desarticulada. In *El Desafío de la competitividad.* Buenos Aires: Ed. Alianza Etudio 21.

_____. 1996. *Business Strategies and Industrial Adjustment: The Case of Argentina.* Working Paper No. 67, ECLAC.

Kravis, I.B., A. Heston, and R. Summers. 1978. *International Comparisons of Real Product and Purchasing Power.* Baltimore: Johns Hopkins University Press for the World Bank.

_____. 1982. *World Product and Income: International Comparisons of Real Gross Product.* Baltimore: Johns Hopkins Press for the World Bank.

Lall, S. 1992. Technological Capabilities and Industrialization. *World Development* 20(2): 165-86.

Landes, D. 1969. *Unbound Prometheus: Technological Change and Industrial Development in Western Europe from 1750 to the Present.* Cambridge: Cambridge University Press.

Langer, E. 1987. La comercialización de la cebada en los ayllus y las haciendas de Tarabuco Chuquisaca a comienzos del siglo XX. In *La participación indigena en los mercados surandinos*, eds. O. Harris, B. Larson and E. Tandeter. La Paz: CERES.

Larrea, C. 1992. The Mirage of Development: Oil, Employment and Poverty in Ecuador 1972-1990. Doctoral thesis, Oxford University.

League of Nations. 1925. *Memorandum on Balance of Payments and Foreign Trade Balances, 1910-24.* Geneva: League of Nations.

——————. 1930-38. *Review of World Trade.* Geneva: League of Nations.

——————. 1938. *Public Finance, 1928-37.* Geneva: League of Nations.

——————. 1945. *Industrialization and Foreign Trade.* Geneva: League of Nations.

Leff, N. 1997. Economic Development in Brazil, 1822-1913. In *How Latin America Fell Behind*, ed. S. Haber. Stanford: Stanford University Press.

LeGrand, C. 1986. *Frontier Expansion and Peasant Protest in Colombia, 1850-1936.* Albuquerque: University of New Mexico Press,

Leopoldi, M.A.P. 1984. Industrial Associations and Politics in Contemporary Brazil. Doctoral thesis, Oxford University.

Lerdau, E., and T.C. Mesmer. 1997. Chile and the Alliance for Progress. Mimeo.

Lessard, D., and J. Williamson. 1987. *Capital Flight.* Washington, D.C.: Institute for International Economics.

Levinson, J., and J. de Onis. 1970. *The Alliance that Lost its Way.* Chicago: Quadrangle Books.

Levitt, K., and L. Best. 1975. Character of Caribbean Economy. In *Caribbean Economy: Dependence and Backwardness*, ed. G.L. Beckford. Kingston, Jamaica: Institute of Social and Economic Research (ISER), University of the West Indies.

Lewis, C. 1938. *America's Stake in International Investments.* Washington, D.C.: The Brookings Institution.

Lewis, W.A. 1949. *Economic Survey, 1919-1939.* London: Allen & Unwin.

——————. 1950. The Industrialization of the British West Indies. *Caribbean Economic Review* 2(1): 1-61.

——————. 1978. *Growth and Fluctuations, 1870-1913.* London: George Allen & Unwin.

Lissakers, K. 1991. *Banks, Borrowers and the Establishment: A Revisionist Account of the International Debt Crisis.* New York: Basic Books.

Londoño, J.L. 1995. *Distribución del ingreso y desarrollo económico: Colombia en el siglo XX*, Bogotá: Tercer Mundo Editores.

Londoño, J.L., and M. Szekely. 1997. Distributional Surprises after a Decade of Reforms: Latin America in the Nineties. Paper presented at the Annual Meeting of the Inter-American Development Bank, Barcelona.

Lora, E. 1997. Una década de reformas estructurales en América Latina: Que se ha reformado y cómo medirlo. Paper presented at the Annual Meeting of the Inter-American Development Bank, Barcelona.

Lora, E, and F. Barrera. 1997. A Decade of Structural Reform in Latin America: Growth, Productivity, and Investment Are Not What They Used to Be. Paper presented at the Annual Meeting of the Inter-American Development Bank, Barcelona.

Love, J. 1971. *Rio Grande do Sul and Brazilian Regionalism, 1882-1930*. Stanford: Stanford University Press.

_____. 1996. *Crafting the Third World*. Stanford: Stanford University Press.

Lowenthal, A.F. 1975. *The Peruvian Experiment: Continuity and Change under Military Rule*. Princeton: Princeton University Press.

Lustig, N. 1992. La medición de la pobreza en México. *El Trimestre Económico* 59(4).

Macario, S. 1964. Protectionism and Industrialization in Latin America. *Economic Bulletin for Latin America* 9(1): 61-102.

Macmillan, W. 1936. *Warning from the West Indies: A Tract for Africa and the Empire*. London: Faber.

Maddison, A. 1982. *Phases of Capitalist Development*. Oxford: Oxford University Press.

_____. 1983. A Comparison of the Levels of GDP Per Capita in Developed and Developing Countries, 1800-1980. *Journal of Economic History* 43.

_____. 1992. *Brazil and Mexico*. Oxford: Oxford University Press for the World Bank.

_____. 1995. *Monitoring the World Economy, 1820-1992*. Paris: OECD.

Maiguashca, J. 1996. Ecuadorian Cocoa Production and Trade, 1840-1925. In *Cocoa Pioneer Fronts since 1800: The Role of Smallholders, Planters and Merchants*, ed. W.G. Clarence-Smith. Basingstoke: Macmillan; and New York: St. Martin's Press.

Mangle, J. 1989. British Caribbean Economic History: An Interpretation. In *The Modern Caribbean*, eds. F.W. Knight and C.A. Palmer. Chapel Hill, NC: University of North Carolina Press.

Manthy, R.S. 1978. *Natural Resource Commodities. A Century of Statistics*. Baltimore: John Hopkins University Press.

Marichal, C. 1988. *Historia de la deuda externa de América Latina*. Madrid: Alianza Editorial.

_____. 1989. *A Century of Debt Crises in Latin America: From Independence to the Great Depression, 1820-1930*. Princeton: Princeton University Press.

Martinez, L.O., C.N. Carruso, J.P. Vallejo, and G.B. Aceveda. 1989. Corporación de fomento de la producción (CORFO): 50 años de realizaciones. Departamento de Historia, Facultad de Humanidades, Universidad de Santiago de Chile. Mimeo.

Maxfield, S., and J. H. Nolt. 1990. Protectionism and the Internationalization of Capital: U.S. Sponsorship of ISI in the Philippines, Turkey and Argentina. *International Studies Quarterly* 34: 49-81.

McCreery, D. 1994. *Rural Guatemala 1760-1940*. Stanford: Stanford University Press.

McIntyre, A., et al. 1996. Jamaica. Social Agenda Policy Group, Inter-American Development Bank, Washington, D.C.

McQueen, C. 1926. *Bolivian Public Finance*. Washington, D.C.: U.S. Bureau of Foreign and Domestic Commerce

Meller, P., R. O'Ryan, and A. Solimano. 1996. Growth, Equity and the Environment in Chile: Issues and Evidence. *World Development* 24(2): 255-72.

Merrick, T.W. 1994. The Population of Latin America, 1930-1990. In *Cambridge History of Latin America*, Vol, VI, Part I, ed. L. Bethell. Cambridge: Cambridge University Press.

Mesa-Lago, C. 1978. *Social Security in Latin America: Pressure Groups, Stratification and Inequality*. Pittsburgh: University of Pittsburgh Press.

_____. 1981. *The Economy of Socialist Cuba: A Two-decade Appraisal*. Albuquerque: University of New Mexico.

—————. 1989. *Ascent to Bankruptcy: Financing Social Security in Latin America*. Pittsburgh: University of Pittsburgh.

—————. 1994. *Changing Social Security in Latin America: Toward Alleviating the Social Costs of Economic Reform*. Boulder, CO and London: Lynne Rienner.

Mikesell, R., ed. 1962. *United States Private and Government Investment Abroad*. Eugene, OR: University of Oregon Books.

Mikkelsen, J.G., and M. Paldam. 1987. Real Wages in 8 Latin American Countries: A Look at the Data 1984-85. Memo 1987-88, Institute of Economics, University of Aarhus.

Mitchell, B.R. 1993. *International Historical Statistics: The Americas, 1750-1988*. Basingstoke: Macmillan.

Moncada, S. 1995. Entrepreneurs and Government in Venezuela, 1944-1958. Doctoral thesis, Oxford university

Morales, J.A., and J.D. Sachs. 1990. Bolivia's Economic Crisis. In *Developing Country Debt and Economic Performance, Country Studies: Argentina, Bolivia, Brazil, Mexico, Vol. 2*, ed. J.D. Sachs. Chicago: University of Chicago Press.

Morgenstern, O. 1950. *On the Accuracy of Economic Observations*. Princeton: Princeton University Press.

Mosk, S. 1950. *Industrial Revolution in Mexico*. Berkeley: University of California Press.

Movarec, M. 1982. Exportación de manufacturas Latino-Americanas a los centros de importancia y significado. *Revista de la CEPAL* 17: 47-78.

Muñoz, O. 1968. *Crecimiento industrial de Chile 1914-1965*. Santiago: Universidad de Santiago de Chile.

—————. 1986. *Chile y su industrialización: pasado, crisis y opciones*. Santiago: CIEPLAN.

—————, ed. 1993. *Historias personales, politicas publicas*. Santiago: CIEPLAN.

—————. 1995. *Los inesperados caminos de la modernización económica*. Santiago: Universidad de Santiago de Chile.

Navarete, I. 1960. *La distribución del ingreso y el desarrollo económico de México*. Mexico City: Instituto de Investigaciones Económicas, Escuela Nacional de Economía, UNAM.

Naya, S., M. Urrutia, S. Mark, and A. Fuentes. 1989. *Lessons in Development: a Comparative Study of Asia and Latin America*. San Francisco: International Center for Economic Growth.

Neves, R.B., and H. Moreira. 1987. Os incentivos às exportações brasileiras de produtos manufaturados 1969-1985. *Pesquisa e Planejamento Econômico* 17(2).

Newland, C. 1991. La educación elemental en HispanoAmérica: desde la independencia hasta la centralización de los sistemas educativos nacionales. *Hispanic American Historical Review* 71(2): 335-64.

Niblo, S.R. 1988. *The Impact of War: Mexico and World War Two*. Occasional Paper No. 10, La Trobe University, Institute of Latin American Studies, Melbourne.

Nickson, A., and P. Lambert. 1989. The Overthrow of the Stroessner Regime: Re-establishing the Status Quo. *Bulletin of Latin American Research* 8(2): 185-210.

Nickson, A. 1997. The Wasmosy Government. In *The Transition to Democracy in Paraguay*, eds. A. Nickson and P. Lambert. Basingstoke: Macmillan; and New York: St. Martin's Press.

Nowzad, B., et al. 1981. *External Indebtedness of Developing Countries*. Occasional Paper No. 3, International Monetary Fund, Washington, D.C.

Obstfeld, M., and A.M. Taylor. 1997. *The Great Depression as a Watershed: International Capital*

Mobility over the Long Run. Working Paper Series No. 5960, National Bureau of Economic Research.

Ocampo, J.A. 1984. *Colombia y la economía mundial, 1830-1910.* Bogotá: Fedesarrollo and Siglo Veintiuno Editores.

_____. 1990. New Economic Thinking in Latin America. *Journal of Latin American Studies* 22: 169-81.

_____. 1991. The Transition from Primary Exports to Industrial Development in Colombia. In *Diverging Paths: Comparing a Century of Scandinavian and Latin American Economic Development*, eds. M. Blomstrom and P. Meller. Washington, D.C.: Inter-American Development Bank.

_____. Terms of Trade and Centre-Periphery Relations, In *Development from Within: Toward a Neostructuralist Approach for Latin America*, ed. O. Sunkel. Boulder, CO and London: Lynne Rienner.

Ocampo, J.A., and S. Montenegro. 1982. La crisis mundial de los años treinta en Colombia. *Desarrollo y Sociedad* 7 (January): 35-96.

_____. 1984. *Crisis mundial. protección e industrialización: ensayos de historia económica colombiana.* Bogotá: Fondo Editorial CEREC.

O'Connell, A. 1994. Economic Reorganization in Latin America. Paper presented at the Istituto Gramsci, Roma, Italia.

Odle, M.A. 1975. Public Policy. In *Caribbean Economy: Dependence and Backwardness*, ed. G.L. Beckford. Kingston, Jamaica: Institute of Social and Economic Research (ISER).

Oral History Project on the Alliance for Progress. 1997. Coordinators: E. Lerdau and T.C. Mesmer. Mimeo.

Organización Latinoamerica de Energía (OLADE). 1996. *Integración energética en America Latina y el Caribe.* Quito: OLADE.

Ortega, L., et al. 1989. *CORFO: 50 años de realizaciones, 1939-1989.* Santiago: Universidad de Santiago de Chile.

Palacios, M. 1983. *El café en Colombia 1850-1970.* 2nd edition. Mexico City and Bogotá: Colegio de México, El Ancora Editores.

_____. 1995. *Entre la legitimidad y la violencia: Colombia 1875-1994.* Bogotá: Editorial Norma.

Palloni, A. 1990. Fertility and Mortality Decline in Latin America. *Annals*, AAPSS: 510.

Palma, J.G. 1979. Growth and Structure of the Chilean Manufacturing Industry from 1830 to 1935. Doctoral thesis, Oxford University .

Pan-American Union (PAU). 1952. *Bulletin of the Pan-American Union* 13(4), October.

_____. 1952. *The Foreign Trade of Latin America since 1913.* Washington, D.C.: Pan-American Union.

_____. 1954. *Fiscal Receipts, Expenditure, Budgets and Public Debt of the Latin American Republics.* Washington, D.C.: Pan-American Union.

_____.1955. *Foreign Investment in Latin America.* Economic Research Series. Washington, D.C.: Pan-American Union.

Pantin, D. 1987. The Political Economy of Natural Gas-based Industrialization in Trinidad and Tobago. In *Development in Suspense: Selected Papers and Proceedings of the First Conference of Caribbean Economists*, eds, N. Girvan and G.L. Beckford. Kingston, Jamaica: Friedrich Ebert Stiftung Foundation and Association of Caribbean Economists.

Papageorgiou, D., M. Michaely, and A. Choksi. 1991. *Liberalising Foreign Trade: Lessons of Experience in the Developing World*. Vol. 7. Oxford: Basil Blackwell.

Peñaloza, L. 1947. *Historia económica de Bolivia*. Vol. 2. La Paz: Editorial Artística.

Pérez Brignoli, H. 1993. América Latina en la transición demográfica, 1800-1980. In *La transición demográfica en América Latina y el Caribe*, Vol. 1, INEGI.

Pérez Brignoli, H., and C.F.S. Cardoso. 1979. *Historia económica de América Latina*. Barcelona: Editorial Crítica.

Pérez-López, J. 1977. An Index of Cuban Industrial Output: 1930-1958. In *Quantitative Latin American Studies: Methods and Findings*, SALA Supplement Series 6, eds. J.W. Wilkie and K. Ruddle. Los Angeles: UCLA.

——————. 1991. Bringing the Cuban Economy into Focus: Conceptual and Empirical Challenges. *Latin American Research Review* 26(3): 7-35.

Persson, T., and G. Tabellini. 1994. Is Inequality Harmful for Growth? *American Economic Review* 84(3): 600-21.

Pfefferman, G., and R. Webb. 1983. Poverty and Income Distribution in Brazil. *The Review of Income and Wealth* 29(2): 101-25.

Phelps, C.W. 1927. *The Foreign Expansion of American Banks*. New York: Ronald Press Company.

Pichón, F.J. 1997. Settler Households and Land-use Patterns in the Amazon Frontier: Farm-level Evidence from Ecuador. *World Development* 25(1): 67-92.

Pietrobelli, C. 1995. Technological Capability and Export Diversification in a Developing Country: the Case of Chile since 1974. Doctoral thesis, Oxford University.

Pinto, A. 1964. *Chile: una economía difícil*. Mexico City: Fondo de Cultura Económica.

Piore, M.J., and C.F. Sabel. 1984. *The Second Industrial Divide: Possibilities for Prosperity*. New York: Basic Books.

Pollitt, B.H. 1984. The Cuban Sugar Economy and the Great Depression. *Bulletin of Latin American Research* 3(2): 3-28.

——————. 1986. Sugar, Dependency and the Cuban Revolution. *Development and Change* 17(2), April: 195-230.

——————. 1997. The Cuban Sugar Economy: Collapse, Reform and Prospects for Recovery. *Latin American Studies* 29: 171-210.

Pollock, D. 1978. Some Changes in United States Attitudes Toward CEPAL over the Past 30 Years. *CEPAL Review* 6: 57-80.

Pollock, D., and C. Rosales. 1989. The 1980s as a Transitional Decade for Latin American Relations with the United States and Canada. *Journal of Latin American Affairs* 5(1).

Posada-Carbó, E. 1996. *The Colombian Caribbean: A Regional History, 1870-1950*. Oxford: Clarendon Press.

Prebisch, R. 1964. *Towards a New Trade Policy for Development: Report by the Secretary-general of the United Nations Conference on Trade and Development*. New York: United Nations.

Programa Regional del Empleo para América Latina y el Caribe (PREALC). 1982. *Mercado de trabajo en cifras: 1950-1980*. Lima: International Labour Organization (ILO).

Psacharopoulos, G., and T. Zafiris. 1992. *Women's Employment and Pay in Latin America. Overview and Methodology*. Washington, D.C.: World Bank.

Puciarelli, A. 1986. *El capitalismo agrario pampeano, 1880-1930*. Buenos Aires: Hyspamérica.

Putnam, R. 1993. *Making Democracy Work: Civic Traditions in Modern Italy*. Princeton: Princeton University Press.

Puyana de Palacios, A. 1980. Economic Integration Amongst Unequal Partners: The Case of the Andean Group. Doctoral thesis, Oxford University.

Rabe, S.G. 1978. The Elusive Conference: U.S. Economic Relations with Latin America, 1945-1952. *Diplomatic History* 2(3): 279-94.

_____. 1982. *The Road to OPEC: U.S. Relations with Venezuela, 1919-1976*. Austin: University of Texas Press.

Ramos, J. 1986. *Neoconservative Economics in the Southern Cone of Latin America, 1973-1983*. Baltimore: Johns Hopkins University Press.

Rangel, D.A. 1969. *Capital y desarrollo: la Venezuela agraria*. Caracas: UCV.

Rangel de Paiva Abreu, A. 1993. Mudança tecnológica e gênero no Brasil. *Novos Estudos* 35, Brazilian Centre for Analysis and Planning, São Paulo.

Restrepo, M. 1958. *El rey de la leña*. Buenos Aires: Capricornia.

Reynolds, C.W. 1970. *The Mexican Economy: Twentieth Century Structure and Growth*. New Haven, CT: Yale University Press.

Reynolds, A., and M. Mamalakis. 1976. *The Growth and Structure of the Chilean Economy from Independence to Allende*. New Haven, CT: Yale University Press.

_____. 1978. *National Accounts: Historical Statistics of Chile*. New York: Greenwood.

_____. 1985. *Historical Statistics of Chile*, Vol. 5. New York: Greenwood.

Rivera, S. 1984. *Oprimidos pero no vencidos*. Geneva: UNRISD.

Rock, D. 1994. Latin America in the 1940s: War and Postwar Transitions. University of California Press.

Rodríguez, E., and S. Griffith-Jones, eds. 1992. *Cross-conditionality, Banking Regulations and Third World Debt*. London: Macmillan.

Roett, R., and R.S. Sachs. 1991. *Paraguay: The Personalist Legacy*. Boulder, CO: Westview Press.

Rojas-Suárez, L., and S.R. Weisbrod. 1995. *Financial Fragilities*. Washington, D.C.: International Monetary Fund.

Romano, C. 1992. Brazil. In "Amazonia—Cause and Case for International Cooperation." Report produced for the European Working Group on Amazonia (EWGA), Amsterdam, July.

Ros, J. 1987. Mexico from the Oil Boom to the Debt Crisis: An Analysis of Policy Responses to External Shocks, 1978-85. In *Latin American Debt and the Adjustment Crisis*, eds. R. Thorp and L. Whitehead. Basingstoke: Macmillan and St Antony's College.

Rowe, F. 1965. *Primary Commodities in International Trade*. Cambridge: Cambridge University Press.

Russell, S., and M. Teitelbaum. 1992. *International Migration and International Trade*. World Bank Discussion Paper 160, World Bank, Washington, D.C.

Sabato, H. 1989. *Capitalismo y ganadería en Buenos Aires: la fiebre del lanar, 1850-1890*. Buenos Aires: Editorial Sudamericana.

Sabato, J. 1988. *La clase dominante en la Argentina moderna: formación y características*. Buenos Aires: CISEA/Grupo Editor Latinoamericano.

Sachs, I. 1980. *Studies in Political Economy of Development*. New York, Oxford: Pergamon Press.

Sachs, J., and S. Collins, eds. 1988. *Developing Country Debt and Economic Performance*. Vols. 1 and 2. Chicago: University of Chicago Press.

Sachs, J., A. Tornell, and A. Velasco. 1995. *The Collapse of the Mexican Peso: What Have We Learned?* Working Paper Series 5142, National Bureau of Economic Research, Cambridge, Mass.

Sánchez-Albornoz, N. 1974. *The Population of Latin America: A History.* Berkeley: University of California Press.

_____. 1986. The Population of Latin America, 1850-1930. In *Cambridge History of Latin America*, Vol. 4, ed. L. Bethell. Cambridge: Cambridge University Press.

Santamaría, A. 1995. La industria azucarera y la economía Cubana durante los años veinte y treinta. Ph.D. dissertation, Universidad Complutense, Madrid.

Santana, S. 1987. The Cuban Health Care System: Responsiveness to Changing Needs and Demands. In *Cuba's Socialist Economy: Toward the 1990s*, ed. A. Zimbalist. Boulder, CO and London: Lynne Rienner.

Schneider, R. 1994. Incentives for Tropical Deforestation: Some Examples from Latin America. In *The Causes of Tropical Deforestation: The Economic and Statistical Analysis of Factors Giving Rise to the Loss of the Tropical Forests*, eds. K. Brown and D.W. Pearce. London: UCL.

Schvarzer, J. 1996. *La industria que supimos conseguir.* Buenos Aires: Planeta.

Scott, C. 1996. The Distributive Impact of the New Economic Model in Chile. In *The New Economic Model in Latin America and its Impact on Income Distribution and Poverty*, ed. V. Bulmer-Thomas. London: Macmillan.

Seers, D. 1964. *Cuba: The Economic and Social Revolution.* Chapel Hill, NC: University of North Carolina Press.

Seidel, R. 1972. American Reformers Abroad: The Kemmerer Missions in South America, 1923-1931. *Journal of Economic History* 32(2).

Senghaas, D. 1985. *The European Experience: A Historical Critique of Development Theory.* Berg Publishers.

Sercovitch, C.F. 1984. Jorge Alberto Sabato. *Revista de Ciencias Sociales* 29.

_____. 1987. Un maestro de la praxis y un teórico entre los realizadores. *Argentina Tecnológica* 1(4), January: 26-7.

Serra, J., ed. 1979. *América Latina: Ensaios de interpretação econômica.* Rio de Janeiro: Paz e Terra.

Shafer, R.J. 1973. *Mexican Business Organizations: History and Analysis.* Syracuse: Syracuse University Press.

Sheahan, J. 1987. *Patterns of Development in Latin America: Poverty, Repression and Economic Strategy.* Princeton: Princeton University Press.

Sikkink, K. 1991. *Ideas and Institutions: Developmentalism in Brazil and Argentina.* Ithaca, NY: Cornell University Press.

Silva, A., ed. 1996. Implementing Policy Innovations in Latin America: Politics, Economics and Techniques. Social Agenda Policy Group, Inter-American Development Bank, Washington, D.C.

Silvestrini, B.G. 1989. Contemporary Puerto Rico: A Society of Contrasts. In *The Modern Caribbean*, eds. F.W. Knight and A. Palmer. Chapel Hill, NC: University of North Carolina Press.

Smith, P.H. 1969. *Politics and Beef in Argentina: Patterns of Conflict and Change.* New York and London: Columbia University Press.

Solimano, A. 1996. Economic Growth and Social Equity: an Overview. Paper presented at the Economic Growth and Social Equity Workshop, Santiago, July.

South American Handbook. 1924. London: South American Publications.

Southgate, D.D., and M.D. Whitaker. 1992. *Development and the Environment: Ecuador's Policy Crisis.* Quito: Instituto de Estrategias Agropecuarias (IDEA).

Stallings, B. 1987. *Banker to the Third World: U.S. Portfolio Investment in Latin America, 1900-1986.* Berkeley: University of California Press.

Stolcke, V. 1988. *Coffee Planters, Workers and Wives: Class Conflict and Gender Relations on São Paolo Plantations 1850-1980.* Basingstoke: Macmillan and St. Antony's College.

Strassman, W.P. 1968. *Technological Change and Economic Development: The Manufacturing Experience of Mexico and Puerto Rico.* Ithaca, NY: Cornell University Press.

Sullivan, W. 1976. Situación económica y política durante el período de Juan Vicente Gómez, 1908-1935. In *Política y economía en Venezuela, 1820-1976,* ed. M. Izard. Caracas: Fundación John Boulton.

Sunkel, O. 1973. Transnational Capitalism and National Disintegration in Latin America. *Social and Economic Studies* 22(1): 132-76.

_____. 1980. The Interaction Between Styles of Development and the Environment in Latin America. *CEPAL Review* 12: 15-54.

_____. 1981. Development Styles and the Environment: An Interpretation of the Latin American Case. In *From Dependency to Development Strategies to Overcome Underdevelopment and Inequality,* ed. H. Muñoz. Boulder, CO: Westview Press.

_____, ed. 1993. *Development from Within: Toward a Neostructuralist Approach for Latin America.* Boulder, CO and London: Lynne Rienner.

Sunkel, O., and M. Mortimore. 1997. Transnational Integration and National Disintegration Revisited. Consultancy paper for this book.

Sunkel O., and P. Paz. 1970. *El subdesarrollo latinoamericano y la teoría del desarrollo.* Mexico City: Siglo XXI Editores.

Szekely, M. 1996. Poverty and Equity under ISI: Can Anything Be Said about It? Consultancy paper for this book.

Tannenbaum, F. 1968. *The Mexican Agrarian Revolution* Hamden, CT: Archon Books.

Teitel, S., and F. Thoumi. 1986. From Import Substitution to Exports: The Manufacturing Exports Experience of Argentina and Brazil. *Economic Development and Cultural Change* 34: 455-89.

Thiesenhausen, W.C. 1995. *Broken Promises: Agrarian Reform and the Latin American Experience.* Boulder, CO: Westview Press.

Thomas, C.Y. 1988. *The Poor and the Powerless: Economic Policy and Change in the Caribbean.* New York and London: Monthly Review Press and Latin American Bureau.

Thomson, K., and N. Dudley. 1989. Transnationals and Oil in Amazonia. *The Ecologist* 19(6): 219-24.

Thorp, R., ed. (Companion Volume 2) *Latin America in the 1930s.* Macmillan and St. Antony's College. Second edition. Forthcoming.

_____. 1991. *Economic Management and Economic Development in Peru and Colombia.* Basingstoke: Macmillan for the OECD Development Centre.

_____. 1992. A Reappraisal of the Origins of ISI, 1930-1950. *Journal of Latin American Studies* 24 (Quincentenary Supplement): 181-96.

_____, ed. 1984. *Latin America in the 1930s: The Role of the Periphery in World Crisis.* Basingstoke: Macmillan and St. Antony's College.

Thorp, R., A. Angell, and P. Lowden. 1995. Challenges for Peace: Towards Sustainable Social Development in Peru. Social Agenda Policy Group, Inter-American Development Bank, Washington, D.C.

Thorp, R, and I.G. Bertram. 1978. *Peru 1890-1977: Growth and Policy in an Open Economy.* London: Macmillan.

Thorp, R., et al., eds. 1991. *Las crises en el Ecuador: los treinta y ochenta.* Quito: Corporación Editora Nacional.

Thorp, R., and L. Whitehead, eds. 1979. *Inflation and Stabilisation in Latin America.* Basingstoke: Macmillan and St. Antony's College.

_____, eds. 1987. *Latin American Debt and the Adjustment Crisis.* Basingstoke: Macmillan and St. Antony's College.

Tinsman, H.E. 1996. Unequal Uplift: The Sexual Politics of Gender, Work and Community in the Chilean Agrarian Reform, 1950-1973. Ph.D. dissertation, Yale University.

Tokman, V.E. 1997. Jobs and Solidarity: Challenges for Post-adjustment in Latin America. In *Economic and Social Development into the XXI Century,* ed. L. Emmerij. Washington, D.C.: Inter-American Development Bank.

Tolba, M.K. 1980. Present Development Styles and the Environment in Latin America. *CEPAL Review* 12 (December): 9-15.

Tomassini, L. 1980. Environmental Factors, Crisis in the Centre and Change in International Relations of the Peripheral Countries. *CEPAL Review* 12 (December): 145-74.

Topik, S. 1988. The Economic Role of the State in Liberal Regimes: Brazil and Mexico Compared 1888-1910. In *Guiding the Invisible Hand: Economic Liberalism and the State in Latin American History,* eds. J.L. Love and N. Jacobsen. New York: Praeger.

Treece, D. 1989. The Militarization and Industrialization of Amazonia. *The Ecologist* 19(6): 225- 28.

Triffin, R. 1944. Central Banking and Monetary Management in Latin America. In *Economic Problems of Latin America,* ed. S.E. Harris. New York: McGraw-Hill.

Tussie, D. 1988. La coordinación de los deudores latinoamericanos: cuál es la lógica de su accionar? In *Relaciones financieras externas y su efecto en la economia latinoamericana.* Mexico City: Fondo de Cultura Económica.

_____. 1995. *The Inter-American Development Bank.* London: Intermediate Technology Publication.

Ugarteche, O. 1968. *El estado deudor: economía política de la deuda: Perú y Bolivia, 1968- 1984.* Lima: Instituto de Estudios Peruanos.

UNCTAD. 1983. *Handbook for International Trade and Development.* New York: United Nations.

_____. 1995. *Handbook for International Trade and Development.* New York: United Nations.

_____. 1997. *Trade and Development Report, 1997.* New York and Geneva: United Nations.

UNDP. 1990. *Human Development Report.* New York and Oxford: Oxford University Press.

_____. 1997. *Human Development Report.* New York and Oxford: Oxford University Press.

United Nations. 1948. *Public Debt: 1914-1946.* New York: United Nations.

_____. 1951. *Statistical Yearbook.* New York: United Nations.

_____. 1989. *1989 World Survey on the Role of Women in Development.* New York: United Nations.

_____. 1995. *World Economic Trends.* New York: United Nations.

Urquidi, V. 1945. Problemas económicos planteados en la conferencia de Chapultepec. *Boletín del Banco Central de Venezuela* 16, Caracas.

_____. 1964. *Viabilidad económica de América Latina* Mexico City: Fondo de Cultura Económica.

_____. 1983. Cuestiones fundamentales en la perspectiva del desarrollo latinoamericano. *El Trimestre Económico* 44(198).

Urrutia, M. 1985. *Winners and Losers in Colombia's Economic Growth of the 1970s.* Oxford: Oxford University Press.

Urrutia, M., and M. Arrubla. 1970. *Compendio de estadísticas históricas de Colombia.* Bogotá: Universidad Nacional de Colombia.

Urrutia, M., and A.R. Berry. 1976. *Income Distribution in Colombia.* New Haven, CT: Yale University Press.

Uruzia, C.M. 1997. Five Decades of Relations Between the World Bank and Mexico. In *The World Bank: Its First Half Century, Vol. 2: Perspectives,* eds. D. Kapur, J.P. Lewis and R.C. Webb. Washington, D.C.: Brookings Institution Press.

U.S. Commission on Cuban Affairs. 1935. *Problems of New Cuba.* New York Foreign Policy Association.

U.S. Department of Commerce (USDC). 1950. *Statistical Abstract of the United States.* Washington, D.C.: USDC.

_____. 1957. *U.S. Investments in the Latin American Economy.* Washington, D.C.: USDC.

_____. 1975. *Historical Statistics of the United States.* Washington, D.C.: USDC.

U.S. Department of State. *Bulletin.* April 11, 1948.

U.S. Federal Trade Commission, 1916. *Report on Trade and Tariffs in Brazil, Uruguay, Argentina, Chile, Bolivia and Peru.* Washington, D.C.: Government Printing Office.

U.S. Tariff Commission. 1942. *Recent Developments in the Foreign Trade of the American Republics.* Washington, D.C.: U.S. Tariff Commission.

Vandellos, J.A. 1938. El movimiento económico venezolano durante los últimos años. *Revista de Hacienda* 10: 5-24.

Vázquez Presedo, V. 1990. *Estadísticas históricas argentinas comparadas.* Buenos Aires: Ediciones Macchi and Academia Nacional de Ciencias Económicas.

Vernon, R., ed. 1966. *How Latin America Views the U.S. Investor.* New York: Praeger.

Webb, C. 1977. *Government Policy and the Distribution of Income in Peru, 1963-1973.* Cambridge, Mass.: Harvard University Press.

Webb, R. 1972. *The Distribution of Income in Peru.* Discussion Paper No. 26, Woodrow Wilson School, Princeton.

Webb, R., and G. Fernández. 1991, 1992. *Perú en números.* Lima: Cuanto S.A.

Weinstein, B. 1983. *The Amazon Rubber Boom 1850-1920.* Stanford: Stanford University Press.

Wendell, S.A. 1993. Caribbean Economic Integration. In *Caribbean Economic Development: The First Generation,* eds. S. Lalta and M. Freckleton. Jamaica: Ian Randle.

Whitehead, L. 1972. El impacto de la Gran Depresión en Bolivia. *Desarrollo Económico.*

_____. 1979. Inflation and Stabilisation in Chile: 1970-77. In *Inflation and Stabilisation in Latin America*, eds. R. Thorp and L. Whitehead. London: Macmillan and St. Antony's College.

_____. 1994. State Organization in Latin America since 1930. In *Cambridge History of Latin America*, Vol. 6, Part 2, ed. L. Bethell. Cambridge: Cambridge University Press.

_____. 1997. La economía en México: el poder de las ideas, e ideas de poder. In *Europa en México*. Centro Interuniversitario di Storia Dell'America Latina and Centro Estudios de México en Italia.

_____. 1997a. Beyond Neo-liberalism: Bolivia's Capitalization as a Route to Universal Entitlements and Substantive Citizen Rights? Paper presented at the North-South Center, University of Miami, May.

Wilkie, J.W. 1974. *Statistics and National Policy* (Supplement 3). Los Angeles: University of California.

_____. Various years. *Statistical Abstract of Latin America*. Los Angeles: UCLA.

Wilkie, J.W., and K. Ruddle, eds. 1977. *Quantitative Latin American Studies: Methods and Findings*. SALA Supplement Series 6, UCLA, Los Angeles.

Williams, E. 1970. *From Columbus to Castro: The History of the Caribbean from 1492-1959*. New York: Harper and Row.

Williamson, J.G. 1991. *Inequality, Poverty and History: The Kuznets Memorial Lectures of the Economic Growth Center*. Oxford: Basil Blackwell.

_____. 1996. *Globalization and Inequality Then and Now: The Late 19th and Late 20th Centuries Compared*. National Bureau of Economic Research, Working Paper 5491, Cambridge, Mass.

Willner, R.A. 1949. Case Study in Frustration: Latin America and Economic Issues at Post-war Inter-American Conferences. *Inter-American Economic Affairs* (Spring).

Wionczek, M. 1987. Jorge Sabato: idealista entre pragmáticos, humanista entre tecnólogos. *Argentina Tecnológica* 1(4), January: 19-26.

Womack, J. 1978. The Mexican Economy During the Revolution, 1910-1920: Historiography and Analysis. *Marxist Perspectives* 1(4): 80-103.

World Bank. 1980. *Annual World Bank Conference on Development Economics*. Washington, D.C.: World Bank.

_____. Various years. *World Development Report*. Washington, D.C.: World Bank.

Worrell, D. 1987. Comparative Experience of CARICOM Countries. In *Development in Suspense: Selected Papers and Proceedings of the First Conference of Caribbean Economists*, eds. N. Girvan and G. Beckford. Kingston, Jamaica: Friedrich Ebert Stiftung Foundation and the Association of Caribbean Economists.

Wythe, G. 1941. *Industry in Latin America*. New York: Greenwood Press.

Yates, P.L. 1959. *Forty Years of Foreign Trade*. London: Allen & Unwin.

Zimbalist, A., ed. 1987. *Cuba's Socialist Economy Towards the 1990s*. Boulder, CO: Lynne Rienner.

Statistical Appendix

Pablo Astorga and Valpy FitzGerald

Contents

ACRONYMS

BCRA	Banco Central de la República de la Argentina
BR	Banco de la República (Colombia)
BCV	Banco Central de Venezuela
CELADE	Centro Latinoamericano de Demografía
CEPAL	Comisión Económica para América Latina
CPI	Consumer Price Index
DANE	Dirección Nacional de Planeación (Colombia)
EAP	Economically Active Population
ECE	Economic Commission for Europe
ECLA	Economic Commission for Latin America
ECLAC	Economic Commission for Latin America and the Caribbean
HDI	Human Development Index
HLSI	Historical Living Standard Index
HS	Household Survey
IBGE	Instituto Brasileiro de Geografía e Estatística
IDB	Inter-American Development Bank
ILO	International Labour Organisation
IMF/IFS	International Monetary Fund/International Financial Statistics
INEGI	Instituto Nacional de Estadística, Geografía e Informática (México)
LN	League of Nations
PAU	Pan-American Union
PPP	Purchasing Power Parity
PREALC	Programa Regional de Empleo para América Latina y el Caribe
RLSI	Relative Living Standard Index
SYLA	Statistical Yearbook for Latin America and the Caribbean
UNCTAD	United Nations Conference on Trade and Development
UNDP/HDR	United Nations Development Programme/Human Development Report
UN-DY	United Nations Demographic Yearbook
UNESCO	United Nations Educational, Scientific and Cultural Organization
USDC	U.S. Department of Commerce

INTRODUCTION

This Appendix offers a more detailed presentation of statistical data used in the main text by identifying sources for this data and explaining the procedures used in elaboration of the indices. A comparative exercise of this kind, particularly when extended over a major region of the world and a whole century, is inevitably fraught with methodological problems—many of them insoluble—and cannot satisfy all readers. Nonetheless, producing a set of data permits meaningful quantitative analysis over time. The inevitable alternative is intuitive generalization about regions and periods informed by partial knowledge of particular economies.

In constructing a database for 20 nations over 100 years (that is, up to 2,000 data points for any one variable), the logical criteria to use are consistency in definition over time, the availability of long-run data, and comparability between countries. The resulting database contains some 100,000 items and supporting material on methods of series construction and so on. In consequence, even in a dedicated Statistical Appendix such as this, considerable summarization of the raw data is necessary in order to make it meaningful and presentable. Space does not permit the reproduction of the complete data set, but it is hoped that this will be possible fairly soon in a separate publication. The sources and methods are explained in each section of the Appendix, but students and scholars working on individual countries are advised to refer to the original data sources, which are listed in the bibliography. Most of the data presentation is in the form of tables showing representative years or periods. However, in some cases we summarize data in graph form in order to show a general pattern developing over time, as in that of international commodity prices, Appendix V, or where the behavior of the components of a series is of interest, such as for the terms of trade in Appendix Figure VI.1. When it is more useful to present detailed information by country, we use tables.

Country groups. A common way to summarize data for individual countries is to construct geographic aggregates. The extent to which the resulting averages are representative of group members depends on the degree of homogeneity within the group; so where appropriate we accompany the aggregate values with their respective measures of dispersion. The country groups used are as follows:

LA[6]: Argentina, Brazil, Chile, Colombia, Mexico and Venezuela

CA[5]: Central America - Costa Rica, El Salvador, Guatemala, Honduras
and Nicaragua

LA[13]: Central America plus Bolivia, Dominican Republic, Ecuador, Haiti,
Panama, Paraguay, Peru and Uruguay

LA[19]: LA[6] plus *LA[13]*

Latin America: LA[19] plus Cuba

The LA[6] group includes those countries for which data are available for the entire century in most cases. These are the larger countries in the region, which between them account for over three-quarters of economic activity and about four-fifths of the population and territory of Latin America during the 20th century. In consequence, the appropriately weighted statistics for this group can be taken as representative of Latin America as a whole—at least insofar as economic and social indicators are concerned. The CA[5] group of Central American countries is a more homogeneous group of smaller economies than LA[6]. The other eight countries included in LA[13] are mainly small—with the exception of Peru—so this subgroup is essentially defined by default. Cuba is usually shown separately because statistical comparison is difficult after 1959, particularly for national accounting variables due to the use of the material balance system, and there is no estimate of purchasing power parity (PPP). Where data are comparable (e.g., population, literacy, railways), Cuba is included and a figure for Latin America as a whole can be shown rather than LA[19].

Regional Indicators. Regional estimates in this Statistical Appendix are calculated from individual country data in three ways:

Aggregation. Where absolute numbers are involved, the group totals in the tables simply aggregate the figures for individual countries; the population of Latin America in Appendix Table I.1, for example, is simply the sum of the country values. Similarly, the growth rate for the group is that for the total, rather than an average of the growth rates of the individual members; so in Appendix Table II.2, the growth rate of LA[6] is that for the aggregate GDP of those six countries. This criterion is also applied in Appendix III for manufacturing value added and in Appendix VI for exports and imports.

Simple average. Where our purpose is to give information about the central tendency of a particular variable for a group of countries regardless of their size, we summarize by simple averages. This is the case of Appendix Table V.1 (domestic prices), where we present simple average figures of inflation. But in order to reflect the dispersion of the data and to balance the distortion of the mean by extreme values, we also show the corresponding standard deviation and the median value for each group. A similar approach is adopted in Appendix VII for indicators of external economic dependence.

Weighted average. Where we are attempting to construct an indicator for a whole country group, individual country values are weighted by a relevant variable in order to obtain an average measure for the group. In Appendix VI, for instance, each country index of export quantum is weighted by its exports at 1970 prices to produce a group figure. Again, the net barter terms of trade aggregates (Appendix Figure VI.1 and Appendix Table VI.4) are the result of weighting the export (import) price indices by the exports (imports) in current U.S. dollars. In other cases (e.g., for Living Standards in Appendix IX), we use population size as the appropriate weight in order to obtain an average measure for groups of countries and for Latin America as a whole; while the figures on infrastructure provision in Appendix X are weighted by population or area, as appropriate.

Periodization. In order to summarize the data over time, tables are "periodized" in different ways. In some cases (e.g., population in Appendix Table I.1) the opening year of each decade is appropriate, but this requires interpolation from actual census dates in order to reach a common point of comparison between countries. In other cases (such as Appendix Table II.1 on rates of growth), periods have been chosen within which the variable appears to be more stable for the region as a whole, so as to provide a common basis for comparison, particularly response to major external shocks. A rigorous periodization would imply an econometric estimation of the structural breaks endogenous to the data rather than statistical inspection and historical preconceptions, an exercise we intend to carry out in the near future. Meanwhile, we have accompanied the averages for time periods by measures of dispersion (standard deviation and coefficient of variation) in order to indicate the intra-period stability of the variable under consideration.

Rates of growth. We use two methods for computing the rate of growth for a particular variable in a given period. The compound rate of growth (or "geometric mean") is calculated by applying the formula $(Y_{tf}/Y_{ti})^{1/N}-1$, where Y_{tf} and Y_{ti} refer to the value of Y at the end and beginning of the period, respectively, and N stands for the number of years in each period. Second, we use linear regression analysis to compute the annual average rate of growth for a particular variable in a given period. The average rate of growth is calculated by estimating an equation based on the formula $LogY_n = LogY_0 + Log(1+\alpha)$. N, where Y_n and Y_0 refer to the value of Y at the end and beginning of the period, respectively, α refers to the rate of growth, and N stands for the number of years in each period. In the case of GDP, its volatility (Appendix Table II.3) is expressed as the *standard deviation of the annual rate of growth.*

Geometric mean growth rates are sensitive to the choice of the base year—if a year with a high (low) rate is chosen, this will depress (raise) the growth rate of subsequent years—while the second method is sensitive to the occurrence of extreme values within the period (Morgenstern, 1950). For most of the calculation of growth rates, we use the linear regression analysis. The geometric mean is used to calculate the rate of growth of population and infrastructure in Tables 2.3 and 2.4 included in the main text.

Comparison of levels for a single year. We have adopted the following rule to present data for the absolute levels of variables. When they represent flows (e.g., GDP, terms of trade, exports or imports), we have calculated three-year average values wherever possible. Thus, for example, the figure for 1970 would be the average for 1969-71. The main exception is the figure for 1900, which refers to the average for 1900-02. This transformation makes observations less sensitive to abnormal values on a particular date. When the variable represents a stock, the figure shown corresponds to a particular point in time as indicated by the date—often a census (e.g., population, life expectancy and illiteracy). Indices are also used to show changes through time, as in the terms of trade and purchasing power of exports in Appendix VI and the Living Standard Indicators in Appendix IX.

APPENDIX I. POPULATION AND TERRITORY

Appendix Table I.1.
Population (in thousands) and Territory (square kms in 1971)

	1900	1910	1920	1930	1940	1950	1960	1970	1980	1990	1995	Area
Argentina	4,693	6,836	8,861	11,896	14,169	17,150	20,616	23,962	28,114	32,546	34,587	2,777
Bolivia	1,596	1,758	1,930	2,164	2,434	2,714	3,351	4,212	5,355	6,573	7,414	1,099
Brazil	17,984	22,209	27,329	33,568	41,524	53,444	72,594	95,847	121,286	148,477	161,790	8,512
Chile	2,974	3,364	3,827	4,370	5,093	6,082	7,608	9,496	11,147	13,100	14,210	757
Colombia	3,998	4,890	6,213	7,914	9,174	11,946	15,939	21,360	26,525	32,300	35,101	1,139
Costa Rica	307	364	420	500	620	800	1,250	1,730	2,220	3,035	3,424	51
Cuba	1,573	2,259	2,945	3,647	4,385	5,514	6,957	8,569	9,619	10,610	11,041	115
Dominican Rep.	600	740	895	1,284	1,698	2,136	3,047	4,006	5,499	7,170	7,823	49
Ecuador	987	1,263	1,616	2,061	2,614	3,387	4,439	5,970	7,961	10,264	11,460	284
El Salvador	801	985	1,170	1,440	1,630	1,860	2,450	3,440	4,750	5,172	5,768	21
Guatemala	885	1,096	1,270	1,760	2,200	2,810	3,830	5,270	7,260	9,197	10,621	109
Haiti	1,250	1,687	2,124	2,422	2,827	3,097	3,911	4,292	4,922	6,486	7,180	28
Honduras	420	553	720	950	1,150	1,430	1,950	2,639	3,691	5,138	5,654	112
Mexico	13,607	15,000	14,900	17,176	20,393	27,737	36,945	50,596	67,570	83,226	91,145	1,973
Nicaragua	420	543	640	680	830	1,060	1,410	1,830	2,693	3,676	4,433	130
Panama	263	330	447	467	623	805	1,076	1,428	1,831	2,418	2,631	76
Paraguay	644	620	699	852	1,068	1,408	1,749	2,250	2,896	4,277	4,986	407
Peru	3,760	3,993	4,448	5,037	5,814	6,948	8,672	11,467	15,161	19,518	21,588	1,285
Uruguay	916	1,116	1,481	1,734	1,974	2,195	2,503	2,705	2,869	3,094	3,186	187
Venezuela	2,542	2,805	2,992	3,300	3,784	5,094	7,579	10,721	15,091	19,502	21,844	912
LA[6]	45,798	60,337	70,156	84,990	102,531	131,171	174,111	228,922	294,630	362,188	393,011	16,069
CA[5]	2,833	3,541	4,220	5,330	6,430	7,960	10,890	14,909	20,614	26,110	29,485	423
LA[13]	12,849	15,048	17,860	21,351	25,483	30,650	39,638	51,238	67,107	85,910	95,753	3,836
Latin America	62,120	74,299	86,816	104,820	125,910	158,950	209,556	273,262	350,214	430,916	468,675	20,020

Sources:

The decennial series for population are obtained by interpolation from census data and in some cases backward projection for earlier decades. Unless otherwise indicated, census figures up to 1988 are taken from Mitchell (1993) and from official national sources thereafter. In the following cases we have used estimates provided by Wilkie (1974): *Central America* in 1900 and 1910; *Dominican Republic* in 1900 and 1910; *Haiti* in 1900, 1910, 1920, 1930, 1940; *Panama* in 1900; *Paraguay* in 1910, 1920, 1925; *Uruguay* in 1920, 1930, 1940, 1950. *Central America*: 1920-1984 from Bulmer-Thomas (1987). The 1990 figure for *Central America*, *Dominican Republic*, *Haiti*, *Panama*, *Paraguay* and *Uruguay* is from ECLAC (SYLA, 1995). *Cuba*: 1990 figure from Wilkie (1993). All figures for 1995 are from ECLAC (SYLA, 1996). The area of territory in 1970 is from ECLAC (SYLA, 1992).

APPENDIX II. Gross Domestic Product

The key source for figures on gross domestic product (GDP) is ECLA (1978), which gives estimates at factor cost using 1970 prices. This represents the most thorough attempt by any international institution to ensure consistency between country data for all of Latin America. The series includes all Latin American countries (except Cuba) beginning at different dates according to the country in question and ending in 1976. Broadly, the next step has been to work backwards from this post-WWII foundation towards 1900 by using national sources or authoritative compendia of comparative historical statistics for GDP volume. In most cases, estimates for GDP after 1976 are obtained by applying an index (usually with a subsequent base year) for GDP at constant market prices. In consequence, these series (and those in Appendix IX) are not entirely consistent in their construction over the whole century, although they do have a common core and are probably the best of their kind available at present.

The "splicing" procedure implicit in joining series in this way means that although the rate of change in the series reported here and in the corresponding sources are almost always the same, the resulting levels of the variables may be different in some cases. The precise method used in each case is explained in the notes to the tables. This procedure gives greater weight to comparability between countries and change over time than to consistency in levels or over time for any one country. This approach appears to be justified for a text of this nature, but the series in Appendix Tables II.2 and II.3 should not be seen as a substitute for the original sources where the study of a particular country is concerned.

To make figures comparable between countries and with the United States, and to obtain aggregates for our country groups, constant values in national currencies are converted into U.S. dollars using the purchasing power parity (PPP) exchange rates. PPP rates are commonly used in international income comparisons, not only to adjust for misaligned exchange rates but also to revalue nontraded services on a comparable basis, which generally adjusts the income of developing countries upwards by a considerable margin. The PPP exchange rates for 1970—the base year for the GDP series used here—are taken from ECLA (1978). They are based on a common basket of goods reflecting consumption patterns in the region during the 1960s. Appendix Table II.1 presents official and PPP exchange rates against the U.S. dollar, and the GDP per capita in 1970 that results from applying these as conversion factors. The general effect of applying PPP instead of official exchange rates is to raise the level of GDP per capita relative to the United States by about one-fifth.

Official PPP estimates for Cuba are not available (see Pérez-López, 1991). However, Brundenius and Zimbalist (1989) do make a rigorous estimate using the "physical indicators" approach used in the UN International Comparison Project (ECE, 1970) to produce PPP estimates for Cuba at 1980 international dollars ($2,325 in 1980). Our estimate for per capita GDP in Cuba in 1970 is derived from the Brundenius and Zimbalist 1980 figure by i) using the ratio of the Cuban figure in 1980 at 1980 prices to the Brundenius and Zimbalist 1980 figure for LA[6] ($3,491), and then applying this ratio to our LA[6] at 1970 prices in 1980 to obtain the Cuban estimate at 1970 PPP US$ prices; and ii) applying the growth rate for 1970-80 (see sources for Cuba at the end of this Appendix).

The most recent comprehensive source of PPP estimates is the Penn World Tables developed by Heston and Summers (1991), which cover 139 countries over 1950-88. Latin American countries (except Cuba) are included in the sample, which uses 1980 as the benchmark year. However, in the Penn Tables' own assessment of reliability on a scale of A to D, all the Latin American estimates are C or D. Our choice of the ECLA series enabled us to work with the same base year and was consistent with our use of the ECLA GDP series, and did not imply the rejection of clearly better estimates.

The differences are, however, quite large. The Penn Tables' ratios of PPP to the official exchange rates lie in general in the range of 30 to 40 percent (e.g., Brazil, 46 percent, Chile, 39 percent, Colombia, 34 percent, and Mexico, 40 percent), only Argentina and Honduras having higher values (65 percent and 61 percent, respectively). This would indicate that, in relation to the United States, their estimates of the real value of GDP per capita are generally higher than ours. Because of differences in both the base year and construction method and the composition of the basket of goods, the Penn Tables also give somewhat different relative positions within the region, notably Brazil with a GDP per capita 10 percent higher than Argentina in 1990 (and a fourth position in the country ranking after Venezuela, Uruguay and Mexico) compared to 30 percent lower when the ECLA PPPs of 1970 are used, which rank Brazil in the eighth position.

Appendix Table II.1.
Adjusted Base Values for GDP Per Capita in 1970

	(1) GDP per cap (official $)	(2) Ratio to U.S. (official $)	(3) GDP per cap (ppp $)	(4) Ratio to U.S. (ppp $)	(5) Exch. rate (official)	(6) Exch. rate (ppp)	(7) PPP/ official (%)
Argentina	883	17.3	1,197	23.5	4.0	3.0	73.8
Bolivia	224	4.4	295	5.8	11.9	9.0	75.9
Brazil	370	7.3	447	8.8	5.0	4.1	82.8
Chile	747	14.6	838	16.5	12.2	10.9	89.1
Colombia	301	5.9	538	10.6	19.1	10.7	55.9
Costa Rica	505	9.9	658	12.9	6.6	5.1	76.7
Cuba*	614	12.1	na	na	1.0	na	na
Dominican Rep.	331	6.5	380	7.5	1.0	0.9	87.0
Ecuador	201	3.9	359	7.0	25.0	14.0	56.0
El Salvador	276	5.4	406	8.0	2.5	1.7	68.0
Guatemala	338	6.6	417	8.2	1.0	0.8	81.0
Haiti	96	1.9	120	2.4	5.0	4.0	79.8
Honduras	245	4.8	279	5.5	2.0	1.7	87.5
Mexico	631	12.4	888	17.4	12.5	8.9	71.0
Nicaragua	387	7.6	425	8.3	7.0	6.4	91.2
Panama	674	13.2	887	17.4	1.0	0.8	76.0
Paraguay	245	4.8	361	7.1	126.0	85.4	67.8
Peru	489	9.6	621	12.2	39.0	30.7	78.8
Uruguay	786	15.4	989	19.4	250.0	198.7	79.5
Venezuela	1,023	20.0	1,332	26.1	4.5	4.0	88.0
U.S.	5,103	100.0	5,103	100.0			100.0

Note: Source for United States: GDP from IMF/IFS, population from Mitchell (1993).

*GDP estimates for Cuba correspond to 1965 prices.

(1) GDP per capita in U.S. dollars at official exchange rate in 1970; (2) Ratio of GDP per capita in U.S. dollars to U.S. GDP per capita at official exchange rates in 1970; (3) GDP per capita in U.S. dollars at purchasing power parities (PPP) in 1970 from ECLA (1978); (4) Ratio of GDP per capita in U.S. PPP dollars to U.S. GDP per capita in 1970; (5) Official nominal exchange rate in 1970 (local currency per dollar) from Wilkie (1974); (6) Implicit PPP-adjusted exchange rate obtained by dividing (1) by (3); (7) Ratio as a percentage of the PPP estimate relative to the official exchange rate, that is (6)/(5).

Appendix Table II.2.
GDP: Average Rate of Growth
(In percent)

	1900–13	1913–29	1929–45	1945–72	1972–81	1981–96	1945–96	1900-96
Argentina	6.3	4.1	3.4	3.8	2.5	1.9	3.0	3.3
Bolivia				2.5	3.8	2.1	2.9	
Brazil	4.1	5.1	4.4	6.9	6.6	2.4	6.1	5.5
Chile	3.6	3.7	3.0	4.1	3.6	5.4	3.6	3.3
Colombia	4.4	4.9	3.8	5.1	5.0	4.0	4.9	4.7
Costa Rica		2.1[d]	2.9	6.9	4.8	3.9	5.4	5.1[d]
Cuba	7.6[b]	*1.1*	3.5	2.4	7.3	-2.2	3.0	2.6[b]
Dominican Rep.				5.9	5.3	2.1	5.2	
Ecuador	5.0	4.1	3.3	5.3	7.0	2.6	5.1	4.8
El Salvador		3.4[d]	2.7	5.4	2.3	3.0	3.6	3.8[d]
Guatemala		3.8[d]	4.6	4.9	5.1	2.6	4.3	4.0[d]
Haiti				1.2	3.8	-1.5	1.5	
Honduras		5.2[d]	-0.4	4.2	4.4	3.1	3.8	3.4[d]
Mexico	3.4[a]	1.4[a]	4.2	6.5	5.5	1.5	5.2	5.0[a]
Nicaragua		3.5[d]	2.2	6.2	-0.3	-1.4	3.0	3.5[d]
Panama				5.8	4.2	1.7	3.0	
Paraguay				3.4	9.3	3.1	4.7	
Peru	4.5	5.3	2.8	5.3	3.4	0.4	3.7	3.9
Uruguay			0.7[c]	1.7	3.5	2.7	1.7	1.9[c]
Venezuela	2.3	9.2	4.2	5.7	4.7	2.2	4.2	5.9
LA[6]	4.3	3.3	3.8	5.6	5.2	2.3	4.8	4.3
CA[5]		3.8[d]	2.9	5.4	3.8	2.7	4.1	4.0[d]
LA[13]				4.4	4.3	1.9	3.8	
LA[20]				5.3	5.1	2.2	4.6	

Notes: Series for GDP per capita are presented in Appendix IX. In italics: values not significantly different from zero at a confidence level of 95 percent. For a description of the methods followed to calculate the growth rates, see p. 312.

[a] There are no data on Mexico between 1911 and 1920 due to the revolution. [b] Data start in 1903. [c] Data start in 1935. [d] Data start in 1920.

Appendix Table II.3.
Volatility of GDP Growth
(In percent)

	1900–13	1913–29	1929–45	1945–72	1972–81	1981–96	1945–96	1900–96
Argentina	8.0	9.5	5.3	4.7	4.3	5.4	4.8	6.4
Bolivia				4.0	3.2	3.2	3.7	
Brazil	5.2	4.8	4.5	3.2	5.1	3.9	4.2	4.5
Chile	3.0	12.4	12.2	3.4	7.0	5.7	4.9	8.0
Colombia[1]			3.0	2.2	2.1	1.5	2.1	2.2[1]
Costa Rica		8.3	9.7	4.6	3.6	3.7	4.6	6.5
Cuba	23.4	17.6	21.1	7.0	3.3	6.9	6.9	15.0
Dominican Rep.				7.0	3.3	3.7	5.8	
Ecuador[1]			3.0	3.5	2.7	3.6	3.8	3.1[1]
El Salvador		9.9	7.6	7.1	6.0	4.3	6.2	7.0
Guatemala		6.1	14.7	3.6	2.7	2.6	3.4	7.6
Haiti				4.7	3.0	4.2	4.6	
Honduras		8.4	7.7	4.6	4.0	2.7	4.1	5.3
Mexico	5.7	4.1	6.4	2.5	5.0	3.8	4.0	4.8
Nicaragua		11.6	13.1	5.1	11.6	4.4	7.1	9.2
Panama				3.8	4.6	5.5	4.7	
Paraguay			10.8	5.0	2.7	2.9	4.7	
Peru		3.8	6.8	2.7	2.3	7.5	4.9	4.9[1]
Uruguay			6.5	3.7	3.1	5.0	3.9	
Venezuela	6.2	11.6	9.6	6.5	4.1	5.0	6.3	8.0
LA[6]	4.4	4.4	4.5	1.8	2.3	2.0	2.5	3.6
CA[5]		3.0	7.2	2.1	3.3	2.6	2.8	4.3
LA[13]				1.3	1.4	2.8	2.3	2.3
LA[20]				1.6	2.1	1.9	2.4	2.4

Note: Volatility of GDP growth is defined as the standard deviation of the annual rate of growth.
[1] Colombia and Ecuador (1900–29), and Peru (1900–13) figures have been omitted because they are mostly based on GDP estimates which assume a constant rate of growth during those years. For data start dates, see Appendix Table II.2.

Sources for GDP estimates:

All series are completed up to 1995 using the rate of growth of GDP at market values in constant prices given by ECLAC (SYLA, 1981-96) and up to 1996 based on ECLAC (1996).

Argentina: 1936-94 from Hofman (1997); the series is completed backwards using the rate of growth of GDP estimates from Cortés Conde (1994) in constant values at 1914 prices.

Brazil: 1947-88 from IBGE (1990). The series is completed for 1900-49 using the rate of growth of the Haddad output index (IBGE, 1990).

Central America: 1920-84 from Bulmer-Thomas (1984).

Chile: 1940-76 from ECLA (1978). The series is completed backwards using the rate of growth of GDP estimates from Hofman (1997) between 1900-07, and Ballesteros and Davis (1963) during the period 1908-39.

Colombia: 1925-93 from BR (1993), rebased to obtain constant values at 1970 prices. The original bases are: 1925-49 at 1950 prices; 1950-70 at 1958 prices; 1970-93 at 1975 prices. The series is completed backwards for 1900-24 using the GDP growth estimates from Hofman (1997).

Cuba: The core of the output series is the estimated values of GDP at 1965 prices for 1958-81 calculated by Brundenius (1984) based on net material product figures. The series is completed as follows: 1900-02 GDP is assumed to grow at the same rate as exports in current dollars; 1903-58 national income estimates at 1926 prices (quoted in Brundenius, 1984) are based on Alienes (1950) but use the Cuban CPI as deflator instead of the U.S. wholesale price index; 1982-84 growth of net material product at 1981 prices from ECLAC (SYLA, 1995); 1985-95, ECLA estimates of GDP at 1981 market prices (SYLA, 1996).

Ecuador: 1939-76 from ECLA (1978). The series is completed backwards for 1900-38 and forward for 1977-95 using the rate of growth of GDP estimates from Hofman (1997).

Mexico: 1900-79 from Cárdenas (1987) based on estimates of *Banco de México* at 1960 prices; 1980-94 official estimates in constant values at 1980 prices taken from Cárdenas (1996). There is no information on GDP during 1911-20 due to the Mexican revolution.

Paraguay: 1938-76 from ECLA (1978).

Peru: 1945-76 from ECLA (1978). The series is completed backwards for

1900-44 and forward for 1977-95 using the rate of growth of GDP estimates from Hofman (1997).

Uruguay: 1935-76 from ECLA (1978).

Venezuela: 1900-20 in Baptista (1997) at 1936 prices; 1920-94 in Baptista (1997) at 1968 prices. The original series was rebased to obtain values at 1970 prices.

Bolivia, Dominican Republic, Haiti and *Panama*: 1945-76 from ECLA (1978).

APPENDIX III. MANUFACTURING

Appendix Table III.1.
Manufacturing Growth: Annual Change in Value Added at 1970 Prices
(In percent)

	1900–13	1913–29	1929–45	1945–72	1972–81	1981–95	1945–95	1900–95
Argentina	10.6	3.3	4.9	4.4	*-0.8*	1.0	2.8	3.5
Bolivia				3.2[h]	9.3	2.1	4.0[h]	
Brazil		3.7[d]	6.0	8.4	6.2	1.1	6.6	6.7[d]
Chile	4.4[b]	3.3	6.1	5.2	*0.4*	5.3	3.2	4.0[b]
Colombia		2.3[c]	8.6	6.6	5.2	3.6	5.6	6.4[c]
Costa Rica		3.7[d]	4.8	8.3	6.1	4.2	6.6	6.2[d]
Cuba			4.3[f]	2.9	6.5	*-1.4*	4.3	3.7[f]
Dominican Rep.				6.4[h]	5.3	3.3	5.7[h]	
Ecuador				5.2	9.3	*-0.1*	5.4	
El Salvador		7.0[d]	2.5	7.3	1.8	3.1	4.4	4.8[d]
Guatemala		4.2[d]	1.6	5.8	5.8	1.5	4.8	4.3[d]
Haiti				1.8[h]	5.0	-7.7	1.9[h]	
Honduras		2.3[d]	3.3	6.8	5.7	2.8	4.8	5.1[d]
Mexico	3.7[a]	6.0[a]	7.4	7.4	6.2	2.3	6.0	6.5
Nicaragua		-3.0[d]	9.6	8.6	1.5	-3.1	4.8	5.7[d]
Panama				9.4	6.3	1.6	6.6	
Paraguay				3.9	10.0	2.4	5.0	
Peru				7.3	2.1	0.1	4.5	
Uruguay			-0.1[g]	2.8	3.1	0.8	1.7	
Venezuela			4.3[e]	9.9	5.0	2.2	6.3	
LA[6]			5.9	6.7	4.5	1.8	5.3	
CA[5]		3.9[d]	3.0	7.0	4.4	2.1	5.1	5.0[d]
LA[13]				5.6[h]	4.6	1.1	4.1[h]	
LA[19]				6.8[h]	4.5	1.7	5.0[h]	

Note: Italicized values are not significantly different from zero at a confidence level of 95 percent.
[a] There are no data between 1911 and 1920 due to the revolution. [b] Data for Chile start in 1908. [c] Data for Colombia start in 1925. [d] Data start in 1920. [e] Data for Venezuela start in 1936. [f] Estimates for Cuba start in 1930. [g] Data start in 1935. [h] Data start in 1950.

Sources:

All series are completed up to 1995 from the last date given below by applying the rate of growth of value added in manufacturing at market prices in constant prices given by ECLAC (SYLA, 1981-96).

Argentina: 1936-76 from ECLA (1978); the series is completed using the rate of growth of value added estimates from the following sources: Cortés Conde (1994) for 1900-35 based on values at 1914 prices; BCRA (in Vázquez Presedo, 1990) for 1977-90.

Central America: 1920-84, Bulmer-Thomas (1984).

Chile: 1940-76 from ECLA (1978). The series is completed backwards for 1908-39 using the estimates of the rate of growth of manufacturing output in Ballesteros and Davis (1963). These authors assumed constant values during the years 1913-16.

Cuba: 1930-58 estimates from Pérez-López (1977); 1959-80 figures correspond to net material product at 1965 prices in Brundenius (1984) based on official figures; 1981-95 figures calculated from rates of growth given in ECLAC (SYLA, 1992, 1996).

Venezuela: 1937-95 from Baptista (1997). Original values at 1968 prices were rebased to obtain constant values of 1970. Figures exclude oil refining activities.

ECLA (1978) up to 1976 for *Brazil* from 1920; *Colombia* from 1925; *Ecuador* from 1939; *Panama* from 1945; *Paraguay* from 1938; *Peru* from 1945; *Uruguay* from 1935 (figures between 1935 and 1940 include mining); *Bolivia, Dominican Republic, Haiti* from 1950.

APPENDIX IV. Sectoral Productivity

This Appendix presents estimates for total and sectoral (agriculture and manufacturing) output per economically active person (as proxy for labor productivity) in the six leading economies: Argentina, Brazil, Mexico, Colombia, Chile and Venezuela. For purposes of estimation, sectoral productivity values for a particular country are defined as the ratio of sectoral GDP (i.e., value added in that sector) to the economically active population in that sector. For purposes of comparison, the sectoral GDP is estimated in "PPP dollars" (see Appendix II). The series presented should be taken only as an indicator of changes in trend in the long term and not as a reliable figure for productivity in one particular year, for the following reasons. First, by using economically active population as a proxy for the sectoral labor force we are not allowing for unemployment and in consequence our figures underestimate the output per worker employed. Second, workforce figures are based on census data where possible, but for years before 1941, estimates based on shares of employment are often used, as is interpolation to fill the gaps between observations. Third, the presence of a significant nonmonetized rural economy during the first half of the century means that output estimates for agriculture are probably biased downwards.

In Appendix Figures IV.1-3, the resulting productivity trends are shown on vertical axes expressed in thousands of U.S. PPP dollars at 1970 prices on a natural logarithmic scale. Next, Appendix Table IV.1 summarizes growth rates of output per economically active person for periods defined by clear changes in the trend of the series. For each sector and period, the annual average rate of growth of the productivity proxy accompanied by its standard deviation is included, as are the growth rates of sectoral GDP and the sectoral economically active population (EAP), so that the changes in output can be attributed to increased productivity or increased labor utilization, respectively. The standard deviation figures indicate the stability of growth during each period.

Appendix Figure IV.1.
GDP Per Economically Active Person
(In thousands of 1970 $PPP, log scale)

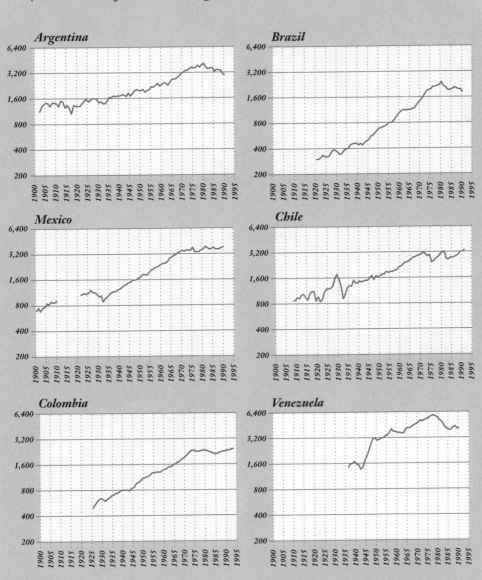

Appendix Figure IV.2.
Value Added Per Economically Active Person in Manufacturing
(In thousands of 1970 $PPP, log scale)

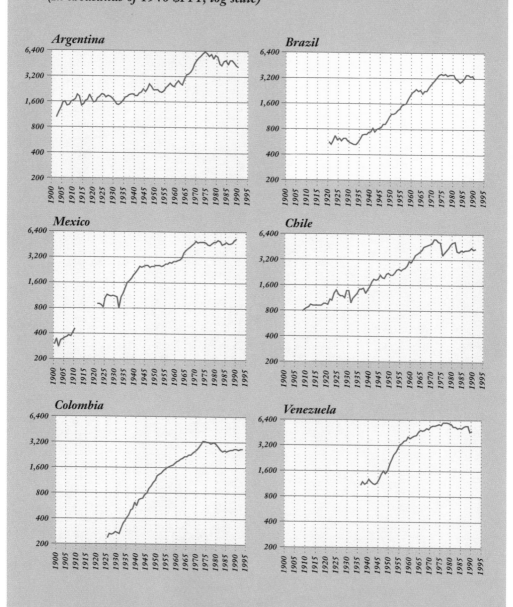

Appendix Figure IV.3.
Value Added Per Economically Active Person in Agriculture
(In thousands of 1970 $PPP, log scale)

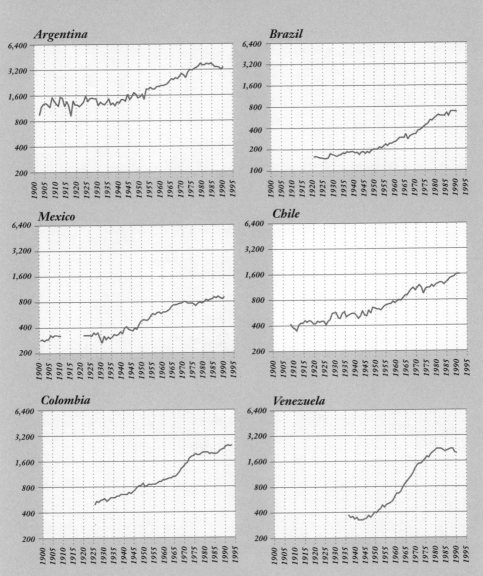

Appendix Table IV.1.
Growth in Productivity
(Average annual growth rates, in percent)

I) TOTAL

	Pvty	Sdev	GDP	EAP
Argentina				
1903–13	2.6	(7.4)	7.0	4.2
1914–33	0.1	(8.6)	2.2	2.0
1934–54	1.9	(4.6)	3.9	2.0
1955–74	3.1	(4.1)	4.6	1.4
1975–90	-1.1	(4.8)	0.5	1.6
1903–90	1.3	(6.1)	3.4	2.1
Brazil				
1901–20	3.7	(5.3)	4.4	0.6
1921–47	0.9	(3.2)	3.2	2.2
1948–67	3.4	(3.0)	6.0	2.6
1968–80	5.5	(2.9)	9.1	3.4
1981–90	-0.6	(4.6)	3.4	4.0
1901–90	2.4	(4.4)	4.8	2.3
Mexico				
1901–10	2.9	(5.7)	3.3	0.4
1922–40	1.0	(6.0)	2.0	1.0
1941–63	3.3	(2.3)	6.0	2.6
1964–73	3.1	(2.8)	7.1	3.9
1974–90	0.7	(4.5)	3.4	2.7
1921–90	2.0	(4.3)	4.4	2.4

II) AGRICULTURE

	Pvty	Sdev	GDP	EAP
Argentina				
1903–52	1.7	(13.8)	3.1	1.4
1953–79	3.9	(7.6)	2.9	-1.0
1980–90	-0.7	(4.1)	1.3	2.0
1903–90	2.1	(11.3)	2.8	0.8
Brazil				
1921–48	0.8	(4.7)	2.5	1.7
1949–81	3.7	(5.2)	4.5	0.7
1949–70	2.6	(5.6)	3.8	1.2
1971–81	5.9	(3.9)	5.8	-0.1
1982–90	1.1	(6.6)	2.0	1.0
1921–90	2.2	(5.3)	3.4	1.1
Mexico				
1901–10	1.3	(5.1)	2.5	1.2
1922–47	0.9	(7.9)	1.8	0.9
1948–70	3.3	(3.8)	5.2	1.8
1971–90	0.6	(3.4)	1.6	1.0
1971–76	-1.8	(1.5)	1.1	3.0
1977–90	1.6	(3.5)	1.8	0.2
1921–90	1.6	(5.7)	2.9	1.3

III) MANUFACTURING

	Pvty	Sdev	GDP	EAP
Argentina				
1903–13	5.7	(8.4)	10.7	4.7
1914–33	-0.6	(8.6)	1.5	2.1
1934–63	1.9	(6.1)	4.3	2.3
1964–74	8.5	(4.7)	7.9	-0.6
1975–90	-2.2	(8.1)	-1.7	0.5
1903–90	1.9	(7.9)	3.8	1.9
Brazil				
1921–45	1.8	(6.4)	4.6	2.8
1946–80	4.3	(4.9)	8.9	4.4
1946–61	6.6	(3.7)	9.8	3.0
1962–80	2.4	(5.1)	8.1	5.5
1981–90	-1.0	(7.4)	0.0	1.1
1921–90	2.6	(6.1)	6.1	3.3
Mexico				
1901–10	5.1	(11.4)	4.9	-0.2
1921–33	3.1	(15.1)	3.9	0.9
1934–61	3.5	(5.2)	7.4	3.8
1962–73	4.4	(4.2)	8.9	4.3
1974–90	0.5	(4.5)	3.7	3.2
1921–90	2.9	(7.8)	6.1	3.2

I) TOTAL

	Pvty	Sdev	GDP	EAP
Chile				
1908–22	0.8	(10.5)	1.6	0.7
1923–41	3.4	(13.4)	4.7	1.3
1942–72	2.5	(3.3)	4.1	1.5
1942–59	2.3	(4.0)	3.9	1.6
1960–72	2.9	(2.1)	4.4	1.5
1973–90	0.5	(6.9)	3.1	2.5
1908–90	2.0	(8.5)	3.6	1.6
Colombia				
1926–43	2.4	(3.9)	4.0	1.6
1944–81	2.6	(2.2)	5.1	2.4
1982–93	0.5	(2.0)	3.6	3.1
1926–93	2.2	(2.8)	4.6	2.3
Venezuela*				
1926–45	2.5	(8.4)	5.4	2.8
1946–63	3.7	(6.8)	7.1	3.3
1964–78	4.1	(2.7)	7.5	3.2
1979–90	-2.9	(5.3)	0.1	3.1
1926–90	2.4	(7.1)	5.5	3.1

II) AGRICULTURE

	Pvty	Sdev	GDP	EAP
Chile				
1909–41	0.7	(7.1)	1.5	0.7
1909–26	0.6	(7.2)	1.4	0.8
1927–41	0.8	(8.9)	1.9	1.1
1942–71	3.3	(6.9)	3.0	-0.2
1973–90	1.8	(6.5)	3.0	1.2
1908–90	1.9	(7.2)	2.5	0.6
Colombia				
1926–66	2.1	(3.5)	2.9	0.8
1967–93	3.0	(3.5)	4.9	-2.1
1926–93	2.4	(3.5)	3.4	0.7
Venezuela*				
1926–50	1.2	(7.1)	2.5	1.3
1951–80	6.0	(4.1)	5.2	-0.8
1981–90	-1.1	(3.5)	2.0	3.2
1926–90	3.1	(6.0)	3.6	0.6

III) MANUFACTURING

	Pvty	Sdev	GDP	EAP
Chile				
1909–20	1.7	(3.3)	2.2	0.5
1921–38	2.4	(12.2)	4.0	1.5
1939–72	4.6	(5.5)	6.1	1.4
1939–59	4.2	(6.3)	6.2	1.9
1961–72	5.4	(3.7)	6.0	0.5
1973–90	-1.0	(10.0)	1.7	2.7
1919–90	2.5	(8.9)	4.3	1.7
Colombia				
1926–32	3.8	(6.8)	2.8	-0.9
1933–74	6.0	(5.5)	7.8	1.8
1975–93	-1.1	(3.3)	3.5	4.6
1926–93	3.8	(5.9)	6.1	2.3
Venezuela*				
1937–50	2.5	(8.8)	6.1	3.6
1951–76	5.5	(4.7)	10.0	4.2
1977–90	-1.4	(5.4)	2.4	3.8
1937–90	3.0	(6.5)	5.1	4.0

Note: Pvty: productivity; GDP: Gross Domestic Product; EAP: Economically Active Population; Sdev: standard deviation of the annual rate of growth.
* GDP figures without the oil sector and manufacturing without oil refining.

Notes and sources for economically active population figures:

The number in brackets preceding the (+) sign (e.g., [C 14+]) refers to the lower age limit of those persons considered to be economically active. The higher end is usually assumed to be 65 years.

Argentina: between 1900-45 we use five-year estimates from Díaz-Alejandro (1970), based on ECLA; for 1947 and 1960 census data from Bairoch, et al. (1968); ILO (1993) for censuses of 1970 [C14+] and 1980 [C14+]; PREALC (1993) for 1990 total, agriculture and industry.

Brazil: Bairoch, et al. (1968) for 1900; IBGE (1990) for 1920, 1940, 1950, 1960, 1970, 1980; ILO (1993) for 1990 [Household Survey, 12+]; IBGE for 1993 [HS, 12+]. The total for industry in 1920 was disaggregated assuming a similar manufacturing share as that for 1940 (80 percent).

Chile: Palma (1979) for 1907, 1920, 1930 based on censuses; Bairoch, et al. (1968) for 1940, 1952, 1960. In 1920 and 1930, industry includes only manufacturing and construction; ILO (1993) for 1970 [C12+] and 1982 (C15+); 1992 census [15+] for 1992.

Colombia: ECLA (1966) for estimates for agriculture and manufacturing in 1925, 1930, 1935, 1940; ILO for 1951 [C10+], 1964 [C10+]; DANE for 1973 [C10+], 1985[C12+]. Bairoch, et al. (1968) has estimates for 1938 (EAP of 4.5 millions) but they are inconsistent with the figures in the 1951 census (3.7 millions), so they are not included. Figures for 1973 are from the census of that year. For 1993, due to the high proportion of persons in "undefined" census activities, we use the sectoral shares in the HS [12+] to allocate the total EAP. The 1985 census did not include information for EAP by sectors. The only data available circa 1980 come from household surveys covering the seven main cities. The household surveys only have national coverage since 1988. A sectoral estimate for manufacturing EAP in 1982 was obtained by using the 1990 household surveys to calculate the shares of the seven cities in the sectoral totals and then to extrapolate the figures from the restricted survey of 1982 to the whole economy. The agricultural share of EAP in 1982 was obtained by interpolation between 1973 and 1993.

Mexico: INEGI (1990) for 1900, 1910, 1921, 1930, 1940, 1950, 1960, 1970, 1980-85; ILO 1970 [C12+], 1980 [C12+], 1990 [C12+]. The 1980 census has 29 percent of the workforce in the "undefined" category, so to obtain an estimate circa 1980 we have applied the sectoral shares given in the 1979 HS to the census figure for total EAP. The datum for agriculture circa 1990 is taken from HS (1991) [12+]. The census datum for EAP in agriculture is not included because its low value is inconsistent with the rest of the observations; instead, estimates were obtained by interpolating between 1960 and 1980.

Venezuela: ECLA (1966) for 1925, 1930, 1935, 1945; Bairoch, et al. (1968) for 1941, 1950 based on censuses; ILO for 1961 [C10+], 1971 [C15+], 1981 [C12+] and 1992 [C12+].

APPENDIX V. PRICES

Domestic Prices and Inflation

Inflation is measured by the annual average rate of growth of the consumer price index in metropolitan areas, except in Argentina, 1900-14, where the implicit GDP deflator is used, and Mexico between 1912-16, where the rate of devaluation of the nominal exchange rate is used as a proxy.

Appendix Table V.1.
Inflation by Decade
(Annual average percent change in CPI)

	1900s	1910s	1920s	1930s	1940s	1950s	1960s	1970s	1980s	1990–95
Argentina	3	7	-3	0	36	31	21	142	787	43
Bolivia					17	69	6	20	203	12
Brazil	-2	7	3	2	13	21	45	37	605	1,270
Chile	8	6	2	7	18	38	27	175	20	19
Colombia	20	12	2	4	13	7	12	21	24	25
Costa Rica					10	2	2	11	27	19
Cuba	2	4	-2	-1	10	1	na	na	na	na
Dominican Rep.					10	1	2	11	26	16
Ecuador					15	2	4	13	37	40
El Salvador					10	3	1	11	19	13
Guatemala					11	1	1	10	15	16
Haiti					0	3	12	7	19	
Honduras					6	2	2	8	8	21
Mexico	7	62	-2	2	11	8	3	17	69	12
Nicaragua					15	5	4	14	5,121	749
Panama					6	1	1	7	2	1
Paraguay					25	33	3	13	22	17
Peru		11	-2	1	15	8	9	32	1,224	113
Uruguay				1	5	17	48	59	63	62
Venezuela	3	7	-4	-3	8	2	1	9	25	45
LA[6]										
Average	3	17	0	2	16	18	18	67	255	236
Sdev	10	32	8	8	23	19	18	92	374	511
Median	2	7	-1	1	12	12	15	25	52	24
LA[19]										
Average					13	13	10	33	437	125
Sdev					19	24	17	57	1,416	403
Median					10	5	3	14	25	19

Notes: Average: simple average values for each decade; Sdev: standard deviation of inflation rates during each decade. For exact definitions, see original sources.

Sources:

Data for Argentina, Brazil, Chile, Colombia, Mexico and Venezuela between 1900 and 1994 are from Hofman (1997) and ECLAC (SYLA, 1996) thereafter, except Argentina 1900-14 (Cortés Conde, 1994); Colombia 1900-10 is the compound rate of growth of the CPI between 1901 and 1910 (Mitchell, 1993); Mexico 1912-16 (Cárdenas and Mann, 1987).

Mitchell (1993) for the rest of the countries up to 1988 and ECLAC (SYLA, 1996) thereafter, with the exception of Cuba 1903-57 from Brundenius (1984); Peru 1983-89, based on Webb and Fernández (1991); and Nicaragua 1968-73, where we use an interpolation based on ECLAC (SYLA, 1981).

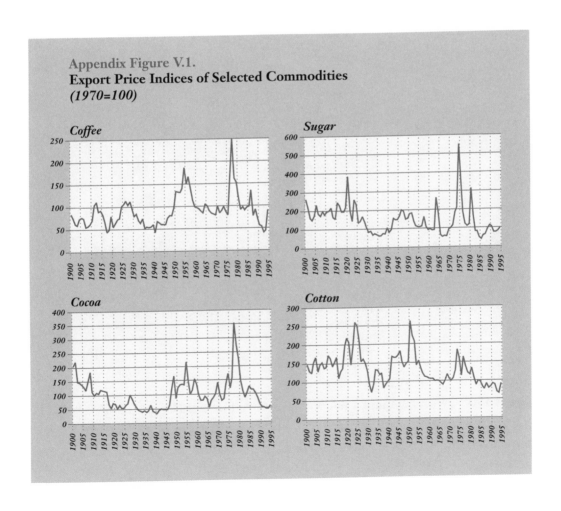

Appendix Figure V.1.
Export Price Indices of Selected Commodities
(1970=100)

International Commodity Prices

Commodity trends are shown in Appendix Figure V.1. The prices reported are those obtained in the main export markets for Latin America—usually the United States—deflated by the U.S. wholesale price index in order to give their "real" value.

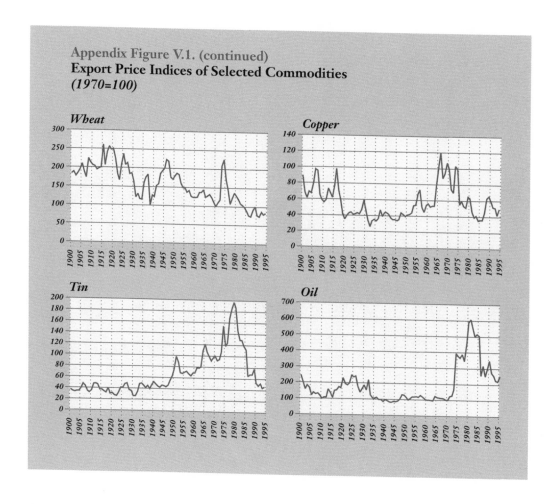

Appendix Figure V.1. (continued)
Export Price Indices of Selected Commodities
(1970=100)

Sources:

Cocoa: 1900-24 average unit value f.o.b. of U.S. imports (USDC, 1950); 1925-47 (Grunwald and Musgrove, 1970) and 1948-92 (IMF/IFS) average value of U.S. imports from Brazil; 1993-94 average of daily prices New York/London, three-month futures (UNCTAD, 1995).

Coffee: 1900-12 average unit value f.o.b. of U.S. imports (USDC, 1950); 1913-92 average annual price of Colombian coffee in New York (BR, 1993); 1993-94 Colombian mild Arabicas, ex-dock New York (UNCTAD, 1995).

Copper: 1900-56 price quoted in New York (Dore, 1988); 1957-92 (IMF/IFS) prices quoted in London; 1993-94 prices quoted at the London Metal Exchange, high grade, cash, (UNCTAD, 1995). During World War II, prices were fixed by the U.S. government.

Cotton: 1900-12 the Sauerbeck Statistical Index for U.S. Middling (Lewis, 1938); 1913-24 average unit value f.o.b. of U.S. exports (USDC, 1950); 1927-39 and 1946-66 prices of U.S. Middling quoted at Liverpool (Grunwald and Musgrove, 1970); 1940-45 figures correspond to U.S. wholesale prices (Manthy, 1978); 1967-92 average price of U.S. cotton in 10 different markets (IMF/IFS); 1993-94 U.S. Orleans/Texas, Mid 1, c.i.f. North Europe (UNCTAD, 1995).

Oil: 1900-19 U.S. well price (American Petroleum Institute, 1958); 1920-70 from Baptista (1989) Venezuelan oil price index (1968=100); 1971-95 from BCV average price of Venezuelan crude.

Sugar: 1900-24 average unit value f.o.b. of U.S. imports (USDC, 1950); 1925-62 average price c.i.f. based on Cuban exports (Grunwald and Musgrove, 1970); 1963-92 imports from the Caribbean in the New York market (IMF/IFS); 1993-94 Caribbean Ports, f.o.b. bulk basis (UNCTAD, 1995).

Tin: 1900-41 (Peñalosa, 1947); 1942-67 (Grunwald and Musgrove, 1970); 1968-92 (IMF/IFS); 1993-94 (UNCTAD, 1995). All prices quoted in London.

Wheat: 1900-12, the Sauerbeck Statististical Index of U.S. wheat in London (Lewis, 1978); 1913-39 average unit value f.o.b. of U.S. exports (USDC, 1950); 1940-49 based on U.S. wholesale prices in Manthy (1978); 1949-92 (IMF/IFS) and 1993-94 (UNCTAD, 1995) U.S. export prices f.o.b. in Gulf ports.

APPENDIX VI. FOREIGN TRADE

The following tables present data for the value (Appendix Table VI.1) and volume (Appendix Table VI.2) growth in exports, and the level of imports (Appendix Table VI.3). The net barter terms of trade (Appendix Figure VI.1 and Appendix Table VI.4) is the ratio of exports unit value to imports unit value. The income terms of trade—often known in Latin America as the "purchasing power of exports"—is the ratio of the current value of exports to the unit value of imports.

Appendix Table VI.1.
Export Value Growth
(Percent annual rate of growth in current US$)

	1900–13	1913–29	1929–45	1945–72	1972–81	1981–95	1900–29	1916–95	1900–95
Argentina	9.0	3.3	*1.4*	1.9	17.3	6.3	6.4	4.3	4.0
Bolivia		-1.9[a]	9.1	2.8	16.6	*1.6*		5.0	
Brazil	5.9	4.0	4.3	3.4	19.0	5.5	3.2	7.2	6.0
Chile	6.5	-0.4	*4.0*	5.7	20.1	11.1	*0.9*	5.9	4.4
Colombia	8.6	9.8	2.3	3.5	18.1	8.4	9.6	7.0	7.1
Costa Rica		4.7[a]	-1.6	8.4	16.2	8.0		8.0	
Cuba	8.9	*1.9*	7.1	*0.8*	17.6	-2.7	7.3	4.5	4.4
Dominican Rep.		0.4[a]	6.4	4.7	11.1	-2.9		6.1	
Ecuador		-0.4[a]	4.3	7.1	22.6	3.2		8.8	
El Salvador		3.6[a]	4.6	7.9	16.1	*0.3*		6.9	
Guatemala		9.5[a]	2.1	7.2	17.4	2.7		7.4	
Haiti		4.6[a]	0.0	1.1	18.7	-5.4		4.1	
Honduras		18.6[a]	-5.6	6.7	17.7	1.6		6.4	
Mexico[b]	5.9	*3.0*	6.4	3.7	30.5	4.7	6.6	7.3	6.6
Nicaragua		4.8[a]	5.6	9.5	8.8	-1.7		6.8	
Panama		-1.6[a]	0.0	10.1	11.0	4.3		8.3	
Paraguay		*1.8[a]*	1.7	3.5	19.0	16.0		7.0	
Peru	7.1	5.2	*1.0*	8.4	16.9	2.9	8.2	6.2	6.0
Uruguay		-0.4[a]	4.6	*0.2*	19.4	5.6		4.5	
Venezuela	5.6	11.4	7.1	5.9	18.2	0.1	7.2	9.3	9.2
LA[6]	7.0	3.7[c]	3.7	3.8	20.3	4.9	4.7	6.6	5.7
CA[5]		8.3	-0.3	7.8	15.7	3.3		7.1	
LA[13]		-0.5[a]	4.2	4.2	16.2	2.1		5.5	
Latin America		2.5[a]	3.8	4.0	19.5	4.5		6.4	

Note: In italics: values not significantly different from zero at a confidence level of 95 percent. For the method used to calculate growth rates, see p. 312.
[a] Data start in 1916. [b] Data on Mexico exclude the period 1913–19. [c] From 1913 to 1919, the rate of growth is calculated excluding Mexico.

Appendix Table VI.2.
Export Volume Growth
(Annual average rate of growth of quantum index)

	1880–1900	1900–13	1913–29	1929–45	1945–72	1972–81	1981–95	1880–29	1929–95	1900–95
Argentina	6.2	4.6	4.9	-0.9	2.2	7.3	6.1	4.7	1.9	1.6
Bolivia				3.1	0.1	0.0	4.3		1.1	1.1
Brazil	3.1	1.6	1.5	2.6	1.1	8.7	6.2	3.0	3.8	2.7
Chile	3.4	4.7	3.4	4.2	2.3	9.6	8.5	2.6	3.8	2.8
Colombia		5.5	6.8	2.6	2.3	1.6	8.5	6.5[a]	3.0	3.7
Costa Rica			0.5[d]	-0.7	6.6	2.6	7.4		5.0	4.1[d]
Cuba	-10.8[b]	12.0	4.6	0.0	0.7	4.2	-13.0	7.2[b]	1.4	1.9
Dominican Rep.				2.1	2.4	2.4	-0.9		2.4	
Ecuador				3.1	7.2	2.0	7.4		5.9	
El Salvador			3.5[d]	0.7	6.2	-3.1	4.3		2.7	2.8[d]
Guatemala			0.9[d]	2.6	5.9	3.9	3.0		4.5	4.0[d]
Haiti				1.5	0.7	6.1	-3.4		1.7	
Honduras			11.4[d]	-6.6	4.6	4.6	1.5		3.3	2.9[d]
Mexico[h]		2.7	2.5	-0.2	5.0	10.2	6.6	5.0[a]	5.3	4.1
Nicaragua			5.4[d]	-3.6	9.1	0.2	0.2		4.4	4.3[d]
Panama					8.8[e]	2.1	4.4		5.0[e]	
Paraguay					3.0	7.7	13.0		5.3[g]	
Peru	5.1	7.2	6.8	-0.7	7.6	1.7	2.1	6.3	3.3	3.6
Uruguay	-4.4[c]	2.5	2.5	-0.6	0.2	10.6	4.1	0.6[c]	2.1	1.2
Venezuela	1.3	2.5	15.5	4.4	5.0	-6.2	3.2	3.5	2.8	6.1
LA[6]		2.8	3.4[f]	0.8	2.4	8.8	6.5	2.8[a]	3.7	2.7
LA[13]				2.3	3.3	2.7	6.6		3.2	
LA[19]				1.0	2.5	7.7	6.7		3.6	

[a] Data start in 1900. [b] Data start in 1890. [c] Data start in 1895. [d] Data start in 1920. [e] Data start in 1900. [f] From 1913 to 1919 the rate of growth is calculated excluding Mexico. [g] Data start in 1938. [h] Excludes 1913–17. *Notes:* In italics: values not significantly different from zero at a confidence level of 95 percent. Group aggregates are obtained by weighting indices of individual countries by the values of exports in constant values at 1970 prices (deflated by each country's export price indices).

Appendix Table VI.3.
Import Volume
(Three-year average values in US$ millions at 1970 prices)

	1900	1910	1920	1930	1940	1950	1960	1970	1980	1990	1995
Argentina	289	707	575	933	1,003	1,344	1,445	1,756	2,700	1,345	4,499
Bolivia			30[b]	38[b]	58	69	83	166	263	232	389
Brazil	502	651	599	848	908	1,724	1,794	2,898	6,151	5,531	11,601
Chile	103	225	155	285	299	386	560	945	1,460	1,904	3,143
Colombia	50	56	84	193	282	419	546	815	1,685	1,884	4,543
Costa Rica			27	34	42	54	113	302	459	575	905
Cuba	202[b]	248[b]	519[b]	319[b]	289[b]	672[b]	720	1,254	1,196	1,679	510
Dominican Rep.			31[b]	23	35	57	90	263	522	592	761
Ecuador			14[b]	17	26	71	119	269	897	1,185	1,955
El Salvador			19	29	23	56	116	224	357	235	408
Guatemala			32	52	45	94	152	280	435	376	572
Haiti			23[b]	28[b]	18[b]	47	40	49	120	115	138
Honduras			34	40	29	51	79	201	334	313	327
Mexico	196	323	321[a]	351	464	1,056	1,401	1,969	7,221	11,727	16,436
Nicaragua			22	24	21	38	72	198	256	192	209
Panama			21[b]	40[b]	67[b]	95	147	354	353	266	389
Paraguay			11[b]	25[b]	19[b]	37[b]	44	81	180	622	1,389
Peru	37	52	78	92	169	259	445	701	1,120	794	1,603
Uruguay			137[b]	191[b]	184	232	220	214	503	451	905
Venezuela	37	52	50	128	346	1,230	1,982	1,717	4,561	3,673	4,252
LA[6]	1,177	2,014	1,736	2,738	3,302	6,160	7,728	10,100	23,778	26,063	44,474
LA[13]			475	632	736	1,060	1,721	3,302	5,800	5,949	9,949
LA[19]			2,255	3,370	4,038	7,320	9,450	13,401	29,578	32,012	54,423

[a] Figure corresponds to average for 1921–22.
[b] Figures are deflated by the U.S. export price index.

Appendix Table VI.4.
Net Barter Terms of Trade
(Three-year average values, 1970=100)

	1900	1910	1920	1930	1940	1950	1960	1970	1980	1990	1995
Argentina	102	146	81	101	115	137	105	100	88	63	62
Bolivia	80	113	50	49	76	59	66	100	124	106	96
Brazil	76	90	82	71	47	97	91	100	71	60	60
Chile	57	74	53	94	62	59	59	100	51	48	48
Colombia			56	79	74	113	96	100	121	122	124
Costa Rica				89	49	102	93	100	90	75	85
Cuba[1]	125	111	145	60	133	215	115	100	138	114	118
Dominican Rep.				28	43	87	67	100	101	78	74
Ecuador				77	55	135	108	100	226	191	173
El Salvador			63	58	72	93	83	100	163	64	56
Guatemala			56	93	58	125	115	100	72	50	55
Haiti				89	69	127	93	100	87	85	63
Honduras			82	109	140	102	93	100	100	90	98
Mexico	116	135	124	178	144	149	97	100	275	202	212
Nicaragua			126	84	138	136	90	100	82	60	51
Panama			40	81	53	127	107	100	69	80	78
Paraguay					67	143	110	100	100	129	123
Peru	171	148	138	103	87	116	85	100	131	95	107
Uruguay					109	121	95	100	108	119	131
Venezuela	161	202	113	111	163	217	185	100	553	461	379
LA[6]	93	119	82	101	104	130	116	100	206	137	124
LA[13]					85	108	89	100	120	88	92
LA-nonoil					83	110	90	100	83	67	68
LA[19]					100	126	110	100	192	129	120
U.S. Pm/Px[2]	128	127	92	101	94	126	109	100	142	133	131

Note: LA-nonoil: Latin American non-oil exporters during 1970–90—that is, LA[19] excluding Ecuador, Mexico and Venezuela.
[1] Terms of trade 1900–60 are proxied by the ratio of unit value of Cuba's export of cane sugar to the United States by the U.S. export price index.
[2] The U.S. inverse terms of trade 1900–70 is obtained by dividing the index price of non-manufactured imports by the price index of exports. Thereafter we divide the general price of imports by the price of exports. Group aggregates are obtained by weighting export and import price indices of individual countries by their exports and imports in current dollars, respectively.

Appendix Table VI.5.
Income Terms of Trade (Purchasing Power of Exports)
(Three-year average values, 1970=100)

	1900	1910	1920	1930	1940	1950	1960	1970	1980	1990	1995
Argentina	19	41	38	55	85	72	68	100	144	159	224
Bolivia				29	57	48	38	100	120	117	138
Brazil	28	44	25	40	39	65	60	100	189	308	429
Chile	23	39	15	27	34	33	45	100	93	171	254
Colombia	6	8	14	36	39	66	68	100	191	341	432
Costa Rica			13	19	9	27	38	100	140	199	299
Cuba[1]	17	32	61	38	38	83	68	100	100	106	45
Dominican Rep.				12	25	50	72	100	168	102	89
Ecuador				9	11	36	72	100	477	678	925
El Salvador			11	14	14	33	49	100	154	43	59
Guatemala			12	19	14	32	47	100	124	85	125
Haiti				68	76	126	87	100	162	132	72
Honduras			15	64	38	43	42	100	159	152	153
Mexico	17	36	40	42	53	78	74	100	429	730	972
Nicaragua			14	14	15	30	40	100	110	50	56
Panama			4	7	9	31	34	100	78	58	86
Paraguay				16	28	72	56	100	204	795	1,527
Peru	5	7	12		23	28	52	100	135	101	132
Uruguay					95	99	63	100	146	227	277
Venezuela	2	2	2	10	36	80	142	100	281	262	282
LA[6]	15	26	18	30	46	64	78	100	210	300	382
LA[13]			24	24	26	40	51	100	151	135	185
LA-nonoil			33	33	43	54	57	100	148	202	276
LA[19]			28	28	41	58	71	100	196	259	334

Note: LA-nonoil: LA[19] excluding Ecuador, Mexico and Venezuela.
[1] For Cuba, we use the U.S. export index price as deflator from 1900 to 1960. To obtain the group values, exports are accumulated and then deflated by an import price index weighted by the value of imports in current dollars.

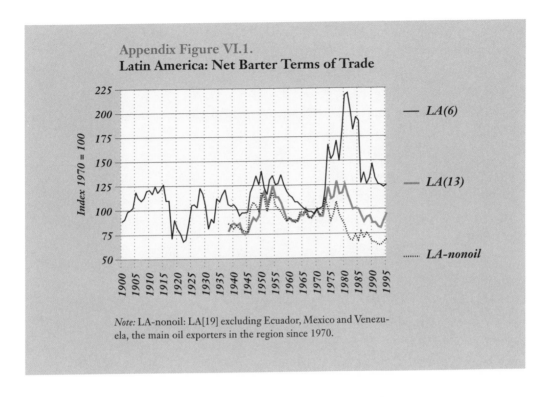

Appendix Figure VI.1.
Latin America: Net Barter Terms of Trade

Note: LA-nonoil: LA[19] excluding Ecuador, Mexico and Venezuela, the main oil exporters in the region since 1970.

Sources for exports and imports in current U.S. dollars:

Unless otherwise indicated, all series are completed up to 1995 from the IMF/IFS. Data are usually recorded as exports f.o.b. (free on board at frontier of exporting country) and imports as c.i.f. (cost plus insurance and freight at frontier of importing country) except the Dominican Republic 1948-62, and Ecuador, Haiti, Panama, and Paraguay prior to 1948, where imports are recorded as f.o.b. (Wilkie, 1974).

Argentina: 1900-15 Hofman (1997); 1916-71 Wilkie (1974).

Brazil: 1900-15 Hofman (1997); Wilkie 1916-39 (1974); 1940-87 IBGE (1990).

Central America: 1913 PAU (1952); 1916-19 Wilkie (1974); 1920-87 Bulmer-Thomas (1987).

Chile: 1900-06 based on growth rates in sterling (Palma, 1979); 1907-15 from Hofman (1997); Wilkie (1974) for 1916-71.

Colombia: 1900-15 Hofman (1997); 1916-22 Wilkie (1974); 1923-92 BR (1993).

Cuba: 1900-88 Mitchell (1993); thereafter ECLAC (SYLA, 1996).

Mexico: 1900-87 INEGI (1990).

Peru: 1900-12 and 1914-15 based on rate of growth of figures in gold *soles*

(Thorp and Bertram, 1978); 1913 PAU (1952); 1916-29 Wilkie (1974); 1930-92 Webb and Fernández (1991, 1992).

Venezuela: 1900-15 Baptista (1997), 1916-39 Wilkie (1974); 1940-95 BCV (1966, 1990).

Bolivia, Dominican Republic, Ecuador, Haiti, Paraguay, Panama, Uruguay: PAU (1952) for 1913; Wilkie (1974) for 1916-71.

Sources for export quantum:

The indices are constructed using the Laspeyres formula. All series are completed up to 1995 using the rate of growth of the export quantum index in ECLAC (SYLA, 1981-96).

Argentina: 1900-63 from Diéguez (1972); 1964-72 from ECLA (1976).

Brazil: 1880-1979 from IBGE (1990).

Central America: 1920-87 from Bulmer-Thomas (1987).

Chile: 1880-1900 from Palma (1979); 1900-49 from ECLA (1951).

Colombia: 1905-45 from Ocampo and Montenegro (1984) "series A" spliced with "series B;" 1920-21 refers only to coffee; 1946-72 ECLA (1976).

Cuba: 1900-59 includes exports of sugar only, from Mitchell (1993, 279-80). 1960-94 from UNCTAD (1986, 1995).

Mexico: 1900-37 from ECLA (1951); 1938-77 from INEGI (1990).

Peru: 1880-1962 from Hunt (1973); 1901, 1903 figures are interpolations; 1963-91 from Webb and Fernández (1991, 1992).

Uruguay: 1895-1970 from Finch (1981). The index is built by splicing three series: 1895-1913 (1913 = 100), 1913-40 (1938 = 100), and 1935-70 (1961 = 100).

Venezuela: 1881-1989 calculation by authors based on coffee, cocoa, and hides and skin exports from 1881 to 1920 using 1907 prices as weights; during 1920-47, oil is included and the weights correspond to 1937 (Izard, 1970); 1948-80 includes only oil exports.

ECLA (1976) up to 1972 for *Bolivia* from 1929, *Dominican Republic* from 1930, *Ecuador* from 1928, *Haiti* from 1930, *Paraguay* from 1938. *Panama* values from 1945 to 1995 correspond to constant value of merchandise exports in U.S. dollars at 1970 prices.

Sources for export unit value indices:

All series are completed up to 1995 using the rate of growth of the unit value index computed by ECLAC (SYLA, 1981-96).

Argentina: 1900-29 from Diéguez (1973); 1930-72 ECLA (1976).

Brazil: IBGE (1990) for 1900-79 (1900-13 in sterling, in US$ thereafter)

Central America: 1920-84 based on Bulmer-Thomas (1987).

Chile: 1900-27 from ECLA (1951); 1928-72 from ECLA (1976).

Colombia: Ocampo (1984) for 1900-06 spliced with the series in Ocampo and Montenegro (1984) up to 1945; 1946-72 from ECLA (1976). For 1920-21, the export price index is calculated from the unit value of price of coffee exports only.

Cuba: 1900-60 the export price index is proxied by the price of sugar cane in U.S. dollars per pound; 1900-18 price of U.S. sugar imports (USDC, 1975); 1919-39 price of Cuban sugar exports to the United States (Santamaria, 1995); 1940-67 price index of Cuban sugar export prices (Grunwald and Musgrove, 1970); 1960-95 export unit value (UNCTAD, 1983, 1995).

Mexico: 1900-24 from ECLA (1951); 1925-60 from Cárdenas (1994); 1961-77 from INEGI (1990). We use the rate of growth of the U.S. import index of non-manufactured goods to fill the gap of the revolution, 1913-18.

Peru: 1900-27 based on Hunt (1973) rate of growth of export index in national currency; 1928-59 ECLA (1976); 1960-88 from Webb and Fernández (1991, 1992).

Venezuela: Baptista (1997) for 1900-72.

ECLA (1976) up to 1972 for *Bolivia* from 1929, *Dominican Republic* from 1930, *Ecuador* from 1928, *Haiti* from 1930, *Paraguay* from 1938. *Panama* values from 1950 up to 1971 from IMF/IFS. *United States* 1900-70 from USDC (1975), IMF/IFS thereafter.

Sources for import unit value indices:

Unless otherwise indicated, series are completed up to 1995 using the rate of growth of the unit value of imports index calculated by ECLAC (SYLA, 1981-96).

Argentina: 1900-09 based on growth rates of the UK export price index (Feinstein, 1972); 1910-28 from ECLA (1951); 1946-72 from ECLA (1976).

Brazil: 1900-79 from IBGE (1990).

Central America: 1920-84 based on Bulmer-Thomas (1987).

Chile: 1900-27 from ECLA (1951); 1928-72 from ECLA (1976).

Colombia: 1900-09 based on growth rates of U.S. export price index; 1910-45 from Ocampo and Montenegro (1984, Table A-2, Series B); 1946-72 from ECLA (1976).

Cuba: We use the U.S. export price index up to 1960 as proxy for the unit value of imports. UNCTAD (1983, 1995) thereafter for unit value of imports.

Peru: 1900-28 based on growth rates of an index that results from combining the export price index of the United States (with a weight of 75 percent) and the UK (25 percent); 1929-59 from ECLA (1976); 1960-84 from Webb and Fernández (1991, 1992).

Mexico: 1900-24 from ECLA (1951); 1925-60 from Cárdenas (1994); 1961-72 from ECLA (1976). We use the rate of growth of the U.S. export price index to fill the gap in data between 1914-18.

Venezuela: 1900-82 from Baptista (1997).

ECLA (1976) up to 1972 for *Bolivia* from 1929, *Dominican Republic* from 1930, *Ecuador* from 1928, *Haiti* from 1930, *Paraguay* from 1938. *Panama*: 1950-71 from IMF/IFS.

United States: 1900-70 index of nonmanufactured imports (weights: 70 percent crude materials; 30 percent crude food) from USDC (1975), IMF/IFS thereafter for general import index.

APPENDIX VII. EXTERNAL ECONOMIC EXPOSURE

This Appendix presents figures and tables with measures of "vulnerability" for a sample of countries—that is, the extent to which domestic economies are exposed to external shock. Appendix Tables VII.1 and VII.2 show the respective shares of customs receipts and income tax in current government revenues, reflecting the fiscal exposure to foreign trade. Appendix Tables VII.3 and VII.4 present the share of the leading products in total exports and an index of commodity concentration. The commodity concentration index measures the weight of the two principal commodities in total exports:

$$\sqrt{\sum_{i=1}^{2} \left(\frac{x_i}{\sum_{j=1}^{2} x_j} \right)^2} *100$$

where xji are the main export categories and xi is the export of the two main commodities. The index takes a value of 100 when a single commodity accounts for 100 percent of exports, and a value of 1 (i.e., close to zero) when the two leading commodities represent only 1 percent each of total exports. Appendix Tables VII.5 and VII.6 show the proportion of imports and exports, respectively, going to the United Kingdom and the United States as a measure of market dependence. Each figure also includes the standard deviation for the sample of countries to indicate dispersion.

Appendix Table VII.1.
Customs as Percentage of Total Receipts
(Three-year average values)

	1900	1910	1920	1930	1940	1950	1960	1970	1980	1988[a]
Argentina	46.3	54.9	47.5	45.1	23.4	5.8	2.8	17.7	9.0	9.1
Brazil	53.6	54.4	35.9	38.0	22.3	9.5	11.2	5.0	3.0	1.1
Chile	61.4	89.0	66.1	43.7	40.9	20.0	18.7	11.2	4.8	8.8
Colombia	na	77.9	54.7	45.3	29.3	19.2	25.9	16.7	11.6	16.8
Mexico	44.2	44.9	na	30.7	33.0	22.6	17.1	6.3	7.7	1.0
Peru	56.0	45.8	44.2	30.7	26.7	39.7	8.6	23.7	28.2	18.0
Venezuela	61.4	65.3	47.0	46.1	33.1	20.2	8.9	5.6	6.5	10.3
Average	52.2	64.0	49.2	39.9	29.8	19.6	13.3	12.3	10.1	9.3
Sdev	21.2	16.6	10.7	7.8	7.1	11.4	8.0	8.4	8.5	6.4

Note: Average: simple average over the sample of seven countries; Sdev: standard deviation.
[a] Average for 1987–88.

Appendix Table VII.2.
Income Tax as Percentage of Total Receipts
(Three-year average values)

	1900	1910	1920	1930	1940	1950	1960	1970	1980	1988[a]
Argentina	3.4	3.1	3.2	3.9	18.8	33.9	19.1	23.0	6.5	12.4
Brazil				4.1	9.2	28.4	27.8	24.7	28.6	22.8
Chile	0.9	1.3	6.9	19.3	23.4	30.0	34.5	39.0	17.4	18.6
Colombia				6.4	25.1	45.6	46.6	50.3	25.2	27.3
Mexico				10.2	14.5	24.3	32.0	39.3	37.6	26.5
Peru	3.2	8.6	6.9	10.9	16.1	24.1	32.8	31.5	27.0	25.3
Venezuela				0.4	24.0	32.0	47.6	66.8	43.6
Average	2.5	4.3	6.2	9.1	15.1	30.0	32.0	36.5	29.9	21.7
Sdev	1.4	3.8	1.8	5.9	8.8	8.1	8.9	11.0	19.2	6.4

Note: Average: simple average over the sample of seven countries; Sdev: standard deviation.
[a] Average for 1987–88.

Appendix Table VII.3.
Principal Commodities Exported
(In percent)

	1900	1910	1920	1930	1940	1950	1960	1970	1980	1990	1995
Argentina	wool(24) wheat(19)	wheat(23) wool(15)	wheat(24) meat(18)	wheat(19) meat(18)	meat(23) wheat(16)	wheat(17) meat(15)	meat(22) wool(14)	meat(25) wheat(6)	meat(13) wheat(10)	meat(7) wheat(6)	oil(8) wheat(5)
Bolivia[1]	silver(39) tin(27)	tin(54) rubb(16)	tin(68) silver(11)	tin(84) copp(4)	tin(80) silver(6)	tin(67) lead(9)	tin(66) lead(7)	tin(50) anti(16)	tin(43) gas(25)	gas(26) zinc(16)	zinc(11) gas(10)
Brazil	coff(57) rubb(20)	coff(51) rubb(31)	coff(55) cocoa(4)	coff(68) cott(3)	coff(34) cott(18)	coff(62) cocoa(7)	coff(55) cocoa(6)	coff(32) iron(7)	soya(12) coff(10)	soya(9) iron(8)	soya(8) iron(6)
Chile	nit(65) copp(14)	nit(67) copp(7)	nit(54) copp(12)	nit(43) copp(37)	copp(57) nit(19)	copp(52) nit(22)	copp(67) nit(7)	copp(79) iron(6)	copp(46) iron(4)	copp(46) fish(4)	copp(39) wood(6)
Colombia[2]	coff(49) gold(17)	coff(39) gold(16)	coff(62) gold(13)	coff(64) oil(22)	coff(62) oil(29)	coff(72) oil(16)	coff(75) oil(18)	coff(59) oil(11)	coff(54) oil(4)	oil(23) coff(21)	coff(20) oil(19)
Costa Rica	coff(60) bana(31)	bana(53) coff(32)	coff(51) bana(33)	coff(67) bana(25)	coff(54) bana(28)	coff(30) bana(56)	coff(53) bana(24)	coff(29) bana(29)	coff(27) bana(22)	bana(24) coff(17)	bana(24) coff(14)
Cuba	sugar(61) toba(23)	sugar(70) toba(24)	sugar(87) toba(10)	sugar(68) toba(17)	sugar(70) toba(8)	sugar(82) toba(5)	sugar(73) toba(8)	sugar(75) toba(4)	sugar(82) nick(5)	sugar(74) nick(7)	sugar(50) nick(22)
Mexico	silver(44) copp(8)	silver(28) gold(16)	oil(67) silver(17)	silver(15) oil(14)	silver(14) zinc(13)	cott(17) lead(12)	cott(23) coff(9)	cott(8) coff(5)	oil(65) coff(4)	oil(32) coff(2)	oil(10)
Peru	sugar(25) silver(18)	copp(20) sugar(19)	sugar(35) cott(26)	oil(33) copp(21)	oil(26) cott(21)	cott(34) sugar(15)	cott(18) copp(17)	fish(27) copp(25)	oil(20) copp(18)	copp(18) fish(13)	copp(19) fish(15)
Uruguay	wool(29) hides(28)	wool(40) hides(23)	wool(40) meat(30)	meat(37) wool(27)	wool(45) meat(22)	wool(48) meat(19)	wool(57) meat(20)	wool(32) meat(32)	wool(17) meat(17)	wool(16) meat(11)	meat(14) wool(9)
Venezuela	coff(43) cacao(20)	coff(53) cacao(18)	oil(42) cacao(18)	oil(82) coff(10)	oil(88) coff(3)	oil(94) coff(1)	oil(88) iron(6)	oil(87) iron(6)	oil(90) iron(2)	oil(79) alum(4)	oil(75) alum(4)

Note: In brackets share of each commodity in total exports of goods f.o.b. Alum: aluminum; anti: antimony; bana: banana; coff: coffee; copp: copper; cott: cotton; gas: natural gas; gua: guano; iron: iron ore; nit: nitrate of soda; oil: oil and products; hides: hides and skins; nick: nickel; tung: tungsten; toba: tobacco.

[1] Bolivian exports of silver circa 1900 correspond to 1901, and exports of rubber circa 1910 to the 1912–13 average.

[2] Colombian data on exports circa 1900 corresponds to 1898; gold exports circa 1910 to the average for 1912–13, and circa 1920 to the average for 1921–22.

Appendix Table VII.4.
Commodity Concentration Indices
(*Three-year average values*)

	1900	1910	1920	1930	1940	1950	1960	1970	1980	1990	1995
Argentina	30.6	27.5	30.0	26.2	28.0	22.7	26.1	29.7	16.4	9.2	10.6
Bolivia	47.4	56.3	68.9	84.1	80.2	67.6	64.4	52.5	49.7	30.5	14.9
Brazil	60.4	59.7	55.1	68.1	38.5	62.4	55.3	32.8	15.6	12.0	10.0
Chile	66.5	67.4	55.3	56.7	60.1	56.5	67.4	76.2	46.2	46.2	39.5
Colombia	51.9	42.2	63.3	67.7	68.4	73.8	77.1	60.0	54.1	31.1	27.6
Costa Rica	67.6	62.2	60.2	71.8	60.9	63.9	58.1	40.9	34.9	28.8	27.8
Cuba	65.2	74.0	87.6	70.1	70.5	82.2	73.4	75.1	82.2	74.3	54.6
Mexico	45.1	32.2	69.1	20.5	19.1	20.8	24.7	9.4	65.1	32.1	10.2
Peru	32.0	27.6	43.6	39.1	33.4	37.2	24.8	36.8	26.9	22.2	24.2
Uruguay	40.3	46.1	50.0	45.8	50.1	51.6	60.4	45.3	24.0	19.4	16.6
Venezuela	47.4	56.0	45.7	82.6	88.1	94.0	88.2	87.2	90.0	79.1	75.1
Average	50.4	50.1	57.2	57.5	54.3	57.5	56.5	49.6	45.9	35.0	28.3
Sdev	13.2	16.1	15.4	21.8	22.3	23.2	22.1	23.3	25.4	23.0	20.8

Note: Average: simple average over the sample of 11 countries; *Sdev:* standard deviation.

Appendix Table VII.5.
Percent Share of Exports to the United Kingdom and the United States
(Three-year average values)

	1900	1910	1920	1930	1940	1950	1960	1970	1980	1988[a]
Argentina	22.9	30.3	43.2	44.4	57.8	35.5	29.9	16.9	11.3	15.0
Bolivia		81.5	91.5	93.8	90.9	95.2	78.8	73.7	38.7	30.0
Brazil	55.2	56.0	47.2	49.4	58.2	60.1	48.7	35.9	21.6	29.9
Chile	52.1	55.8	51.8	42.3	59.6	59.0	53.5	25.0	16.7	25.9
Colombia		66.2	78.2	83.3	63.9	78.7	69.2	39.4	26.4	38.3
Mexico	77.8	79.7	72.7	71.5	87.3	80.6	63.3	64.3	62.2	61.2
Peru	65.8	63.4	78.3	59.8	51.1	45.7	41.9	35.1	30.0	23.3
Uruguay	15.4	13.4	45.3	41.5	52.2	58.3	32.8	16.6	12.6	17.5
Venezuela	42.1	45.2	38.2	22.0	35.1	32.0	50.1	46.4	31.6	49.8
Average	48.0	52.5	60.3	56.5	63.2	63.2	53.4	40.5	27.5	32.3
Sdev	26.6	21.8	21.2	22.9	18.9	21.4	16.6	20.0	15.9	15.3

Note: Average: simple average over the nine countries shown; *Sdev*: standard deviation.
[a] Average for 1987–88.

Appendix Table VII.6.
Percent Share of Imports from the United Kingdom and the United States
(Three-year average values)

	1900	1910	1920	1930	1940	1950	1960	1970	1980	1988[a]
Argentina	46.7	42.7	49.2	40.9	48.9	29.0	33.1	28.9	25.3	17.1
Brazil	40.6	41.0	59.8	49.4	56.6	50.8	36.2	35.6	20.3	24.0
Chile	46.6	43.9	61.4	49.7	54.6	61.2	53.9	38.6	26.6	22.8
Colombia	na	61.8	75.9	56.7	73.7	70.0	62.0	48.3	40.6	37.9
Mexico	54.6	57.3	71.8	74.8	79.5	86.5	76.0	65.4	65.1	52.7
Peru	54.8	58.0	71.2	54.5	59.8	72.6	55.4	31.4	25.2	21.8
Venezuela	75.3	78.6	84.5	73.4	88.6	93.3	78.9	65.3	70.2	63.3
Average	53.4	54.0	67.1	57.0	65.9	62.4	56.5	45.1	39.1	34.6
Sdev	14.2	14.2	13.2	12.9	14.8	21.8	18.8	15.8	20.7	18.4

Note: Average: simple average over the seven countries shown; *Sdev*: standard deviation.
[a] Average for 1987–88.

Sources:

Appendix Tables VII.1-2 and VII.5-6 are based on primary data from Mitchell (1993). In the case of Appendix Tables VII.3 and VII.4, data between 1900 and 1988 from Mitchell (1993), ECLAC (SYLA) thereafter, with the exception of Bolivia, values for rubber and silver exports in 1901 from PAU (1902) and in 1912-13 from League of Nations (1925), exports of lead in 1960, antinomy in 1970 and silver in 1980 from Wilkie (1996); Colombia data in 1898 from Ocampo (1984), gold exports in 1912-13 and 1921-22 from League of Nations (1925); Cuba 1980-95 from UNCTAD (1995); Peru exports of guano circa 1900 and 1910 are from Hunt (1973).

APPENDIX VIII. INCOME DISTRIBUTION

Income distribution is presented here in the form of Gini coefficients for household incomes, which although not a technically ideal measure, is the only one available in Latin America over half the century for a number of countries. The Gini coefficient is derived from the "Lorenz curve," which summarizes the cumulative size distribution of incomes over the population. It ranges from zero (equivalent to a completely equal distribution of national income between households) to unity (equivalent to one household receiving all the national income) so that a rising coefficient over time reflects a worsening income distribution, while a country with a lower coefficient than another enjoys a more egalitarian distribution of income.

Appendix Table VIII.1.
Gini Coefficients
(Distribution of households according to total household income)

	Argentina	Brazil	Chile		Colombia		Costa Rica	Mexico		Uruguay	Venezuela
	Urban	National	Santiago	National	National	Urban	National	National	Urban	Montevideo	National
1938					0.45						
Early 1950s	0.37		0.44		0.51						
1960		0.57	0.46								
1961	0.41										
1963								0.59			
1964			0.46		0.54	0.57		0.61	0.57		
1967								0.59	0.55	0.33	
1968			0.50								
1969	0.41										
1970		0.63									
1971			0.47		0.52	0.57	0.44				0.49
1973										0.33	
1974	0.42										
1977							0.39	0.55			
1978			0.52		0.47	0.56				0.44	
1979		0.61				0.57					
1980	0.46	0.62	0.52				0.42				
1981						0.51		0.48		0.43	0.39
1984						0.51		0.48			
1985							0.39				
1986	0.50									0.41	0.42
1987		0.63	0.54				0.43				
1988					0.47	0.52	0.43				
1989		0.65						0.52			0.40
1990	0.52	0.63	0.52				0.41			0.41	0.40
1991										0.44	
1992	0.51		0.52		0.46	0.56	0.42	0.53			
1993						0.56	0.42			0.38	
1994	0.54					0.56					
1995						0.54					

Source: Altimir (1997a, Figure 1). Data revised by Altimir for this book in order to include only those estimates which can be considered as reasonably comparable.

APPENDIX IX. LIVING STANDARDS

This Appendix contains data on GDP per capita, illiteracy and life expectancy as basic measures of human development. In addition, a Living Standards Index computed by the authors of this Appendix is presented, based on the approach in the UNDP *Human Development Report*.

Appendix Table IX.1.
GDP Per Capita: Absolute Values by Decades
(US$ per capita at 1970 PPP prices, three-year averages)

	1900	1910	1920	1930	1940	1950	1960	1970	1980	1990	1995
Argentina	439	557	513	559	645	773	852	1,191	1,377	1,147	1,402
Bolivia						261	215	294	352	289	310
Brazil	71	82	97	126	160	215	324	450	775	788	809
Chile	283	341	315	502	482	576	679	851	959	1,098	1,392
Colombia	118	146	172	230	291	360	420	536	674	749	856
Costa Rica			278	278	325	371	469	655	884	808	880
Cuba[1]	272	412	402	366	374	380	390	373	649	686	480
Dominican Rep.						244	298	379	543	509	545
Ecuador	89	109	132	154	159	230	285	358	542	520	549
El Salvador			164	178	190	274	329	407	409	355	429
Guatemala			235	246	382	309	337	419	514	447	475
Haiti						129	120	121	157	118	85
Honduras			216	264	195	227	237	280	307	276	294
Mexico[2]	261	316	346	313	357	458	611	879	1,163	1,107	1,090
Nicaragua			173	200	185	219	288	426	314	193	175
Panama						457	561	892	1,098	943	1,099
Paraguay					317	295	302	359	619	563	559
Peru	104	150	192	270	309	370	485	613	702	497	562
Uruguay					662	864	915	971	1,156	1,155	1,351
Venezuela	106	115	143	408	502	974	1,128	1,328	1,533	1,248	1,248
LA[6]	185	228	235	277	320	413	521	707	973	938	990
LA[13]						323	367	457	557	466	505
Latin America						394	487	649	884	837	879
United States	1,478	1,718	1,901	2,151	2,484	3,299	3,844	5,153	6,301	7,379	7,742

[1] See note on the calculation of Cuba's GDP in Section II of this Appendix.
[2] Figure circa 1910 corresponds to the 1909–10 average, and circa 1920 to the 1921–22 average.
Sources: Calculated from data for population and GDP in Statistical Appendices I and II.

Appendix Table IX.2.
Illiteracy Rate
(Percent of population age 15 and over)

	1870	1880	1890	1900	1910	1920	1930	1940	1950	1960	1970	1980	1990	1995
Argentina	76.5	67.2	57.9	48.7	39.6	31.8	25.1	18.3	12.4	8.6	7.4	6.1	4.2	3.8
Bolivia				81.5	79.8	77.5	75.1	72.1	67.9	55.9	44.0	32.6	22.0	16.9
Brazil	84.0	85.2	75.3	65.3	65.1	64.9	60.5	56.1	50.6	39.7	33.8	25.5	20.6	16.7
Chile		67.8	63.1	56.5	46.8	36.6	25.3	27.1	21.0	16.4	11.0	9.3	6.3	4.8
Colombia				66.0	60.7	56.2	48.1	43.1	38.2	30.4	21.8	14.9	10.3	8.7
Costa Rica	81.7	77.8	73.9	64.4	53.5	42.5	33.0	26.8	20.6	17.1	12.9	8.9	6.2	5.2
Cuba				54.0	43.2	35.9	28.9	23.7	22.1	20.8	13.0	7.0	4.7	3.5
Dominican Rep.						70.8	74.2	69.6	57.1	35.5	33.0	26.6	20.8	17.9
Ecuador				66.9	62.3	57.7	53.7	49.4	44.3	34.5	28.0	18.5	11.7	9.9
El Salvador				73.7	73.4	73.2	72.4	65.0	57.6	51.6	43.7	35.7	27.7	23.7
Guatemala		93.7		88.1	86.8	85.4	80.7	75.7	70.6	64.5	56.7	45.8	39.1	36.0
Haiti			90.1	92.0	91.8	91.7	91.5	90.8	89.4	84.3	79.2	67.7	58.9	55.0
Honduras			73.5	71.7	70.0	68.2	66.5	65.3	60.4	55.5	46.8	39.3	33.0	29.9
Mexico				75.6	70.2	64.7	63.6	53.9	39.5	34.6	25.8	17.0	12.4	10.4
Nicaragua						61.3	61.4	61.5	61.6	53.0	43.5	38.5	30.2	25.8
Panama				82.7	73.4	58.4	53.9	41.5	33.3	26.7	21.7	14.4	11.2	9.2
Paraguay			75.5	68.6	61.7	54.9	48.0	40.7	34.2	27.2	21.0	14.0	10.3	7.9
Peru		80.9	78.3	75.7	71.2	66.8	62.6	57.6	48.7	39.8	29.6	19.1	14.1	11.3
Uruguay				40.6	35.1	29.5	23.9	18.7	14.3	10.5	7.5	5.4	3.7	2.7
Venezuela				72.2	70.8	68.2	64.1	58.0	49.0	37.9	24.8	16.1	10.0	8.9
LA[6]				66.1	62.1	57.9	52.7	47.1	39.9	32.5	26.2	19.2	14.6	12.2
LA[13]						67.4	64.6	60.2	53.8	45.5	37.7	29.0	23.0	20.3
Latin America						58.9	54.3	49.0	42.0	34.6	28.0	20.7	16.1	13.6
Jamaica	83.4	76.2	66.0	57.3	48.8	43.9	36.5	28.9	23.0	18.1	14.0	10.6	8.2	7.3
Trinidad &Tobago				61.8	52.2	42.6	37.9	30.5	24.1	19.5	15.4	11.9	9.0	
Canada			19.8	15.9	8.8	6.5	4.9	3.7	2.5	1.7	1.0			1.0
United States	19.8	16.5	13.9	11.2	8.2	6.5	4.8	4.2	2.6	2.1	1.0	0.5		1.0

Sources:

All data is from a consultancy report by Hunt, 1997, for this book. The sources are national censuses or linear interpolations between censuses. The 1995 figures are UNESCO estimates in most cases. Nicaragua figure in 1995 from the national census. Figures for Argentina (before 1940) and the United States (after 1930) refer to adult population aged 14 and older. Other figures refer to population aged 15 and over. Early censuses reporting adult literacy using a different minimum age were adjusted to 15 and over using ratios from other censuses showing similar demographic and educational characteristics. Censuses adjusted in this way were those of Bolivia (1900), Canada (1911, 1901, 1891), Chile (1895, 1885, 1875), Colombia (1928, 1918), Costa Rica (1927, 1892, 1864), Dominican Republic (1935, 1920), Guatemala (1921, 1893, 1880), Honduras (1950, 1927, 1887), Jamaica (1953, 1943, 1921, 1911, 1891, 1881, 1871, 1861), Mexico (1921, 1910, 1900), Nicaragua (1920), Panama (1950, 1940, 1930, 1920, 1911), Paraguay (1886), Peru (1876), Trinidad and Tobago (1946, 1931, 1921, 1911), and Venezuela (1926).

In cases where several decades elapsed between censuses (such as Bolivia 1900-50, Paraguay 1886-1950, Peru 1876-1940, and Uruguay 1908-63), estimates for intervening years were made not by linear interpolation but by tracking the relative size of specific cohort groups with known literacy rates. In some countries, this technique was also used for projecting literacy estimates to decades prior to the first available census containing literacy data (e.g., Colombia before 1918, Ecuador before 1950, El Salvador before 1930, Haiti before 1950, Panama before 1911). It was also used for recent forward projections in the cases of Cuba (since 1979), Jamaica (since 1960), and Trinidad and Tobago (since 1946). For further detail on sources and methods, see Hunt (1997).

Appendix Table IX.3.
Life Expectancy
(Years at birth)

	1880	1890	1900	1910	1920	1930	1940	1950	1960	1970	1980	1990	1995
Argentina			39	44	49	53	56	61	65	67	70	72	72
Bolivia		28	26	28	31	33	36	40	43	46	52	58	60
Brazil	28		29	31	32	34	37	43	55	59	63	66	66
Chile			29	30	31	35	38	49	57	62	69	74	75
Colombia				31	32	34	38	49	57	61	66	69	70
Costa Rica	29		32	33	37	42	49	56	62	67	72	76	77
Cuba		30	32	36	39	42	45	56	64	70	74	75	76
Dominican Rep.						26	34	44	52	58	64	69	70
Ecuador								48	53	58	63	68	69
El Salvador			24	24		29	36	44	50	57	57	66	69
Guatemala		24	24		25	25	29	38	46	52	58	63	66
Haiti								36	42	47	52	56	54
Honduras						34	36	39	46	53	60	67	68
Mexico		24	25	28	24	34	39	48	57	61	67	71	72
Nicaragua						28	34	39	47	54	59	64	67
Panama						36	42	50	61	65	70	72	73
Paraguay	23	25	25	29	33	38	42	48	55	61	67	69	69
Peru								40	48	54	60	66	67
Uruguay									68	69	70	72	73
Venezuela				31	31	32	38	51	60	65	68	71	72
LA[6]			29	31	35	37	40	48	57	61	65	68	70
LA[13]								44	50	55	60	66	67
Latin America								47	56	60	64	68	69
Canada						61	64	68	71	73	75	77	79
United States	43	43	48	52	57	59	64	68	70	71	74	75	76
Trinidad & Tobago				39	41	40	46	52	58	66	68	71	73
Jamaica				40	37	44	52	57	63	68	71	73	74

Sources:

All data is from Hunt (1997) consultancy paper for this project with the exception of estimates for Cuba and Uruguay before 1950 taken from Pérez Brignoli (1993), and data for 1995 from UNDP (1997). The sources by country are as follows:

Argentina: 1955-90: CELADE. 1915-1950: UN-DY.

Bolivia: 1955-90: CELADE. 1900: Arriaga (1968). 1910-50: Interpolated between 1900 and 1955.

Brazil, Colombia, Costa Rica, Chile, Mexico, Dominican Republic, Ecuador, Peru: 1955-90, CELADE; 1950 and earlier, Arriaga (1968).

Cuba: 1900 to 1940 are estimates from Pérez Brignoli (1993) based on inverse projection method. 1955-90: CELADE. 1950 projected from 1955 and 1960.

Haiti: 1955-90: CELADE. 1950 projected from 1955 and 1960.

El Salvador, Guatemala, Honduras, Nicaragua, Panama, Venezuela: 1955-90: CELADE. 1950 and earlier: Arriaga (1968), reduced by ratio of CELADE to Arriaga figures for 1960 (0.90). (0.90 for El Salvador, 0.92 for Guatemala, 0.88 for Honduras, 0.96 for Nicaragua, 0.99 for Panama, 0.96 for Venezuela).

Paraguay: 1960-90: CELADE. 1950 and earlier: Arriaga (1968), reduced by a ratio of CELADE to Arriaga figures that declines in linear fashion from the actual rate of 1.18 in 1960 to 1.00 in 1880.

Uruguay: 1900 to 1940 estimates from Pérez Brignoli (1993) based on inverse projection method. Hunt (1997) based on CELADE after 1950.

Canada, Jamaica, and Trinidad and Tobago: all years from UN-DY.

United States: All years: U.S. Bureau of the Census. Figures for 1850-95 are for Massachusetts only. Massachusetts figures diverged from equivalent national figures by less than 1 percent in 1900 and 1910.

Living Standard Indices

Appendix Tables IX.4 and IX.5 contain estimates of the average standard of living by country over the century. The methodology is derived from the Human Development Indicator (*HDI*) established by the UNDP in 1990 as a central element of the *Human Development Report* (UNDP, 1990), which has appeared annually since then. Two separate indices are computed from the data shown above on per capita incomes, literacy rates and life expectancy; the methodology is set out fully in Astorga and FitzGerald (1998). The first is the Historical Living Standard Index (*HLSI*) for each country, which is basically a simplified form of the *HDI* that tracks changes in the standard of living over time for any one country in relation to its own median value. The second is the Relative Living Standard Index (RLSI), which permits the welfare level in any one country to be compared with the index value for the United States at any one point in time, and thus by extension a comparison can be made between Latin American countries. Both indicators are based on three variables already reported in this Appendix:

    Y: GDP per head (at 1970 constant purchasing power dollars)

    L: Life expectancy at birth (years)

    E: Educational attainment (adult literacy rate)

    In principle, the appropriate weights for the three components should be determined by reference to the relative marginal utility of income, longevity and education. However, in the absence of relevant information, equal weights for the three indices have been applied, which is also the solution adopted by the UNDP *HDR*.

    For any one country (*i*) in any one year (*t*) the *Historical Living Standard Index (HLSI)* is defined as

$$HLSI_{i,t} = \left[\frac{Y_{i,t}}{Y_{i,1950}} + \frac{L^*_{i,t}}{L^*_{i,1950}} + \frac{E_{i,t}}{E_{i,1950}} \right] * 100$$

    Where life expectancy (*L*) is scaled across the 20-85 year range which are its approximate minimum and maximum values.

$$L^*_{i,t} = \frac{L_{i,t} - 20}{85 - 20}$$

    The literacy rate (*E*) is scaled across 0 - 100.

    The *HLSI* for Latin America (or any group of countries therein) is found by weighting the index for each of the (*n*) countries by its population (*P*) share in that year (*t*)

$$HLSI_{LA,t} = \sum_{i=1}^{n} HLSI_{i,t} \frac{P_{i,t}}{\sum_{i=1}^{n} P_{i,t}}$$

    The *Relative Living Standard Index (RLSI)* shown in Appendix Table IX.5 is defined in a somewhat different way from the *HLSI*. Education *(E)* and longevity

(L) indices are defined and scaled as before. However, an adjustment is made to per capita GDP in order to reflect the widespread acceptance of a declining marginal income criterion in comparing countries with widely different per capita incomes. The welfare content *(W)* of the relevant income level *(Y)* is now measured by the square root of per capita GDP, which is a compromise between the acceptance of uncorrected GDP per capita as a measure of welfare on the one hand, and the notion of welfare as independent of income levels on the other.[1] The *RSLI* for any one Latin American country *(i)* is then defined as the arithmetic mean of the ratios between the annual values of each of the three components and the same components for the United States in that year *(t)*:

$$\text{RLSI}_{i,t} = \left[\frac{W_{i,t}}{W_{us,t}} + \frac{L_{i,t}}{L_{us,t}} + \frac{E_{i,t}}{E_{us,t}} \right] x \frac{100}{3}$$

The *RLSI* for any group of countries *(n)* is then simply weighted by population as before, so that

$$RLSI_t = \sum_{i=1}^{n} RLSI_{i,t} \frac{P_{i,t}}{\sum_{i=1}^{n} P_{i,t}}$$

The results for the *HSLI* and the *RSLI* over the century are presented in the following tables. The coefficient of variation for the various groups is shown in Appendix Table IX.5, as an indicator of the degree of convergence within the region. As can be seen, there is a considerable degree of convergence within Latin America over the century, but little or no convergence between Latin America and the United States.

---

[1] In other words, a general form of the utility function such that utility *(u)* is a function of income *(y)*, of the form $u = a.y.^e$ where $1 > e > 0$ in order to ensure the convexity consistent with a declining yet positive marginal utility of income. The two extreme values correspond, respectively, to the widespread use of unweighted per capita income as a measure of welfare as in Appendix Table IX.1 *(e = 1)* on the one hand; and the belief that utility is independent of income *(e = 0)* on the other. The formulation in the text thus falls midway between these two extremes *(e = 0.5)*.

Appendix Table IX.4.
Historical Living Standard Index (HLSI) by Decades
(Three-year average values, 1950=100)

	1900	1910	1920	1930	1940	1950	1960	1970	1980	1990	1995
Argentina	55	67	72	79	89	100	108	125	136	128	140
Bolivia						100	111	139	168	182	193
Brazil	48	51	56	66	78	100	140	170	231	241	248
Chile	45	54	57	78	80	100	118	136	151	166	185
Colombia	40	47	54	66	79	100	119	140	162	175	187
Costa Rica			65	74	87	100	116	140	167	164	172
Cuba	56	75	80	83	88	100	109	116	146	152	135
Dominican Rep.						100	135	158	193	199	208
Ecuador						100	120	140	178	185	192
El Salvador			52	56	73	100	121	145	152	163	180
Guatemala			51	59	85	100	124	154	186	197	208
Haiti						100	125	153	206	231	232
Honduras			75	91	86	100	118	142	164	177	185
Mexico	39	48	62a	60	74	100	125	155	187	190	192
Nicaragua			68	78	85	100	132	172	168	167	173
Panama						100	122	154	177	171	184
Paraguay					92	100	112	129	169	168	168
Peru					83	100	129	157	182	176	187
Uruguay	31	33	38	51	85	100	105	109	118	120	128
Venezuela					64	100	122	143	159	157	158
LA[6]	45	53	60	69	80	100	124	147	177	181	188
LA[13]						100	119	142	166	168	176
Latin America						100	123	145	175	178	184
United States	65	71	76	82	88	100	107	121	135	147	151

a 1921–22 average.

Appendix Table IX.5.
Relative Living Standard Index (HLSI) by Decade
(Three-year average values)

	1900	1910	1920	1930	1940	1950	1960	1970	1980	1990	1995
Argentina	65	70	70	73	75	76	78	79	78	77	78
Bolivia	40	43	48	54	58	61	56	60	65	67	68
Brazil	41	40	39	41	43	47	56	73	74	77	79
Chile	51	54	54	62	60	65	70	73	74	77	79
Colombia	42	44	45	48	51	56	62	66	69	71	72
Costa Rica			55	59	63	65	69	73	76	76	76
Cuba	54	60	61	62	63	65	68	71	75	75	74
Dominican Rep.						45	56	59	63	66	67
Ecuador						51	57	60	65	68	69
El Salvador			36	36	40	46	50	55	56	60	64
Guatemala			32	32	37	39	44	49	54	57	58
Haiti						28	31	34	39	42	42
Honduras			40	43	40	42	46	50	55	58	60
Mexico	41	38	37[a]	45	49	56	63	68	72	73	74
Nicaragua			38	40	40	41	48	54	54	57	59
Panama						60	67	71	74	74	75
Paraguay					55	56	60	64	69	70	70
Peru					45	48	55	60	65	66	68
Uruguay					76	78	79	78	78	77	78
Venezuela	39	38	39	45	50	60	68	73	75	75	75
LA[6]	45	46	47	49	52	56	62	66	70	71	72
LA[13]						48	53	57	61	63	64
Latin America						55	61	64	68	69	70
Coefficient variation											
LA[6]	0.22	0.27	0.28	0.24	0.21	0.16	0.11	0.09	0.07	0.05	0.06
LA[13]						0.27	0.23	0.20	0.18	0.15	0.15
LA(20)						0.25	0.21	0.19	0.16	0.14	0.14

Note: The coefficient variation is the standard deviation divided by the mean value.
[a]1921–22 average.

APPENDIX X. Iɴꜰʀᴀsᴛʀᴜᴄᴛᴜʀᴇ

This Appendix presents the available information on the availabilities of motor vehicles, railroads, electric energy and telephones.

Appendix Table X.1.
Motor Vehicles

	Registered vehicles (veh. thousands)					Density (veh. per thousand sq km)					Vehicles per capita (veh. per thousand persons)				
	1929	1940	1950	1970	1990	1929	1940	1950	1970	1990	1929	1940	1950	1970	1990
Argentina	412	428	557	2,195	5,785	148	154	201	791	2,083	36	30	32	92	178
Bolivia	3	6	13	48	261	2	6	12	44	238	1	3	5	11	40
Brazil	193	177	398	3,020	13,071	23	21	47	355	1,536	6	4	7	32	88
Chile	36	49	72	326	1,072	48	65	95	431	1,416	8	10	12	34	82
Colombia	16	30	58	402	1,451	14	26	51	353	1,274	2	3	5	19	41
Costa Rica	2	4	8	66	264	43	71	152	1,302	5,207	4.5	5.8	10	38	87
Cuba	50	46	106	192	504	437	402	921	1,680	4,398	14	10	19	22	47
Dominican Rep.	4	2	8	60	341	88	47	158	1,232	7,007	3	1.4	4	15	48
Ecuador	2	4	11	63	386	8	13	39	222	1,362	1.1	1.4	3	11	38
El Salvador	2	3	9	47	117	103	159	435	2,196	5,467	1.6	2.1	5	14	23
Guatemala	3	5	13	67	188	28	41	118	615	1,726	1.8	2.0	5	13	20
Haiti	4	3	4	13	49	140	96	137	482	1,755	2	0.9	1.2	3	8
Honduras	1	1	3	29	102	7	12	30	259	913	0.9	1.2	2	11	20
Mexico	84	146	303	1,823	9,875	43	74	154	924	5,006	5	7	11	36	119
Nicaragua	1	1	3	46	64	8	6	22	350	493	1.5	1.0	3	25	17
Panama	6	15	23	61	184	82	202	305	807	2,435	13	24.6	29	43	76
Paraguay	1	2	3	28	191	3	6	8	69	469	1.4	2.2	2	12	45
Peru	13	26	60	348	605	10	20	47	271	471	3	4	9	30	31
Uruguay	52	63	63	209	430	278	338	337	1,118	2,300	30	32	29	77	139
Venezuela	18	37	131	764	2,046	20	41	144	838	2,243	6	10	26	71	105
Latin America	904	1,048	1,845	9,807	36,987	45	52	92	490	1,848	20	19.2	19.9	49	94

Appendix Table X.2.
Railroads

	Track length (thousands of km)								Density (km of track per thousand sq. km)						
	1870[a]	1900	1913	1929	1940	1950	1970	1995	1870	1900	1913	1929	1950	1970	1995
Argentina	7.3	168	335	375	413	429	399	358	0.3	6.0	12.1	13.5	15.4	14.4	12.9
Bolivia	na	10	13	21	23	23	35	37	na	0.9	1.2	1.9	2.1	3.2	3.4
Brazil	7.5	153	246	320	343	367	318	304	0.1	1.8	2.9	3.8	4.3	3.7	3.6
Chile	7.3	44	81	85	86	85	83	64	1.0	5.8	10.7	11.2	11.2	10.9	8.5
Colombia	0.3	6	11	26	33	35	34	21	0.02	0.5	0.9	2.3	3.1	3.0	1.9
Costa Rica	0.8	3.9	6.2	6.7	6.7	6.7	6.2	6	1.62	7.7	12.2	13.1	13.1	12.3	11.5
Cuba	13.8	20	38	49	49	49	52	47	12.1	17.1	33.2	43.2	42.4	45.7	41.0
Dominican Rep.	na	1.8	2.4	2.4	2.7	2.7	2.7	1	na	3.7	4.9	4.9	5.5	5.5	2.9
Ecuador	0.4	0.9	5.9	10.3	10.6	11.2	9.9	10	0.14	0.3	2.1	3.6	4.0	3.5	3.4
El Salvador	na	1.2	3.2	6.0	6.1	6.2	6.2	6	na	5.4	15.0	27.9	28.9	28.9	26.4
Guatemala	0.2	6.4	9.9	11.6	11.6	11.6	8.2	11	0.19	5.9	9.1	10.6	10.6	7.5	10.5
Haiti	na	0.4	1.8	2.2	2.5	2.5	1.2	1	na	1.3	6.5	7.8	9.1	4.4	4.4
Honduras	0.6	1.0	2.4	14.6	12.6	13.0	10.3	10	0.54	0.9	2.1	13.0	11.6	9.2	8.9
Mexico	3.5	136	205	232	230	233	245	266	0.2	6.9	10.4	11.8	11.8	12.4	13.5
Nicaragua	na	2.3	3.2	3.3	3.7	4.3	4.0	2	na	1.7	2.5	2.5	3.3	3.1	1.7
Panama	0.8	0.8	0.8	1.6	1.6	1.6	1.6	5	1.01	1.0	1.0	2.1	2.1	2.1	6.4
Paraguay	0.9	2.4	3.7	4.7	5.0	5.0	4.4	4	0.22	0.6	0.9	1.2	1.2	1.1	1.1
Peru	6.7	18	33	29	29	31	22	21	0.5	1.4	2.5	2.2	2.4	1.7	1.7
Uruguay	0.2	17	26	27	30	30	30	30	0.11	9.3	13.8	14.6	16.1	15.9	16.1
Venezuela	0.1	9	9	10	10	10	2	6	0.01	0.9	0.9	1.1	1.1	0.2	0.7
Latin America		600	1,035	1,237	1,309	1,357	1,276	1,211		3.0	5.2	6.2	6.8	6.4	6.0

[a] Ecuador and Costa Rica, 1875; Cuba, Guatemala and Honduras, 1880.

Appendix Table X.3.
Electric Energy

	Generation (gigawatt hours)						Per capita supply (kilowatt hours per head)					
	1913	1929	1940	1950	1970	1993	1913	1929	1940	1950	1970	1993
Argentina	na	1,285	2,552	4,673	21,788	61,666	na	111	180	272	908	1,825
Bolivia	na	22	83	190	786	2,578	na	7	34	70	186	364
Brazil	na	532	1,292	8,192	46,032	252,585	na	16	31	153	480	1,614
Chile	na	285	564	3,004	7,763	23,872	na	66	111	493	818	1,733
Colombia	na	na	258	861	8,802	39,922	na	na	28	76	422	1,065
Costa Rica	na	na	na	185	1,026	4,434	na	na	na	151	588	1,356
Cuba	na	255	356	761	4,725	11,054	na	71	81	138	552	1,017
Dominican Rep.	na	na	26	82	978	5,879	na	na	15	38	243	777
Ecuador	na	na	na	128	950	7,592	na	na	na	38	159	691
El Salvador	na	na	na	68	677	2,880	na	na	na	24	196	520
Guatemala	na	na	29	76	775	3,019	na	na	13	27	148	300
Haiti	na	na	na	14	118	395	na	na	na	3	27	57
Honduras	na	na	na	51	315	2,477	na	na	na	23	118	454
Mexico	481	1,436	2,505	4,553	28,525	136,041	32	85	122	166	563	1,546
Nicaragua	na	na	na	81	612	1,670	na	na	na	76	333	404
Panama[c]	na	na	37	89	951	3,267	na	na	60	110	664	1,283
Paraguay	na	na	13[a]	44	222	31,486	na	na	12[a]	31	99	6,681
Peru	na	41[b]	98	271	5,589	14,211	na	8[b]	17	39	487	672
Uruguay	22	125	273	624	2,217	8,164	18	73	138	284	819	2,593
Venezuela	na	na	136	796	12,529	71,321	na	na	36	155	1,175	3,411
Latin America				24,637	145,379	684,513				118	449	1,418

[a] Paraguay, 1941. [b] Peru, 1931. [c] Panama excludes the Canal Zone throughout.

Appendix Table X.4.
Telephones

	Network (thousand lines)						Density (lines per thousand inhabitants)					
	1913	1929	1940	1950	1970	1990	1913	1929	1940	1950	1970	1990
Argentina	74	269	460	798	1,748	4,622	10	23	32	47	73	142
Bolivia	3	3	4	10	41	201	1	1	2	4	10	31
Brazil	39	160	297	550	2,001	14,125	2	5	7	10	21	95
Chile	15	40	90	132	357	1,096	4	9	18	22	38	84
Colombia	3	28	42	90	809	2,902	1	4	5	8	39	82
Costa Rica	1	3	3	9	61	450	2	6	5	12	35	148
Cuba	16	75	59	113	269	610	6	21	13	20	31	57
Dominican Rep.	1	2	3	7	47	297	1	2	2	3	12	41
Ecuador	3	6	7	9	130	540	2	3	3	3	22	53
El Salvador	0	4	4	5	39	250	0	3	3	3	11	48
Guatemala	2	3	4	5	49	192	2	2	2	2	9	21
Haiti	na	2	3	3	5	56	na	1	1	1	1	9
Honduras	0	2	4	4	14	92	0	2	3	3	5	18
Mexico	42	87	180	286	1,506	10,103	3	5	9	10	30	121
Nicaragua	1	1	2	3	26	56	1	1	2	3	14	15
Panama	3	9	8	14	85	256	7	20	12	17	60	106
Paraguay	1	2	4	5	24	128	1	2	3	4	11	30
Peru	4	15	26	47	228	769	1	3	4	7	20	39
Uruguay	10	32	55	90	215	579	8	19	28	41	79	187
Venezuela	5	20	29	68	406	1,794	2	6	8	13	38	92
Latin America	221	763	1,284	2,248	8,060	39,118	4	9	12	17	36	89

Sources:

All figures for infrastructure provision up to 1988 are based on primary data from Mitchell (1993). Railway length 1989-95 from ECLAC (SYLA, 1996). Electric output, motor vehicles in use and telephones in use 1989-90 from Wilkie (1996).

APPENDIX

ADVISORY COMMITTEE

Leslie Bethell

Roberto Cortés Conde

Aldo Ferrer

Albert Fishlow

Winston Fritsch

Ricardo Hausmann

Albert Hirschman

Alan Knight

Eduardo Lizano

Sir Alister McIntyre

Juan Antonio Morales

Oscar Muñoz

José Antonio Ocampo

David Pollock

Nohra Rey de Marulanda

Gert Rosenthal

Ignacy Sachs

Osvaldo Sunkel

Victor Urquidi

Richard Webb

COMPANION VOLUMES

CV1: *The Export Age: the Latin American Economies in the Late Nineteenth and Early Twentieth Centuries*, eds. E. Cárdenas, J.A. Ocampo and R. Thorp. Macmillan Press and St. Antony's College (forthcoming). Spanish version published by the Fondo de Cultura Económica.

Contributors:

Marcelo de P. Abreu

Afonso Bevilaqua

María Mercedes Botero

Héctor Pérez Brignoli

Roberto Cortés Conde

Manuel Contreras

Paulo Drinot de Echave

Alan Knight

José Antonio Ocampo

Gabriel Palma

Antonio Santamaría García

CV2: *Latin America in the 1930s*, ed. R. Thorp., 2nd ed. Macmillan Press and St. Antony's College, 1998. Spanish version (*América Latina en los Años Treinta*) Published by the Fondo de Cultura Económica, 1998.

Contributors:

Marcelo Abreu

Victor Bulmer-Thomas

Dionisio Dias Carneiro

Carlos Díaz-Alejandro

Enrique Cárdenas

Charles Kindleberger

Arturo O'Connell

Carlos Londoño

José Antonio Ocampo

Gabriel Palma

Rosemary Thorp

CV3: *Industrialisation and the State in Latin America: the Black Legend of the Post War Years*, eds., E. Cárdenas, J.A. Ocampo and R. Thorp. Macmillan Press and St. Antony's College (forthcoming). Spanish version published by the Fondo de Cultura Económica.

Contributors:

Marcelo de P. Abreu

Pablo Astorga

José Miguel Benavente

Afonso Bevilaqua

Enrique Cárdenas

Isaac Cohen

Gustavo Crespi

Valpy FitzGerald

Jorge Katz

Bernardo Kosacoff

Ricardo Ffrench-Davis

Oscar Muñoz

Demosthenes Pinho

José Antonio Ocampo

Camilo Tovar

Richard Webb